Marriage in a Changing World

Gerald R. Leslie
University of Florida

Elizabeth McLaughlin Leslie

John Wiley & Sons
New York · London · Sydney · Toronto

This book was set in Helvetica Light by
York Graphic Services and printed and
bound by Kingsport Press, Inc.
The text and cover was designed by Nancy
Axelrod. Photograph by Dan Lenore.
Photo credit to NASA.

Library of Congress Cataloging in Publication Data

Leslie, Gerald R
   Marriage in a changing world.

   Includes bibliographies and indexes.
   1. Family life education. 2. Family—United States.
3. United States—Social conditions—1960–
I. Leslie, Elizabeth McLaughlin, 1928–   joint author.
II. Title.
HQ10.L45   301.42'0973   76-26613
ISBN 0-471-52801-3

Printed in the United States of America

10 9 8 7 6 5 4 3 2 1

Preface

Continuity and change in human experience are unending: People are born into families, grow up in them, marry, and create families for their own children. Each generation improvises on the cultural script provided to it and alters the style of life of its predecessor, sometimes almost indiscernibly and sometimes drastically.

This book is intended for use in the many college and university courses whose purpose is preparation for marriage and family living. They are called by various names, among the more popular being Marriage, Marriage and Family Relationships, and Family Living. The breadth of the coverage also makes it appropriate for use in courses that enroll students beyond the age of most freshmen and sophomores, such as the evening divisions of many community colleges and metropolitan universities.

The last decade or so has been one of unusually rapid and often disconcerting change. Social relationships among young people have been transformed almost beyond recognition. The expectations of women are creating new conceptions of men's and women's roles in marriage and out. Legalized abortion has accompanied the most rapid drop in birth rates we have ever experienced, and divorce rates have climbed equally sharply. Historians of the future are not likely, however, to pick the year 1965, or 1970, or 1975 or any other one year as the date of a major revolution in American life. Instead, they will interpret all of these seemingly radical changes in terms of evolution from patterns that existed before and toward those that came after.

Our title was chosen very carefully to reflect the book's special approach. *Marriage in a Changing World* preserves the substantial amount of information contained in traditional marriage textbooks, but it rejects their orientation to social conditions that existed a generation or more ago. It incorporates the new material on alternative life styles that has been appearing in *avant garde* books, written in rebellion against the traditional texts, but it resists naive arguments that the solution to complex human problems can be found in some special life style.

A recurrent theme is the profound effects that changes in masculine and feminine roles are having upon marital and parent–child relationships. This material is too important to be confined to a single chapter on "alternative life styles." In the early chapters, we introduce the theme in terms of recent research on gender identity formation. Later it is developed in terms of the relationships of teenagers and young adults and, subsequently, detailed attention is given to the ways in which adult men and women work out their role problems. Instructors have long complained of textbooks that deal almost exclusively with preparation for marriage and parenthood; this book covers the entire life cycle from birth to death.

The analyses of the many topics covered in this book are carefully informed by the latest research findings available. Students need to know not only what conclusions their authors have reached, but also how they have reached them. Tables and charts are used to summarize information, but their construction has been kept simple. Footnotes, we think, are far more useful to teachers than to most students, so we have followed a style that leaves the text largely uncluttered but permits the instructor to locate sources quickly in the main list of references at the end of the book. An annotated list of additional readings is provided at the end of each chapter for students who wish to pursue specific topics further.

We think that the courses for which this book is written are, inherently, the most exciting courses in the curriculum; in many ways they are also the most useful. We have tried to write a book that will make such courses both more challenging and more helpful.

G. R. L.
E. M. L.

Contents

Chapter 1
Life in
Modern
Society

We live in a period of drastic change. If a person could have fallen asleep twenty years ago, like Rip Van Winkle, think how different he or she would find things upon awakening today. Twenty years ago the phrase "Women's Liberation" did not even exist, to say nothing of NOW (the National Organization for Women), the National Women's Political Caucus, the Equal Employment Opportunity Act, or the proposed Equal Rights Amendment to the Constitution. If our slumbering friend were male, he would likely be startled at the new militance of many girls and women. If female, our friend might be confused about how to interact with both women and men.

Changes in other areas of life have been equally drastic. The organized shared exchange of sexual partners among married couples—"swinging"—began to receive public attention only in the mid-1960s. Until then, "wife-swapping" and "key clubs" were furtive activities that only rarely came to light, perhaps when one of the more unwilling participants filed for divorce or took a shot at one of the others. The sexist nature of these activities went unrecognized, because the concept of sexism had not come into use yet.

Similarly, our sleepy friend probably would have heard of group marriage only in the context of exotic or primitive societies. Likewise, the phrase "communal living" might suggest some little-known nineteenth-century social experiments or, perhaps, the *kibbutzim* in Israel. The idea that middle-class Americans might consider such arrangements to be legitimate alternative life styles was a concept, again, whose time had not yet come.

Many other examples could be cited to illustrate how different the conditions of life in general, and those of marriage and family life in particular, have become in only a few short years. Such drastic changes create a certain amount of anxiety in all of us. Inexperienced persons, or sensationalists, sometimes take advantage of this anxiety to cry "revolution"; they proclaim that morality, marriage, the family, male domination, or what have you, are on the point of collapse. More careful analysts examine such changes carefully to see how time-proven basic values will be expressed in the new circumstances.

VALUES THAT ENDURE

A basic theme of this book is that there are certain fundamental human values that are widely shared—by both sexes, by different social classes and races, and even by different nations and peoples. They have persisted over long periods of time, and they are as important today as they ever were. These values, which reflect the very essence of what makes us human, include at least the following:

THE WORTH OF THE INDIVIDUAL

Each human being is a creature of inestimable worth. His or her welfare should be a goal of high priority, first for the individual, and then for all of the groups to which the individual belongs and all of the associations in which he or she participates. Human welfare is inextricably linked with the welfare of the individual.

INTIMACY IN INTERPERSONAL RELATIONS

Individuals acquire and nurture their sense of worth in loving relationships with other people. In early childhood, love is received from and taught by parents, or by those who take the place of parents. As one grows, peer relationships with people of both sexes continue one's development toward emotionally healthy adulthood. For most people, a basic transition occurs in adolescence. At that time, heterosexual relationships become the major source of perceived self-worth. (Among a small minority, and for reasons not yet understood, love and security are sought from members of the same sex.) The need for interpersonal intimacy continues throughout life.

Given these values, each individual should strive to become the healthiest, most creative person he or she is capable of being. We witness the prevalence of this value most clearly in childhood, as parents aid and encourage their children to develop into strong, trustworthy, considerate, and helpful adults. We also judge relationships between teenagers and young adults by how much they foster such traits in one another. It has also long been recognized that marriage should allow the continued personal growth of the husband and wife. But only recently has it been emphasized that such continued growth not only should be possible, but is a highly desirable goal.

PERSONAL GROWTH AND DEVELOPMENT

Finally, self-esteem, love, and personal growth flourish best in an atmosphere of security and responsibility. Children grow and develop most easily when they are not threatened with the loss of their parents' love and care. Teenagers must learn to trust members of the opposite sex if they are to live with them in harmony. And adult men and women can give completely of themselves only in relationships that they can depend upon to last, and that they can trust not to hurt them.

RESPONSIBILITY FOR THE WELFARE OF OTHERS

This list of enduring human values is not complete, of course. Surely there are other ways to list and describe even the values stated here. But any such catalogue serves to remind us of an important fact: despite the appearance of near-revolutionary change in recent years, most of the people around us have not actually changed that much. They still hold very basic human values, around which people have organized their lives and relationships over the centuries. To be able to love others, people must first love themselves. They learn to love themselves and others in secure relationships with parents, relatives, and friends. They build later relationships upon the lessons learned in earlier ones. For most people, this process culminates in marriage and parenthood. Continuity and change in human relationships are what this book is all about.

For the rest of this chapter we will look more closely at the interplay between enduring values and new social forms in the 1970s. This interaction has affected a whole range of human events: marriage rates, divorce rates, remarriages, single living, and widowhood. There have also been new social inventions, such as group marriages and communal living. These developments pose challenges to old values but, at the same time, they are also affected by them. We will come back to all of these topics in later chapters. The goal for now is to provide a general perspective within which we can analyze preparation for successful living.

OLD
VALUES
IN NEW
SETTINGS

*VIRTUALLY
EVERYONE
MARRIES*

If marriage and family life are breaking down, as alarmists maintain, marriage rates in the United States do not reflect the decline. A welter of commercial facilities—apartment houses, restaurants, commercial laundries, and so on—make it easier for people to remain unmarried today than ever before. Women do not have to marry to have an economic livelihood, and men do not have to marry in order to have their meals prepared and their socks mended. Yet people of both sexes are more likely to marry than ever before.

The proportion of the adult population that is currently married actually rose dramatically in the last half century or so, from 58 percent in 1920 to 75 percent in 1973. But this figure is not a very good measure, because it tells us only what proportion is married at any one time. If we focus instead upon the proportion who *ever* marry, it rises to approximately 95 percent.[1] Now stop to think: some three percent of the population is mentally retarded, and others suffer from chronic physical or mental illness, to say nothing of those who are more or less permanently held in prisons. Under these circumstances, the fact that 95 of every 100 adults marry, at least eventually, is quite remarkable. Almost all Americans today are married for some part of their adult lives.

*SINGLE
LIVING*

In the late 1960s and early 1970s, the stereotype of unmarried persons as "lonely losers" began to yield to a new stereotype, the "swinging singles" (Jacoby, 1974). Apartment complexes in urban centers advertised a life style organized around the swimming pool and the club room, featuring nightly cocktail parties and the presumption that everyone paired off by bedtime. Magazines such as *Playboy* and *Penthouse, Playgirl* and *Viva,* helped other elements in the mass media convey the attractiveness of this new single life. News magazines ran features which assumed that a rapidly growing proportion of the population would remain permanently single.

The idea gained credibility from two facts. First, the number of unmarried adults in the United States increased from 12.9 million in 1960 to 16.2 million a decade later. Second, the median age at marriage, which had declined rather steadily from 1900 to 1960, began to climb again. In the decade after 1960, the median age at marriage increased by about half a year for both men and women. The figures are presented in Table 1-1.

On close examination, however, these data are inadequate to tell us whether a new life style of permanent singlehood is emerging. They could simply reflect the fact that we have a temporary population bulge in the young adult years: people may marry as much as ever, but at slightly older ages (Glick, 1975). A few statistics support the second theory. For

[1] *U.S. Statistical Abstract,* 1973, p. 65.

YEAR	MEN	WOMEN
1900	25.9	21.9
1910	25.1	21.6
1920	24.6	21.2
1930	24.3	21.3
1940	24.3	21.5
1950	22.8	20.3
1960	22.8	20.3
1965	22.8	20.6
1970	23.2	20.8
1973	23.2	21.0

**TABLE 1-1
MEDIAN AGE AT FIRST
MARRIAGE, 1900–1973**

Source: National Center for Health Statistics.

instance, the number of single adults grew by 3.3 million between 1960 and 1970, but at the same time, the total number of persons between the ages of 14 and 24 increased by 13.8 million (Moynihan, 1973). The mere *number* of single young adults, therefore, is not enough to tell us whether the *rate* of singlehood is increasing. It is possible that many of today's young singles are merely delaying marriage. This theory is also supported by the fact that the proportion of the population over 30 that is single has actually fallen over the past 15 or 20 years. If younger people are remaining single longer, older people are more married than ever!

Whether singlehood will become a continuing life style or not, substantial numbers of people are living it, at least temporarily, and it needs to be related to our traditional value system. The first point that must be made is that there is no one life style for singles. Age, residential area, and economic status all influence one's life style. Twenty-five-year-old singles have no more in common with 45-year-old singles than 25- and 45-year-old married people have in common with one another.

Only in fairly large cities are there likely to be special facilities catering to singles, such as apartment houses and bars. In fact, in smaller communities, single adults often are discriminated against by employers and landlords. They tend to be regarded as irresponsible and "wild."

The "swinging single" life style of the stereotype is most possible for urban, educated, professional and technical people; only they can afford the high rents, the lavish entertainment, and so on that are required. Blue-collar and many white-collar people find little excitement in living singly when it means having to live in run-down apartments, or with several people sharing expenses and crowding into a more desirable one.

Several studies have shown that single people are not very different from married people in either social or personality characteristics (Baker,

1968; Rallings, 1966; Spreitzer and Riley, 1974). The same applies to personal happiness: some single people, like some married people, are relatively happy with themselves and their lives; others range from merely satisfied to quite unhappy (Jacoby, 1974).

Even in the best of circumstances, single living has its share of problems. Take the growing numbers of single women, for instance. Although most of them manage their finances quite well, they seldom make investments for the future as married couples are likely to do. They do not use life insurance, stocks, bonds, and real estate to accumulate equity, to protect themselves against catastrophe, and to provide for the needs of old age.

The popular impression that there are large numbers of ''singles'' apartments and bars is also misleading. Most such establishments are rather rigidly segregated by age and economic status. Middle-aged men soon stop going to places where they are scorned by the younger women they approach; middle-aged women find it easier to stay home or go to the movies than to be ignored by available, attractive young men. Similarly, many white-collar men and women do not want to frequent blue-collar bars. Establishments catering to professional people do not welcome others.

After all, even married people do not always have available and willing bed partners. Therefore, it seems obvious that most singles either devote an inordinate amount of time and energy to cultivating hetero-sexual relationships, or they experience frequent loneliness; most often it is both. Singlehood seems to be most attractive to prosperous young people in their early twenties living in large cities. Even among them, however, the passing years increasingly bring a yearning for deep emotional relationships in which they may find lasting security. They favor marriage in principle, and they gradually move toward it as a personal alternative. What is equally apparent is that they are determined to avoid early, or hasty, marriages. Most of them probably will marry. Moreover, their older ages and accompanying maturity, their years of single living, and the realism with which they approach marriage, may result in their making better marriages than they might otherwise have done.

RISING DIVORCE RATES

If people are marrying more than ever, they also are divorcing one another much more frequently. In the ten years from 1966 through 1975, the number of divorces in the United States more than doubled to about one million per year (see Table 1-2). The divorce rate almost doubled also, from 2.5 per 1000 population per year, to 4.7.

Currently, over two million people in the United States are divorced each year. If the magnitude of this figure is too overwhelming to grasp, it translates into the probability that between one-third and one-fourth of all

**TABLE 1-2
THE INCREASE IN
DIVORCE**

YEAR	NUMBER OF DIVORCES	RATE PER 1000 POPULATION
1965	479,000	2.5
1967	523,000	2.6
1969	639,000	3.2
1971	773,000	3.7
1973	913,000	4.4
1975	1,026,000	4.8

Source: National Center for Health Statistics.

30-year-old married people today eventually will be divorced (Glick and Norton, 1971; Glick and Norton, 1973). Moreover, some five to ten percent of the men and women who divorce one partner also will divorce a second one.

Divorce has become so common that stand-up comics and cartoonists make fun of it. Young people, in an attempt to allay their fears about their impending marriages, sometimes remark flippantly, "Well, we can always get a divorce if it doesn't work out." But marriage counselors and most people who have been divorced know that divorce is far more serious than that attitude implies. They know that heartbreak, guilt, feelings of rejection, conflicts over children, and money problems are only too real in most divorces. They also know, however, that continuing an unsatisfactory marriage may also impose heavy costs upon embattled spouses and their children.

Half a century ago, when the divorce rate was one-third what it is today, some people proclaimed that high divorce rates would mean the destruction of family life. Their counterparts today will probably keep right on predicting catastrophe. We know, however, that such fears are grossly exaggerated. The fact is that most divorced people remarry. In other words, they are disillusioned with particular marriages rather than with marriage itself. Moreover, most of those people have stable remarriages, and most of them describe themselves and their children as being happier and better off than before (Goode, 1965).

Divorce is seldom, if ever, a positive experience. Nevertheless, it often may be a necessary step in the growth of the two people toward greater emotional and social maturity (Rogers, 1968). No one can predict whether U.S. divorce rates will continue to climb. What is certain is that many of the young adults approaching marriage today will have to cope with divorce sooner or later.

HIGH RATES OF REMARRIAGE

About one out of four persons marrying today has been married at least once before. Official statistics on remarriages are not compiled and released as regularly as those on marriage and divorce, so we must use

YEAR	WOMEN	MEN
1965	407,000	410,000
1966	423,000	426,000
1967	437,000	439,000
1968	466,000	467,000
1969	496,000	499,000

**TABLE 1-3
ESTIMATED NUMBERS OF
REMARRIAGES IN THE
UNITED STATES,
1965–1969**

Source: National Center for Health Statistics, Series 21–Number 25, *Remarriages: United States* (Dec. 1973), p. 2.

figures that are a few years old. Some of them are presented in Table 1-3.

Two things should be noted about the figures presented in this table. First, the figures follow the increases in divorces shown in Table 1-2, although not precisely. In 1965, for example, there were 479,000 divorces and approximately 408,000 remarriages. By 1969 there were 639,000 divorces, but the number of remarriages had climbed only to about 498,000. In today's period of rapidly rising divorce rates, remarriage rates are not quite keeping up. This fact is related to a simultaneous rise in group marriage and communal life styles.

The second thing to be noted from the table is that the number of remarriages is slightly higher for men than for women; men hold an advantage in the likelihood of remarriage following divorce. This fact can be seen more clearly if we use rates instead of numbers and extend the comparison to a full decade. From 1960 to 1969, the remarriage rate for men increased from 167.7 per 1000 to 220.8. For women, over the same period, the increase was from 122.1 to 135.4. Not only were men more likely to remarry throughout the decade, but the difference in rates was almost twice as great at the end of the decade than at the start.

We might question, of course, whether the greater likelihood of remarriage for men is an advantage or a disadvantage. Logically, at least, it is possible that more women might have decided that they do not want to remarry; they may be contributing to the development of a new life style in which divorce is not followed by remarriage. But no responsible conclusion can be based upon such scanty and short-term data. A more likely possibility is that some men and women are simply not remarrying quite as soon after divorce as they used to. Whether this change in life style is temporary or permanent, however, it is common enough so that we will devote a whole chapter of this book to parents without partners.

*GROUP
MARRIAGES*

The significance of group marriage lies not in the number of people involved. Even the most extravagant estimates hold that only a few thousand people are participating in group marriages (Ellis, 1973; Pomeroy, 1973), and in-depth studies of group marriages have been based only upon thirty couples or so (Constantine and Constantine, 1971). Nevertheless, group marriage is a significant development on the American scene. It has helped some people find intimacy, a sense of self worth, and growth in interpersonal relationships. Moreover, many people who have not tried group marriage are open to it as a possibility.

Group marriages can involve as few as three people—two women and a man, or two men and a woman—and they sometimes include as many as six or seven. The most popular arrangement, however, is two couples. The pairs usually have lived together before entering upon the group marriage arrangement. They may or may not bring children into the group living (Constantine and Constantine, 1970; Ramey, 1972).

Group marriages rarely involve maritally inexperienced persons. Instead, they usually begin with couples who find that the joy and challenge have gone out of their own marriages. Two such couples, who are intellectually, emotionally, and physically attracted to one another, gradually come to share more and more; and eventually they decide to make a common household. The participants need not be unconventional in other respects. The men typically hold regular jobs and go to work each morning as other men do. The women may be somewhat more likely than most women to work outside the home, but one woman or both often continues to play the role of housewife. Fairly frequently, at least one of the couples either has been divorced from each other in the past or views the group marriage as a way of warding off an anticipated break. The participants are likely to be people in their late twenties, thirties, or even forties.

No generalization will fit all cases. Nevertheless, most members of group marriages seem to be committed not only to one another, but to ideals of interpersonal intimacy that they believe cannot be realized in conventional marriages. They usually advocate love of all members of the group by all members. They also use techniques such as group discussion and mutual criticism to try to eliminate the defensiveness about personal shortcomings that plague many conventional marital relationships. Sexual sharing in group marriages is part of the more general sharing of resources, pleasures, and problems; the participants believe it enhances the welfare of all.

Two other advantages claimed for group marriages relate to finances and children. Obviously, it costs less to maintain one household than two separate ones for the same number of people. Moreover, there may be less stereotyping of masculine and feminine roles in group marriages, with more men doing household chores and child care, and more women having active lives outside the home. This arrangement is believed to lead to fewer sex-role problems in the children. Advocates believe that group marriages may produce a new generation that is better prepared than this one for true intimacy, for giving to and receiving from others.

Group marriage on the American scene is new and, as yet, too little studied; it cannot be evaluated in other than the most general terms. It does appear to appeal to the maritally dissatisfied and to those who are separated or recently divorced. That is why we discuss it in the context of divorce and remarriage; if often becomes part of these processes. Since group marriages are not legally sanctioned in the first place, formal divorces are not required to end them. Yet one of the ironies is that group marriages appear especially vulnerable to dissolution; they are far more likely to break up than conventional marriages are (Constantine and Constantine, 1972; Salsberg, 1973).

We believe that the most useful way to regard group marriage is as an attempt by the people involved to realize the time-honored human values discussed earlier in this chapter. These values are difficult to achieve in a world characterized by almost chaotic change, and group marriage is anything but a simple solution to marriage and family problems. Instead, the achievement of a stable, growth-enhancing intimacy is infinitely more difficult among four or more adults than it is when only a couple is concerned. But it is unwise to dwell too long on the unconventionality and the problems that attend it. For some of today's young adults, group marriage may be a temporary part of the search for truly fulfilling relationships. For a very few, it may be the source of such fulfillment.

COMMUNAL LIVING

Communal living should not be confused with group marriage. It represents a quite different way in which people attempt to cope with the problem of creating lasting, rewarding relationships. There have been as many as 3000 communes in the United States in recent years. Some of them have been in cities and some in isolated rural areas; some have emphasized drug use; some were created only for financial advantage; and some have included conventionally married couples living monogamously (Kovach 1971; Otto, 1971).

Communes may contain only a few people. Typically, though, they involve from ten or twelve to a hundred or more. Some commune members may be only in their teens, but more are in their twenties or thirties; practically no one is of old age. People join and leave most communes informally, and there is a high membership turnover. The ownership of private property often is disapproved, and the commune strives to be a self-sufficient economic unit. Conventional sex roles are spurned, and men and women ostensibly share all productive tasks, all household and community chores, and child rearing.

Group marriages usually follow some experience of living with a member of the opposite sex. Many people try communal living, however, while they still are in their late teens or very early twenties. There probably are more communes near college and university campuses than

anywhere else. We need not dwell on the financial advantages in having ten or 12 people share the cost of just one house. Moreover, no particular ideological commitment, or even rebellion against the status quo, is required of the members. This kind of communal living need not involve sex relationships even with one person, let alone with all of the members of the group. It is true, however, that many unconventional people are attracted to communal living, and the chance of sexual involvement, including involvement with several persons, is greater than it is in most college and university circumstances. This kind of communal living seldom lasts beyond the college years, if that long. The participants go on to develop other kinds of relationships just as most of their peers do.

Communes other than student-based ones can be found in urban areas, but the typical self-sufficient commune is rural and agriculturally based. Some of the members may be students who have dropped out for a while, but more of them are older people whose joining reflects marital and family experiences not unlike those of members of group marriages. Some are separated, some are divorced, some join with their spouses in an attempt to revitalize their marriages, and some are married couples who are deeply committed to the ideals of communal living. All of them are searching and working for the creation of a better world (Kanter, 1974).

Little is known about communes, other than that most of them do not survive for more than a few years. But even less is known about what happens to ex-commune members after they leave the commune. A few such people have written their private histories, describing moving from one commune to another in the search for that elusive better way of life (Fairfield, 1972). But most ex-members simply seem to disappear into the larger society. Few people grow old in communes, and virtually no one has yet grown to adulthood in a commune.

Only a fraction of a percent of the population ever spends time in a commune. And even for most of the members, the experience is a transitory one, coming during college years, in a "drop-out" period before entering upon adult life, as a reaction to a marital break-up, and so on. Nonetheless, the experiences acquired during those months or years may be very important, and we will have more to say about them in later chapters.

Half of all married people are destined to live alone after their spouses die. This is hardly a recent development, but we have arrived at a new awareness of it in the past few years. Most people know that women outlive men, on the average, by some seven years. Also, we know that men marry women who are, on the average, some three years younger than themselves. These facts mean at least two things: First, women are much more likely to be widowed than men are. In 1971, of all

THE INEVITABILITY OF WIDOWHOOD

persons over age 65, more than 70 percent of the men had wives with whom they were living, but only 35 percent of the women had husbands. Second, women who are widowed live in that state for an average of some ten years. The last years of many women are lived out in increasingly lonely isolation.

There are only one-fourth as many widowers as widows in the United States. Not only that, but the men who do manage to outlive their wives are also much more likely to move from widowhood into remarriage. Widowers have a large pool of women available as prospective marriage partners, whereas widows find that there are not nearly enough men to go around. As might be expected, the remarriage rate for widowers is approximately four times as high as that for widows (Carter and Glick, 1970).

Although most young people know intellectually that they will one day face widowhood, the conditions of life that people face in their twenties are so different from those of old age that the prospect of widowhood seems quite unreal to them. Mate selection, career prepara-

tion, and even financial planning seldom are done with the inevitability of widowhood clearly in mind. But effective education for living must include preparation for the older ages as well as for the young and middle years.

With each passing moment, the future begins anew. We need not engage in fanciful speculation about what "the family" will be like in the year 2000, or at some other future date. Instead, let us indicate how family life has already changed, what it is today, and what it will be like during the years when the users of this book will be setting the patterns of their adult lives.

MARRIAGE AND THE FAMILY IN THE FUTURE

First, there is today a range of choices wider than has ever existed before. People have, and will have, the right to remain single, with or without informal sleeping and living arrangements with members of the opposite sex. Homosexuals will find themselves freer of harassment by the heterosexual world. Multiple-person living arrangements, including group marriages and communes, will suffice for some people. Not all officially sanctioned marriages will produce children, and some couples will concentrate their resources and energies upon their own personal and pair growth. Older people, widows, and widowers will be freer to form new relationships, clear in their own consciences and less subject to censure by their children or public authorities.

A WIDER RANGE OF CHOICES

Paradoxically, high rates of marital break-up may help produce better marriages. Though some unsatisfactory marriages may continue, for most people, the day has passed when they would be willing to remain bound in unrewarding, hurtful marriages. As many unsatisfactory marriages are terminated and replaced by better ones, the quality of married life in general may rise. Permanence in marriage already has come to depend upon whether the relationship continues to meet the emotional, physical, and intellectual needs of the partners. More of the marriages that survive in the future will be better marriages.

MORE VARIED MARRIAGES

There will be more emphasis upon husbands and wives as *persons,* apart from their marital roles. Partners will communicate more openly about their needs. In the resulting non-defensive atmosphere, they will be more able to give to, and receive from, one another. Spouses will continue to grow and change long past the ages when such development formerly ceased. Parents and even grandparents will view themselves as being in a state of "becoming," rather than "having been."

MORE COMMUNICATION AND GROWTH

Children will be less often the automatic and expected products of marital unions, and will more likely be the consciously desired fruit of stable unions. Though not all parent–child relationships will be idyllic,

CHILDREN IN A LOVING ENVIRONMENT

many children will receive more uncomplicated love from their parents, and will themselves experience fuller emotional and social growth. They will be more likely to see their parents as persons, not merely as parents; using the parents as models, they will more often become authentic persons themselves.

SUMMARY

Conditions of personal, marital, and family living have changed remarkably in recent years, as symbolized by the Women's Liberation and Gay Liberation movements, group marriages, communal living, and "swinging." These changes cause many people to wonder whether past experience any longer provides useful guides for successful living. Yet, through the seeming turmoil, certain basic human values remain as important as ever. These values include the following:

1. the worth of each individual as a person

2. the need for intimacy in interpersonal relationships

3. the desirability of continued personal growth

4. the responsibility of each person for the growth and welfare of others.

The broad context of current social life is formed in the interplay between enduring social values and emerging social conditions. Some generalizations are possible. First, married life is the norm for virtually all adults. Second, the evidence is unclear whether a new life style of singlehood is emerging; at the minimum, many young adults are delaying the time of marriage and seeking to assure themselves that their eventual marriages will be good ones. Third, rapidly rising divorce rates indicate that they have reason for concern. Fourth, remarriage rates also are high, suggesting that disillusionment with a particular marriage does not extend to marriage in general. Fifth, group marriages and communal living represent attempts by some people to cope with a need for intimacy and growth in a situation of marital instability. Finally, increasing longevity magnifies the problem of lonely widowhood.

With this background to provide perspective, we can make several judgments about marriage and family life now and in the near future. People now have an unprecedentedly wide range of choices of life style, ranging from singlehood, through informal heterosexual or gay cohabitation, group or communal living, and childless marriage, to conventional family life with children. Although many marriages do not survive, the majority that do may be better marriages than have existed in the past. There is more open communication between marital partners, and this freedom encourages their continued growth and development as persons. When babies are produced, they are more likely to be wanted and to be raised in a socially and emotionally healthy environment.

FOR ADDITIONAL READING

Bernard, Jessie, *The Future of Marriage* (New York: World, 1972). A distinguished scholar presents a provocative analysis.

DeLora, Joann S., and Jack R. DeLora, eds., *Intimate Life Styles: Marriage and Its Alternatives* (Pacific Palisades, California: Goodyear, 1975). A collection of readings that reflects the breadth of its title.

Gordon, Michael, ed., *The Nuclear Family in Crisis: The Search for an Alternative* (New York: Harper and Row, 1972). Emphasizes communal alternatives to the conventional family.

Perucci, Carolyn C., and Dena B. Targ, *Marriage and the Family: A Critical Analysis and Proposals for Change* (New York: David McKay, 1974). Constructive analysis from a feminist perspective.

Streib, Gordon, ed., *The Changing Family: Adaptation and Diversity* (Reading, Mass: Addison–Wesley, 1973). Issues, variations, and projections into the future.

STUDY QUESTIONS

1. How do you reconcile the extensive social change of recent years with the persistence of age-old basic values in human relationships? What are its implications concerning preparation for successful living?

2. Has a new life style of permanent singlehood come into existence? Evaluate the evidence for and against.

3. What has happened to divorce rates over the past decade? How can increasing divorce rates be consistent with the belief that the quality of individual marriages is improving?

4. What proportion of U.S. marriages today are remarriages? Who are more likely to remarry, men or women? What do you think produces this difference?

5. Describe how group marriages are attempts to implement enduring human values. In what ways are these attempts successful? unsuccessful?

6. How do communes around college campuses typically differ from other communes? What role does each kind of commune usually play in the lives of its members?

7. Justify the statement that preparation for marriage should include preparation for widowhood. How does the situation of women differ from that of men?

8. How are current social changes altering the quality of marriage and family life?

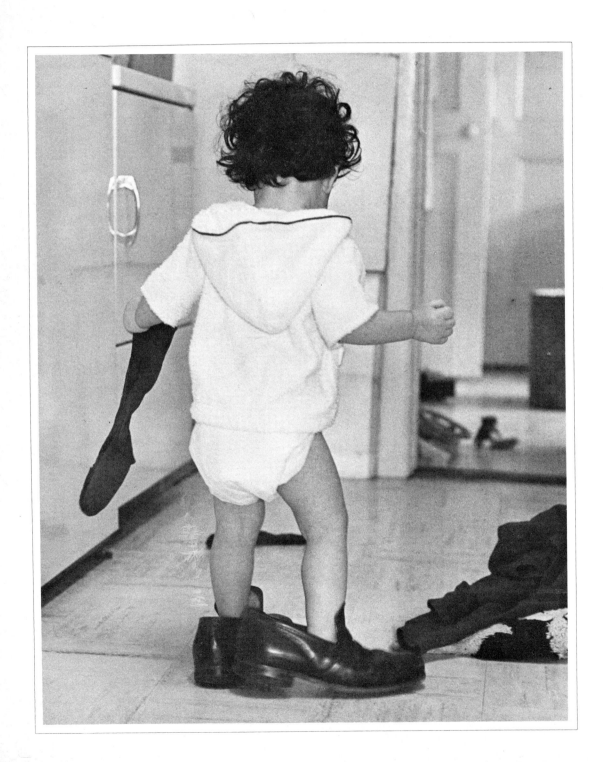

Chapter 2
Personality
Preparation
For Pair Living

A person today may choose from a variety of life styles. But virtually all of them emphasize the importance of love, intimacy, and trust in interpersonal relationships. Moreover, except among persons who are exclusively homosexual, such relationships develop primarily between men and women. We may be talking about one man and one woman in a fairly conventional relationship, or about several men and women in a group or communal setting. Whatever the case, the relationships are built upon personality foundations laid at the moment of conception and developed throughout fetal life, infancy, childhood, and adolescence. That is what this chapter is about; how human beings become the kind of adult men and women they are, and what difference it makes.

GENETICS AND SEX DIFFERENCES

Genetic, constitutional and learning influences are all inextricably intertwined in the development of a human personality. Genetic influences are only one set of factors among many. But we must start somewhere. Genetic influences are those upon which all subsequent influences must operate.

SEX RATIOS AND THEIR INFLUENCES

In ways that are not completely understood, but that are nonetheless important, unequal numbers of the two sexes are created at conception. This inequality is related to the sexes' unequal survival rates.

More conceptions result in male fetuses than in female ones. Estimates of the degree of the discrepancy are based upon laboratory study of early abortions and are not precise, but they indicate that somewhere between 120 and 160 male conceptions may occur for every 100 female conceptions (Money, 1973). *Sex ratios* are conventionally stated as the number of males per 100 females. Hence, we say that there is a sex ratio of between 120 and 160 at the time of conception. This figure is called the *primary* sex ratio.

Apparently, male fetuses are more vulnerable from the moment of conception than females are. More males fail to survive until birth, and by the time of birth the sex ratio is down to 105 or 106. The sex ratio at birth is called the *secondary* sex ratio.

We know more, of course, about what happens from birth onward. What happens is that males continue to die in larger numbers than females do. Fifty-four percent more males die of birth injuries, and 54 percent more males die during the first year of life. Males also are more vulnerable to organic disorders such as mitral stenosis (a heart deformity), color blindness, and hemophilia (failure of the blood to clot) (Oakley, 1972). Higher male death rates during childhood and adolescence bring the sex ratio down to near 100 by the time of adulthood. This figure is the *tertiary* sex ratio. As Table 2-1 shows, women tend to outlive men by a few years and, at older adult ages, women outnumber men.

The question arises of how much the higher adult death rates of males are due to genetic factors and how much they are due to the more active and hazardous lives that males often lead. To test the latter possibility, one ingenious researcher compared groups of monks and nuns, both of whom were teachers. Presumably, their conditions of life were virtually identical, and the social risks they encountered were approximately the same (Madigan, 1957). Yet, even in this sheltered life, the males had higher death rates. The results strengthen the belief that males are physically more vulnerable than women.

**TABLE 2-1
INCREASED LONGEVITY
OF UNITED STATES
MEN AND WOMEN**

YEARS	WOMEN	MEN
1959–1961	73.2 years	66.8 years
1974	75.8 years	68.1 years

Source: Metropolitan Life Insurance Company, *Statistical Bulletin* 56 (April 1975), p. 5.

On the other side of the ledger, males appear to be genetically larger and stronger than females. On the average, newborn males are larger and heavier than females; they also generally are more active, cry more, sleep less, and demand more attention (Alexander, 1971). It has been suggested that even these infant differences may be learned. Similar differences, however, are found in other species, such as rhesus monkeys. Young rhesus males wrestle, push, tug, and bite, but young females turn their heads away when challenged (Bardwick, 1973).

Human males as adults are also physically larger and stronger, on the average, than females. This fact, along with the physical handicaps that traditionally have accompanied menstruation, pregnancy, and nursing in women, probably accounts for the fact that men generally have dominated and controlled women to some degree.

Thus, we have a paradox. More males are conceived, but they have higher death rates. Males are physically more powerful, and tend to dominate females. But males continue to be more vulnerable, and females tend to outlive them; females have the power of survival.

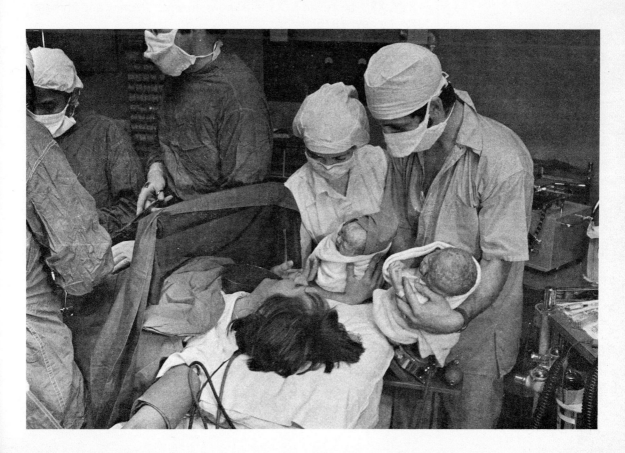

CHROMOSOMAL SEX

Most people know by now that the genetic instructions for the individual are embodied in the chromosomes. Each human body cell contains 46 chromosomes in 23 pairs. One chromosome of each pair is contributed by the mother, and the other 23 come from the father.

The sex of the individual is determined through one of the chromosome pairs, the X and Y chromosomes. Females have a pair of X chromosomes, and males have an X and a Y. Since the mother always contributes an X chromosome. if the fetus also receives an X from the father, it will develop as a female, XX. But if it receives a Y from the father, it will develop as a male, XY. A bit of male chauvinism often intrudes here, as people say that the sex of the child is determined by the father. The father cannot consciously influence the process, of course, and it might lead to less confusion if we said that the sex of the child is determined *through* the father.

For reasons not yet understood, the process does not always work as clearly and simply as this; occasionally, sex chromosomes may be either gained or lost during cell division. Chromosomal anomalies such as XYY, XXY, and even XXXY, are known to occur (Money and Ehrhardt, 1972; Money, 1975).

The XYY combination, having two of the chromosomes known to work in the direction of maleness, might be expected to result in an unusually aggressive male. We do not know whether this supposition is always true, but it is known that such men are found disproportionately in maximum-security mental institutions (Mazur and Robertson, 1972). It is estimated that the XYY combination occurs in only one to four men in a thousand in the general population. Yet men with this chromosomal pattern make up from one to three percent of the inmate population. Such males often are unusually tall and tend to be sterile.

The XXY combination also is rare (one or two in a thousand in the general population). But, strangely enough, this pattern also appears to be overrepresented about tenfold in maximum security mental institutions. It seems that chromosomal sexual abnormalities *of all sorts* may be found disproportionately in institutionalized populations. The simple fact that an abnormality exists may be more important in causing adjustment difficulties than the specific nature of the abnormality. Men with the XXY combination appear generally to be normal in body type, although the penis may be small. They also tend to be sterile, and there sometimes is severe mental retardation.

In the vast majority of cases, the chromosomal distinction between males and females is relatively clear-cut. It also is accompanied by physical differences between men and women. We have already observed sex differences in longevity and physical strength. In addition, female infants appear to be more sensitive to cold, touch, and sounds than males are. They also smile more. By the age of 12 weeks, when there still has been little opportunity for differential learning, male infants look for longer periods at all kinds of pictures than female infants do. Females tend to look longer at pictures of faces than at geometric figures; males show no such preference. Later on, when more learning has occurred, boys prefer the geometric figures (Alexander, 1971).

In adulthood, women's hearts beat eight to ten times a minute faster than men's do. The center of gravity of the female figure is around the hips, while that of males is around the chest and shoulders. Finally, the angle of the arms and legs from the body tends to be more parallel in men and somewhat more flared in women. Their build makes it easier for men to do vigorous physical activities such as running and throwing.

INTRAUTERINE INFLUENCES

The distinction between genetic and environmental influences is always hazy. Environmental influences begin to affect the fetus well before birth. Hormones, which are chemical substances secreted into the bloodstream by the endocrine glands, are among such influences. Hormones affect the development of maleness–femaleness (biological sexuality) and masculinity–femininity (personality characteristics).

In the earliest weeks of pregnancy, the embryo is not differentiated as to sex. The differentiation into male or female occurs primarily from the seventh week through the third month. Unless the fetal testes secrete sufficient quantities of the male hormone, androgen, at a very critical period, the fetus inevitably develops as a female. This point cannot be emphasized too strongly! It takes something extra to produce development as a male, the process is more complicated, and it is more subject to error. Hence, the emphasis upon males when we speak of sexual anomalies: male sexual development is simply more likely to include abnormalities.

The interactions between chromosomal sex and hormonal influences are extremely complex. A few specific instances may help to show how rather subtle changes in hormones can profoundly affect development. We will look at three different illustrations. Although all three situations involve influences that continue after birth, they all begin *in utero* (in the uterus).

PREGNANCY-SAVING HORMONES

Some women have a history of spontaneous abortions. During the 1950s, doctors began prescribing hormones as a means of helping these women avoid further miscarriages and carry their pregnancies to term. The drugs used were progestins, which closely resemble the pregnancy hormone, progesterone. But the full nature and action of progestins were not known at that time. It was discovered, subsequently, that some progestins tend to act as masculinizing hormones on female fetuses. Some babies whose mothers received the hormones were born with hermaphroditic characteristics, that is, with a mixture of male and female traits. These features included enlargement of the clitoris, some fusion of the labia, or even a penis with an empty scrotum. The internal reproductive organs of these babies were female, but the external sexual organs were ambiguous.

Ten such girls were treated systematically at Johns Hopkins University. By 1972, when the findings were published, they had been treated through mid-adolescence (Money and Ehrhardt, 1972). The masculinization of their external organs had been corrected surgically, and the subjects had all been raised as girls. Since the progestin was an "outside" influence during the pregnancy, and was discontinued at birth, no subsequent hormone treatment was necessary.

To determine the effects of the fetal masculinization, each of the ten girls was matched for age, I.Q., socioeconomic background, and race with a "normal" control subject. The results of this comparison turned out to be virtually identical with those for girls subjected to the *androgenital syndrome.* Before returning to the Johns Hopkins study, it is worthwhile to look at that condition. Then the results for the two groups can be discussed together.

THE ANDROGENITAL SYNDROME

The androgenital syndrome is a condition in which a genetic defect causes a malfunction of the adrenal glands. The glands fail to produce the proper hormone, cortisol, and instead produce a hormone similar to the male androgen. In these circumstances, when the fetus is a chromosomal female, the internal reproductive structures are not affected. But, again, the external genitalia may be masculinized. There may be an enlarged clitoris, some fusion of the labia, or even a penis with an empty scrotum. There may also be distortion of the vagina that requires surgical correction when the girl reaches adolescence.

Most such cases are quickly diagnosed after birth because of related problems. But in a few instances, mistakes in diagnosis have led surgeons to correct the sexual organs as male. In these cases, chromosomal females have been raised as boys. These "boys" developed conceptions of themselves as male and masculine and learned to act in masculine ways. Their success indicates how complex the relationship between chromosomal sex, intrauterine influences, and learning can be.

John Money, a medical psychologist, and his associates studied systematically a sample of 15 girls with the androgenital syndrome. All of the subjects were surgically corrected as females and raised as girls. Unlike the progestin-induced hermaphrodites, girls with the androgenital syndrome continue to produce the androgen after birth, so they must have cortisone therapy throughout their lives. But with such treatment the girls develop physically at a relatively normal rate and develop the usual female secondary sexual characteristics. The onset of menstruation may be delayed, but usually the girls are eventually able to both bear and nurse babies.

By coincidence, the discovery of cortisone therapy for the andro-genital syndrome was discovered at about the same time that progestins were being used to prevent miscarriages. Consequently, Money was able to study both groups together.

Money found that both groups of girls displayed more "tomboy" behavior than did the "control" girls with whom they were matched. They liked outdoor activities, particularly ball games, and preferred to play with boys rather than with girls. They liked traditionally masculine toys such as guns, cars, and trucks better than they liked dolls. They also preferred slacks and shorts to dresses, and were not much interested in jewelry, perfume, or having their hair done.

They also were more likely than their controls to wish that they had been born boys, although none of them had actually wanted to change her sex. Their early lack of interest in dolls was followed by a later lack of interest in babies and in working as babysitters. Some expressed anxiety about awkwardness in handling babies. Most did not reject the idea of having children themselves, but neither did they display much enthusi-asm for it.

In response to questions on the matter, these girls expressed more interests in occupational careers than did the control girls, and they tended to give their careers priority over marriage. A totally unanticipated finding was that career interests were associated with high I.Q. levels, and I.Q. elevation appears to be one of the consequences of fetal androgenization.

Few significant findings appeared in the area of specifically sexual behaviors. No differences were found in childhood sex play, but this fact may only mean that both groups kept most of their sex play secret from adults. In adolescence, the experimental girls appeared to lag behind the controls in becoming interested in boys, in dating, and in beginning love play. There were, however, no signs of lesbianism in either group.

Money and other scientists (Bardwick, 1971; Hamburg and Lunde, 1967; Oakley, 1972) believe that androgen may act upon the brain to produce one type of brain circuitry in males and another in females. The masculine brain may be programmed for dominance, assertion, and high energy levels, with tender, caretaking behavior somewhat inhibited (Money and Ehrhardt, 1972). If they are correct, this finding suggests that there are very real limits on how far societies can successfully go in altering masculine–feminine roles. In any event, these phenomena sug-gest the complexity of the interaction between chromosomal sex, hor-monal influences, and learning.

Before leaving this matter altogether, let us consider the case of a boy baby who lost his penis through a bizarre accident and who was subsequently raised as a girl. This case offers an interesting contrast to chromosomal females, androgenized before birth and reared as females: here we have a chromosomal male, normally androgenized *in utero*, but reared as a female.

CHROMOSOMAL MALE
WITH DESTRUCTION
OF PENIS

This case involves a set of male twins who were born without any sexual abnormality. At the age of seven months, during electrical circumcision, a too-powerful current accidentally burned off the penis of one twin. With no other solution apparent, the decision was made to reconstruct the infant's external genitals as female, delaying the construction of a vagina until full growth was achieved. Thus, when the child was 17 months old, its parents changed its name to a girl's and began to rear it as female with the aid of estrogen therapy. Medical authorities gave the parents continuing guidance on how to accomplish the sex reassignment, assuring them that she would develop a female identity and appropriate feminine behavior, and that one day she would marry and have children by adoption. At the time the results were described, the "girl" and her twin brother were about seven-and-a-half years old.

From the time the decision was made, the mother dressed the child in girl's clothes, let her hair grow, and emphasized feminine adornment. Gradually, the child came to prefer dresses to slacks and to be proud of her long hair. She became much neater than her brother and, unlike him, disliked being dirty. She preferred dolls and other female toys, imitated her mother in doing housework, and decided she wanted to be a teacher or a doctor when she grew up. She did not emphasize getting married but seemed to feel that she would.

Before the sex change, the sexually reassigned twin had been the dominant one. After the change, she gradually became rather maternal in relation to her brother, who remained very boyish and wanted to be a police officer or fire fighter when he grew up. The girl combined tendencies toward increasing daintiness and femininity with tendencies toward some tomboyishness, high energy levels, and dominance in girls' groups (Money and Ehrhardt, 1972). In this case, hormonal influences and learning substantially overcame genetic influences.

DEVELOPMENT
OF GENDER
IDENTITY

Environmental influences, especially hormones, begin to operate before birth. As we have seen, it has even been suggested that prenatal hormonal influences may dispose people to either masculine or feminine patterns of behavior. This is certainly true in very extreme cases: abnormally large doses of androgen in the fetus do affect behavior after birth. But we still cannot say how much, if any, of the childhood and adult behavior of most people reflects prenatal influences. What is certain, however, is that the development of masculine and feminine personalities is greatly affected by new and complex learning patterns that begin to operate at birth.

Regardless of the possible effects of hormones, human infants at birth are not *psychologically* differentiated as male or female. That is, they do not know of their sex and their sexuality, and they do not know that males and females are expected to think, act, and feel differently. But from birth onward, parents and others, intentionally and unintentionally, begin to teach such differences.

The process may begin with the development of the layette. Parents often stress "neutral" colors until the sex of the child is known, at which time the layette is completed in the appropriate pink or blue. No one would claim that the color of the baby's blankets and clothes makes a difference by itself. Nevertheless, it should be obvious that the pink or the blue provides other people with clues as to how the baby should be treated.

Most people, including the parents, admire large size and other signs of robustness in male babies. Likewise, they favor "cuteness" and regular features in female babies. Many new parents get upset when someone mistakes their boy for a girl, or vice versa. This reaction shows the importance they place upon the norms of what boys and girls are supposed to be like.

Within the first few months, other differences in treatment are evident. Both mothers and fathers are likely to cuddle a female baby more than a male baby. They speak to it more tenderly and tend not to think its occasional crying is inappropriate. Boy babies are likely to be bounced around more, shaken gently, and lifted over the parent's head. More physical reaction is expected from boy babies as a kind of infantile expression of "toughness." Their crying also is more likely to be interpreted as "temper."

As today's parents become more sophisticated about how young children are socialized to sex roles, such differences may become less pronounced than they were in the past; parents may make a conscious effort to treat boys and girls as nearly as alike as possible. Nevertheless, perhaps as early as 18 months, children show some awareness of sex differences and some idea of themselves as either male or female. The way they are treated by the parents reinforces their own perception of those differences. It also encourages them to model themselves after the parent of the same sex. Psychologically, they assume the gender of their own sex. Sociologically, they take on the behavior our culture defines as appropriate for that sex.

The term *gender identity* refers to the person's persistent, unambiguous definition of self as either male or female. The development of such a definition is crucial to the formation of later heterosexual relationships. Ordinarily, children acquire firm gender identities as a result of receiving

clear, consistent messages from adults. Their parents and others give instruction, either explicitly or by example, in what it is like to be male or female, and in how to behave as a male or female. This process can mean, of course, that stereotyped sex roles are uncritically repeated, generation after generation. But it need not.

The content of the masculine and feminine roles played by the parents can be quite varied without confusing the child. The mother may hold a responsible job and the father may wash dishes and change diapers, without either parent losing his or her gender identity; the child can still be given a firm sense of sexual identity.

Money likens the situation to what happens in a bilingual home. If each person in such a home uses the two languages predictably, the child soon learns how to respond to each person; it has no difficulty learning both languages. If, however, people use the two languages randomly, the child is likely to become confused and disturbed, and may suffer a permanent learning disability (Money and Ehrhardt, 1972).

So it is with the development of gender identity. The child normally learns two sets of gender roles, one masculine and one feminine. The female child learns that the female role is the one she is supposed to assume and the male role is the one she should respond to. The male child learns to play the male role and to respond to the female role. The essence of these male and female roles is not their content—that is, who does what around the house—but the ease and comfort with which the parents relate to one another and accept themselves as parents. The daughter of an aggressive, businesswoman mother will have no difficulty learning how to relate to boys, as long as the mother comfortably relates erotically to her own husband, and so on. Successful heterosexual relationships in adulthood are built upon the foundation provided by parental roles.

ANOMALIES OF GENDER IDENTITY

HOMOSEXUALITY

The ways in which homosexual preferences develop in human beings remain little understood, and we will not try to explain all homosexual behavior. For one thing, homosexual behavior is of many different kinds, requiring many different explanations.

At one extreme is the compulsively homosexual person who has a life-long and exclusive attraction to members of the same sex. Then there are people whose basic orientation is homosexual, but who can, and do, respond heterosexually on some occasions. Bisexuality is defined as being able to "go either way" comfortably and doing so. It, in turn, may shade off into behavior that is predominantly heterosexual, with homosexual behavior developing only in special situations. Some homosexual behavior in prisons, for example, is never repeated on the outside; some women who otherwise are exclusively heterosexual, participate in lesbian activity in group-sex situations.

We can at least speculate on the ways in which some distortions of gender identity develop. In a few cases, chromosomal factors may operate. The XXY pattern, for example, sometimes seems to be associated with bisexuality. At the hormonal factor level, also, too much androgen in females and too little androgen in males may result in brain circuitry that disposes the individual to an uncertain gender identity. Finally, the sex-role models presented to some young children may sometimes be ambiguous enough to hinder the development of a clear gender identity.

TRANSEXUALISM

Homosexuals accept their own genitals, as do heterosexuals. Transexuals, however, despise the bodies with which they were born, and particularly their genitals. A profound disturbance of gender identity is evident in such people from as early as three years of age. They reject activities appropriate to their own sex, adopt the dress and play of the opposite sex, and become determined to rid themselves of their hated genitals and to acquire the body of the opposite sex, which they believe to be their true sex. Male transexuals have been known to castrate themselves as part of their effort to assume the opposite sex.

Transexuals ordinarily are not considered to be mentally ill in the conventional sense. Except for their compulsion to change their bodies, they often function quite well in the role of the opposite sex. It was once believed that particular family conditions, such as weak fathers and domineering mothers, might be the cause. But attempts to identify such conditions generally have been unsuccessful. For one thing, younger and older siblings in the families of transexuals are usually not affected. Virtually all forms of psychotherapy have been tried with transexuals, and none with any success.

The ratio of male to female transexuals is at least three-to-one, and it may be as high as seven-to-one. This fact makes one suspect that there may be some pattern of hormonal causation before birth. An excess of androgen in a female fetus, particularly beyond the third month, could produce an infant with female genitals but a masculine-programmed brain. Similarly, a male fetus that received too little androgen could be born with a feminine-programmed brain. Sexual development is more complex in the male fetus than in the female, and hence easier to disturb.

In physical development, outwardly, male transexuals seem normal. Their testes function normally, their hormonal levels fall within normal ranges, and they develop the usual secondary sexual characteristics at puberty. But the onset of puberty, which signals readiness for reproduction, often provokes a crisis. At this time, they may be isolated further from their peers, intensifying their determination to join the opposite sex.

Some male transexuals conceal their sexual problems from both themselves and others. They marry heterosexually and even father children. But ordinarily, such men have very low levels of heterosexual activity. They become normally sexually active only if they adopt homosexual behavior.

The only successful therapy for transexuals that has been found is sex-conversion surgery. In a series of operations, the external genitalia are reconstructed as those of the opposite sex. The surgery is supplemented by hormone treatment that aids in transforming the secondary sexual characteristics (Benjamin, 1966). Many such conversions have now been done, and the procedures have gained increased acceptability in medical circles. The converted transexuals assume the public role of their new sex, often fall in love, and even marry.

SEX HORMONAL INFLUENCES IN ADULTHOOD

Our discussion up to now has emphasized the role of the male sex hormone, androgen, in the development of male sexuality. But we should now point out that there are male hormones (androgen, testosterone) and female hormones (estrogen, progesterone). Both male and female hormones are produced by both sexes. Females produce more estrogen, and males produce more testosterone.

Large differences in the production of the sex hormones do not occur until puberty. At that time, the increased production of estrogen slows the growth of the long bones in females. In boys, testosterone similarly increases. Adult males apparently produce about ten times as much testosterone as adult females do.

Estrogen influences ovulation, conception, menstruation, gestation, and vaginal lubrication in females. Testosterone appears to be responsible for heightened levels of sexual interest and activity. When testosterone is administered medically to women, it tends to increase their physical activity, sexual interest, and aggression. These characteristics decline again to former levels when the testosterone is discontinued. Similarly, men with inadequately functioning testes often are treated with testosterone. When it is discontinued, their frequency of erections, erotic dreams, masturbation, and coitus decline markedly. Men placed on testosterone therapy experience dramatic increases in sexual fantasy and overt behavior.

Thus, testosterone appears to be related to sexual drive in adults of both sexes. When given to sexually responsive women, testosterone increases heterosexual interest, but it does not cause homosexual interest. Sexually unresponsive women also report more sexual arousability through testosterone therapy.

Estrogen therapy in men inhibits androgen secretion by the testes. Consequently, it reduces sexual interest. Women who discontinue estrogen therapy, however, report little change in their sexual reactions. Many postmenopausal women, in whom the production of estrogen has declined, report unchanged or even increased levels of sexual activity.

In summary, the bio-psycho-sexual nature of men and women appears to be the product of very complex interaction among chromosomal, hormonal, and learning influences. Thus far, we have focused primarily upon chromosomal and hormonal influences. But the effects of learning are equally profound.

EARLY SOCIALIZATION

We have already seen some of the different ways in which male and female infants are treated. There is no question that such influences affect the development of gender identity. Even parents who strive not to develop traditional masculine and feminine qualities in their children continue to do so subtly, and not so subtly, throughout early childhood and into the school years.

Most girls learn at a very early age to respond to verbal and non-verbal cues from adults, particularly the mother, that will bring them love and approval. By the age of six months, for example, girl babies gaze longer and more steadily at human faces than boy babies do (Bardwick, 1973). As young girls become able to move about and interact with others, they are less likely than boys are to oppose their parents directly or to behave aggressively. They develop language skills earlier, and they employ those skills in getting along with adults. Adults approve of this girlish dependent behavior; They encourage and reward it and, thus, perpetuate it. As another consequence, girls become better prepared to do well in school.

The same parents who encourage dependency in girl children are likely to reject it in young boys, believing that it is inappropriately feminine or "sissy" behavior. Now, in all probability, young boys have as much need as girls do to be dependent upon their mothers, and to receive affection and approval from them. But they are rarely treated in the same way. A hypothetical example may help to show how girls are supported in passive, feminine modes of adjustment, while boys are coerced toward aggressive, masculine forms.

Suppose that we have a pair of twins, a boy and a girl, four or five years of age, and playing together. Somehow, the girl hurts herself: pinches her finger in a door, hits it with a toy hammer, or something. Almost surely she will cry and run to her mother for comfort, and the mother will take the girl on her lap and soothe her hurt, "kissing it to make it well." Thereby she gives tacit consent to the little girl's sobs. In a few minutes it is all over and the little girl goes back to play, secure in the knowledge that mother is there to protect and comfort her.

Now let the little girl's twin brother hurt himself in precisely the same way. What does he do? Well, if we have set the age of these hypothetical children young enough, he will probably do the same thing as his sister: run crying to his mother for comfort. And if the mother is at all sensitive, she will treat him much as she would treat his sister, comforting and reassuring him.

But unless she is a very unusual mother, she will probably do something else as well. She will convey to him directly or indirectly that boys should model their behavior after that of their fathers. She may not say it in so many words, but she will communicate the message that men are not supposed to cry. Daddy may swear when he hurts himself, but he does not cry! The little boy, whose finger hurts just as badly as his sister's, ''manfully'' stifles his tears and goes back to play, having begun to learn that men are tougher than women and that they conceal hurts behind some kind of aggression.

To emphasize the significance of the different ways in which boys and girls are socialized for their adult interaction, take one more brief illustration. Little boys and girls, interested in everything, also are likely to be especially interested in sex. And even in situations that involve no overt sex play, they again receive different kinds of messages from their parents.

Suppose, in this case, that a group of children of both sexes are roughhousing, wrestling, standing on their heads, competing with one another. Until they learn that there are limits upon the ways in which girls may compete, the girls may do very well. Sooner or later, however, one of the girls will be wearing a dress rather than jeans or slacks and, in vigorous play, that dress will end up around her waist. The boys may or may not trigger a response from one of the mothers by giggling or otherwise showing interest in her panties; a wise mother would try to ignore the whole episode. But again, whether the mother intervenes or not, and no matter how subtly, both boys and girls will get the message: ''Girls should keep their dresses down.''

The little boys and girls who are taught that women cry, but men don't, will grow up to live with similarly conditioned members of the opposite sex. The women will know that society says it is quite proper for married women to have their dresses around their waists when they are alone with their husbands; but years of modesty conditioning will make it difficult for them to be as free with their men as they would like to be. At least some of the men will react with frustration and anger at their partners' inhibitions.

When a fight starts, the woman may run off to the bedroom and cry in the manner that she has been taught is appropriate for women. The man who has learned not to cry also is likely to be unable to cope with a woman's tears, so he reacts as he has been taught: he shouts and swears and, perhaps, slams the door. Such obvious insensitivity, which is not at all what she had been led to expect, aggravates the woman's crying. It becomes increasingly difficult for either partner to end the vicious cycle.

There is yet another way to interpret the differential conditioning of young boys and girls. Girls gain security and learn to adjust by identifying with their mothers, and by being passive and dependent. But little boys are taught that they must give up their identification with the mother and their dependence upon her. Instead, they must gain approval through achievement, first in peer competition and, later on, in school or business. Thus boys, more than girls, are conditioned toward aggressiveness and independence.

In recent years, some parents have gained some awareness of how these things happen, and they have begun to attempt to minimize the differences. Such parents try hard to accept tenderness and dependence in their young sons, believing that doing so will make their sons more able as men to give and to accept love. If the parents wonder whether such men will also be less ambitious and competitive occupationally, it is a price that increasing numbers of people are willing to pay.

Similarly, more parents are encouraging aggression and independence in their young daughters. They believe that traditional femininity has stifled the development of the full potential of girls and women. Such parents see true equality of the sexes as necessarily being based upon the elimination of biases in child rearing. Less traditionally masculine men may be less occupationally focused, but less traditionally feminine women will be more so. Husbands and wives, from this point of view, will become more nearly partners in earning a living and in maintaining a home.

INFLUENCES IN THE SCHOOLS

The schools generally reinforce and extend the masculinity–femininity differences that boys and girls learn in the home. They do so through the instructional materials that are used, and by continuing to encourage boys toward aggression and achievement and girls toward passivity and domesticity.

The books that children are given to read, both pre-school and school, are filled with the stereotyping of masculine and feminine roles. In picture books, for example, women very rarely appear as the central figures. Boys' and men's activities are emphasized, with girls and women appearing mostly as shadowy figures in the roles of wives and sisters. Boys occupy leadership roles, doing things and accomplishing things, while girls essentially stand by, watching.

Men are portrayed in active occupational roles: fire fighter, police officer, airplane pilot, and even mechanic and plumber. Women are identified chiefly as mothers and wives. And motherhood is presented as a full-time job, so girls are not encouraged to think of following most occupations or of combining work and motherhood (Weitzman, Eifler, Hokada, and Ross, 1974).

Teachers and counselors, wittingly or unwittingly, help to reinforce

the stereotypes. Girls are 'counseled' into home economics and book-keeping, while boys are advised to take science and math. The implications are clear enough: boys are being prepared for careers; girls are being prepared to be wives (Safilios-Rothschild, 1974; Weitzman, 1975).

Most people would agree that such sexual stereotyping is unfair and harmful to girls and women, effectively denying to much of our population the opportunity to lead full, productive lives. Many also would agree that men's lives are impoverished too, by rigid, unyielding demands that men place occupational goals ahead of everything else, as well as by the denial of opportunity to women.

Patricia Cayo Sexton has developed an interesting thesis. In her view, the schools are essentially *feminine* institutions that feminize males and make it difficult for them to become strong men. Consequently, they make it hazardous for such men's wives to assert themselves without fear of tragedy. She points out that most teachers are women who emphasize obedience and conformity, and who provide little opportunity for healthy young males to express their natural ebullience. Either boys are stifled by school, or they must rebel against it and fail academically in order to escape with their masculinity intact. Sexton recommends both the masculinization of the schools—putting many more men in position to be role models—and the liberation of women; as mothers, such women would be able to encourage both their sons and their daughters to make maximum use of their strengths and abilities (Sexton, 1973).

CULTURAL CONTRADICTIONS AND SEX ROLES

The personalities that are formed in the home and in the schools provide the foundations upon which heterosexual relationships are built later in life. Young people enter adolescence with biologically ascribed sexuality, a masculine or feminine gender identity, and more than a decade of conditioning to masculine and feminine roles. Yet they now find themselves confronted with relationship demands for which they are not wholly prepared. In Mirra Komarovsky's phrase, they are confronted with "cultural contradictions and sex roles."

Girls are likely to reach adolescence having learned to some degree that they should be domestically oriented and subordinate to men—or, in other words, traditionally feminine. But at the same time, they are likely to have learned that women are as capable as men and that they should seek to develop their capacities to the fullest. As far back as World War II, Komarovsky reported that up to 40 percent of college women had problems with men that arose from conflicting sex roles (Komarovsky, 1946). These women felt under pressure to defer to their dates: 40 percent of them admitted that they had knowingly "played dumb" on occasion to permit their dates to win in games or contests. Since then, even more girls have probably become troubled by the consequences of being completely themselves in their heterosexual relationships.

Light was thrown on the contemporary situation in a 1973 study of 62 Ivy League college males and their conflicts in dating situations (Komarovsky, 1973). The results showed clearly that women are more likely today to present themselves honestly on their dates. About a third of college men suffer some intellectual insecurity with their dates as a consequence. Some of these men solved their problem by confining their dating to women to whom they felt superior. Others continued to date intelligent, capable women but were tormented by their own inability to be consistently superior.

Of at least as much interest is the two-thirds of the men who did not report such difficulties. They seemed to be divided into five different groups. First were those men who still felt superior to their women friends and, thus, did not experience this kind of problem. Second, and probably a growing group, were those men who were able to have equalitarian relationships with women, based upon intellectual companionship. Third, at the other extreme, there were relationships based upon "fun" and sexual attraction in which there was little or no intellectual component. Fourth, there were relationships that presented other problems so pressing that the problem of intellectual competition was completely overshadowed. Finally, there were cases in which the woman's obvious intellectual superiority was compensated for by some handicap, such as being physically plain, socially dependent, or emotionally unstable. Some superior women played an essentially maternal, supportive role with their men instead of a competitive one.

TOWARD ROLE FLEXIBILITY

Underlying this whole discussion of sex-role socialization are two basic themes. One is that differences in masculine and feminine personalities are systematically created. The other is that new social trends are lessening those differences. Both those themes will now be made fully explicit.

By the time they reach college age, women typically have come to value being liked and approved of more than they value achievement. This is true particularly in the occupational sphere. Paradoxically, women do well in school, reading and writing better than men, and displaying, in the abstract, high motivation to achieve. But they also fear that high achievement will cause them to be rejected as persons, that they will lose their femininity, and that they will suffer emotional breakdown (Horner, 1972). In short, they appear to have been conditioned effectively to the traditional feminine role in this society.

There are paradoxes resulting from the way males are socialized, too. Males typically are aggressive and occupationally ambitious. But at the same time, they have learned to inhibit tender feelings and overt expressions of affection (Knox and Kupferer, 1971). Balswick and Peek have called this pattern "the tragedy of the inexpressive male" (Balswick

and Peek, 1971). They see the traditional view of masculinity as one requiring toughness, courage, and aggression, and forbidding the display of love, tenderness, and sentiment. In their view, this results in many males coming to fit either of two stereotypes: the ''cowboy'' or the ''playboy.''

The cowboy, epitomized by John Wayne's screen image, is a strong, silent, two-fisted type who feels real affection for women but is unable to show it. He treats women in courteous, reserved fashion and is unable to develop relationships of any depth. The playboy is epitomized either by the stereotyped men featured in *Playboy* magazine or, perhaps, by James Bond. He is not merely unable to express affection for women—he doesn't feel it. Instead, he is a skilled, unfeeling manipulator, who ''knows when to turn the lights down, what music to play on the stereo, which drinks to serve, and what topics of conversation to pursue.'' He measures success in terms of getting a woman into bed without becoming emotionally involved with her.

Now take these images of men and women and pair them in a heterosexual relationship. The prospect is somewhat discouraging. The male partner is handicapped in his ability to give and receive affection, and the female partner is ambivalent about being loved and still being a creative, productive person. In real life, men and women do experience these problems, and we shall have more to say about them in subsequent chapters. But there is another side to it: many men and women now do not suffer much from these handicaps, and the trend is toward further reduction in the future.

One clue to how masculine–feminine differences have diminished over the last decade comes from a study employing the Rorshach ink blot test. Psychologists have found that men are giving more of the responses that women used to give, and that women are giving more traditionally masculine responses.[1]

Changes in teenage heterosexual relationships probably have much to do with this development. These days, boys and girls are freer to associate with one another outside of the old formal dating situation; they are able to talk with one another seriously about what they think and feel. This opportunity should cause them both to understand one another better and to become somewhat more alike.

Some research support for this conclusion exists in a study of college men. The subjects were compared in the degree to which they disclose personal information about themselves to their parents, their brothers, their sisters, their men friends, and their women friends (Komarovsky, 1974). In the area of "money," the parents were most involved. But in all other areas, more of the men's preferred confidants were their women friends. This was especially true in the sensitive areas of "personality" and "body."

SUMMARY

Adult relationships of intimacy and trust are built upon personality foundations laid down from the moment of conception and developed through infancy, childhood, and adolescence.

Up to 50 percent more males than females are conceived, but males have higher death rates, resulting in a secondary sex ratio of approximately 106 and virtually equal numbers of men and women in early adulthood. Apparently, genetic factors cause males to be physically larger and stronger on the average than females, but also more vulnerable to illness and death.

Normally, an X chromosome from the mother and either an X or a Y from the father determine the sex of a child. Occasional anomalies appear, such as XYY or XXY. They are associated with both physical and behavioral abnormalities. Normal males and females differ in body structure, with the male body being better suited for some kinds of vigorous physical activity and the female body being structured for child bearing.

The operation of hormonal influences during the fetal period makes it difficult to separate genetic influences from environmental ones. Production of androgen between the seventh and twelfth weeks of preg-

[1] *Behavior Today,* Vol. 2, May 24, 1971.

nancy seems necessary for development of the fetus as a male. That process is more complex than development as a female and more subject to error. Studies of female infants androgenized before birth show the influence of the male hormone in the development of ambiguous external sex organs and some masculinization of behavior. Correspondingly, an infant boy who suffered the loss of his penis is being raised successfully as a female with the assistance of reconstructive surgery and hormone therapy. Apparently, hormonal and learning influences can almost nullify the influences of chromosomal sex.

Psychological sexuality, or gender identity, develops during the first years of life. The child learns of its physical sex, and it is treated differently by other people according to whether it is a boy or a girl. By age three, the child ordinarily has modeled itself after the parent of the same sex and has become firmly identified as male or female. Distortions of gender identity formation, including homosexuality and transexualism, may result in various ways from the interaction of chromosomal, hormonal, and learning factors.

Both males and females produce both male and female sex hormones. Adult males produce about ten times as much testosterone as adult females do. Testosterone appears to regulate sexual drive in both sexes.

From infancy onward, most parents condition their daughters to seek love and approval in dependent relationships with others, whereas they condition their sons to ambition, competitiveness, and independence. The schools continue the process by using sex-stereotyped instructional materials and by counseling girls toward traditionally feminine subjects and occupations.

Cultural demands are inconsistent. They emphasize that women are as competent as men, but that women should defer to men in many situations. Such demands cause conflicts and problems for many young men and women in their heterosexual interaction. They also create difficulties for men by conditioning them either against feeling tender emotions toward women, or against expressing those feelings openly.

Many parents have come to believe that the traditional socialization of children to masculine and feminine behavior has interfered with both full equality for women and satisfying marital and parental relationships. Such people are trying to encourage the development of active competence in their daughters and the capacity for tenderness in their sons. The next generation may have fewer such problems than this one has.

FOR
ADDITIONAL
READING

Chafetz, Janet Saltzman, *Masculine / Feminine or Human: An Overview of the Sociology of Sex Roles* (Itasca, Illinois: Peacock, 1974). Introductory-level analysis of changing sex roles in the U.S.

Hutt, Corinne, *Males and Females* (Baltimore: Penguin, 1972). A more extended treatment of the topics covered in this chapter.

Seward, Georgene H., and Robert C. Williamson, eds., *Sex Roles in Changing Society* (New York: Random House, 1970). Analysis of sex roles in primitive, ancient, and modern societies.

Stoll, Clarice Stasz, *Male and Female: Socialization, Social Roles, and Social Structure* (Dubuque, Iowa: Wm. C. Brown, 1974). Attempts to counteract sexism in the analysis of men's and women's roles.

Yorburg, Betty, *Sexual Identity: Sex Roles and Social Change* (New York: Wiley–Interscience, 1974). Includes cross-cultural and historical data in analysis of sex roles in modern society.

STUDY
QUESTIONS

1. Define the primary, secondary, and tertiary sex ratios. How are these ratios related to the kinds of relationships that exist between men and women?

2. How is the sex of a child determined? How does chromosomal sex influence behavior?

3. What role do hormonal influences before birth play in the development of sexuality? How far can they go in nullifying the influences of chromosomal sex?

4. Define the concept of gender identity. How is it developed? What is its significance for behavior?

5. Evaluate this proposition: when mothers and fathers do not play conventional masculine–feminine roles, it becomes difficult for their children to assume a firm sense of gender identity.

6. How do hormones influence adult sexual drive? in men? in women?

7. Describe how parents and others influence growing children toward masculine and feminine behavior patterns.

8. Elaborate on the phrase "cultural contradictions and sex roles." Is time working to reduce such contradictions? If so, how?

Chapter 3
Pairing Off

PRE-TEEN INVOLVEMENT

Most children develop a firm sense of themselves as either male or female by the age of three. Subsequently, people continue to encourage them in the direction of masculine and feminine personalities. It would therefore be surprising if children did not soon begin to take special interest in members of the opposite sex. This is not to say that they necessarily begin overt sexual play (although, as we shall see in the next chapter, many children do), but members of the opposite sex do form a significant part of most children's environments. Boys react to girls differently from the way they react to other boys, and vice versa.

By adult standards, or even those of teenagers, the first heterosexual adventures of young children are immature indeed. The *Peanuts* strip reproduced on the next page makes the point well. Linus wants to show his interest in the little girl, but either he doesn't know how, or his sense of male identity is not yet secure enough to allow him to show affection directly. Little boys are taught, of course,

that hitting is manly and that "sissy" behavior Is not acceptable. So what is a red-blooded five-year-old boy to do? He makes his first clumsy effort to relate to a little girl, and he immediately runs to share the experience with Charlie Brown.

We might imagine this same occurrence from the viewpoint of the little girl. There is some chance that she was aware of Linus's interest before she was hit. She probably feels a mixture of pleasure at the attention received and distress at being hurt. She is likely to share those feelings with her girlfriends. But if parents and others have been socializing her adequately, she also is likely to want to tell adults: first her teacher, perhaps; then her mother; then her doting grandparents, and so on. One can almost see the mischievous look in her eye as she tells the teacher, "Linus hit me!" She watches for the responding twinkle in the teacher's eye which tells her, "Yes, you are an attractive little girl," and "Boys are like that and it is all right for little girls to enjoy it."

The point is not that all little girls have their first crushes at age five. Nor is it that all little boys show affection, perversely, by hitting. Some boys and girls don't begin significant heterosexual interaction until beyond their mid-teen years. But the personality foundations for such interaction are laid down early. Some boys and girls feel the first stir of romantic attraction before they even start school.

Two other points are implicit in this story. The first is that boys generally share their heterosexual experiences with their peers more than girls do. The second is shown in the little girl's reaction: among girls, success in attracting boys becomes a means of securing approval and status from adults and from other children.

THE MASCULINE SUBCULTURE

Many little boys learn early that other little boys, and older boys too, will approve of their efforts to divest little girls of their panties. Most little boys don't need much encouragement to become interested in sex, anyway. They discover the pleasure that results from handling their own genitals. They find graphic drawings with Anglo-Saxon descriptions on the walls of restrooms to help stimulate their curiosity.

Our interest at this point is not in sex as such, but in the ways that male peers encourage sexual activity. We are also concerned with the kinds of activity they encourage and the rewards they offer for accounts of sexual exploits—either real or imagined.

Boys talk about sex in much more personal terms, on the average, than girls do. They do not talk about sex in the abstract, but rather, they emphasize what they would like to *do to* girls or women they know, or to movie and TV stars whose curves "turn them on." Often, they share their fantasies with groups of their peers in graphic detail. Both the teller and his listeners live the experiences vicariously and become motivated to attempt such exploits with available girls.

Usually there is more than a subtle overtone of hostility toward females in these discussions. Young boys talk in terms of lusting after women, not of "making love" to them. Lust is masculine and approved; making love has dangerous connotations of sentimentality and tenderness. Their image of girls and women usually fits right in with these attitudes. They see females as either wantonly reveling in sexual activity (which they really want, even if it does almost have to be forced upon them!), or as deliberately frustrating the males' pleasure by refusing to participate.

Much of the activity described privately among groups of boys is fantasy. Few boys are as successful or experienced as they pretend to be. But to the extent to which their pretense succeeds, they are admired, envied, and emulated by other members of the group. Factors other than sexual accomplishment bring status in boys' groups, of course, but sexual achievement is one of the things that identifies boys as leaders.

One important byproduct of this masculine subculture goes generally unrecognized. It is the anxiety that it fosters in many boys about their adequacy as males. Each boy recognizes that he is not as sophisticated as he pretends to be to the others. However, he is not experienced enough to be sure that they themselves are exaggerating. Consequently, he is pressured to acquire experience to gain status within the group. He also comes to need it for himself to reassure himself of his adequacy as a male. The boy's orientation to sexual participation with girls comes to be increasingly exploitative and self-centered.

COMPETITION FOR STATUS

Girls ordinarily do not gain status with other girls by being sexually experienced and sexually active. An occasional teenager may gain some notoriety and attention by boasting of her ability to attract boys. But she is usually a girl who cannot compete successfully in other ways, and the attitudes of her female peers are generally quite disapproving. Even the boys who pursue her in the hope of sexual intercourse hold her in contempt privately and in their peer sessions.

Girls gain status from their relationships with the opposite sex in a different way that was implied in the reaction of our hypothetical five-year-old to being struck by her inept suitor. Girls seek approval from adults and use that adult approval to create envy in other girls. Adults, of course, rarely would sanction an explicitly sexual encounter. As a result, girls learn that a combination of attractiveness to boys and restraint in behavior with them brings continuing approval both from adults and peers.

**EARLY
DATING**

The relationships between teenaged boys and girls have changed considerably over the past few years. These changes have almost made the term "dating" inapplicable at that level. However, it still usefully describes some of the common experience of pre-teenagers. These ten-to-12-year-olds imitate in some ways the teenagers' dating patterns of the 1950s and 1960s.

Various studies show that many youngsters begin a kind of dating by the time they are in the fifth or sixth grade (Bayer, 1968; Broderick and Rowe, 1968). At least, by that time they are heterosexually oriented and are beginning to become emotionally involved with boyfriends or girlfriends. One study of several hundred fifth to seventh graders in Pennsylvania and Missouri illustrates the point. Many of those youngsters had already singled out a boyfriend or girlfriend, and they viewed that person in the context of one day getting married. Not all of these children were deeply involved, of course; in some instances the other child did not even know of the attraction. But the majority of these students reported that they had "been in love" (Broderick and Rowe, 1968).

Studies also have shown considerable variation at these age levels. Urban youngsters, and those from higher socioeconomic groups, tend to become involved somewhat earlier. Dating activities at this age are likely to be rather structured, including such activities as going to the movies and attending parties at one of the youngsters' homes.

**HIGH-SCHOOL
PATTERNS**

*DATING
STAGES*

Slightly more structure enters boy–girl relationships as youngsters move through middle school, or junior high, into high school. A recent study of over 2000 high-school students in Kentucky, for example, compared rural and urban patterns. The study classified the students into three groups: those not dating, those playing the field, and those going steady (Wittman, 1971). The results are shown in Table 3-1.

As among pre-teenagers, the urban high schoolers were more likely to date. The urban girls were also more likely to be going steady. When asked about their reasons for dating, they were more likely to emphasize companionship and the opportunity to get to know a variety of other people. The rural boys who were going steady tended to have more serious interests in selecting marriage partners.

Other findings in the table are also of interest. Notice that from one-fifth to over one-fourth of the students had not yet begun to date.

	URBAN (PERCENT)		RURAL (PERCENT)	
	BOYS	GIRLS	BOYS	GIRLS
Not Dating	21	21	28	27
Playing the Field	50	40	42	39
Going Steady	13	19	14	16

**TABLE 3-1
DATING PATTERNS OF
RURAL AND URBAN
HIGH-SCHOOL
STUDENTS[a]**

[a]Percentages do not add to 100 because other students were already engaged or married.

Source: James S. Wittman, ''Dating Patterns of Rural and Urban Kentucky Teenagers,''
   The Family Coordinator 20 (Jan. 1971), p. 64.

The very largest groups described themselves as playing the field, and up to one-fifth were going steady. Note also that more girls than boys were going steady. This finding is consistent with their younger average age at marriage.

This study reported students to be involved in a fairly traditional dating system. But it also showed them adapting that system to suit their needs for companionship and spontaneity in boy–girl relations. Those

going steady reported, for example, that they were not interested in either the prestige it brought or the security of always having a date. Instead, they emphasized the satisfactions received from "being with someone you enjoy." They also saw the biggest disadvantage of steady dating as being that "you can't date others."

NEW RELATIONSHIP NORMS

Both teenagers and young adults today are increasingly critical of the traditional dating system in the United States. Many are seeking to replace it with patterns that permit them to get to know one another better as people, without the rigid structure and the artificiality that the term "dating" implies (Olson, 1972).

When they can avoid it, they shun situations that require the boy to telephone the girl or otherwise make arrangements far in advance. They also de-emphasize dressing up and attending formal events, whether they be dances, movies, concerts, sports events, or what have you. They object to the sexism implicit in requiring or permitting the male to plan the event. Finally they abhor the anxiety that traditional dating creates in both sexes. Boys and men should not have to make formal overtures and worry about having them rejected; and girls and women should not have to worry about whether they will be asked. Neither males nor females should be forced to put on their best behavior when in the company of the other.

Pair dating is being replaced to some extent by groups of boys and girls who get together informally to buy a pizza, to listen to music, or often just to "hang around." The activities ideally develop spontaneously, and the boys have no special responsibility for planning or for paying. The casualness and the lack of explicit pairing-off in this arrangement permits both males and females to be included without worrying about being accepted. The emphasis is more upon being together than upon doing specific things. Particular boys and girls are discouraged from "playing little games," in which one seeks to involve the other emotionally or to hurt and take advantage of the other. Sometimes, obviously, attraction does develop between a particular boy and girl. When it does, they pair off to some degree and participate in the group more as a couple. Gradually they may withdraw in order to have more private time together.

HIGH-SCHOOL MARRIAGES

It should come as no surprise that few very youthful marriages occur among people who are destined to become college students. Such young people are counseled and led from a very early age not to become seriously emotionally involved until they have secured their education, the foundation of a successful career. In the meantime, they tend to take a "fun" approach to boy–girl relationships. The situation is different for many who are not likely to attend college; they often learn that boy–girl

relationships in high school may lead to intimate sexual involvement and early marriage. There also tends to be a rural–urban difference in this regard, as Table 3-1 suggests.

Non-college-oriented boys frequently pair off in high school with girls a year or two younger than themselves. For these young men, a major transition occurs with their graduation from high school and their entry into the job market. This time is seen as the appropriate time to marry. Only about 18,000 young men under 18 years of age marry in the United States each year. Between 18 and 19 years, however, the figure jumps to over 160,000. An additional 180,000 marry between their 19th and 20th years.[1]

Girls often are a year or two younger than the boys with whom they become involved. Thus, many of their marriages occur while they are still in high school. About 130,000 girls under 18 years of age marry in the United States each year. Almost 300,000 more marry between their 18th and 19th years, and over 400,000 more marry between their 19th and 20th years.

A very high proportion of teenage marriages are brought on by premarital pregnancy. Official government data show, for example, that in 42 percent of the marriages involving 15-to-19-year-old brides, the interval from the wedding to the birth of a child is less than eight months. As might be expected, infant mortality rates also are higher when the mothers are very young.

Most husbands in high-school marriages expect to go to work without seeking further education, and the early arrival of a child confirms them in that path (Bartz and Nye, 1970; de Lissovoy, 1973). Early marriage, lack of formal education, and early childbearing all combine to keep the family at inadequate income levels, and generally to compound its problems (Bacon, 1974; Coombs and Freedman, 1970). These problems include a higher than average probability of divorce. Through 1970, teenage marriages were about twice as likely to end in divorce as were other marriages.

COLLEGE PATTERNS

Most of the students who read this book will not yet be married. Most college students have grown up having some contact with subcultural influences that encourage competition, status striving, and sexual exploitation in male–female relationships. They also have had many of the high-school dating experiences already described. For some students, the transition to college will have little direct effect upon their relationships with the opposite sex; for others, striking changes will occur.

[1] Vital and Health Statistics, Series 21, No. 23.

College students, like other younger people, find customs governing male–female relationships in rapid change. The old dating system, stemming from the post-World War II years, exists side by side with newer patterns formed in rebellion against the old.

**Values
in Dating**

Children learn the subtleties of sexual aggression and coquetry from models unknowingly provided to them by parents and others. But even as they are doing so, most boys and girls are formally taught that there are positive values to be sought in dating experiences. They are admonished to de-emphasize sex, and not to focus upon such superficial qualities as good looks and the possession of money. Instead, the wise boy or girl is urged to date different people, learning all the while to evaluate them for the significant traits of character and personality that will, one day, make good marriage partners.

As a consequence, even at the high-school level, many people of both sexes consciously seek certain values in dating and certain qualities in their dating partners. By the time they reach college, the process often is almost wholly explicit. Young men and women can tell you both what they look for in their dating partners and what they hope to find in marital partners.

In the late 1960s, at three universities in the United States and one in Canada, a study was done of the qualities that men and women value most highly in one another (Hudson and Henze, 1969). Of the 18 characteristics that the men and women were asked to rank, they placed them in the following order, from most important to least important.

MEN	WOMEN
1. Dependable character	1. Emotional stability
2. Mutual attraction	2. Dependable character
3. Emotional stability	3. Mutual attraction
4. Pleasing disposition	4. Pleasing disposition
5. Desire for home—children	5. Desire for home—children
6. Good cook—housekeeper	6. Ambitious—industriousness
7. Refinement	7. Education—intelligence
8. Ambition—industriousness	8. Refinement
9. Good health	9. Similar educational background
10. Education—intelligence	10. Good health
11. Good looks	11. Similar religious background

12. Sociability	12. Good financial prospects
13. Similar educational background	13. Sociability
14. Similar religious background	14. Favorable social status
15. Chastity	15. Chastity
16. Favorable social status	16. Good cook—housekeeper
17. Similar political background	17. Good looks
18. Good financial prospects	18. Similar political background

The lists for men and women are really remarkably similar, with most traits appearing within a place or two of one another. Only in the case of traditionally sex-linked qualities, such as being a good cook or having good financial prospects, is there much difference in the rankings.

Obviously, at conscious levels, many college students believe that such qualities as dependability, emotional stability, being pleasant, and being family-oriented constitute a good basis for marriage when coupled with mutual attraction. Other studies confirm that these preferences are stable over time. They are also widespread geographically (Moss, Apolonio, and Jensen, 1971; Wakil, 1973).

Relationships as Exchange

A more or less explicit bargaining element exists in many traditional dating situations. The young man and woman "trade" favors, and each seeks to get the best of the bargain, or at least to make sure he or she doesn't get "cheated." Men often bargain for sex, seeking to get the woman into bed in exchange for showing her a good time. According to these norms, the more time, money, and effort he invests in the dating, the more sexual play he is entitled to expect in return.

Traditional norms de-emphasize the sexual interests and needs of women. For them, sexual activity is supposed to be a bargaining commodity to be offered in exchange for other desired goods. Women, in this context, are viewed as being interested in dating the most desirable men in order to marry as well as possible. In the process, they also raise their status among other females by demonstrating their desirability (McCall, 1966).

At the crudest level, generally in early adolescence, the bargaining may center around whether the young man is entitled to a good-night kiss on the first date or just how much of a further investment is required. Later on, the bargaining may become much more complex. Ultimately it can involve all sorts of demands the woman may make upon the man's time, money, and patience in exchange for varying levels of sexual activity.

The persons with whom one bargains (that is, whom one dates) and the kinds of bargains struck, depend upon the resources one brings into the dating situation. After all, people shop at stores they can afford, and they receive deference from sales clerks according to how much money they appear to be able to spend. Dating bargains are struck in much the same way. The most attractive men usually date the most attractive women, and vice versa. But physical attractiveness is just one factor. Such assets as having money to spend, having a car, dressing appropriately, and knowing the "in" places to go and the "in" things to do also bring dating status.

Studies have shown that campuses generally have a dating stratification system that most students clearly recognize. Fraternity and sorority members are at the top, and most people can distinguish among the more desirable and less desirable organizations (Larson and Leslie, 1968). Most of the time, most people date at or near their own prestige levels and strike rather even bargains. But in those instances in which a man or woman dates below (or above) his or her level, the stage is set for an exploitative relationship (Waller and Hill, 1951).

The Principle of Least Interest

Whether we are talking about the traditional dating system, with its formally arranged dates, emphasis upon mate selection, and dominance of the man, or about the emerging patterns that emphasize spontaneity, informality, sharing, and equality, one of the partners often has more to gain from the relationship than the other one does (Eslinger, Clarke, and Dynes, 1972). This lack of balance may develop either from the unequal statuses (and hence, bargaining power) of the partners, or from the greater emotional involvement of one partner.

When a high-status, desirable woman dates a man of lower status and bargaining power, she is not likely to be admired for doing so. Indeed, other people may tease her, make jokes behind her back, or forthrightly disapprove of her poor choice.

But she gains some corresponding advantages. She has less to lose than the man does by ending the relationship; she probably could find a more attractive man, whereas he would probably have to settle for a less desirable woman. Consequently, she is likely to assume control of the relationship. She can decide where and when the couple should go and what they should do when they get there. Not only does she wield a great deal of power, but she can also use the power to survey the field with an eye to attracting other men. A man who would not tolerate such behavior from his status-equal, must do so if he doesn't wish to risk a break with his higher-status partner. In addition, the man also is in a poor position to claim his share of the bargain. If the woman refuses to reward his tolerance with appropriate love making, there is little that he can do about it. If he accepts these circumstances, it is probably in the hope that his dating partner will eventually come to return his interest and yield to him or marry him.

In the reverse situation, where a higher-status man dates a lower-status woman, he is in a position to exploit her comparably. He can be less considerate of her wishes, and he can demand more sex. The woman must either yield or be prepared to break off the relationship. She may yield in the hope of inducing the man to fall in love with her. She may even permit herself to become pregnant in the hope that the prospect of a child may help her attain her goal.

This sort of differential bargaining power between partners, with its accompanying risk of exploitation, is not confined to relationships between persons of unequal status. It probably develops to some degree in many relationships. Most dating partners are at least potentially attracted to one another, or they wouldn't continue dating. Often, however, one is more strongly attracted than the other, and the partner with the lesser interest in continuing the relationship is in a position to dominate and control it. Exploitation may follow.

Studies have shown that both men and women systematically misperceive the expectations of members of the opposite sex in dating situations. Women tend to see men as expecting women to be sexually more permissive than they really are. Men perceive women as expecting them to be more aggressive than they really are (Balswick and Anderson, 1969). Small wonder that the efforts of men and women to discover the desired qualities in dating partners become confused, when the situation rests essentially upon bargaining and when some inequality in bargaining power is common. Fortunately, there is a mechanism, not generally recognized as such, that serves to equalize the balance of power within the couple.

The Function of Lovers' Quarrels

Whatever the source of the unequal bargaining power, most men and women do not suffer exploitation by the dating partner for very long without becoming at least intuitively aware of it and upset by it. Thereby they set the stage for a "lovers' quarrel." The function of such conflicts is either to terminate the relationship or to minimize the exploitation.

Quarrels work this way because most people disapprove of exploitation; they can engage in it blatantly only as long as they are not really aware of what they are doing. The upper-status woman, for example, who uses her lower-status date for personal advantage is likely to be shocked when he confronts her with the accusation. If she truly has no interest in him, the quarrel is likely to distress them both and they will probably stop dating one another.

More likely, however, she will meet his anger, the legitimacy of which she at least senses, by denying that she exploits him. She will respond with professions of warmth and interest, if not love, for him. Consciously seeking qualities such as dependability, stability, and mutual attraction in dating, she responds in terms of those ideals. In the process, she actually becomes more interested in her partner. Both partners are thus somewhat reassured about the relationship, and they are likely to move on to deeper levels of both emotional and physical involvement.

The process works similarly when it is the man who does the exploiting, and when the exploitation results from unequal emotional involvement rather than unequal social status. Moreover, lovers' quarrels of this sort are likely to erupt not just once but whenever the power in the relationship gets grossly out of balance. If it is the man who is exploited at first, it may be the woman later on. Or the relationship may continue to be one-sided, with the lower-status, more involved partner repeatedly seeking redress as the relationship moves hesitantly toward marriage.

Most young men and women today have been somewhat involved in these aspects of the traditional dating system, and many still are. Increasingly, however, young people are coming to perceive the artificiality, the harmful effects, and the inherent subordination of women in these patterns. Gradually, they are helping to create new relationship norms.

EMERGING RELATIONSHIP NORMS

Spontaneous, informal hanging around together in heterosexual groups, which was described in the context of high-school students, continues at the college level. Here, too, there is a similar conscious rejection of arranged dates and all that they imply. Because the people are older, however, and because both biological and social pressures impel them toward greater and more exclusive intimacy, there also is more pairing off.

College Dating Patterns

There have been very few studies focusing explicitly upon changes in college dating patterns in recent years. One valuable study, however, was done upon men from the Harvard University classes of 1964, 1965, 1970, and 1973 (Vreeland, 1972). The study reported differences in dating patterns between groups, and it also traced changes within groups as the students progressed through the university.

Analysis of data from the classes of 1964 and 1965 revealed the existence of four distinct dating patterns. They can be called, in turn, companionship, instrumental, traditional, and intellectual.

The need to have a friend who is a sympathetic listener was prominent in the *companionship* pattern. In these relationships, recreational activities, particularly formal ones, were de-emphasized in favor of private and intimate activities. Sexual activity generally was present, but it appeared to be subordinate to the couples' search for their individual and paired identities.

In the *instrumental* pattern, operation of the traditional masculine subculture was prominent. In these cases, the men were out for sexual conquest that would enhance their reputations among their fellows. They emphasized dress and manners, and they took their dates to popular places, sports events, nightclubs, and dances.

The *traditional* dating pattern was most in line with the values men and women tell researchers they look for in dating partners. These men were conscious of looking for wives, and they sought women they could "take home to mother," women who were of a status equal to their own, religious, sexually conservative, and of good reputation.

Finally, the *intellectual* pattern, which may have been widespread only at elite colleges and universities, was found among brilliant but socially rather inexperienced men. They emphasized the woman's intellectual qualities and their ability to share ideas and questions with her.

Analysis of the data from the classes of 1970 and 1973 showed that all four of these patterns continued to exist, but that significant changes had occurred in them. One notable change was in the variety of dating activities among those following the companionship pattern. It had broadened to include forms of recreation, such as concerts, sports events, and parties. Recreation now weighed as heavily among these men as did having a good listener.

The instrumental pattern changed the most, with the formerly desired qualities of "effervescent personality," "well dressed," and "sexually attractive" giving way to approval of interest in political activities, using drugs, and making love. Preoccupation with sex was still there, but there was more emphasis upon "swinging" than upon making and displaying conquests.

The traditional dating pattern also had been transformed. Some men still were looking for wives, but they now devalued the very traits in women that they had sought earlier. Now they wanted women who were liberated and unconventional, not those who could be taken home to mother. The companionship and intellectual patterns, which had appeared only recently, remained relatively unchanged.

In summary, the two older dating patterns, the traditional and the instrumental, had changed markedly. The "beautiful bad girl" stereotype had been replaced by what we might call one of "radical hedonism," in which women who were independent and rebellious were sought after. The only overall trend in dating patterns as the men moved from the freshman to the senior year was for there to be less emphasis upon the traditional pattern and more upon the companionship one.

Several other observations from this study are also pertinent. First, formal introductions of men and women had almost disappeared; informality was now the keynote. The establishment of coed dormitory living in the late 1960s, changed things considerably, and just sitting around the dorm or going out for something to eat had now become popular. The proportion of men who did not date at all dropped from 12 percent to four percent. This drop suggests both more opportunity and more interest in dating on the part of men (Vreeland, 1972). More men also were going steady. But, paradoxically, men often resisted too much commitment to a particular woman. Men who had years of professional preparation still ahead of them sometimes felt pressured by their girlfriends, who knew the college years offered them their best opportunities to make appropriate marriages.

Although few systematic studies of the new dating patterns have yet been made, two other significant trends have become evident over the past several years. The old taboos against dating persons unlike oneself in religion and in race have been breaking down.

Dating often leads to marriage, of course, and virtually all the representatives of organized society have discouraged interfaith dating because they are opposed to interfaith marriages. Nevertheless, as long as 25 years ago, approximately half of all young people affirmed that they would be willing to enter a mixed religious marriage. By 1971, a striking 91 percent said they would marry a person of different faith (Landis and Landis, 1973).

Interreligious Dating

There are no statistics on the proportion of people who date outside their own religious faiths. Obviously, though, it is high and increasing. Undoubtedly, the devoutness of the individual is an important factor. People who are deeply involved in their religions are likely to regard interfaith dating as wrong or unwise. They are also likely to heed the official rules of their churches. Even some devout people these days, however, are committed to ecumenical ideals; that is, they might accept interfaith dating as a means of bridging religious differences, as long as there is a clear understanding that it cannot become serious.

For growing numbers of young people, interfaith dating is looked upon more as an opportunity than as a problem. Jewish, Catholic, and Protestant young people, including Protestants from different denominations, consciously seek to learn and appreciate one another's traditions, beliefs, and outlooks. Their rationale is that such contacts will make them better persons, regardless of whom they ultimately marry. Such dating also may be tending to lower the levels of religious antagonism in the country.

Much dating, particularly among college students, takes place away from the scrutiny of parents and in a generally supportive liberal atmosphere. As a result, much interfaith dating never leads the young people to confront the potential or active disapproval of others. If the relationship becomes serious, of course, these factors must eventually be faced. The topic of interfaith marriage will be treated systematically in Chapter 6.

**Interracial
Dating**

Interracial dating certainly is more apparent, on college campuses and off, than it was only a few years ago. Public opinion polls demonstrate both more favorable attitudes toward it and more participation in it. A Louis Harris poll in 1971 reported that almost one person in five had dated interracially; the greatest level of acceptance was found among the young, the more affluent, and the better educated.

Later, a Gallup poll reported an increase in the acceptance of interracial marriage between 1968 and 1972. On the average, approval of black–white marriages increased nationwide from 20 to 29 percent in that interval. However, there were striking differences in the attitudes of blacks and whites. Sixty percent of the blacks queried expressed approval, while only twenty percent of the whites did so. The level of white approval, however, had risen from only five percent four years earlier. Again, younger and better educated people were the most favorable.

Few studies of interracial dating in any social context have yet been reported, for obvious reasons. The persons involved know that many people disapprove of their activities; consequently, they are loath to talk to strangers about them. Interracial dating is still a minority practice, and it is not easy to get access to participants. Finally, many potential researchers are sympathetic to these feelings and are reluctant to intrude upon the couples' privacy.

Despite these obstacles, one perceptive study was done in a midwest city. A husband–wife team interviewed, informally, both black and white students at a desegregated high school of some 3000 students

(Petroni, 1974). All of the students agreed that white boys do not date black girls. But they did not agree on why. Some white girls rationalized their own privileged positions by stating that the white boys were too proud to date black girls. White boys tended to think that black girls aren't as pretty as white girls; they also emphasized the problems they would encounter: hostility from other people, the possible loss of friends, and the lack of suitable places to go.

Black girls faced special pressures not to date white boys. The black girls of the highest status, who were headed for college, generally faced strong parental disapproval. This opposition was reinforced by possible loss of reputation. Many of these girls who had strong achievement motivation were not, themselves, opposed to interracial dating, however, and they might be more likely to do it once they are in college and away from direct parental control. Other black girls emphasized the belief that white boys interested in black girls were only after sex. If the girls accepted such dates, they felt, they would face sexual demands from the boys. Furthermore, other black students would believe them guilty whether or not they yielded. And finally, black boys pressured black girls not to date white boys. They themselves approved of dating white girls, but their racial pride was offended at the reverse situation.

Dating between black boys and white girls also met with widespread disapproval, although in this case not enough to stop it. White girls who dated blacks were harassed and rebuffed. They tended to be regarded as "immoral" on the basis of even the most casual contacts with black boys, such as stopping to talk to them in the hall. Many sensitive black boys stated that they had avoided dating white girls because they didn't want to be responsible for ruining the girls' reputations. White girls who dated black boys and then broke off with them continued to be ostracized by other whites, both boys and girls.

The black boys who dated interracially suffered, too. Other blacks attacked them for lack of racial pride and for "thinking they were white." The black girls were particularly hostile. They resented the fact that white girls had some access to boys of both races, whereas they themselves were prevented from dating white boys.

Interracial couples also were opposed, threatened, and punished by parents and school personnel. Even parents who perceived themselves to be "liberal" generally disapproved, and they disapproved more of their daughters dating interracially than of their sons. Less avowedly liberal parents sometimes used beatings to enforce their demands.

School principals, teachers, and counselors did not interfere directly with interracial dating, particularly by lower-status students. But they often were more coercive with upper-status students. Upper-status white girls who dated blacks sometimes were forbidden to run for school offices, or to try out for cheerleader; or they were discouraged from seeking scholarships. High-status black boys, who often were athletes, were threatened with loss of scholarships or even removal from the team.

Thus, we have all the symptoms of a troubled situation in rapid change. Most high-school-age people defend in principle the right to date whomever one chooses and not be punished for it. Older people, particularly parents, are likely to be opposed because of both racial prejudice and fear for their children's welfare. When confronted with actual interracial dating situations, even young people tend to react with bigotry and self-interest.

All of these problems should not obscure, however, the fact that interracial dating has recently become much more common. Clearly, it is proving rewarding enough to some young people to cause them to withstand the pressures against it. Some young people are putting their egalitarian ideals into practice as they grow toward maturity. If we had comparable analyses of interracial dating at the college and adult levels, doubtless they would show similar problems and pressures. Doubtless, they would also show that people become somewhat less vulnerable to these pressures as they get older and become more independent. There has been considerable research on interracial marriage, which will be analyzed in another chapter.

COLLEGE MARRIAGES

Somewhere around 20 percent of college students today are married. College marriage occurs more often in urban universities than in small residential colleges, more often among graduate students, and more often among upperclassmen than among freshmen and sophomores. In most ways, marriages that occur while one or both partners are still in college probably do not differ from other marriages of college educated people. But college marriages have some special features.

Many college marriages represent an unexpected termination of the usual college dating pattern. This fact is indicated by one study, of a sample of 196 college marriages, which reported that something over 30 percent of them followed premarital pregnancies (Price-Bonham, 1973). These same 196 marriages had, at the time of the study, an average of about one child each. Some had two children, of course, and eleven of the couples had more than two. Not only had these couples been hastened into marriage, but their tasks of completing their educations and achieving marital adjustment had also been complicated by early childbearing.

We should emphasize the fact, of course, that most college marriages are not the result of pregnancy. Among most of them, the processes of falling in love and mate selection are the same as for other couples; the marriages simply occur at an earlier time.

College marriages in the 1970s have changed markedly from earlier ones (Busselen and Busselen, 1975; Hepker and Cloyd, 1974). Marriage was not common among college students until after World War II. At that time, returning war veterans entered college in large numbers under the G.I. Bill. Older than most other students, they either brought their wives to campus with them or refused to delay mate selection and marriage any longer. Many of these men also held outside jobs, and many of the wives worked to help their husbands complete their educations.

The pressures on these marriages were great. Many of the husbands who were not particularly academically oriented had to work very hard to get through school. They often held jobs on nights and weekends, leaving many wives to entertain themselves as best they could. Few of these marriages had adequate incomes, either. Tempers often became short, and campus counseling agencies were kept busy. The more recent Korean and Vietnam wars were not so large in scale, nor were veterans' educational benefits as adequate. As a result, the veteran-linked marriage ceased to be the major form of college marriage by about the mid-1950s.

Once the barriers to college marriages were broken, however, they were not to be erected again. Older men continued to go back to college in small numbers, but most of the college marriages from the mid-1950s on occurred among 20 to 22-year-old people. Couples who wanted to marry often agreed that the woman would drop out of school, get a job, and support the completion of the man's education; then, after his graduation, they would share the rewards of their joint efforts.

For many couples, this arrangement worked well. There were unanticipated pregnancies, quarrels over the husband's having to study most of the time, and other adjustment problems that plague most young marriages. But many college marriages weathered the problems well; the husbands today have good jobs, and the couples enjoy very adequate standards of living. After graduation, many of the wives quit work to have and enjoy their families, and many of them today are still content and satisfied with their choices. Some of them, however, regret not having completed their educations and yearn for a life more challenging than marriage and motherhood alone. We will have much more to say about this problem later.

Others of these marriages did not fare quite so well. Some of the wives gave up most of their outside interests when they quit school, while their husbands continued to expand their horizons, first in college and then on the job. Some of these couples grew apart. The wives tended to become increasingly bitter over their husbands' lack of appreciation of their sacrifices; the husbands, in turn, grew to resent their wives' inability to take an interest in the husbands' careers or the world in general. Some of these husbands eventually found more interesting, more vital, and younger women.

As a result, outsiders tended to cluck their tongues disapprovingly when women college students announced their intention to drop out of school and marry. To do so, they counseled, was to one day be discarded by the man for whom the sacrifice was to be made.

This pattern of marriage carried over from the 1950s and 1960s into the next decade. But as we entered the 1970s, a more equalitarian form of college marriage, which had always existed in small numbers, began to emerge alongside the older form. Of the sample of 196 college marriages mentioned above, 125 were relatively traditional ones, in which only the husband was a student. However, 71 were more modern ones in which both partners were students (Price-Bonham, 1973).

In over 40 percent of the college marriages of both types, the husband and the wife both held paying jobs. In addition, over half of each group received some outside financial assistance, such as checks from parents, loans, trust funds, gifts, and so on. Still, both groups indicated that their most serious problems were financial. Only in rare instances do married college couples have enough income to live on comfortably.

Somewhat surprisingly, and discomfortingly for people who believe in equality in man–woman relationships, there was evidence of more strain in the marriages in which the wives continued their educations. These wives, but not their husbands, made lower scores on a standardized marital adjustment scale than did their counterparts in more traditional marriages. Children also were more of a problem when the wives were in school than when they were not. Employment itself posed problems when the wife also was in school.

It should be emphasized, of course, that these measurements were made at one time, while the spouses were still in college. They do not tell us anything about the quality of these marriages in the long run. Perhaps the strains encountered by the modern college marriages must be endured in order to lay the foundations for more equalitarian, growth-enhancing relationships later on. It may even be (indeed, we suspect it to be) that there is a continuing price to be paid for equality and sharing. Equalitarian marriages should be expected to produce special kinds of problems, not only in the early years but throughout married life. They should also be expected to produce special rewards and benefits.

SUMMARY

For many youngsters, the first stirs of romantic attraction are felt in early childhood. Sexual curiosity and developing sexual urges provide some of the motivation; also, both boys and girls learn that success with the opposite sex brings approval both from peers and from adults.

Many boys and girls are beginning to pair off and to have "crushes" by about the fifth to seventh grades. By high-school age, most youngsters have had some dating experience and describe themselves as playing the field. Up to one-fourth have not dated yet, and almost as many are dating steadily. Girls tend to move into steady dating earlier than boys do, and boys who are not college-oriented are more likely to go steady in direct anticipation of marriage.

At the high-school level, there is now a widespread rejection of the old system of formal dating, which is regarded as sexist, anxiety-producing, and hypocritical. Spontaneous, informal activities are preferred, with couples pairing off from the group only as they become serious about one another.

Non-college-oriented young people are more likely to pair off seriously in high school, and to marry young. Many of these marriages are precipitated by pregnancy and complicated by early childbearing. Occupational training ends with high-school graduation or before. Teenage marriages are about twice as likely as other marriages to end in divorce.

At both high school and college levels, many young men and women consciously seek qualities in dating partners that they believe are desirable in marriage partners. They emphasize such qualities as stability, dependability, family orientation, and mutual attraction.

Many people, also, are aware of bargaining elements in the traditional dating situation: trading sex for going places, spending money, and the like. Most campuses have a recognizable hierarchy of groups and organizations, and people as well as groups differ in prestige and attractiveness. When people date outside their own levels, exploitation often results.

Some exploitation eventually occurs in many relationships. It arises either from status differences between the two people, or because one partner becomes more emotionally involved than the other. Sooner or later, this unbalance is likely to result in a crisis. It appears as a quarrel in which one partner confronts the other with the charge of exploitation; the quarrel leads either to a break or to a greater commitment to the relationship by the exploiting partner. Such crises may recur, and they may move the relationship toward marriage.

College dating patterns have changed significantly in recent years. There is now more emphasis upon informality, sharing, and just doing things together; there is less emphasis upon sexual conquest, and more upon love making. The old image of the sexually reluctant female has given way to a new image of the liberated woman.

Although most official agencies continue to oppose it, interreligious dating is becoming much more common. Many young people accept it as an opportunity to learn more about other people and other groups.

Interracial dating also is more common and is looked upon more favorably by younger, better educated people, but it still is strongly resisted by many. Many interracial couples are harassed by parents, school authorities, and peers. The persistence of the pattern, however, testifies to the dedication of many young people to ideals of equality and to the rewards with which their relationships provide them.

Between one-fifth and one-fourth of all college students today are married. Many college marriages are precipitated by pregnancy, and many college couples have children. Fewer wives these days drop out of college to support their husbands through school, recognizing that to do so many result in their eventually growing apart. Increasingly, both partners stay in school and both work to support the marriage. But still they suffer financially. In some ways, these modern college marriages undergo more strain than more traditional ones do. That is part of the price to be paid for equality and partnership.

FOR ADDITIONAL READING

Lopata, Helena Znaniecki, ed., *Marriages and Families* (New York: D. Van Nostrand, 1973). Good selections on the role of fraternities and sororities in college dating, and on interracial dating.

Roleder, George, ed., *Marriage Means Encounter* (Dubuque, Iowa: Wm. C. Brown, 1973). Contains a perceptive analysis of the American Dating Game.

Skolnick, Arlene, and Jerome H. Skolnick, eds., *Intimacy, Family, and Society* (Boston: Little, Brown, 1974). See the section on "Love and Pairing."

Winch, Robert F., and Graham B. Spanier, eds., *Selected Studies in Marriage and the Family* (New York: Holt, Rinehart and Winston, 1974). The section on adolescence contains selections relating to the subject matter of this chapter.

Wiseman, Jacqueline P., ed., *People as Partners* (San Francisco: Canfield Press, 1971). Section II has articles on courtship as exchange, interreligious and interracial dating, sororities, and values in dating and mate selection.

STUDY QUESTIONS

1. How does the masculine subculture affect pre-teen dating patterns? Is status seeking a factor in the heterosexual experiences of little girls? How?

2. How have high-school dating patterns changed in recent years? What factors produce high-school marriages? How do they affect the nature of the marriages?

3. What values do college students consciously seek in dating partners?

4. Are there any parallels between bargaining in dating relationships and the social class structure of the larger society? How is bargaining related to differences in personal attractiveness?

5. How does exploitation enter into dating? Describe the forces that tend to eliminate it again.

6. What changes in college dating patterns have occurred in recent years? Relate these changes in dating to changes in the status of women.

7. What is your attitude toward interracial dating by others? by yourself? Why do you feel as you do?

8. Distinguish between traditional and modern college marriages. Does it seem reasonable to you that modern college marriages should have some strains that more traditional ones do not have? Why?

Chapter 4
Sexual
Involvement

The relationships of adult men and women are based upon personality foundations built up in infancy and childhood. Some of the interaction between men and women is explicitly sexual. The foundations for that behavior, too, are laid down early in life.

CHILDHOOD SEXUAL BEHAVIOR

In 1948, a team of researchers under Dr. Alfred C. Kinsey published the first of two books on human sexuality based upon thousands of interviews. The so-called Kinsey reports startled many people with their frank accounts of sexual behavior, which directly challenged many cherished assumptions (Kinsey, Pomeroy, and Martin, 1948; Kinsey, Pomeroy, Martin, and Gebhard, 1953). Not the least of their findings was in the area of infant sexuality.

The Kinsey team reported, for example, that orgasm-like responses had been observed in infants of both sexes at only four to five months of age. A later study, using motion picture records of the behavior of naked 20-week-old babies, reported that the boy babies had penile erections at the average rate of 2.3 per hour (Shuttleworth, 1959). Finally, in the 1960s, William H. Masters and Virginia Johnson discovered that girl babies display comparable sexuality, experiencing vaginal lubrication. We need not impute any sexual motives or even any conscious awareness to these babies, of course. The fact is simply that many infants display primitive sexual responses almost from birth.

The Kinsey studies showed that about half of all adults had experienced some sex play, most commonly masturbation, as children. A tenth of the women respondents and one-fifth of the men had achieved orgasm that way by age twelve. If these figures seem high, more recent investigators (Simon and Gagnon, 1970) believe that they may actually be far too low, because some adults may be unable or unwilling to recall their childhood behavior. Simon and Gagnon believe that as many as three-fourths of all persons may engage in some childhood sex play.

Other studies have shown that boys are more commonly and more frequently involved in sex play than girls are (Broderick, 1966; Spanier, 1975). This finding raises the question again of whether males are endowed with more compelling sex drives than females are. We can only say that we have no final answer. Males traditionally have not been discouraged from sex play, whereas girls have. In fact, males often have received positive support from their peer groups in doing so; girls, on the other hand, generally have been discouraged from sex play by adults, and there has been little support for it from their peers. What is virtually certain is that differences between boys and girls in sexuality have been overemphasized. Sexual responses in female infants, infant vaginal lubrication, and the trend toward more female sexual activity in childhood and adolescence all indicate the potential that is there.

We also know that, apart from encouragement or discouragement, boys and girls receive very different *kinds* of sexual conditioning. Boys typically begin masturbation either before puberty or very shortly thereafter. Although they may have fantasies about sexual intercourse, their sex behavior is somewhat "privatized." That is, it focuses upon genital pleasure, rather than upon a heterosexual relationship within which that pleasure might be experienced. In fact, the masculine subculture encourages boys to approach adolescence having had very little experience with, or orientation toward, romantic relationships.

Among girls, the reverse is typical. They have been encouraged to focus upon relationships and romance rather than upon sexuality. In their early heterosexual relationships, however, they must interact with boys who are sexually oriented and relatively inexperienced in the language and actions of romantic love. Not surprisingly, the boys and girls often have difficulty understanding one another.

Early in life, and early in the history of a particular dating relationship, the boy is likely to press vigorously for sexual involvement. But the girl, who has been taught that sex is acceptable only in the context of love, is confused by his behavior and tends to resist it. As the relationship develops and emotional involvement occurs, the situation often reverses. The boy becomes romantically involved with the girl and lets up on trying to seduce her. But she, sensing his affection for her, becomes more ready to accept sex play with him.

Simon and Gagnon report a study that bears on this subject. It shows, indirectly, that males seek sex in casual relationships, whereas females accept it in more serious, stable ones. Focusing upon the number of times that males and females had intercourse with their first coital partners, they report that the males typically had intercourse with those women only from one to three times. The women, in contrast, had intercourse ten or more times with their first sexual partners.

ADOLESCENT SEXUAL BEHAVIOR

The line between preadolescent and adolescent sexual behavior is not a sharp one. Some boys and some girls begin masturbation and heterosexual play early in childhood. Generally, however, sexual activity becomes more explicit and more common with the onset of puberty.

MASTURBATION

In the early 1970s, a research team of a man and a woman did a questionnaire study of 435 students on three university campuses in the New York City area. Two hundred and thirty of the respondents were men and 205 were women (Arafat and Cotton, 1974).

Some of the results are shown in Table 4-1. They indicate a high frequency of masturbation by both sexes; male–female differences were surprisingly small. These results suggest again that innate differences between males and females have been overemphasized, and that male and female behavior are becoming more alike with the passage of time.

Unlike earlier studies, this one did not ask whether the respondents had *ever* masturbated. Instead, it inquired whether they were mastur-

**TABLE 4-1
AGE AT FIRST
MASTURBATION, BY SEX
(330 UNIVERSITY
STUDENTS)**

AGE AT FIRST MASTURBATION	MALES		FEMALES	
	NUMBER	PERCENT	NUMBER	PERCENT
5–8 years	30	14.6	25	20.0
9–12 years	85	41.5	40	32.0
13–16 years	80	39.0	40	32.0
17–21 years	10	4.9	20	16.0
Totals	205	100.0	125	100.0

Source: Ibtihaj S. Arafat and Wayne L. Cotton, ''Masturbation Practices of Males and Females,'' *The Journal of Sex Research* 10 (Nov. 1974), pp. 293–307.

bating *at present.* Eighty-nine percent of the male respondents reported that they were masturbating, and 61 percent of the females did so. These figures are about as high as those reported by Kinsey for the whole *lifetime* experience of people two generations ago. It is probable, of course, that people who masturbate were more likely to respond to the questionnaire than those who do not (there was a 27-percent non-response rate). But these figures are also far higher than those reported for earlier generations.

The figures in Table 4-1 are based only upon those men and women who stated that they do masturbate. Note that over half of the students of both sexes reported that they began masturbating before reaching age 13, and virtually all of the men had begun before age 17. Roughly one woman in six began at age 17 or older.

One-third of both the men and the women stated that they masturbate a few times a week. Another one-third masturbate a few times a month. About 10 percent of the students of both sexes report masturbating several times a day. And 20 percent of both sexes reported that they continue to masturbate with the same frequency even when they have other sexual activity regularly with a partner. Almost 60 percent of both sexes discovered masturbation by themselves, while about half that many more of both sexes learned about it from their friends.

Their feelings about masturbation were mixed. Nearly 70 percent of the men and nearly 60 percent of the women reported receiving physical satisfaction from it. However, something under one-fourth of the men and one-third of the women reported experiencing either guilt or depression.

This study did not delve deeply into the emotional reactions of men and women to masturbation. Nevertheless, it does appear to indicate at least two things. First, many young persons of both sexes today are much more matter-of-fact about masturbation than people used to be. Second, there still is a minority who are emotionally troubled by it.

THE INFLUENCE OF PORNOGRAPHY

It has long been known that the sharing of explicit sexual materials—"dirty" books and pictures—has been widespread among adolescents. Until recently, however, the subject was "hush-hush"; most people tried to ignore its existence and simply assumed that pornography is a corrupting influence for young people. In 1967, however, Congress created the U.S. Commission on Obscenity and Pornography to evaluate the influences of pornography on the American people, and to recommend means for dealing with whatever problems they found. The commission did its work between 1968 and 1970, undertaking and coordinating studies of numerous subjects: the extent of availability of pornography, the extent of exposure to it, and its effects on youth, on women, and on men (Wilson, 1972).

One study dealt with a national random sample of 769 adolescents, aged 15 to 20, who were living at home. It showed that about half of all boys see sexually explicit material by the time they are 15 years old. Girls reach that level of exposure about a year later. By 18 years of age, fully 80 percent of the males and 70 percent of the females have seen pictures or read descriptions of sexual intercourse.

Both males and females report being sexually aroused by these materials. Laboratory measurements of heartbeat, rate of breathing, blood pressure, and so on, confirm this fact. But, contrary to earlier beliefs, females report as much and as frequent arousal as males do.

The studies do not show, however, any systematic acting out of this arousal by people of either sex. People exposed to pornography show no more sexual activity during the 24 hours after exposure than they did in the previous 24 hours. People who are accustomed to masturbating continue to do so. Those who are engaging in sexual intercourse have intercourse if the partner is available; if not, they are somewhat more likely to masturbate.

Many people have worried whether prolonged exposure to sexually explicit materials might not distort the values and attitudes of young people, encouraging them to deviant or violent sexual patterns. The commission conducted elaborate studies to find out.

One study compared people who have been imprisoned or hospitalized for sex offenses with a matched group of persons who were not known to be sex offenders. Surprisingly, there was actually a *negative* relationship between exposure to explicit sexual materials in adolescence and later sex offenses. That is, the sex offenders had had less exposure to sexual materials than had their normal counterparts. The essentials of this study were repeated four different times in four different parts of the country, by four different teams of researchers, always with the same result.

Other studies focused upon whether people tend to become "addicted" to sexual materials, and on whether bad moral character results. Again, the findings were negative. Overexposure to pornographic materials leads to boredom. Bad moral character seems to precede such exposure rather than to result from it.

Apparently, most young people are quite capable of dealing constructively with sexually explicit materials. In fact, the commission's principal recommendation was that a massive sex education program should be launched in the United States, on the assumption that much of the public concern about pornography stems from people's inability to talk directly and frankly about sex.

The commission did not endorse the distribution of sexually explicit materials to adolescents, however; in fact, the opposite is true. Although it recommended the repeal of all existing laws restricting the access of adults to sexual materials, it also urged stronger laws against the commercial distribution of such materials to minors. As we have seen, the commission found no evidence that such materials are harmful to minors. Nevertheless, it endorsed the traditional principle that parents should control their children's access to sexual materials and should have the primary responsibility for shaping their attitudes and values.

CHANGED SOCIETAL ATTITUDES

Although to select any one date would be arbitrary, public attitudes toward the sexual behavior of adolescents and young adults apparently began to liberalize substantially beginning about 1965. Gallup polls, for example, taken in 1963 and again in 1974, showed an increase in the number of people who approved of sexual relations between engaged persons, from 12 percent to 43 percent.

The outcomes of polls depend partly upon the wording of the questions asked, of course. Thus, it is interesting to note that other Gallup polls that asked whether people *objected* to premarital sexual intercourse found a similar development. Between 1969 and 1973, the proportion *not* objecting rose from 21 percent to 43 percent. None of the polls has yet shown that most people approve of premarital sex. But it does appear that much of the harsh condemnation of such behavior that once existed has now diminished or disappeared.

The findings of these national polls have been supported by in-depth studies of the attitudes of college students. One study at a large southern university, for example, compared attitudes of students, both men and women, in 1965 and 1970. Over those five years, the proportion of men who believed that premarital intercourse is immoral dropped from 35 percent to 15 percent. Proportionately greater change occurred in the attitudes of the women, though they were originally and finally more conservative than the men. The proportion of women believing premarital intercourse to be immoral dropped from 70 percent to 34 percent (Robinson, King, and Balswick, 1972). The emerging attitudes of both college students and the general public seem to be typified by the huge majority, 96 percent of the men and the 94 percent of the women, who said in 1970 that "sexual behavior is a person's own business."

Another study of university students, in both the South and the Midwest, catalogued changes between 1968 and 1972. Again, both men and women were found to have become much more liberal in their attitudes. They showed greater acceptance of heavy petting, sexual intercourse, and oral–genital contacts (Croake and James, 1973).

Not only have people become much less disapproving of sexual intimacy among young unmarried people, but more young men and women are having sexual intercourse. This statement is true for adolescents in general and for college students in particular.

PARTICIPATION IN SEXUAL INTERCOURSE

One pair of researchers studied the sexual behavior of high school students in a west-shore Michigan community in 1969 and again in 1973. They found that almost identical percentages of 17-year-old boys and girls, 34 and 35 percent, reported that they had had sexual intercourse at least once. Surprisingly, this equality was arrived at by the girls having shown an increase over those years, while the boys showed a slight decrease. This study also showed increases in the proportions of boys and girls who had had intercourse with more than one partner (Vener and Stewart, 1974).

Something between one-fourth and one-third of all girls in the United States have had sexual intercourse by age 17, according to a national study done in 1971. The Commission on Population Growth and the American Future questioned 4240 girls. It reported that 27 percent of the 17-year-olds and 37 percent of the 18-year-olds had had sexual intercourse (Kantner and Zelnik, 1972).

College and university students are somewhat older on the average, of course, than these general samples of adolescents. Consequently,

they should be expected to be sexually more active. This theory is confirmed by one of two recent studies.

One of the studies involved 419 students at a southeastern university and a midwestern college. It found that 63 percent of the men, and 34 percent of the women, had at some time had intercourse. These figures represent an increase over the figure reported above for 17-year-old men, but no increase for women. As will be shown in a moment, however, these women, who averaged slightly over 20 years of age, were more conservative than many. This same study reported that 39 percent of the sexually experienced men had had two or more coital partners; only 11 percent of the sexually experienced women had done so (Lewis, 1973).

A strongly contrasting picture is provided by a study done at another southeastern university, an institution with a reputation for being politically and socially liberal. This study was also done originally in 1968 and repeated in 1972. Some of its findings are summarized in Table 4-2.

High percentages of both the men and women reported having had intercourse, and the numbers for both sexes underwent substantial

EXPERIENCED COITUS	MEN		WOMEN		TABLE 4-2
	1968 (N = 98)	1972 (N = 107)	1968 (N = 88)	1972 (N = 68)	**PERCENTAGES OF STUDENTS AT ONE UNIVERSITY WHO HAD EXPERIENCED COITUS, 1968 AND 1972**
Yes	56	73	46	73	
No	44	27	54	27	
Total	100	100	100	100	

Source: Adapted from Karl E. Bauman and Robert R. Wilson, "Sexual Behavior of Unmarried University Students in 1968 and 1972," *The Journal of Sex Research* 10 (Nov. 1974), p. 330.

increases between 1968 and 1972. Moreover, by 1972, the proportions of men and women with coital experience were exactly equal, amounting to almost three-fourths of the students sampled. These findings should not be overgeneralized, however. The samples are relatively small, and this is a liberal institution. On the other hand, these figures probably show where America is heading: toward a higher level of premarital sexual involvement and more sexual equality (Bauman and Wilson, 1974).

Interestingly, however, these socially liberal young men and women did not show a large variety of sexual partners; the mean number of partners was approximately two for both sexes. What is more, this figure did not show any significant increase between 1968 and 1972. We might assume, therefore, that much of the increase in sexual intimacy among young people occurs within the context of relatively stable relationships. That this conclusion is likely will be shown later when we examine coed dormitory living and living together.

Considerable research documents an increased likelihood that young people will become sexually involved before marriage. Nevertheless, there has been relatively little study of the circumstances surrounding their first experiences in sexual intercourse. These experiences, of course, are bound to vary from group to group. We will focus here upon a study of 98 men and 88 women at a major university (Eastman, 1972).

Almost half of the men first had sexual intercourse while they were still in high school; for the other one-half it occurred when they were 18 or 19 years of age. Nearly one-fourth of the women had also had their first sexual intercourse in high school, but over one-third of them had been 20 years of age or older. This discrepancy is related to another fact: over half the men had their first experience with women they did not love, but fully four-fifths of the women said that they had been in love with their first partners. In fact, almost half of the women were not only in love with their partners, but planned to marry them. These data reinforce an earlier

FIRST SEXUAL INTERCOURSE

conclusion: many young men have an interest in sex for its own sake, and the masculine subculture supports sex without emotional commitment. The behavior of most women, on the other hand, reflects their lifelong encouragement to develop sexual interest in the context of serious love relationships.

The circumstances in which intercourse first occurs vary with the living situations of those involved. When young women live at home, a substantial proportion of them have intercourse there (Jackson and Potkay, 1973). In fact, the woman's residence is the most likely place for it to occur whether she lives with her parents or in an apartment. However, dormitory living still is not private enough in most circumstances. From one-fourth to one-third of first experiences occur in automobiles; motels are used somewhat less often.

As might be expected, women are much more likely than men are to be anxious during their first sexual encounters. They are concerned not only with the risk of pregnancy, but also with a variety of other things: guilt feelings, parental reactions, the physical circumstances, and the possibility of being hurt. Men, too, express some fear about the possibility of pregnancy, but report much less anxiety about it than women do (Eastman, 1972).

Later reactions to the first sexual experience also reflect the different situations of men and women. About 90 percent of the men in this study reported having been happy following their first experiences. A small minority experienced dissatisfaction over the act's being purely a physical one for them. In contrast, only about three-fifths of the women were happy about the experience. However, the women's enthusiasm tended to increase rather than decrease with the passage of time. This development probably reflects the growth of the total relationship with the man, and the acceptance of sex as one part of it.

Over two-thirds of the women said their relationships became stronger following sexual intercourse. One in six reported no change, and slightly fewer said it became weaker. Among men, however, there was either no change or a weakening of the relationship in almost three-fifths of the cases; presumably, these men were more interested in sex than in their partners. Somewhat surprisingly, however, the remainder of the men reported that their relationships with their women partners had been strengthened. This fact may reflect two things. First, a substantial proportion of men probably are seeking emotional as well as physical intimacy. Second, the fact of having had intercourse may tend to bind some men to their partners even when a deep relationship was not their original intention.

That sex has different meanings for men and for women is also shown by these couples' subsequent experiences. Over half of the men do not have intercourse with their first partners again, or have it only once or twice. These are the men who are not relationship-oriented. At the other extreme, though, over a third of the men become involved enough with their first partners to have intercourse more than ten times. Women tend to stay with their first partners longer. Among the women, almost three-fourths have intercourse with those partners at least three times, and some 45 percent have it more than ten times. Apparently these women tend to use sex to strengthen their relationships; or they continue having intercourse until they determine that the relationship is not a good one, at which time they break it off.

Given the age and the educational level of these young people, we might expect them to be knowledgeable about contraception and to use it effectively. But this is not true, at least during the first intercourse. This finding reflects in part the fact that almost 90 percent of the women say they did not plan for their first intercourse. Apparently they wished for it to be a spontaneous love experience.

Only about two percent of the women surveyed were currently using the pill, and none of them used other feminine contraceptive methods, such as diaphragms, spermicidal jellies, or intrauterine devices. The men were somewhat more calculating, and about a third of them used condoms. Some couples attempted coitus interruptus (withdrawal before ejaculation), and a few claimed to be using the rhythm method. But, all in all, there was little contraceptive protection in some two-thirds of the cases. The students who were worried about pregnancy had good reason to be worried.

THE DYNAMICS OF INVOLVEMENT

Statistics on the proportions of people who engage in sexual intercourse, and the conditions under which they do so, indicate what people in general are doing. They tell us little, however, about why they do it: what meaning their behavior has in their lives. One of the themes running through this book is the existence, side by side, of older heterosexual patterns that came to us roughly from the World War II era and new patterns that still are emerging. This duality also exists in the area of premarital intercourse.

Several studies show that old patterns still survive. Men still pursue women for the physical pleasure and the boost to self-esteem that conquest brings (Berger and Wenger, 1973); and women still tend to be more conservative and concerned about the possibility of exploitation (Hobart, 1974; Kaats and Davis, 1970). One study involving interviews with 1177 students at 12 colleges and universities, for example, emphasized not how many people had had intercourse but how they had reacted to the experience—specifically, how many other people they had told about it. Some of the results are summarized in Table 4-3.

The difference between the men's behavior and the women's is apparent. Most people of both sexes told someone about their experi-

**TABLE 4-3
NUMBER OF FRIENDS
TOLD OF FIRST
INTERCOURSE**

NUMBER OF FRIENDS TOLD	MEN (N = 328)	WOMEN (N = 184)
None	17.7%	26.6%
One or Two	14.0	29.3
Three or Four	14.9	21.7
Five or More	53.4	22.3
Totals	100.0%	99.9%

Source: Adapted from Donald E. Carns, "Talking About Sex: Notes on First Coitus and the Double Sexual Standard," *Journal of Marriage and the Family* 35 (Nov. 1973), p. 680.

ence. But over a fourth of the women told no one at all, and approximately 30 percent more told only one or two close friends. Among the men, by contrast, over half of them told five or more people. While it might be argued that the men have many close friends, it is more likely that there was some "displaying of trophies" involved (Carns, 1973).

Even if they recognize such behavior in themselves, most young people today disapprove of it. Most often, they express new youth values that hold that virility and glamor are false goals and that it is far more important to be honest with oneself and with other people (Toussieng, 1971). Part of being honest with oneself involves accepting one's body and the bodies of others. In heterosexual relationships, it involves enjoying the other person to the fullest. Such young people become involved in sex, seeking to find one another in what they perceive to be wholly artificial constraints that society imposes upon sex and marriage.

To the confounding of many of their elders, such young people ordinarily do not make sex the center of experience. They view it instead as just one part of the total experience. Sex helps to give completeness to a situation, just as loud music, natural dress, long hair, and other characteristics do, helping them respond to one another as unique persons.

*THE CONTINUING
SEARCH FOR
SELF-ESTEEM*

Modern young people have not given up the search for self-esteem. Nor have they given up searching for it through sex. What they have done is to alter the nature of the search.

Adolescence is a critical time for people to receive confirmation from their peers that they are adequate and desirable. Boys and young men have always sought this confirmation in sexual experience; their self-esteem is bolstered by sexual success and deflated by failure. Many a young man has thus been impelled to "make it" with his women friends regardless of the level of attraction between them, and regardless of the nature of their relationship. Traditionally, the young women often have been confused and somewhat frightened by such male aggression (Kanin, 1969). In fact, their own self-esteem is jeopardized, because their favorable self-concepts have depended upon not having too much sex too soon or with the wrong person (Schimel, 1971).

Recent changes have, in some ways, made the situation easier for both men and women. Disapproval of conquest has relieved males of the necessity to try to seduce their partners; it has also freed women to respond on the basis of their true feelings rather than outside pressures either to accept or to resist involvement.

In another way, though, the new patterns have created problems as well. The new emphasis upon "scoring," for example, represents almost explicit recognition that people can "gain points" for themselves through success in sex. Both men and women come under pressure from their peers to score. Moreover, in the traditional pattern, women were exempt from the expectation that they be adept in premarital sex; the only question was whether or not they would engage in it. As heterosexual relationships have become more equalitarian, however, the self-esteem of both men and women has come to depend upon their being capable sexual performers.

Now, the fact is that initial sexual experiences often are not very successful as athletic events. Young men, unsure of themselves and under the pressure of great sexual excitement, often fumble, and they are subject to premature ejaculation. Young women—inexperienced, somewhat frightened, and unsure whether what they are doing is proper—frequently are ill-prepared either to reassure their companions or to respond well themselves. The result often is somewhat unsatisfactory for both partners, and both of them may have their self-doubts increased by the experience.

THE RIGHT TO SAY NO

In our preoccupation with discovering how many young people are having sexual intercourse, and what their adjustment problems are, we sometimes overlook the fact that most people enter college as virgins; furthermore, substantial numbers of them graduate from college still without having had intercourse. Recent years have seen enough change in sexual attitudes to produce real problems for some members of this group (Hicks and Taylor, 1973).

It probably is inevitable that people should rationalize their own situations, whatever they are. Some sexually liberated young people have not only done that, but they have almost convinced other young people that there must be something wrong with them if they are not enjoying the pleasures of sex. They use the term "virginity" disdainfully, suggesting that it means immaturity at best, and homosexual tendencies at worst.

Human relationships, including those that involve sexual intercourse, are never simple and uncomplicated. The sexually active relationships of teenagers and young adults usually involve ambivalences and anxieties that are concealed from outsiders. Many young women do not have orgasm in their first encounters, and they worry about that failure. Many of them also have doubts, at least, about whether they are emotionally ready for intercourse with a particular man. They worry about whether the man really loves them, about discovery by their parents, about becoming pregnant, and so on.

Men, too, often are less than sure of themselves in their first sex relationships, although they may hide their uncertainty behind a screen of braggadocio. Frequently, they are unable to continue intercourse for more than a few seconds before ejaculation. This failure leaves them and their partners somewhat dissatisfied. With their fantasies of the great sexual experience shattered, men sometimes embark on a compulsive round of further sexual conquests, with the same woman or others, to reassure themselves of their sexual adequacy. This need to gain reassurance from others may help account for the fact that many men do not long continue having intercourse with their first partners. Often, fearing that they have "failed" her, they move on to other conquests and complicate their subsequent partners' lives in the process.

The point of all this is not that premarital intercourse is always a disappointing experience. It is not. With time and experience, and a loving relationship, it usually becomes very rewarding. What is unfortunate, however, is that some young people seek to allay their own anxieties by coercing other young people prematurely into the same situation. These pressures gain support from the general trend in our society toward sexual permissiveness.

The odds against any young man or woman remaining a virgin permanently are overwhelming. Time and experience will take care of that. Moreover, there is absolutely no reliable evidence either way to suggest that whether one has had intercourse or not is related to one's subsequent personal or marital adjustment (Ard, 1974). What is true is that sex in a loving relationship is likely to be far more satisfactory than sex as a means of proving something to oneself, or of gaining the approval of others. Loving sex is far more independent of performance standards, and far more likely to strengthen the overall relationship.

The results of a recent study lend further support to this view. The study, of 584 students at a western university, was directed at their reasons for *not* having sexual intercourse (Driscoll and Davis, 1971). The results are summarized in Table 4-4. Among men, the fear of pregnancy was cited more frequently than any other reason. Almost as frequently, the men reported that the woman couldn't be talked into it. The third reason, "decision not mine" seems quite similar to the second one. The fourth most common reason was that the man did not love the woman involved.

Among women, "did not love" was given far more often than any other reason. A belief that premarital intercourse is morally wrong came

REASONS	MEN	WOMEN
Did not love	26	106
Fear of pregnancy	42	43
Morally wrong	17	47
Couldn't talk into	39	1
Decision not mine	27	12
Ashamed after	7	43
Would worsen relationship	20	24
Risk of being caught	3	7
Ruin reputation	4	5
Totals	185	288

**TABLE 4-4
UNIVERSITY STUDENTS'
REASONS FOR NOT
HAVING INTERCOURSE**

Source: Adapted from Richard H. Driscoll and Keith E. Davis, "Sexual Restraints: A Comparison of Perceived and Self-Reported Reasons for College Students," *The Journal of Sex Research* 7 (Nov. 1971), p. 255.

second, followed by a feeling that they would be "ashamed after," and by fear of pregnancy; fear that intercourse would worsen the relationship came next. The women's reasons, even more than the men's, indicate a belief that the quality of the relationship is the most important thing.

COMPLICATIONS OF PREMARITAL SEX

Although we have discussed some of the emotional and relationship complications of premarital sex, there are medical, social, and legal ones as well. Venereal disease, for one, has become almost epidemic. Illegitimate births are also common, with still other pregnancies being aborted. Nationally and locally, teenagers are beginning to seek the legal right to medical care for such problems.

VENEREAL DISEASE

Social change has brought the problem of venereal disease (V.D.) almost full cycle. Syphilis and gonorrhea were the scourge of sexually active young people some two generations ago, but the development of penicillin and other antibiotics greatly diminished their threat for people growing up in the 1950s and early 1960s. During the later 1960s, however, the rates of gonorrhea and syphilis began to climb precipitously. After the common cold, they are now the most common infectious diseases in the United States. Teenagers in some cities have a one-in-five chance of contracting gonorrhea before their high-school graduation (Saxton, 1972).

Treatment for these diseases is quite effective when they are diagnosed promptly. The problem is that venereal disease may produce so few initial symptoms that people do not know they have it; gonorrhea in women, in particular, may remain hidden. A second problem is that many people fail to seek treatment because of the stigma associated with V.D.

They seldom become sexually inactive, however, so they continue to spread the disease.

Much of the recent increase in venereal disease must be attributed to our increasing sexual permissiveness and to some degree of promiscuity. Loving couples who have not had intercourse before do not give each other venereal disease. But when a young man or woman has intercourse with a sexually experienced person, the risk of infection is always present. The more frequently that casual sex is engaged in, the greater the risk.

CONCEPTION AND ILLEGITIMACY

Apparently the increasing public acceptance of sexual intercourse among young adults is somewhat informed, because repeated polls show comparable increases in the acceptance of contraceptive services and legal abortion for teenagers. The proportion of people who favored making birth control information available to anyone who wants it rose from 64 percent in the mid-1930s to 90 percent in 1971. In 1972, about two-thirds of three national samples approved of providing birth control services to sexually active unmarried teenagers (Pomeroy and Landman, 1972).

Table 4-5 summarizes a national survey of 4611 young women, 15 to 19 years of age, done in 1971. This study showed that although most sexually experienced women had used contraception at some time, most of them did not use it consistently. Fifty-three percent, for example, had failed to use contraception the last time they had intercourse. Sixteen percent had never used contraception. Moreover, almost one-fourth of

**TABLE 4-5
CONTRACEPTIVE METHOD
MOST RECENTLY USED
BY NEVER-MARRIED
WOMEN, AGES 15–19[a]**

METHOD	PERCENT USING (N = 1319)
Pill	21.4
Condom	27.3
Withdrawal	24.1
Intrauterine device	1.2
Douche	4.5
Other[b]	5.5
Never Used	16.0
Total	100.0

[a] Base includes those who gave no answer to the question. Percents are based on numbers weighted so as to conform for each of the 45 geographic strata with females of the same age and race in the 1970 U.S. Census of Population. N's, however, are unweighted totals from the interview sample.

[b] Foam, jelly, cream, diaphragm, and rhythm.

Source: John F. Kantner and Melvin Zelnik, "Contraception and Pregnancy: Experience of Young Unmarried Women in the United States," *Family Planning Perspectives* 5 (Winter 1973), p. 26.

the contraceptive users depended upon the unreliable method of coitus interruptus. Fewer than half used the generally reliable condom, intra-uterine devices, or the pill (Kantner and Zelnik, 1973).

This same study was later expanded to include women who had married before age 20. The authors reported that nearly 30 percent of those who had premarital intercourse also became pregnant before marriage. Of those women, 35 percent married while they were pregnant, and another ten percent married after the baby was born. Considering only those women who did not marry, almost 60 percent of them had live births, about 20 percent had abortions, and 15 percent still were pregnant at the time of the study (Zelnik and Kantner, 1974).

Figure 4-1 Ages of consent for medical care, 1974. (Reprinted by permission from *Time,* the weekly news magazine, November 25, 1974, p. 81; copyright Time, Inc., 1974.)

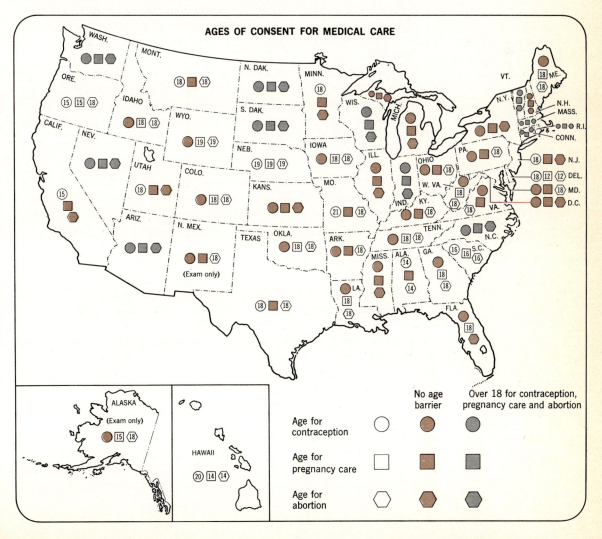

What we find, then, is that despite the alleged availability of contraceptives, most young people do not learn to use them consistently until some time after intercourse is begun and the risk of pregnancy is relatively high (Cvetkovich, Grote, Bjorseth, and Sarkissian, 1975). Traditionally, parents and other adults have sought to cope with the problem by discouraging their offspring from having sex and by denying them contraceptives. This method does not work, however (Furstenberg, 1971); in fact, it may actually compound the problem.

Teenagers and young adults are well aware that a pregnancy, with or without a resulting marriage, may damage both their chances in life and those of their offspring. But until the 26th Amendment to the Constitution was adopted in 1971, lowering the national voting age from 21 to 18, most states rigidly circumscribed the rights of minors to V.D. treatment, contraceptive service, pregnancy care, and abortion without parental permission.

The adoption of the amendment set off a chain reaction in many states, and 41 of them quickly lowered the legal age of majority from 21 to 18. This action had the effect of making most medical care available to 18-year-olds without either parental knowledge or parental consent. As Figure 4-1 shows, the trend is toward lowering the age barriers still further or eliminating them altogether.

COED DORMITORY LIVING

Obviously, coed dormitories were not intended by college or university officials to increase student sexual involvement. Indeed, many institutions resisted the idea precisely because they feared such developments. But coed dorms are becoming increasingly common.

Most of the young people who agitated for coed dorms emphasized that they are adults and that it is not right for universities to dictate their living arrangements. They sought primarily to create a casual, relaxed environment in which men and women could get to know one another without the hypocrisy and the artificiality of the traditional dating situation. One estimate held that, by 1974, coed dorms had become so widespread that more than half of the nation's resident college students lived in them.[1]

Most residents agree that, after a brief period of hesitant adjustment, both men and women settle easily into coed dorms. They quickly get used to seeing one another in robes or nightclothes and attach little more significance to it than they do with parents and siblings. In some respects, people of both sexes appear to be under less tension than they are in sex-segregated situations. Men show less need for the boasting and boisterousness typical of many male dormitories and fraternities, and women appear to be relieved of some of the competitiveness that is

[1] *Time,* June 3, 1974, p. 45.

common when they live apart from men. Many women report that their relationships with women, as well as with men, are improved.

The man–woman friendships that develop under such conditions appear to be both casual and deep. Women walk into men's rooms easily, and vice versa, just as they would in a same-sex situation. They talk as friends or would-be friends, not as potential bedmates. Much of the interaction is more on a group basis than on a pair basis; a woman or a group of women may invite one or more men to join them in whatever they are doing (Lief and Guthrie, 1972).

Many women residents are pleased to be treated by their male companions as human beings and not merely as potential sexual conquests. They find, too, that sexual stereotyping of attitudes and interests tends to break down; they can better pursue ideas and careers without being labeled as unfeminine. At the same time, however, some women appear to miss the pursuit aspect of traditional dating; they would like to be sought after by one special man "because he thinks she is very special." Thus, there is a price to be paid for being "just one of the guys."

There are few formal barriers to sexual activity in coed dormitories. Few people disapprove of it, and sex is viewed in the context of the total relationship. Some couples slip into sex easily, while others find it difficult to do so. Sexual attraction may not flower in a friendship situation, and some people report holding back either because they don't want to jeopardize the friendship or because they are afraid of being rejected. Interestingly, those people who do sleep with someone often choose a person outside the intimate dorm group.

As in other situations, however, some students are not yet ready for full sexual involvement. And in coed dorms, they can be confronted with sex in ways that are embarrassing or uncomfortable. They may have to sit and watch as their roommates "make out" with boyfriends or girlfriends. The friend may even move in and intrude upon the nonparticipant's privacy and convenience. In a more traditional living situation, any disapproval would be visited upon the sexually active couple. But in most coed dorms, the roommate who objects is likely to be regarded as reacting unreasonably and as the victim of "hang-ups."

The one thing that does not appear to be true of coed dorms is that there is a great deal of promiscuous sexual activity. Instead, most relationships are quite monogamous, and the people involved seem to be seeking emotional intimacy and deep commitment as well as physical sex. In so doing, however, they face several kinds of complications.

Some students have boyfriends or girlfriends at other colleges or at home whom they don't want to betray by having sex with someone else. If they are encouraged by someone in the dorm, they face a conflict. They may resist the overtures of the dorm-mate without telling that

person why; in so doing, they create confusion and anxiety in the friend. And if they do tell why, they may threaten that friendship. The temptations may be difficult to resist, of course, and the person who is tempted may wonder whether the absent boyfriend or girlfriend is also being faithful.

The dorm resident who does succumb may suffer guilt and anxiety. He or she may be unable to become deeply involved with the dorm partner, or may regret betraying the absent partner. Sometimes these triangles surface, of course, when the guilty person confesses all or when the third party arrives for a visit. The chance that at least one of the three people will be deeply hurt by the situation is, of course, great.

Both men and women suffer some conflict between their ideals of freedom and spontaneity and their fears of ''using'' other people sexually. Believing that sexual involvement implies emotional involvement, a surprising number of persons of both sexes find it very difficult to engage in casual sex.

In summary, most coed dorm residents seem to be seeking love and affection in exclusive relationships that embody the highest ideals of married love. Many such relationships lead to marriage, but other relationships break, with trauma to one or both partners. In addition to the loss suffered, there may be damage to self-esteem. Such problems may arise in other situations too, of course. But in coed dorms, many people will know what has happened, and the hurt student must go on living not only with them but with the former partner as well (Rimmer, 1973).

LIVING TOGETHER

Even though most people probably would still be reluctant officially to report such behavior, the 1970 U.S. Census indicated that some 143,000 couples are living together without benefit of marriage. The practice has become especially evident around college and university campuses, where most officials, landlords, and others generally ignore it.

Studies of students living together have been conducted widely, from upstate New York and New York City through the mountain states and the Southwest. These studies have reported that up to one-fourth of all students have lived with someone, at least for a while. And up to 40 percent of students may do so by the time of graduation (Arafat and Yorburg, 1973; Henze and Hudson, 1974; Macklin, 1972; Peterman, Ridley, and Anderson, 1974).

Most couples do not plan to live together as they might plan to get married; rather, they just gradually drift into it. As they begin to have sexual intercourse regularly, it becomes more and more inconvenient for one of them to get up late at night and go home, so he or she falls into the habit of staying overnight. Chances are that they are eating some meals together, too, and it is cheaper to prepare some of those meals where they live than to eat in restaurants. They may also drift into living together if the one partner has lost his or her apartment, or if someone else has moved in with a former roommate of the same sex, leaving that person no place to go.

There are still further reasons for deciding to live together. More men than women say that their primary motivation is sex, whereas more women indicate that they have marriage in mind; they are afraid that if they don't live with the man, some other woman will. Some people state that they were curious to see what the experience would be like; they say that they would be reluctant to get married without testing their compatibility first. When pressed on the matter, however, many couples deny that living together indicates that they will marry. "No permanent commitment" seems to be a common part of the arrangement.

THE NATURE OF THE ARRANGEMENT

The term "living together" has different meanings. Sometimes it appears to include almost all cases of sleeping together (Peterman, Ridley, and Anderson, 1974). Other times it refers only to relatively structured, lasting relationships (Macklin, 1972). We can analyze the pattern most usefully by restricting ourselves to the more lasting relationships.

The most detailed study yet reported was done at Cornell University. It was based upon interviews with women who either had lived with someone or were doing so at the time (Macklin, 1972). Only relationships in which the couple had spent at least four nights a week together for at least three consecutive months were included.

Most commonly, in such arrangements, the woman partially moves in with the man, who may be sharing the apartment or house with other men. She does not usually give up her own living quarters, but instead returns there some nights, keeps some of her clothes and eats some of her meals there, and receives her mail there. This arrangement helps hide the situation from her parents and enables her to keep up relationships with her women friends. It also provides a place to go when she and her boyfriend do not get along well.

Few couples share their finances completely. Each partner retains his or her own income, but they share some of the expenses of food and entertainment. This separation symbolizes and assures the woman's continued independence. The partners also share some chores, such as shopping and doing the laundry, but the woman usually does most of the cooking and cleaning. This unequal division of labor often is the source of disagreements and quarrels.

ADVANTAGES AND PROBLEMS

Most people living together report that their relationships are quite successful, maturing, and pleasant. They emphasize how much they have grown emotionally in the relationship. Most of them also state that they would not consider marrying someone without living together first.

Up to one-third of the couples studied report some emotional problems, nevertheless. Sometimes one of the partners becomes over-involved and wants to become more serious than the other one does. This leads the other partner to feel "trapped" in the relationship, while the first one feels that he or she is being "used." The situation may be aggravated by increasing isolation from friends as the relationship becomes more serious. Few people feel guilty about living together, but when one does it is usually the woman; her anxiety most often centers around having to hide the relationship from her parents.

Three-fourths of the women report that their relationships are sexually satisfying. About two-thirds of them, though, also report that there are specific sexual problems. Different degrees or periods of sexual interest are cited most often. Following closely is lack of orgasm. Almost all of these couples use contraception, but most of the women say that they are still anxious about the possibility of pregnancy. These problems are, of course, ones that married couples have been reporting for decades, indicating how closely these relationships approximate marriage. It also suggests how little today's more permissive patterns have changed those enduring relationships.

One of the most serious and most common problems involved in living together is the parents. Most women in the Cornell study feared discovery by their parents, felt guilty about deceiving them, or had received ultimatums from parents who had learned of the relationship. About half of the women believed they had succeeded in concealing the relationship from their parents. About one-fourth stated that their parents knew, and about one-fourth were unsure whether the parents knew. The man's parents were much more likely to know and were less likely to cause problems for the couple.

COMMUNAL SEX

At the mention of the word "commune," some people, particularly older ones, conjure up images of sexual orgies. And there are communes that emphasize freedom and variety in sex. As was pointed out in Chapter 1, however, most of the people in such communes are older and more experienced than most college students are.

Some communes around college campuses are not very different in ambience from coed dorms. The decor may be less conventional and less luxurious, but the commune members share the same basic values and needs as other students. Their sexual experiences may not differ much, either. Some members are sexually inexperienced and remain so without undue pressure from others. Some couples sleep together regularly just as they do in the dorms; they experience a similar range of satisfactions and problems. Some of these people may be rebelling against conventional society, but others are merely looking for a cheap place to live where they won't be "hassled."

One of the things that delays the entry of people into sexual intercourse is, of course, the disapproval of others; another is the lack of a suitable place. College-related communes are likely not to disapprove, and they often do provide the place. It would be naive not to believe that people's chances of becoming sexually involved are greater in such situations.

We might hazard the guess that some commune members are more idealistic, and some less so, than most other students. The less idealistic males may be quite exploitative and try to seduce as many females as possible. Inexperienced and dependent women may be very vulnerable to such pressures.

Some women who have problems gravitate toward communes also. If one is rebelling against authority, the commune is a good, safe place to do it. If one is afraid of the intimacy of a one-to-one relationship, one can hide that fact from oneself and from others in a group setting.

One way to avoid true intimacy while giving the appearance of sophistication is to espouse a philosophy of sexual freedom and to engage in sex indiscriminately. This happens in communes also, just as it happened around campuses before communes became popular.

The experience of most young people with this kind of communal living is not very radical, and it does not last very long. Some people who try communal living during their junior years are living in coed dorms or private apartments as seniors. Some couples who become involved with each other in a commune subsequently move out and live together. Some simply reassume whatever their situation was before joining the commune. For the vast majority of students, few traces of the experience are left after a year or two.

SUMMARY

Infants of both sexes display rudimentary sexual behavior, and many preadolescent children engage in explicit sexual play. Boys receive less discouragement from such play than girls do. The attitudes they develop also are different. Boys become interested in sex for its own sake, while girls more often view sex within the broader context of love and romance.

Explicit sexual play becomes more common with the onset of puberty. Studies show that the majority of teenagers of both sexes masturbate fairly regularly, with or without other sexual experience. Most young people are exposed to pornography by mid-adolescence and are sexually aroused by it. There is no evidence, however, that their behavior is significantly affected by it. If anything, sex offenders have less exposure to pornography during adolescence than most people do.

Public attitudes toward sexual intercourse among unmarried people have become much less harsh in recent years, and the incidence of such relationships has been increasing. There is less evidence of a double sexual standard than before, with the experience of men and women tending to equalize.

Men still become involved in sexual intercourse somewhat earlier, on the average, than women do; they are also less likely to be in love with their partners. First intercourse most often occurs at the woman's residence, and automobiles are the second most likely place. Most couples do not use effective means of contraception and worry about pregnancy. Women suffer more anxiety and guilt than men do. The women are also more likely to continue their relationships with their first partners and to report that intercourse strengthened the relationship.

Persistence of the double standard and the influence of the masculine subculture is shown by the fact that men tell more people about their experience in intercourse than women do. These patterns conflict with new standards that value openness and honesty in interpersonal relationships, including sexual ones. The new patterns have relieved young people of some kinds of pressures but have introduced new ones. One such problem is the pressure to have sexual intercourse whether or not one is socially and emotionally ready for it.

The new sexual permissiveness has brought some unpleasant consequences. Venereal disease has become almost epidemic among groups having casual sex. Contraceptive practice also leaves much to be desired, and the risk of pregnancy is rather high. Some forced marriages result, some women resort to abortion, and some bear their babies without marriage. The 26th Amendment to the Constitution spurred social changes that are giving teenagers increased access to private medical assistance and counseling.

Coed dorm living on many campuses has fostered a relaxed, comfortable living style in which men and women are better able to know one another as persons, and not simply as dates and prospective sexual partners. Sexual relationships do develop, but they tend to be serious, involved, and responsible. Some people are troubled, however, by explicit and implicit pressures toward involvement. And relationships that break up produce as much trauma as ever.

Some campus couples live together with an openness that was impossible until only recently. They drift into it gradually, and many almost defensively deny that they are permanently committed to one another. Most report that their relationships are successful and maturing. They are candid, however, about problems they encounter. These include quarrels over housework, unequal degrees of involvement and dependency, problems of sexual adjustment, and relationships with parents. Women, especially, try to hide their relationships from their parents to avoid conflict with them.

Campus communes provide environments conducive to sexual participation, but many of them are not as radical as they are reputed to be. In such communes, both men and women work out the same kinds of problems they experience in other settings.

FOR ADDITIONAL READING

Cottle, Thomas J., *A Family Album: Portraits of Intimacy and Kinship* (New York: Harper and Row, 1974). Includes an exquisitely sensitive account of young people's struggles to develop their sexuality in a context of personal integrity and interpersonal intimacy.

Edwards, John N., ed., *Sex and Society* (Chicago: Markham, 1972). See the section on "Nonfamilial Relationships" for analysis of sexual codes among teenagers.

Johnson, Cecil E., ed., *Sex and Human Relationships* (Columbus, Ohio: Merrill, 1970). Has good articles on sexual research on college

campuses, and on the relation between sexual attitudes and behavior.

Morrison, Eleanor S., and Vera Borosage, eds., *Human Sexuality: Contemporary Perspectives* (Palo Alto, Cal.: National Press Books,
1973). Includes many thought-provoking articles on moral and
ethical issues in sexual behavior.

Rist, Ray C., *The Pornography Controversy: Changing Moral Standards
in American Life* (New Brunswick, N.J.: Transaction Books, 1975).
A report and analysis of the research and conclusions of the
Commission on Obscenity and Pornography.

STUDY QUESTIONS

1. Do you believe that the sexual interests of preadolescent girls are
greater than, equal to, or less than those of boys? Why? In what ways are
their interests different?

2. How do the boys and girls differ in their adolescent sexual activities? in
exposure to sexually explicit materials? in masturbation? in intercourse?
What conclusions do you draw from these facts?

3. How much change has there been in recent years in the extent of
college student participation in sexual intercourse? How well prepared
emotionally are most men and most women for these initial sexual
experiences?

4. What dilemmas confront college-age persons who are not yet ready
for sexual intercourse? What are the different ways of handling the
problem, and what are the costs and rewards of each?

5. How are problems of venereal disease, contraception, and pregnancy
linked to the new sexual permissiveness? What legal rights and problems
do teenagers have in these areas?

6. Analyze the effects of coed dorm living on the sexual experiences of
college students. In what ways are they beneficial? In what ways are they
potentially harmful?

7. How many couples on your campus live together openly? What
proportion later marry? What are the effects in the lives of those who do
not marry?

8. Are student communes visible around your campus? How radical are
they? How beneficial or how harmful are their sexual patterns?

Chapter 5
Love:
The Search
for Fulfillment

People use the term "love" in a bewildering variety of ways. It frequently refers to the passionate attraction of a man and woman for each other, which many people believe to be the preferred basis for marriage, if not the only proper one. That is the kind of love we are most interested in in this chapter. But "love" is also used to describe an infant's helpless dependence on its parents and their tender, nurturant affection for their baby. It is also applied to the erotic, mutually supportive, and cooperative relationship of a husband and wife. It even describes a child's affection for a dog or a favorite toy. Our goal is to understand how love develops between men and women, how it is involved in their making commitments to one another, and how love grows and changes over the years. To begin to do so, we must trace its development from childhood forward.

DEVELOPMENTAL TASKS

The idea that a person develops through a series of biological stages in life is familiar enough. Particular periods in life have specific characteristics and problems associated with them. We use terms such as infancy, childhood, adolescence, adulthood, and old age to refer to these stages. Similarly, the concept of "developmental tasks" assumes that certain kinds of achievement are associated with specific periods in life. These achievements are necessary to facilitate the emotional and social progress of the individual from one stage to the next (Duvall, 1971).

Let us take an example that is already familiar. We have seen how the development of gender identity in the very young child is crucial to its later emotional growth. Unless a child establishes a firm sense of self as male or female, he or she will be severely handicapped later in life in building rewarding relationships with other children and adults. The child who accomplishes this task by the age of three or so, on the other hand, has his or her preparation for life's later needs enhanced. The development of gender identity, in short, is a "developmental task" of this period of life.

The development of gender identity depends upon the child's having established a satisfactory love relationship with its parents. That sort of relationship may thus be viewed as an earlier developmental task. And once gender identity is established, the child must go on to form play relationships with other children if it is to approach school age as a relatively happy, healthy, well-adjusted child. At that time, adjustment to principals, teachers, and schoolmates becomes the next developmental task. Becoming attracted to members of the opposite sex, and learning how to interact specifically with them, begins early in childhood and persists, for most people, throughout adolescence. Eventually, adjustment to college is accompanied by or followed by courtship and marriage; these are appropriate developmental tasks for early adulthood. Parenthood and grandparenthood extend the process of development into old age.

The accompanying box summarizes schematically how the process works. Our goal here is not to try to define precisely the developmental tasks that are appropriate to each stage of life. These tasks are too subject to cultural variation; such a list inevitably would reflect the values of the person who drew it up. But we can all agree on the way the process works, whatever one's cultural values: approximate stages and developmental tasks exist in the life of each individual. Moreover, it is apparent that personal adjustment depends upon the success with which one accomplishes these tasks. A person who fails a given task or who becomes fixated at a certain level inevitably encounters frustration, unhappiness, and social disapproval.

**PRINCIPLES IN THE ACCOMPLISHMENT
OF DEVELOPMENTAL TASKS**

1. Development is influenced by both biological and social factors.

2. Development tends to be orderly, regular, and predictable.

3. Development rates vary somewhat for different individuals.

4. Each development is built upon earlier ones.

5. The stages of development are culturally prescribed.

6. Norms for given ages and stages act as prods or brakes on development.

7. Societal values determine personal goals for individuals.

8. Successful accomplishment of tasks brings fulfillment and happiness.

9. People face certain responsibilities for maturing at every stage in life.

10. Developmental tasks successfully accomplished lead to further developmental levels.

Source: Adapted from Evelyn Millis Duvall, *Family Development* (Philadelphia: Lippincott, 1971), p. 141.

STAGES IN LOVE DEVELOPMENT

For each of the major stages in life, it is possible to describe a corresponding stage in love development. Although it is useful to identify them, we must be careful not to define these stages too rigidly. We must also remember that there are not sharp breaks in most people's lives as they move from one stage to the next. Rather, infancy merges almost imperceptibly with early childhood; the oedipal period persists well into preadolescence; and so on. In this chapter, we will define and describe nine stages through which love develops. Although any such scheme must be somewhat arbitrary, these broad stages do reflect most people's experience, and they provide a valuable framework within which to examine the emotional development of the individual (Orlinsky, 1974).

INFANCY

Because of their obvious limitations, infants cannot be very active participants in the love relationships with their parents. Although their physical dependence is total, they do, however, accept and respond to the nurturing care of mother and father. They receive the physical comfort associated with being fed, washed, clothed, held, and cuddled and respond with pleasure. They learn to smile and coo and, further, they learn that such behavior elicits more attention and affection from those who care for them.

From the perspective of the parents, of course, the relationship is one of being nurse and protector. The parents give actively to the infant, receiving their satisfaction from seeing the infant as an extension of themselves; they delight in its primitive emotional responses.

EARLY CHILDHOOD

By early childhood, the primitive emotional responses of the infant are transformed by awareness of other people. The child is now forming a conception of itself as male or female and as a person capable of giving love as well as receiving it. The objects of affection are still basically the parents, but the field is gradually expanded to include others in the immediate environment: grandparents, perhaps, and brothers and sisters.

The adult role toward the young child retains major elements of nurse and protector, but now it increasingly becomes that of loving teacher. Adults confirm, encourage, approve, and reward the child's developing conception of itself as a person worthy of love. The child responds to love and approval with open affection and joy, less complicated emotions than those it will experience later in life.

The oedipal period was defined by Sigmund Freud as one in which children of both sexes develop sexual attraction to the parent of the opposite sex. The child immediately represses that attraction because of the danger it presents from the potential wrath of the parent of the same sex. The attraction continues to manifest itself, however, in flirtatious, seductive behavior directed toward the parent of the opposite sex. Daughters become "Daddy's little girls"; sons become "Mommy's little boys." They tease, they share "secrets," and they "innocently" crawl into bed with the desired parent whenever they get the chance.

Well-adjusted and knowledgeable parents recognize that their children at this stage are learning and "rehearsing" behavior that they soon will redirect to their own age-mates. Ideally, they neither reject nor over-encourage the budding eroticism of their offspring. The children, in turn, incorporate into their affectional relationships an erotic component that will be evident in virtually all their heterosexual relationships, at least from then on.

THE OEDIPAL PERIOD

A new emphasis on intimacy with one's age mates often emerges in the pre-adolescent years, those between six or eight and puberty. The first peer relationships of great interpersonal intimacy are formed at this time. Often, these relationships are with members of the same sex rather than the opposite sex. The youngsters become "best friends" or "pals." They spend most of their waking moments together, swear undying loyalty, and form and reveal their most private hopes, fears, and wishes. Significantly, these same-sex friends often become confidants and supporters as the child makes its fumbling first efforts to act upon "crushes" for members of the opposite sex.

As indicated in Chapter 3, some people form cross-sex relationships and begin dating before puberty. Occasionally, these relationships develop into real intimacy; however, the dependence of boys and girls of this age on planned social events usually makes it difficult for them to do so. More often, pre-adolescent boys and girls rehearse with friends of the same sex the intimacy they will one day have with members of the opposite sex.

PRE-ADOLESCENCE

Youth is more difficult than the previous stages to define chronologically. It does not fit neatly between preadolescence and adolescence—or anywhere else for that matter. The emotions and relationships that characterize it are in some ways more mature than those just discussed, but they still do not indicate full adult heterosexuality.

A crucial feature of this stage is an overt identification with adult role models of the same sex. This process is likely to have begun way back in early childhood, when little girls donned aprons and mimicked their mothers' housekeeping duties, and little boys strutted around with their

YOUTH

fathers' pipes in their mouths. By some time in mid-development, how-ever, the imitation has ceased to be play and is no longer so superficial. The young man or woman actually takes on many aspects of the role of an adult of the same sex, and also the values, attitudes, and behavior appropriate to that role.

A second, but related, feature of this stage is the tendency of the youth toward idealization. The young man or woman not only takes on the role of an adult model but, literally, idolizes that model. Athletes, movie stars, singers, and other public performers often are the subjects of this worshipful identification. The role models frequently change, but the need to identify, and the awe in which the model is held, will persist.

In this stage, both males and females transfer their tendency toward idealization to heterosexual relationships. In immature form, this process can be seen in the frenzied adoration of popular music groups and stars. A few boys and girls physically pursue the objects of their fascination, and many more idolize from a distance.

More pertinent to the development of a capacity to love others is the fact that many young men and women also idealize, to some extent, the people of the opposite sex with whom they actually interact and with whom they seek to become involved. Thus, "star-struck" young men become bumbling clods as they try to talk with perfectly ordinary young women, whom they have transformed in their imaginations into figures of perfection and grace. And young women become mute on dates with equally ordinary young men whom they perceive as Adonises and heroes.

TEENAGE AND YOUNG ADULT

People in the teen and young adult years combine some qualities of both youth and adulthood. In them, the idealization of selected members of the opposite sex persists alongside the full flowering of sexual passion. Teenagers are often not yet fully comfortable with their maturing sexual-ity. As a result, they develop a rich fantasy life, in which the relationship with the loved one is anticipated, lived, and relived. The partner may be unaware of this fantasy relationship, or at least of its details. The partner either is relatively unaffected by it or creates a reciprocal fantasy of his or her own.

Novelists and poets have often told us of the tremendous power of such romantic love. It is almost as though the person's will has been seized by an overwhelming outside force. Every waking thought is directed to the beloved, and the lover is alternately lifted to ecstasy or plunged into agony. The phrase "falling in love" symbolizes the lover's loss of control over his or her destiny and the propulsion into a euphoria that can only end with fulfillment of the relationship.

As young people put into words the worshipful adoration that they feel for each other, emotional and physical intimacy build together to move the couple toward commitment. For many couples, that development means moving rapidly toward marriage. Couples are frequently somewhat aware, however, of the irrationality of the forces that grip them. Counseled by parents and others to go slowly, many couples deliberately try to put the brakes on their relationship at this point. They strive to de-romanticize the relationship and to view themselves and their partners realistically. They do so in part because divorce rates indicate that romantic love does not last, and they do not want to make a mistake. Some couples deliberately choose to live together until the romance fades and they determine what other bases they have for being married to one another.

If romantic passion flowers in the young adult years, it gradually is replaced by a less intense and demanding love among mature adults.

CONJUGAL LOVE

People who have lived together for many years no longer fantasize about what it would be like to be together—they are together. This fact does not mean that their relationships are necessarily less erotic. Indeed, they may be more richly sensual than the most passionate younger couples could imagine.

But conjugal love is less *exclusively* erotic than romantic love. It is based upon the broader, deeper intimacy that comes with years of shared experiences and with the knowledge of great commitment to one another. Sex becomes something to be shared openly and fully in a context of domestic cooperation. If passion is less overwhelming, affection is far more pervasive.

PARENTAL LOVE

Parental love is the reciprocal of infant and childhood love, and what was said about it in those sections leaves little to be added here. Parental love is nurturant, but its particular qualities change as the child grows older. The physical nurturing of the infant gives way to the personal nurturing of the young child, which gives way in turn to the erotic nurturing of the pre-adolescent. Later still, parents provide adult role models with whom their youthful offspring can identify.

Parental love has another dimension, however, for it often is turned toward one's own parents as well, as old age makes them more dependent. The parents who were nurtured in their youth come to nurture their parents in turn, as the older generation moves into retirement, ill health, widowhood, and dependency. The reversal of roles often is not complete, because part of this selfless nurturing process is allowing the aging grandparents to retain some nominal authority and dominance. As age and ill health take their toll, physical dependence may result. In the final years, the nurture of parents may become almost as physical as that of infants.

GRANDPARENTAL LOVE

The vigorous, physically healthy love that married persons feel for one another and for their children gradually becomes transformed into the more tender, considerate love that old men and women feel for one another and for their grandchildren. Sensuality and eroticism can, and often do, persist until very old age. The balance gradually shifts, however, as spouses become increasingly aware of physical decline in themselves and in one another. Even as they receive nurturance from their adult children, so do they physically care for one another in ways that were not necessary in earlier years.

Tenderness becomes more prominent in the love that old people feel for one another, and it is often characteristic of love for grandchildren. Grandparents do not have to discipline their grandchildren, so their relationships are spared the ambivalence and strain that discipline implies. Grandfathers, particularly, are relieved of the authority role and

the demand for masculinity that complicated their relationships with their wives and children. They can be tender and loving and undemanding. Grandmothers, too, are relieved of the need to be disciplinarians, and they can be indulgent sources of refuge for their grandchildren.

The stages of love development are closely linked to the individual's overall personal growth (Orlinsky, 1974). Progress toward emotional maturity is facilitated when a person experiences the kind of love that is appropriate to his or her present stage in life; it also is encouraged when the person gives up that form of love upon moving to the next stage. The seductive cuteness of the beginning schoolchild, for example, signals the child's progress beyond the simply nurturant stages. But if he or she is still flirting with the parent of the opposite sex at age 15, rather than with

LOVE AND FULFILLMENT

peers, this behavior signals emotional problems and is likely to provoke disapproval from both age groups. So it is with other stages of life and love.

As a general rule, society looks more favorably upon prolonging those forms of love that involve giving to and nurturing others than upon those in which the individual primarily receives and takes. Thus, there is relatively strong pressure upon children to give up dependent relationships, but much more tolerance and approval of parental nurturance even beyond when it is strictly necessary. Approved relationships are given labels such as "healthy" and "mature," whereas disapproved ones are called "unhealthy," "neurotic," or "immature."

It is characteristic of all developmental tasks, including those of love development, that they almost totally preoccupy and fascinate the individual while he or she is involved in them; but once they have been successfully accomplished, they cease to be the center of attention. The toddler, for example, may be enthralled by his or her first days at nursery school, only to have become very blasé about the whole business less than a year later. Similarly the excitement of the first semester of the freshman year at college contrasts strongly with the bored sophistication of the senior year.

Comparable preoccupation, excitement, and fascination mark people's progress through the stages of love development. Most of us can remember the ecstasy of our first romantic crushes, although now we may recall them with some amusement. Similarly, our early adult experiences with romantic love cause us to function at levels above and beyond ourselves for a while. But eventually we must move on to other tasks of life, such as earning a living and raising children; and we develop other forms of love that are compatible with those tasks.

Some young people find this inevitability threatening. They may ask if they are doomed to fall out of love with their partners and to live out most of their lives in the absence of a truly fulfilling love. But such fears miss the point. Adolescents are convinced that their intimate relationships with their closest friends will always be the most important things in their lives, only to discover a few years later that they no longer have much in common with those friends. So it is with romantic love. Wonderfully rewarding at the time, and to be fondly remembered, it nonetheless must wane. But it gives way to the richly rewarding love of two people who know each other well, who have shared problems and tragedies as well as fulfillment, and who require more of each other than purely romantic involvement can provide.

Each stage of love development is a means to personal growth. By passing through each stage successfully, the individual becomes prepared for the next. The process continues, not just through early adulthood, but throughout life.

Writers have always been fascinated with how people fall in love and marry. Young people, who are most immediately concerned with the process, share their interest. But despite the general appeal of the subject, there is little definitive research on how men and women fall in love as a prelude to marriage. Consequently, we must piece together the findings from scattered small research projects.

Research supports the idea that a substantial proportion of college men and women, up to one-third, experience the sudden, overwhelming attraction to someone that we call "love at first sight" (Kanin, Davidson, and Scheck, 1970). What the evidence does not tell us, however, is the effects of such irrational attraction on the subsequent development of the relationship.

One school of thought has been highly suspicious of such relationships. It labels them as "infatuation" and decries infatuation as a basis for marriage. The reasoning is straightforward enough. In these people's view, infatuation cannot be based upon adequate knowledge of the other person as a whole person; rather, it must be based on just one or a few characteristics, such as sex appeal or neurotic personality needs. Such attraction cannot last in a situation of continued intimacy such as marriage. These people see marriages based on infatuation as leading to disillusionment and divorce.

When we analyze the situation carefully, however, it appears more complicated. For one thing, parents and others have often used the label, "infatuation," as a kind of epithet to discourage relationships of which they do not approve. We might guess, for example, that when a young man or woman becomes enamored of a person from a different religious, racial, or economic background, people are more likely to cry "infatuation" than they are when that person is attracted to someone they consider a more "suitable" marriage partner.

The underlying argument is somewhat disguised by this strategem, but it boils down to, "You must break up with this unsuitable person or you are doomed to unhappiness." Moreover, those who cloak their disapproval in such terms cannot lose. If the couple persists in spite of the opposition and eventually does have serious trouble, their detractors can say, "See, we told you so." If, on the other hand, the relationship endures as a good one, the detractors may say, "It was infatuation in the beginning, but it developed into true love." Infatuation is easily twisted in this way, a fact that ensures its continued availability as a weapon, regardless of the outcomes of particular relationships.

One component of infatuation is idealization, the tendency to perceive the loved one more favorably than other people do. Thus the idealized woman may be seen to be incredibly beautiful, gracious,

LOVE AND MOVEMENT TOWARD MARRIAGE

INFATUATION

IDEALIZATION

talented, and creative; the idealized man is perceived as strong, brilliant, aggressive, and kind. If the lovers are less sexist, they may reverse the images, picturing the woman as strong and aggressive and the man as gracious and creative. In any event, each person is viewed in terms somewhat larger than life.

Idealization of the loved one does not occur only in those situations commonly labeled as infatuation, however. Substantial proportions of both men and women idealize their loved ones, particularly early in the relationship. Some studies show women to be the more romantic ones at this stage (Kephart, 1967), but others show men to be more romantic and to idealize more than women do (Knox and Sporakowski, 1968).

People who disapprove of infatuation in love relationships also tend to disapprove of idealization. They predict tragic outcomes for relationships in which they discern its presence. Little research has been done on the matter, but one study using engagement adjustment scales has shown that idealistic couples make scores as high as, or higher than, those of more realistic couples (Schuman, 1974). Another study of married couples reports that romanticism is associated with the finest that marriage has to offer (Spanier, 1972).

MOVEMENT TOWARD MARRIAGE

The evidence is contradictory about which sex is the more realistic as the relationship moves toward marriage. Some studies show men becoming more romantic as they become more involved (Fengler, 1974), and some show that women become more romantic and idealistic as they fall in love (Kanin, Davidson, and Scheck, 1970). The most consistent finding is that, regardless of which sex is the more romantic, both men and women idealize their partners less and become more realistic about their relationships as they get older and move closer to marriage. College seniors, for example, are more realistic than freshmen (Knox and Sporakowski, 1968); engaged people are more realistic than non-engaged people.

One study compared teenagers, young adult married couples, and couples who had been married for 20 years or more. Not only the teenagers, but the older married couples as well, were more romantic than the young married couples (Knox, 1970). Apparently, the experience of heady, exhilarating romantic love is common enough as people begin to form serious heterosexual relationships; we may even regret that not all people seem to experience it. Some idealization of the loved one is a normal accompaniment of such falling in love. But as they move closer to marriage, most couples show increasing awareness of the realities of their situations. Most couples approach mate selection with a good deal of conscious awareness.

SUMMARY

Our understanding of the way the capacity to love develops is facilitated by the concept of developmental tasks. Developmental tasks are goals appropriate to particular stages in life; achievement of them brings happiness and satisfaction and enables the individual to go on to other tasks well prepared. Formation of gender identity, development of a heterosexual orientation, falling in love, marriage, and parenthood are all developmental tasks.

The learning of certain kinds of love relationships at each stage of the life cycle may be viewed as developmental tasks. In infancy, the baby exists in a state of physical dependence upon the parents, but it learns gradually to behave in ways that elicit attention and affection. In early childhood, the individual develops awareness of other people and begins to learn to give love as well as to receive it. Slightly later on, the child differentiates between its parents; at this time an erotic component that will influence all later relationships enters its love relationships.

Emotional intimacy with one's age mates, particularly those of the same sex, often develops before puberty. These relationships provide a foundation upon which to build the first tentative relationships with members of the opposite sex.

Cross-cutting several of these stages is another process: the selection of adult role models of the same sex. These models serve as guides in the development of mature heterosexual relationships. Idealization of the adult role models is transferred easily to the objects of the young person's first serious romantic attractions.

The experience of romantic love—heady, ecstatic, and overpowering—often comes with the teen and young adult years. Sexually explicit and demanding, it moves people rapidly toward commitment and marriage. Older and younger people alike, aware of the power of such feelings, often try to moderate them before deciding to marry.

The passion and vigor of young adulthood may survive well into the married years. Gradually, though, they tend to be replaced by a richer, more sensual, and deeper conjugal love, based upon many shared experiences and an increasing sense of commitment to the partner. Conjugal love and parental love tend to be linked; the parental role adds elements of tenderness, nurturance, and responsibility to the relationship. As people move into grandparenthood and old age, their ability to display tenderness is uncomplicated by the need to discipline their grandchildren. Ultimately, they themselves may become the objects of both physical and emotional nurturance.

The various stages of love development and personal growth are closely linked. Each stage is fascinating as one moves through it, and each prepares the individual to move on to the next. In this fashion, they serve as vehicles of personal growth and development.

A substantial proportion of young people report having had the experience of "falling in love at first sight." Many adults disapprove of love at first sight, especially if it is with someone they consider an inappropriate marriage partner. They label it as "infatuation," and use the label as a weapon to try to break up the relationship. Idealization of the loved one also is a common feature of romantic love relationships, and also is widely disapproved. Some research indicates, however, that it is associated with good adjustment in both engaged and married couples. Both men and women tend to become increasingly realistic about their partners and their relationships as they move toward marriage.

FOR ADDITIONAL READING

Crosby, John F., *Illusion and Disillusion: The Self in Love and Marriage* (Belmont, Cal.: Wadsworth, 1973). Contains a section on "Romance, Sex, and Marriage," and one on "Need Fulfillment in Marriage."

Murstein, Bernard I., ed., *Theories of Attraction and Love* (New York: Springer, 1971). See the selection on "Passionate Love."

Powers, Edward A., Mary W. Lees, *et al.,* eds., *Process In Relationship: Marriage and Family* (St. Paul: West Publishing Co., 1974). Includes five articles dealing with various concepts of love.

Rimmer, Robert H., ed., *Adventures in Loving* (New York: New American Library, 1973). First-hand accounts of loving in unconventional contexts.

Tavuchis, Nicholas, and William J. Goode, eds., *The Family Through Literature* (New York: McGraw-Hill, 1975). Selections on love relationships from ancient Greece to contemporary America.

STUDY QUESTIONS

1. Define a developmental task. Then construct your own list of developmental tasks that people encounter as they move through life.

2. Construct a list of stages of love development. Now relate these stages to the developmental tasks you have specified.

3. Is the feeling of an infant for its parents really love? How do *you* define love?

4. How does romantic love differ from other kinds of love? What do you think of romantic love as a basis for marriage?

5. Relate the stages of love development to personal growth and development. Do you find your view encouraging or discouraging? Why?

6. Differentiate between romantic love and infatuation. How does "love at first sight" fit in?

7. Is idealization of the loved one good or bad? However you answered the question, now turn it around and answer it the other way.

8. Which sex do you think is more idealistic about love and marriage? Why do you think so?

Chapter 6
Mate Selection

If we aren't too serious about it, we can compare falling in love and making the relationship permanent to catching the measles. People usually are in love when they decide to make things permanent. It isn't very helpful, however, to think in terms of love *causing* marriage. For one thing, lots of love relationships don't result in marriage or even in the couple's living together permanently.

Being in love doesn't *cause* long-term commitments any more than the fever that precedes the measles rash causes the rash. In measles, a virus is the underlying cause of both the fever and the rash. Similarly, when we ask why some couples marry and others don't, we need to look beyond the outward symptom (being in love) to the underlying causes. We need to look at what social scientists call factors in mate selection.

The factors that determine who chooses whom for marriage can be classified in many ways. Laws determine who can marry, and at what ages. Place of residence and social characteristics tend to restrict marital choice. Finally, personal attraction narrows the choice still further.

LEGAL REQUIREMENTS

This book is not a textbook in law and these pages should not be read as such. We can, however, summarize the basic legal requirements for marriage in the various states. Individual state laws differ as to prohibited relationships, minimum ages for marriage, required blood tests, and waiting periods. Many of these requirements are summarized in Table 6-1.

PROHIBITED RELATIONSHIPS

Few people are romantically attracted to close relatives. As a result, we seldom are consciously aware that all states have laws forbidding marriage and sexual intercourse with certain relatives. Father–daughter, mother–son, brother–sister, grandparent–grandchild, uncle–niece, and aunt–nephew relationships are forbidden in all states. There, however, the uniformity stops.

Over half of the states prohibit marriage between first cousins, but the remaining states permit it. Again, over half of the states prohibit marriage to half-brothers or half-sisters. Fewer states forbid marriage between second cousins, grandnieces or grandnephews. Some states prohibit marriage with half cousins, half-nieces, and half-nephews.

Such restrictions are designed, of course, to prevent the transmission of genetic defects; they also seek to avert disruptive sexual rivalries within the family. Technically, these prohibitions are based on *consanguinity,* or blood relationship. The law doesn't stop with consanguinity, however. It also forbids marriage between some classes of persons who are related only through marriage, or *affinity.* The object again is to prevent sexual rivalries within the family.

Laws prohibiting affinal marriage generally apply to stepparents and stepchildren, fathers and daughters-in-law, mothers and sons-in-law, men and their wives' mothers, and women and their husbands' fathers. The probability that any one person will want to enter one of these prohibited relationships is slim. Nevertheless, it does happen, and sometimes with serious emotional repercussions for the family. In other instances, such as when the spouse has died, there would seem to be no good reason to forbid marriage with one of the spouse's relatives.

The prohibited relationship that causes the most trouble is that involving first cousins. First cousins may be reared quite apart from one another, meet, and fall in love. Neither they nor their families may see any good reason why they should not marry, and in many states they can do so legally. If they live in a state where it is prohibited and are persistent enough, they may go to another state to marry and then return to their home state to live.

TABLE 6-1 UNITED STATES MARRIAGE LAWS*

STATE	WITH CONSENT MEN	WITH CONSENT WOMEN	WITHOUT CONSENT MEN	WITHOUT CONSENT WOMEN	BLOOD TEST REQUIRED	WAIT FOR LICENSE	WAIT AFTER LICENSE
Alabama (b)	17	14	21	18	Yes	None	None
Alaska	18	16	21	18	Yes	3 days	None
Arizona	16 (h)	16	18	18	Yes	None	None
Arkansas	17	16 (j)	21	18	Yes	3 days	None
California	— (h)	— (h)	18	18	Yes	None	None
Colorado	16	16	18	18	Yes	None	None
Connecticut	16	16	18	18	Yes	4 days	None
Delaware	— (m)	16 (j)	18	18	Yes	None	24 hrs (c)
District of Columbia	18	16	21	18	Yes	3 days	None
Florida	18	16	21	21	Yes	3 days	None
Georgia	18	16	19	19	Yes	None (b)	None (k)
Hawaii	17(e)	16	20	18	Yes	None	None
Idaho	16	16	18	18	Yes	None (l)	None
Illinois (a)	— (e)	15 (e)	21	18	Yes	None	None
Indiana	17	17	18	18	Yes	3 days	None
Iowa	18	16	18	18	Yes	3 days	None
Kansas	— (e, h)	— (e, h)	18	18	Yes	3 days	None
Kentucky	18	16	18	18	Yes	3 days	None
Louisiana (a)	18	16	18	18	Yes	None	72 hours
Maine	16	16	18	18	No	5 days	None
Maryland	18	16	21	18	None	48 hours	None
Massachusetts	— (h)	— (h)	18	18	Yes	3 days	None
Michigan (a)	—	16	18	18	Yes	3 days	None
Minnesota	—	16 (e)	18	18	None	5 days	None
Mississippi (b)	17	15	21	21	Yes	3 days	None
Missouri	15	15	21	18	Yes	3 days	None
Montana	— (h)	— (h)	19	19	Yes	5 days	None
Nebraska	18	16	19	19	Yes	5 days	None
Nevada	—	16	18	18	None	None	None
New Hampshire (a)	14 (e)	13 (e)	18	18	Yes	5 days	None
New Jersey (a)	—	16	18	18	Yes	72 hours	None
New Mexico	16	16	21	21	Yes	None	None
New York	16	14	18	18	Yes	None	24 hours (g)
North Carolina (a)	16	16	18	18	Yes	None	None
North Dakota (a)	— (h)	15	18	18	Yes	None	None
Ohio (a)	18	16	18	18	Yes	5 days	None
Oklahoma	18	15	21	18	Yes	None (f)	None
Oregon	18 (e)	15 (e)	18	18	Yes	7 days	None
Pennsylvania	16	16	18	18	Yes	3 days	None
Rhode Island (a) (b)	18	16	18	18	Yes	None	None
South Carolina	16	14	18	18	None	24 hrs	None
South Dakota	18	16	18	18	Yes	None	None
Tennessee (b)	16	16	21	21	Yes	3 days	None
Texas	16	16	18	18	Yes	None	None
Utah (a)	16	14	21	18	Yes	None	None
Vermont (a)	18	16	18	18	Yes	None	5 days
Virginia (a)	18	16	18	18	Yes	None	None
Washington	17	17	18	18	(d)	3 days	None
West Virginia	18 (h)	16	18	18	Yes	3 days	None
Wisconsin	18	16	18	18	Yes	5 days	None
Wyoming	18	16	21	21	Yes	None	None
Puerto Rico	16	16	21	21	(f)	None	None
Virgin Islands	16	14	21	18	None	8 days	None

Many states have additional special requirements; contact individual state.
(a) Special laws applicable to non-residents. (b) Specials laws applicable to those under 21 years. (c) 24 hours if one or both parties resident of state; 96 hours if both parties are nonresidents. (d) None, but male must file affidavit. (e) Parental consent plus Court's consent required. (f) None, but a medical certificate is required. (g) Marriage may not be solemnized within 10 days from date of blood test. (h) Statute provides for obtaining license with parental or court consent with no stated minimum age. (j) Under 16, with parental and court consent. (k) All those between 19–21 cannot waive 3 day waiting period. (l) If either under 18—wait full 3 days. (m) If under stated age, court consent required.
*as of November 1974.

Source: Adapted from a table compiled by William E. Mariano, Council on Marriage Relations, Inc., for *The World Almanac and Book of Facts, 1975* (New York: Newspaper Enterprise Association, 1975), p. 961.

AGE

All states require that persons reach certain ages before they marry. Traditionally, the ages for men generally have been different from those for women, usually older. In 1975, however, a young man successfully challenged the constitutionality of Utah's law in a state district court on the grounds that it discriminates against men. The required ages also vary according to parental consent. People are generally permitted to marry at younger ages if their parents give written approval.

Until the final constitutionality of such laws is determined, the most common legal ages for marriage are 18 for men, and 16 for women, with parental consent. Without parental consent, the most common minimums are 21 for men and 18 for women. As can be seen in Table 6-1, however, there is great variation from state to state. In New Hampshire, boys of 14 and girls of 13 can marry with consent of the parents and the courts. Several other states permit girls of 14 to marry with parental consent. Without parental consent, several states require both partners to be 21, and all states require both men and women to be at least 18.

As the table indicates, many states also have special age requirements. Some states have special provisions for nonresidents, and some permit marriage at younger ages when the girl is pregnant.

BLOOD TEST

The vast majority of states require a blood test to certify that the partners are free of communicable syphilis. In four states, the District of Columbia, and the Virgin Islands, however, no test is required. In Washington no test is required, but the man must file an affidavit stating that he does not have the disease. In Puerto Rico, a nonspecific medical certificate is required. In a few states, the blood test is required of the man but not of the woman.

WAITING PERIOD

To discourage hasty marriages, most states impose waiting periods before couples may marry. Most commonly the waiting period is three days, but it may be as long as eight. At the other extreme, more than ten states impose no waiting period at all. Apparently, the waiting period at least partly fulfills its function: a substantial number of couples who apply for licenses never return to claim them, and others who get licenses do not use them after the waiting period has ended.

SOCIAL SELECTION

Theoretically, any couple who are of age and not too closely related may marry, as long as they follow the required procedures. Mate selection is not random, however; it tends to occur within certain well-defined categories. This tendency reflects the process of social selection.

SEX RATIOS

Over the country as a whole, there are approximately equal numbers of young men and women, so sex ratios should not be a problem in mate selection. The only trouble is that young people are not equally distributed. There are shortages of men in some places and of women in others.

One prevailing migrational trend is from rural to urban areas. More young women than men make the trip, because there are fewer occupational opportunities for women on the farm. The men left behind have an insufficient number of women to marry. Similarly, the young women who migrate to the cities to work in business and industry find economic opportunity, but they also find a shortage of men. The magnitude of this problem should not be overstated, however. In rural areas the sex ratio hovers around 110, and in urban areas it seldom drops below 95. Most men and women do find mates in these circumstances. That fact may be small comfort, though, to the man or woman who faces a personal shortage.

Of more immediate relevance to most readers of this book is the situation on many campuses. There still are some colleges that are predominantly for students of one sex. This imbalance may be a matter of tradition, or it may be a matter of curriculum: technical schools still attract mostly men, while those specializing in the arts and home economics draw more women. A high degree of sex segregation also occurs on many large university campuses. Male engineering students, for example, may go for days without having the opportunity to really talk with a woman, and women majoring in one of the liberal arts may have almost as little opportunity to interact with men.

Men marry, on the average, around age 23, and women marry, on the average, by 21. Therefore, the college years may be crucial ones in establishing promising relationships. People who are not thrown naturally into heterosexual contacts may have to work harder at it.

The term *homogamy* means, literally, "marrying alike." It describes the fact that most persons select as marriage partners persons who resemble themselves in certain ways. People tend, for example, to marry persons of roughly their own age. We must say "roughly," however, because actually, most people prefer the man to be slightly older, which he is in about three-fourths of all marriages. Men average two-and-a-half years older than their wives. In about ten percent of all cases the couple are of the same age, and in the remaining 15 percent the woman is older (Leslie, 1976). Age homogamy operates most effectively among young adults who marrying for the first time. Age differences tend to be larger among older persons marrying for the first time, and among those who are remarrying.

HOMOGAMY

In general, mates also sort themselves out along lines of social class, there being few marriages between persons of widely disparate statuses. College students often face conflicting social pressures. Their parents and home communities usually urge them to marry someone from their circle of acquaintances, while their peers and much of the college environment emphasize the importance of getting to know people of widely differing backgrounds.

Status homogamy also runs counter to traditional expectations in some respects. Traditional attitudes assumed that there was a *mating gradient,* which meant that men tend to date and marry downward in age, education, and social class, whereas women marry upward. Although most of us know of such cases, recent careful research has failed to confirm that these marriages are anything more than chance occurrences. One study, using data from four national surveys, reports that the mating gradient is largely illusory; it seems to be chiefly a function of the prevailing upward social mobility of the whole population. Most young couples marry before their final social class destinations are evident. As they grow older, their social status tends to rise. These researchers also found considerable downward social mobility, and that women's parents are not successful in discouraging them from entering "unfavorable" marriages (Glenn, Ross, and Tully, 1974).

RESIDENTIAL PROPINQUITY

The awkward phrase *residential propinquity* describes another source of social selection. It is simply the fact that people tend to select marriage partners from among those who live nearby. Several decades ago, studies of city residents showed that up to one-sixth of the persons applying for marriage licenses lived within one city block of one another and up to one-third lived within five blocks. One-half lived within 20 blocks.

This fact really should not surprise anyone. Before people can fall in love and marry, they must have the opportunity to meet. Moreover, residential areas tend to be somewhat segregated by social class, race, religion, and ethnic background. Therefore, the people with whom one is most likely to come into contact are also likely to be similar in background. Homogamy and propinquity obviously are related, and together they provide the general social context within which people choose their mates.

The more mobile people are, and the more varied the circumstances in which they live, the more complex is the operation of propinquity. Using city blocks as the unit of measurement made sense decades ago, when most people had relatively permanent addresses, and most interaction centered around the home. But it makes much less sense when we are dealing with a college student population. Large segments of the college population live in dormitories, fraternity and sorority houses, and apartments.

In these circumstances, many people who live close at hand may be of quite different social backgrounds. Here, propinquity does not imply homogamy as it does in more traditional settings. In fact, propinquity may increase the likelihood of becoming emotionally involved with someone of a different religion, race, or social background.

The situation is complicated, further, by the fact that *residential* propinquity may be less influential than *organizational* propinquity. In the classroom, men and women are seated elbow-to-elbow, and may be required to work on class projects together. This situation may throw them into more meaningful contact than would living across the hall or in adjacent apartments. Extracurricular activities of all sorts may be even more influential in the lives of many people. Activities bring people into day-to-day contact with others who are not thought of as potential partners at first, but who may become so with the passage of time.

Some scholars have used the phrase *field of eligibles* to refer to the total number of persons with whom one might become involved. The field is delimited by the operation of homogamy and propinquity (Winch, 1958). But defining field of eligibles is only the first step. Next we must move on to consider how particular people choose one another out of the total field.

HETEROGAMY

Logically, religion and race as factors in the selection of marriage partners might have been included under homogamy. Most people do marry others of similar religious and racial backgrounds. These are areas, however, in which society is undergoing rapid change. Increasingly, people are challenging the traditional homogamous norms. They are asserting both the right and the desirability of marriage between persons of different groups. In short, they are advocating religious and racial *heterogamy*. The issues are complex, so we will treat interfaith marriages and interracial marriages separately.

INTERFAITH MARRIAGES

Religious homogamy is still the rule; Catholics, Protestants, and Jews all marry within their own groups far more than would occur simply by chance. Because there are unequal numbers of people in the three major religious groups, the statistics are somewhat complicated. Protestants, who represent 66 percent of the population, would marry other Protestants 53 percent of the time if pairings were determined strictly by chance. Actually, 91 percent of Protestants marry other Protestants. Catholics make up 26 percent of the population and would marry other Catholics 16 percent of the time. In practice, 78 percent marry homogamously. Jews are only three percent of the population, and would marry homogamously two percent of the time. But actually, Jews make homogamous marriages in 93 percent of the cases (Carter and Glick, 1970). These facts are summarized in Table 6-2.

Religious homogamy is clearly still the rule. However, the situation is changing very rapidly. One measure of the change is in public attitudes. A Gallup Poll taken in November 1972, for example, showed that acceptance of marriage between Jews and non-Jews went up from 59 percent in 1968 to 67 percent in 1972. A study of college student attitudes in 1971 reported that 91 percent of the subjects were willing to marry a person from a different religious faith (Landis and Landis, 1973).

Not surprisingly, interfaith marriages are increasing rapidly. Some data now indicate that as many as 30 percent of the Catholics marrying today are taking non-Catholic partners. Interfaith marriage by Jews is increasing even faster. A study by the Council of Jewish Federations and Welfare Funds, for example, reported that nearly one-third of American Jews who married between 1966 and 1972 had non-Jewish spouses. This rate was more than double that of the preceding five years, and nearly four times the pre-1960 rate.

**TABLE 6-2
EXPECTED AND ACTUAL
RELIGIOUS HOMOGAMY
AMONG PROTESTANTS,
CATHOLICS, AND JEWS**

RELIGIOUS GROUP	PERCENT OF POPULATION	EXPECTED HOMOGAMY	ACTUAL HOMOGAMY
Protestants	66%	53%	91%
Catholics	26	16	78
Jews	3	2	93

Traditionally, all of the major faiths have opposed interfaith marriages, and all of them continue to do so. Religions are not unaffected by trends in the larger society, however. They also are wise enough to know that their policies must not be too greatly at variance with the attitudes and practices of their members. Consequently, religious opposition to interfaith marriages has been changing and weakening.

Fewer than 20 years ago, Roman Catholics were threatened with excommunication if they entered a mixed marriage in defiance of the church. The church strongly opposed interfaith marriages and was willing to grant dispensation for them only under stringent conditions. The non-Catholic partner had to agree to attend several sessions with the priest on Catholic doctrine and the proper rearing of children, and both partners were required to sign an Ante-Nuptial Agreement. The precise wording of the provisions of this agreement varied from one diocese to another, but there were five essential provisions:

**The Roman
Catholic Policy**

1. There should be only one wedding ceremony, to be performed by the priest.

2. The marriage should be indissoluble and broken only by death.

3. There should be no practice of birth control.

4. All children born of the marriage should be raised in the Roman Catholic Church.

5. The non-Catholic partner should not interfere with the Catholic partner's practice of his or her religion, and the Catholic partner should seek to convert the non-Catholic partner to Catholicism.

These demands represented, of course, extremely strong opposition to interfaith marriages. They caused strong resentment among many partners in mixed marriages, and they also aroused the ire of organized Protestantism. The church's intent, however, was to prevent mixed marriages; failing that, it was to protect the Catholic partner's faith and to see that the children were reared as Catholics.

This position persisted relatively unchanged until the Ecumenical movement of the late 1960s. In 1970, acting upon recommendations of the Ecumenical Council, Pope Paul VI removed the necessity for the written Ante-Nuptial Agreement; he also relieved the non-Catholic partner of the obligation to make any promises or commitments. The Catholic partner still must promise to have the children baptized as Catholics and to rear them in the Catholic religion. But now the non-Catholic partner is merely informed of the promise.

The requirement for a Catholic ceremony also has been eased. The bishop may now grant a dispensation "for serious reasons" for the marriage to be performed by a Protestant clergyman, a rabbi, or even a civil official.

The Jewish Policy

Traditional Jewish opposition to interfaith marriages had a quite different basis from the Catholic. Nevertheless, it was probably equally strong. To understand it requires knowledge of two things about Judaism. First, there are three branches of Judaism: Orthodox, Conservative, and Reform. The three branches have different attitudes toward, and policies on, interfaith marriages; with some oversimplification, the Orthodox and Conservative positions can be treated as one, and contrasted with the Reform position. Second, Judaism does not have an elaborate organizational hierarchy. Although the seminaries provide some leadership and guidance, the local rabbi acts essentially independently.

Jewish opposition to interfaith marriage has always emphasized the threat that it poses to the survival of the Jews as a separate people. Jews are a small proportion of the population, and widespread mixed marriage might cause their faith and traditions to become lost.

Jews distinguish between two different types of interfaith marriage: *intermarriage* and *mixed marriage.* Intermarriage involves a Jew and a gentile who has converted to Judaism. Mixed marriage occurs between a Jew and a gentile. Traditionally, most Orthodox rabbis would perform neither mixed marriages nor intermarriages. Reform rabbis generally would perform intermarriages. And a minority of them would officiate, reluctantly, at mixed marriages.

Many Jews fear and oppose interfaith marriages because of the threat they pose to Judaism. But the Jewish position also is based on social grounds that emphasize the welfare of the family. Generally, for example, Jews believe that the children should be reared in the faith of the mother, whether or not she is Jewish, on the grounds that women more than men can be counted upon to see that children get some religious training.

Many Reform rabbis, also, advise couples contemplating interfaith marriage that both partners should embrace either the Jewish faith or the other partner's faith, so that they will have some common religious home and religious identity. Consistent with that position, many rabbis will perform the ceremony if the gentile partner converts, or will urge a gentile ceremony if he or she does not.

Recent years have seen a sharp increase in the number of Reform rabbis who are willing to perform mixed marriages. In 1972, for example, one-fifth of the members of the Central Conference of American Rabbis reported that they would perform mixed marriages without imposing any conditions. Another one-fifth said they would do so when "special conditions exist,'' such as a pledge to raise the children as Jews. But there remains strong resistance to such liberalization. At the next year's conference, the rabbis voted 321 to 196 to oppose participation by Conference members ''in any ceremony which solemnizes a mixed marriage.''

Stating the Protestant position on interfaith marriage is more difficult. There are numerous Protestant denominations, and Protestantism also constitutes something of a residual category. People who are neither Catholic nor Jewish become labeled as Protestant by default, whether or not they are very religious.

The Protestant Policy

The policy of organized Protestantism has been formulated, in good part, in reaction to that of Roman Catholicism. Many denominations violently opposed the Catholic Ante-Nuptial Agreement, and many also formulated harsh statements opposing the Catholic position and urging Protestants not to enter mixed marriages under such conditions.

Beyond their specific opposition to the Catholic Church, which has softened in many cases since the Ecumenical developments of the late 1960s, Protestant denominations have opposed interfaith marriages on several grounds. First, they believe mixed marriages to be far more unstable than religiously homogamous marriages. Second, the religious faiths and participation of the couple are believed to suffer. Finally, there is the fear that the children will not be educated in the specific religious faith, or even in any faith at all.

Let us consider the influence of religion on divorce rates independently of interfaith marriage for a moment. Religious faith and religious membership have been associated with low divorce rates. Traditionally, Jews, Roman Catholics, and most devout Protestants have had low divorce rates. While this fact tells us nothing about the happiness of the marriages among such groups, it does indicate that many religious people have not considered divorce as a legitimate solution to marital problems.

Interfaith Marriage and Divorce Rates

Studies of divorce in interfaith marriages were undertaken both before and after World War II. These studies confirmed the fact that religiously homogamous marriages had low divorce rates, and they found substantially higher divorce rates in mixed Catholic–Protestant marriages. The highest rates of all were found among those with no religious affiliation (Landis and Landis, 1973).

Subsequent studies from the 1950s into the 1970s have shown smaller differences than before, but the pattern still persists. Catholics and Jews have the lowest divorce rates, and religion in general acts as a deterrent to divorce. Interfaith marriages taken as a whole have higher divorce rates. The recent studies also show, vividly, the effects of age, social status, and degree of commitment to religion. Couples who are older at the time of marriage and of higher social status are more likely to enter interfaith marriages, as are people who have been previously divorced (Monahan, 1973; Rosenthal, 1970). They also have lower divorce rates (Burchinal and Chancellor, 1963). Some of the highest divorce rates occur among Protestants in marriages of fundamentalists to nonfundamentalists (Bumpass and Sweet, 1972).

Religious Participation

Little is known about the impact of interfaith marriage upon the religious participation of the partners or upon the religious upbringing of children. It seems plausible that a disproportionate number of the people who enter such marriages already have grown away from their former religious ties. The marriage may simply confirm them in moving in that direction. Some data indicate that in about one-third of interfaith marriages, one partner converts to the faith of the other; only about five percent of the children of such marriages are reared without religious training. Where separate religious ties are maintained, the children are more likely to be brought up in the faith of the mother (Landis and Landis, 1973).

Jews are a small minority in most communities outside the urban Northeast. In view of this fact, they seem to be especially vulnerable to loss of faith upon mixed marriage. A study of Jews in mixed marriages and living in small midwestern towns, however, revealed no differences between their religious identities and those of their homogamously married counterparts (Schoenfeld, 1969).

INTERRACIAL MARRIAGES

Pressures toward racial homogamy are even stronger than those supporting religious homogamy. Originally, most states forbade interracial marriage, and such marriages were few. Attitudes were changing, however, and finally, a 1967 ruling by the United States Supreme Court had the effect of declaring the remaining laws against racial intermarriage unconstitutional.

The attitude changes were documented in a Gallup poll late in 1972, which reported that approval of marriage between blacks and whites increased from 20 percent of the population in 1968 to 29 percent in 1972. Blacks were far more favorable than whites, with approximately 60 percent approving. White approval, at 20 percent, was up from only four percent four years earlier.

A U.S. government report released in 1973 showed that there were almost 65,000 black–white marriages in 1970. This figure represents a 63-percent increase over the past decade. The percentage increase may be misleading, however, because there simply were more marriages; the proportion of marriages that are interracial marriages increased from only 0.44 percent to 0.70 percent. Although it is questionable whether they

should be counted as interracial, there were also almost 85,000 white–Indian marriages in 1970, and almost 55,000 marriages between whites and people of Japanese extraction (Heer, 1974).

Official statistics on interracial marriage are highly suspect. For one thing, it is well known that the census fails to enumerate minorities adequately. Also, the stigma that still attaches to interracial marriage in most quarters undoubtedly causes many of these marriages to remain ''hidden'' from the census takers. Nevertheless, it is obvious that the number of interracial marriages has increased very rapidly in recent years (Aldridge, 1973; Monahan, 1973; Schmitt, 1971). A study of marriage registrations for the state of Indiana showed, for example, an increase from less than two percent of all marriages in 1962, to 4.3 percent in 1967.

There is no need here for an elaborate statistical analysis of the structural features of interracial marriages. Nevertheless, it is helpful to known how they differ from most other marriages. Several studies have

Demographic Features

been done of the nature of black–white marriages in several different states. The studies reveal some consistent features.

The husbands in black–white marriages most often are black. This fact doesn't necessarily tell us anything about the patterns of romantic attraction between black persons and white persons, but it probably does tell us something about the power relationships between them. As described in Chapter 3, black high school boys may find it easier, in terms of group pressures, to date white girls than it is for white boys to date black girls. And people who cannot date are not likely to marry. Furthermore, once dating or other relationships (perhaps surreptitous) are established, the white woman may be in a stronger position to pressure her black partner into marriage than the black woman is.

Many black–white couples are older at marriage than most couples are, often in their mid-to-late twenties. This older average age often is associated with at least one partner's having been married before. People who have been married and divorced may worry less about what other people think, and may be less afraid to enter interracial relationships. A general rule is illustrated here: homogamy norms exert their greatest force upon the young and inexperienced.

A third feature of black–white marriages, and related to the preceding one, is that they seem to produce relatively few children. Part of the reason probably has nothing especially to do with mixed marriage. The young adult years are the most fecund years, and the likelihood of having children drops off rapidly after the early twenties. Late marriages are not likely to result in large families. Another factor, however, may be directly related to mixed marriage. Many couples probably worry about whether they can make the marriage work, and are reluctant to complicate their situation by having a baby. More directly, most interracial couples encounter much prejudice and discrimination themselves; they know that any children they may have will be victimized by it also.

The final fact to note runs counter to the assertions of many uninformed people. It is that black–white marriages appear to be as stable as most other marriages, and more stable than many. Using divorce rates as the criterion, an analysis of 30 years' data for the state of Iowa showed that black–white marriages as a whole have higher divorce rates than those of homogamous white couples. The rates were lower, however, than those of homogamous black couples. More strikingly, the divorce rates of couples in which the husband is black and the wife is white are lower than those of homogamous white couples (Monahan, 1970). These results generally were confirmed in a study in Kansas (Monahan, 1971).

It should be pointed out that the stability of interracial marriages again tells us little about their happiness. Interview studies of intermarried couples generally have reported an impression of comfort and security. But it probably is true, also, that researchers are more likely to be able to interview the more successful couples than the less successful ones.

Over the years, there have been studies of the adjustment patterns in interracial marriages in Chicago, New York, Philadelphia, and Indianapolis (Leslie, 1976). Recently there have been other studies in San Francisco (Wolf, 1971) and in an unnamed midwestern city (Porterfield, 1974). For obvious reasons, these studies have been based upon small samples and lengthy interviews. Although they vary in details, they have yielded a generally consistent picture of what interracial marriages are like.

In most cases, the fact of being from different races seems not to have been a significant factor in attracting the man and woman to each other. A few of the black men do say that their initial desire to date interracially may have been influenced by a desire to revenge themselves on white people. But the vast majority of couples state that their attraction to one another was based upon shared interests, ideals, and values. In this way, as in most others, interracial couples appear to be not very different from other couples.

From the beginning, however, race complicates the relationship. Black men dating white women may be accused of being traitors to their race and of thinking they are better than other blacks; black women are particularly resentful. Black men sometimes state that the hostility and aggressiveness of black women drives them to seek out more understanding and accepting white women.

Regardless of the sex composition of the couple, they encounter frequent disapproval and hostility from outsiders. The hostility ranges from curious and cold stares on the street and in public places to vicious comments and shouted obscenities. These incidents are shocking and momentarily painful. They are, however, less devastating than the opposition encountered on the job and in trying to find a place to live.

In the large cities where the studies have been done, there is enough separation of work from the rest of life, and enough anonymity, that the nature of the marriage may not become known at work. Thus, hostility is not often a factor on the job. Some people deliberately conceal the relationship, however, for fear of harassment or losing their jobs. In other cases, people report having been fired from their jobs, with or without explicitly being told that the interracial marriage was a factor.

Landlords have proved to be especially difficult, and most couples report a variety of problems. When they go together to investigate a potential rental, unexplainably there are no vacancies. If the white partner goes alone, complications suddenly develop when the landlord discovers that the other partner is black. The leaseholder has changed his mind and will not sublet. Or an unreasonably lengthy lease with an exorbitant deposit is demanded. Cruder landlords may simply state outright that they will not rent to a mixed couple, or they may make lascivious overtures to the woman when they can get her alone.

Most commonly, the white woman partner finds her self-concept

Relationship Dynamics

under attack from many quarters. Landlords, employers, and co-workers are likely to assume that she is "fair game" and available for sexual liaisons. But, once they discover that she is not promiscuous, their "sympathy" for her situation may be equally devastating. Even harder for her to take may be the realization that the couple's black men friends may be just as bigoted and just as ready to take advantage of her situation as white men are. Finally, black women are likely to attack her as a symbol of the subjugation of black people by white people.

Probably the greatest pain is inflicted by parents and other family members. Frequently, they refuse to accept the relationship, and they may ostracize the involved family member. The family of the white partner is more likely to reject the couple than is the family of the black partner. The most fortunate couples are accepted by both families; the least fortunate are rejected by both.

Women, having been encouraged all of their lives to remain emotionally dependent upon their parents, are more likely to be devastated by such rejection than men are. Some men, however, are also deeply hurt. The need for parental approval is so great that some couples, rejected by their families, seek out almost any accepting middle-aged couple and, knowingly or unknowingly, use them as surrogate parents.

Finally, the adjustment of interracial couples seems to be more similar to than different from the adjustments of other couples. Most of them learn to live with the special pressures of mixed marriages. If the couples are conscious of race at all as a factor *in their relationship,* they believe that it helps them to be especially understanding of each other. This does not mean that there are not gross incompatibilities in some interracial marriages; the worst of such marriages surely are as bad as any other bad marriages. But interracial couples don't tend to fight about race; they fight about the division of labor in the home, money matters, disciplining the children, personality differences, and other things, just as other couples do.

PERSONALITY SELECTION

Theoretically, people have almost unlimited choice in the selection of marriage partners. Actually, as we have seen, the field of eligibles for most persons is reduced by social selection in terms of homogamy and propinquity. Even interfaith and interracial marriages usually pair people from similar social and economic backgrounds and people who live and work near one another. We still have not answered the question, however, of how and why two particular people manage to get together out of the remaining field of eligibles. This is the area of *personality selection.*

THE OPERATION OF CHANCE

At the outset, it should be apparent that the process of mate selection is not wholly a matter of fate. If there were only one person (or even a few people) with whom each of us was destined to fall in love, most of us would spend our entire lives looking for the right person. Obviously, chance plays a role.

People do not choose to be reared in a particular neighborhood. Yet the location of the home does influence which eligible persons one will get to know. When a person picks a particular college to attend, large numbers of potential eligibles from other colleges are removed from the area of active choice. A further inevitable narrowing occurs when the student chooses a particular major.

Chance continues to operate, in decisions about where to live on campus, which groups to participate in, and which persons to date. Dating does not automatically lead to marriage, of course; most of us date several different people before becoming serious with someone. But the link between dating and mate selection becomes closer the nearer one moves to marriage age. To put it crassly, dating during the freshman and sophomore years generally is less "risky" than dating during the junior and senior years. For a freshman or sophomore, it is easy to decide that person A whom one dates is not very interesting or is unacceptable for a variety of reasons. On the other hand, if one happened to meet and date person A during the last semester of the senior year, the odds are much higher that A would seem both interesting and attractive. In a very significant sense, you marry "the last person you date."

We should not carry the point too far. After all, people do reject specific dating partners even when the pressures to get involved and to marry are strong. And personality factors, to be described next, are important in the final selection. But there are also a lot of accidental factors operating to determine who is brought together with whom at a particular time. The personality selection factors operate within the context of dating relationships that have been created partly by chance.

One picture of the way people select certain personality types with whom to become involved has been called the *theory of complementary needs* (Winch, 1958). The theory appeals to many people because it seems to be consistent with common sense. It is based on the principle that opposites attract. Briefly, the theory holds that people select marriage partners who give promise of meeting their unfulfilled personality needs. Thus, people with a need to be dominant select submissive partners, autonomous people select dependent partners, and so on. Because the situation obviously is more complicated than this, the theory holds that the complementariness can be of two different kinds. The needs being gratified for the one partner can be different from those being gratified for the second partner; or the needs of the two partners may be the same, but may differ markedly in intensity.

The theory is superficially attractive. The only trouble with it is that a

COMPLEMENTARY NEEDS

large body of research fails to support it. There may be a variety of reasons why (Moss, Apolonio, and Jensen, 1971). First, personality needs are highly abstract and difficult to measure; different research projects may use the same terms but actually refer to different things. Second, dating partners' perceptions of one another are not always accurate. A person may see the partner as being much more nurturant and achievement-oriented than he or she actually is. Thus, people may marry on the basis of *perceived* rather than *actual* personality characteristics. In support of this view, a study showed that women select mates to resemble their ideal selves rather than their actual selves (Karp, Jackson, and Lester, 1970).

THE STIMULUS–VALUE–ROLE THEORY

The most generally useful theory of how people select mates views the process as developing through three stages (Murstein, 1971). They are called the stimulus stage, the value stage, and the role stage.

The Stimulus Stage

The stimulus–value–role theory holds that people are first attracted to one another on the basis of how they perceive their own attractive qualities and those of the other person. Some of these qualities are physical: good looks, sex appeal, age, and so on. Some of them are social, such as being a big person on campus, having promising career prospects, being an athletic star, and so on.

There is more to it than just attractiveness, however. Otherwise, most people would be competing unsuccessfully for the relatively few attractive persons. The perceived attractiveness of the other person interacts with one's perception of one's own attractiveness. Most people, most of the time, approach members of the opposite sex to whom they feel approximately equal. They avoid approaching too-attractive persons because they fear being rejected; they know, realistically, that they haven't much chance with those persons. At the other extreme, they also avoid approaching persons much less attractive than they are because they know they can do better. These assessments characterize the *stimulus stage.*

Although they may not be consciously aware of it, the two partners at this stage are constructing a kind of balance sheet for the relationship, weighing assets against liabilities. If either partner sees the liabilities of the relationship as outweighing its assets, the relationship is likely to be discontinued. Only if the balance for both partners is favorable is the relationship likely to move on to the second stage.

The Value Stage

In the second stage, the *value stage,* the crucial question is whether the couple will go on to discover compatibility of values and attitudes to support their initial attraction. The partners typically discuss their attitudes toward life and toward marriage, and toward the roles of men and

women in it. They explore their feelings about children and their attitudes toward politics and religion. In the process, they either confirm their initial attraction or discover that they have too little in common and break off the relationship.

The more similar the values of the two persons are, the more likely that their attraction will become stronger, because each receives positive reinforcement from the other. Each partner enhances the other's self concept. Similar attitudes and values also tend to lead to shared interests; such couples engage in more activities together and further confirm their suitability for one another.

Whether the relationship develops on into the third stage depends on an interaction between the first two stages: specifically, on how well the initial stimulus attractions are supported by discovered compatibility. In some instances—the extremely wealthy man or the exceptionally beautiful woman, for example—the stimulus attractions may be so strong as to lead to marriage in spite of a general lack of compatibility in values. But this is not ordinarily the case. In most instances, only when the stimulus attractions combine with value compatibility does the couple move on into the *role stage.*

The Role Stage

It is one thing for couples to talk about their attitudes toward sex, family, religion, and politics, and another thing to know how they express those feelings in daily life. Only as they reach an advanced stage of intimacy can the partners reveal to each other how they cope with success and failure, whether they shoulder responsibility well, whether they project blame onto others, and whether they are stable or neurotic, happy or depressed, and placid or angry.

The broader the range of behavior they observe in one another, the more likely they are to become conscious of what it would be like to be married. They measure themselves, each other, and the relationship against ideal standards, and they are reassured or alarmed by what they find. Sexual compatibility generally is measured at this stage, more in terms of the comfort and harmony with which they interact rather than in terms of physical compatibility.

It is doubtful that most couples can escape the artificiality of courtship altogether. Therefore, they never truly fall into the roles that they will play as husband and wife. Even couples who live together before marriage do so knowing that they can end the relationship at any time, and without public censure. The legal obligations and 24-hour-a-day intimacy of marriage change things substantially.

Yet, many couples do test their relationships at increasing levels of intimacy and reality. Each partner comes to know whether the other is strong and dependable or prone to be quarrelsome and irresponsible.

Each discovers whether the other partner is slovenly or compulsively tidy, autonomous or dependent. Each learns whether the other's interest in sex is greater or less than his own. And the partners discover whether their relationship has any tendency to exploitation.

The notion of a balance sheet is appropriate here again. Perhaps the only couples who are likely to enter marriage totally in love with one another, and without some misgivings, are those who marry hastily and on short acquaintance. Most others are aware of both assets and liabilities in their relationship. They decide to marry on the assumption that the assets outweigh the liabilities.

It would be unrealistic to ignore the fact that not all men and women are strong, healthy people, and not all relationships that culminate in marriage have shown extensive compatibility and role-fit. Ideally, couples test their relationships thoroughly before committing themselves to marriage. In practice, however, some couples marry because marriage appears to be the least unattractive of the alternatives confronting them.

SUMMARY

Legal requirements define the boundaries within which mate selection takes place. The state prohibits marriage with persons who are closely related by blood or marriage and extends those prohibitions somewhat arbitrarily. It also imposes minimum legal ages for marriage, blood tests certifying freedom from venereal disease, and a waiting period before the ceremony may be performed.

Within the boundaries set by law, processes of social selection and personality selection operate. Figure 6-1 offers a summary of how these forces work. The law defines the field of eligible dating partners. Thereafter, propinquity, or physical nearness, influences whom any person actually may date. Some people are attracted to one another, and some are not. Most of the time, people are attracted to others who are like themselves (homogamy); increasingly, however, people are willing to cross religious and racial lines.

Personality selection tends to proceed through three stages. First, people are attracted to one another on the basis of external stimulus characteristics. Second, their initial attraction is either confirmed or discouraged through extensive verbal interaction, which establishes their degree of compatibility of attitudes and values. Third, continued intimacy encourages the adoption of roles that forecast what marriage would be like. Most couples assess the balance of assets and liabilities in their relationship before deciding whether to marry.

Figure 6-1 Mate Selection Filters. (Adapted from Udry [1971], p. 213; and Murstein [1971], pp. 110–131.)

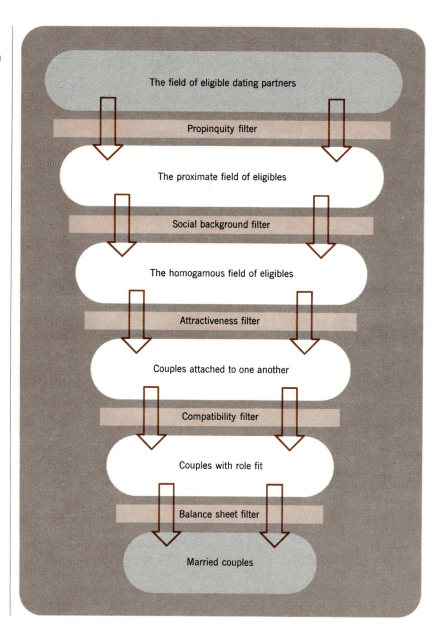

Barron, Milton L., ed., *The Blending American: Patterns of Intermarriage* (Chicago: Quadrangle, 1972). Selections on interracial, inter-ethnic, international, and interfaith marriages.

Besanceny, Paul H., *Interfaith Marriages: Who and Why* (New Haven: College and University Press, 1971). Analysis by a Roman Catholic priest–scholar of factors weakening religious homogamy.

Carter, Hugh, and Paul C. Glick, *Marriage and Divorce: A Social and Economic Study* (Cambridge, Mass.: Harvard Univ. Press, 1970). Contains chapters on "Group Variations in Age at Marriage" and "Intermarriage Among Educational, Ethnic, and Religious Groups."

Eshleman, J. Ross, *The Family: An Introduction* (Boston: Allyn and Bacon, 1974). Basically a textbook on the family as a social institution; contains two chapters on mate selection.

Kieren, Dianne, June Henton, and Ramona Marotz, *Hers and His: A Problem Solving Approach to Marriage* (Hinsdale, Ill.: The Dryden Press, 1975). Contains a chapter on engagement as part of mate selection and making a commitment.

FOR ADDITIONAL READING

STUDY QUESTIONS

1. Look up the laws regulating marriage in your state. Do they vary from the general national pattern? Develop a rationale for them.

2. What is meant by homogamy? How does homogamy work in mate selection?

3. Define propinquity. How does it work in mate selection?

4. Describe the positions of Roman Catholicism, Judaism, and Protestantism on interfaith marriage. Do you agree with these positions? Why or why not?

5. How much interracial marriage occurs? How are interracial marriages similar to and different from other marriages?

6. How big a role do you believe that chance plays in mate selection? Why do you think so?

7. Outline the stimulus–value–role theory of mate selection, describing each of the three stages.

8. Use the concept of mate selection filters to describe the narrowing of the field of eligibles to a specific marital partner.

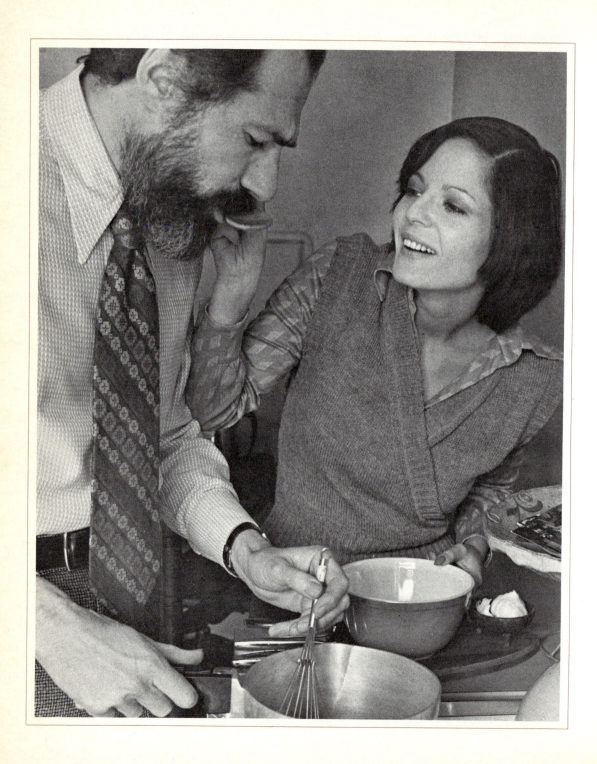

Chapter 7
Learning to Live Together

Little has changed as much in recent years as attitudes, particularly women's, on what marriage should be like. Men's attitudes have changed too, although not to the same degree. These attitudes and the differences between them are extremely important, because they affect the couple's adjustment both early in the marriage and later on.

WOMEN'S ROLE EXPECTATIONS

In chapter 2, we emphasized how young girls are socialized in the direction of traditionally feminine roles. Now, we must point out that many women, particularly college-educated women, do a great deal of further role learning before they approach marriage. This later learning often causes them to question the adequacy of marriage as a source of life fulfillment, and stimulates them to develop occupational as well as family goals (Katelman and Barnett, 1968; King, McIntyre, and Axelson, 1968).

THE INFLUENCE OF ENRICHMENT EXPERIENCES

Some women have always followed or wanted to follow traditionally masculine occupations. But until recently, many people regarded them as deviants, women who had somehow rejected themselves as females and adopted masculine self-images. Such women were widely perceived to be poorly adjusted, likely to remain single, and poor risks if they did marry. For a while, research supported this idea. Studies showed that career-oriented women began dating at later ages, dated less often, enjoyed children less, and were less likely to like domestic activities (Rossi, 1967).

In the early 1970s, however, two enterprising researchers decided to test an alternative hypothesis. Their proposal was that modern career-oriented young women are not deviants; rather, they are people who were subjected to certain kinds of enrichment experiences in the process of growing up. These experiences cause them not to reject the traditional feminine role, but to want to augment it by meaningful careers (Almquist and Angrist, 1972).

The study, of 110 women students over the four years of college, divided the subjects into career-oriented (46%) and non-career-oriented groups (54%). The subjects were then divided again into those who expected to follow typical occupations (teacher, social worker, secretary, and so forth) and those who anticipated atypical occupations, such as lawyer, journalist, and personnel manager. As we might guess, career-orientation and atypical job choices were closely related.

The findings strongly supported the idea that women who want non-traditionally feminine careers have had experiences that lead them to see themselves and the world in other than strictly family terms. The career-oriented women who wanted to follow non-traditional occupations differed from the other women in several ways. First, their mothers were more likely to be currently employed, and also to enjoy their combined family and work roles. Second, these women were influenced by their professors and people in their chosen occupations more than by peers and family. Third, the career-oriented women had worked at more jobs, and more different kinds of jobs, while they were in college.

CHANGE DURING THE COLLEGE YEARS

All but 13 of these 110 women went through all four years of college together and became the subject of further analysis. On the basis of extensive data, they were classified into five "life-style" types. The changes in the distribution of those types were then traced from the freshman through the senior year. The five types were described as careerists, noncareerists, converts, defectors, and shifters.

The largest category was that of *noncareerists* (33%). These women did not aspire to a career life-style at any stage of college. Their interest centered totally on their prospective families, and they were actively looking for husbands. They often became engaged as seniors, and they viewed outside employment only in terms of financial security.

The second largest group was the *converts* (22%). These women started college without career aspirations but developed them some time during the college years. They tended to become better students as their career interests developed. They generally were willing to delay the time of marriage to facilitate their careers and then to make flexible work arrangements with their husbands.

Women who were *careerists* throughout college represented another 18 percent of the class. These women anticipated not only careers but also active participation in their communities. They viewed housework and child care as areas in which other adults could at least partly replace them. The careerists and converts together made up approximately 40 percent of the class by the time of graduation.

The *shifters* (14%) showed a lack of directional trend. They shifted back and forth from career to noncareer orientations. They seemed ambivalent about their adult roles and appeared to be relatively uninfluenced by college in this regard. Finally, 13 percent were classified as *defectors,* having moved away from career interests during their college years. These women often were poor students who wanted to finish college, marry, and concentrate upon raising their children (Angrist, 1972).

If these data hold for college women in general, they suggest that nearly half of today's college women may have serious career interests, while around one-third are ideologically committed to family life and another 10 to 15 percent are family-oriented by default. The remaining 15 percent or so are likely to be ambivalent about either role.

ANTICIPATED ROLES

Confirmation of these findings was provided in a study of 1063 freshman women at the City University of New York. The subjects were asked to project themselves 15 years into the future and to choose one of five roles which they would like to play at that time. The results are summarized in Table 7-1. Approximately half of the women wanted

**TABLE 7-1
COLLEGE FRESHMAN
WOMEN'S DESIRED
ROLES FIFTEEN YEARS
IN THE FUTURE**

PREFERRED ROLE	PERCENT (N = 1063)
Married career woman with children	48
Housewife with children	28
Uncertain	19
Unmarried career woman	2
Married career woman without children	2
Housewife without children	0
Total	99

Source: Gilda F. Epstein and Arline L. Bronzaft, "Female Freshmen View Their Roles as Women," *Journal of Marriage and the Family,* 34 (Nov. 1972), p. 672.

careers, marriage, and children. Between one-fourth and one-third wanted marriage and children without a career, and about one-fifth were either uncertain or ambivalent. Virtually all the women rejected the idea of remaining childless, and only a very few wanted careers without marriage.

The combined evidence is consistent and impressive. Most women today want marriage and children. Something around one-third of them focus on family life to the extent that they do not wish to have gainful employment outside the home. At least as many college-educated women, however, somewhere between one-third and one-half, are not content with marriage and children alone; they also want to be able to work outside the home in meaningful, well-paid occupations. Moreover, they expect their husbands to share in housekeeping and child rearing in ways that will make it possible for them to do so.

For decades, people have talked smugly of egalitarianism in marriage without really having to face up to its full implications. As long as most women thought of outside employment as a necessary evil, a

burden that sometimes had to be borne in addition to wifely and motherly duties, men could afford to be gracious about their wives' desires to be considered as full partners in the relationship. After all, the wife still saw to it that the house was clean and orderly, the children were cared for, meals were ready on time, and the laundry was done. The wife earned less money, subordinated the demands of her job to those of his, and was ready to move to a distant city when he got a transfer or a promotion.

Today, however, the meaning of equality is hitting home hard (Parelius, 1975). More and more women want to be full partners with their husbands in the world of work, and they want their husbands to be full partners in the home. We have seen how young women view the matter. Now let us see it from the male perspective.

Changes in the role expectations of women are receiving considerable attention from researchers. As yet, however, relatively little research has been done on how these changes affect men. On a common-sense level, it seems apparent that some men are able to accept the changes more readily than others are. Also, one might assume that men, on the whole, lag somewhat behind women in both their awareness of the changes and their adjustment to them.

These common-sense generalizations received some support in a study of cultural contradictions in sex roles among 62 Ivy League College men. The analyses of their dating behavior were reported upon briefly in Chapter 2. These men were also specifically asked about their attitudes toward their future wives' occupational roles. Predictably, most of them paid some lip-service to the idea that their wives should be free to seek fulfillment in paid employment. Under further questioning, however, many of them hedged their answers carefully (Komarovsky, 1973).

The results of this part of the inquiry are summarized in Table 7-2. On the basis of their responses, the men were categorized into four overall types: traditional, modified traditional, pseudo-feminist, and fem-

MEN'S ROLE EXPECTATIONS

ROLE TYPE	PERCENT (N = 62)
Traditionalist	24
Modified traditionalist	48
Pseudo-feminist	16
Feminist	7
Views not crystallized	5
Total	100

**TABLE 7-2
COLLEGE MEN'S
PERCEPTIONS OF THEIR
WIVES' OCCUPATIONAL
ROLES**

Source: Mirra Komarovsky, ''Cultural Contradictions and Sex Roles: The Masculine Case,'' *American Journal of Sociology,* 78 (Jan. 1973), p. 117.

inist. Some five percent of the men viewed marriage as so remote a possibility for them that their responses could not be classified.

Approximately one-fourth of the men were classified as *traditionalists.* They were quite confident of their ability to support their families; they intended to marry women who would not seek employment, finding sufficient challenge in family, civic, and cultural pursuits.

Almost half the men were classified as *modified traditionalists.* They anticipated that their wives might work before children were born and again after the children were grown. However, they were firm in their belief that young children need their mothers in the home. Apparently recognizing that their views might not wholly prevail, these men were willing to make minor compromises; particularly, they were prepared to help their wives by hiring maids. They set relatively strict limits on their own direct assistance, however, emphasizing variously that they would not "do the laundry," "clean," or "do the diapers."

The *pseudo-feminists,* about one-sixth of the total, were ideologically somewhat more liberal. They stated that they favored the idea of their wives' working, at least in the abstract. When it came down to specific cases, however, they were inclined to impose conditions that few women, if any, could meet. For example, they favored their wives' working as long as "the home was run smoothly, the children did not suffer, and the wife's job did not interfere with her husband's career."

Only seven percent of the men were classified as *feminists.* These men were willing to make significant changes in their own roles in order that their wives might pursue careers without being unduly hampered by marriage and child rearing. These men seemed to be genuinely aware of women's needs in this area; they were willing to make any adaptations short of a complete reversal of roles. They favored equality, but they were not ready to give up the traditional masculine prerogative of earning a living.

When we compare these data to those on women's views, the potential for conflict is clear enough. Roughly one-third of college women still have fairly traditional views on marital and occupational roles. Among college men, though, at least three in four still hold such views. And whereas about half of all women believe in full equality in home and marketplace, fewer than one man in ten agrees. Other people of both sexes are markedly ambivalent about women's roles.

Men and women approach marriage with a legacy of psychological conditioning that predisposes them to certain patterns of adjustment in lovemaking, in-law relationships, dependence, and so on. They also have conceptions of the proper roles for husbands and wives to play; of what is fair and what isn't, and of what the proper division of labor should be. Adjustment to these psychological differences, and resolution of the role problem, constitutes a large part of learning to live together.

Couples cope with the problem of marital roles in many ways. One that has recently become prominent is a rejection of the whole idea of conventional marriage, with all its attendant "hang-ups." This strategy was a feature of the counterculture that flourished during the late 1960s and early 1970s, elements of which are still with us (Whitehurst, 1972).

The value system of the counterculture sought to embrace all of life, of course, and not just relationships between men and women. Its catchword was "freedom" in all areas of life. Each person was to "do your own thing," with the goal of escaping the "hang-ups" of traditional society. Men and women should be free to relate to one another both physically and emotionally on the basis of mood and inclination, without any idea of developing order and security in the relationship. The ideal situation in this view was the communal one, in which many people related to one another spontaneously and freely, seeking intimacy, naturalness, and unrestrained esthetic satisfaction (Davis, 1971).

Various aspects of communal living have been dealt with in earlier chapters, and others will be analyzed later. Our interest here is upon marriages that are legally solemnized, but in which the partners attempt to live their lives according to countercultural prescriptions rather than the norms governing conventional marriage.

As part of a major study of early marriage conducted by the National Institute of Mental Health, the investigators discovered that some 80 marriages out of a total of 2000 could be classified as unconventional counterculture marriages. They analyzed these marriages, most of which were on the east and west coasts, through extensive personal interviews with more than 40 of the participants (Kafka and Ryder, 1973).

These couples were all legally married and lived primarily with their spouses, but they were determined to create an intimacy that they felt conventional marriage does not allow. They encouraged experimentation with new roles for both men and women; they de-emphasized the traditional division of labor between the sexes; and they accepted intimate relationships outside of the marriage as well as within it. Similarly, there was less emphasis upon the privacy of the home than there is in most conventional marriages. The importance of money was minimized. Rejection of the establishment was symbolized by the men's generally long hair and by the widespread use of "soft" drugs, such as barbiturates, amphetamines, and marijuana.

The interview data produced several generalizations. First, there was considerable unconventionality in the roles played by men and women. In one case, for example, the wife held an office job with an insurance company and provided the family income, while her husband, a poet, slept during the day, spent the evening with his wife and baby, and wrote at night. There was not a total reversal of roles in this case, however. The husband did not assume the housewife role, but rather played the role of

INFLUENCE OF THE COUNTER-CULTURE

"expert in interpersonal relationships." He still somewhat dominated his wife, and her work was viewed not as breadwinning, but as routine drudgery. Later on, this couple rented a house and shared it with several other people. The husband took a part-time menial job and supplemented this income by petty stealing from his friends.

These counterculture couples appeared to be sexually more active than most couples their age, but they also seemed outwardly to be less preoccupied with sex. Since they advocated nonpossessive relationships, there were outside sexual liaisons. In the couple just described, for example, the husband told his wife repeatedly about the women he would like to sleep with and advocated a permissive attitude toward sex. She, then, felt free to sleep with another man and did so for a while.

A third distinctive feature of these marriages was their approach to the handling of tension in the relationship. Unlike the partners in most conventional marriages, these people did not seek to minimize tension or even to reduce it. Instead, they seemed almost to cultivate it because it generated discussions that were used for problem-solving. Confrontation was a valued part of the interaction of specific couples, and it also occurred in encounter-group settings.

Finally, a kind of "psychology of plenty" was part of the social environment of these relationships. The couples seemed confident that there would always be enough money for their limited needs. Thus, they put little emphasis upon getting ahead financially. Some couples lived on as little as $100 to $200 a month, and another couple felt they could get by if they worked for pay only one day out of each two weeks.

More importantly, these couples often had a similarly relaxed attitude about the availability of emotional and sexual relationships. Many couples were geographically mobile, and most of them believed they could find warmth and friendliness, if not love, on any street corner in any major city. Within their own immediate environments, the ready availability of other people reduced the need for exclusive relationships.

As these relationships were studied over time, however, they showed an irregular but nevertheless discernible tendency to revert to more conventional ways. In the couple already described, the husband who advocated sexual permissiveness became intensely jealous when his wife began her affair; the same thing happened in several comparable situations. Eventually, the wife became pregnant again and had to quit her job, their friends moved out of the house, and the husband moved uncertainly toward assuming the role of breadwinner.

The researchers are careful to point out that these are not truly the most radical couples. These people did all get legally married, and they did all emphasize their bonds with their spouses. But their relationships did tend to become increasingly conventional as time went on. There are two ways we can interpret this development. One is that these people were, for a time, on the way to finding a radical solution to the role problem that other, more radical, couples eventually may find. Another possibility is that people reared in our kind of society simply cannot accept the idea of nonpossessiveness in relationships and need some agreed-upon role definitions (Kafka and Ryder, 1973). Marital roles, and how to define them, are a growing concern of young adults. Another recent approach to this problem is the writing of marriage contracts.

MARRIAGE CONTRACTS

A marriage contract is a signed document in which the prospective husband and wife spell out their respective rights and obligations in marriage. It may be surprising to learn that marriage contracts are not new. Mary Wollstonecraft, the early English feminist, and her husband, William Godwin, had such an arrangement in the 1790s. Lucy Stone and Henry Blackwell wrote another marriage contract in the 1850s; and the birth-control pioneer, Margaret Sanger, had such an arrangement with her husband, J. Noah Slee, early in the present century (Edmiston, 1974).

The current interest in marriage contracts grows out of the efforts of many people to make marriage more personally meaningful. It is one device for arriving at agreements that promote satisfying and equalitarian relationships. Instead of depending upon the state to define their rights and duties, the partners to a contract take it upon themselves to do so (Weitzman, 1974). The relationship between the state and married couples is complex, however. Some factual background is essential if we are to analyze how marriage contracts can be used most constructively.

MARRIAGE AS A LEGAL STATUS

Marriage is not, as many people believe, a legal contract. The parties to a legal contract may specify the terms of the agreement, and they may also provide conditions for its termination. Neither of these things is true of marriage.

Marriage is instead a legal status, controlled by the state; the terms of the relationship are the same for all marriages. Moreover, the parties cannot dissolve the relationship themselves or even specify the grounds on which it may be terminated. Again, the state sets the terms, and only the state may relieve the parties of the status that it bestowed upon them.

The state regulates who may marry, what conditions they have to fulfill, and how they may become unmarried again. It also defines the relationship between them while they are married. These definitions, which are descended from traditional common law, have been altered by statute in some cases and not in others.

Basically, the courts have held that the husband is obligated to support his wife financially. In return for this support, he is entitled to her companionship and to sexual intercourse. In practice, the courts have generally defined these conditions in detail only in the event of controversy, such as suits for separate maintenance or divorce. They have also generally held that the legal domicile (residence) of the couple is the husband's residence. The wife must "follow" her husband, and if, for example, she refuses to move to a new location with him, she may be charged with desertion.

These requirements are relevant to the preparation of marriage contracts, because the state generally will not recognize any agreement between the partners that is not consistent with them. Thus, an agreement whereby the husband is required to pay a salary or wages to his wife in exchange for housekeeping probably would not be recognized by the courts; he is legally entitled to those services and has only a general obligation to support his wife in turn. Similarly, an agreement that the husband will not have to support the wife has no legal force. Agreements not to have sexual intercourse are not legally binding; nor are ones that permit the wife to maintain her own domicile.

Another area about which there is great confusion, and where conflict sometimes develops, is that of property rights. In states where common law still prevails, wives have a *dower* right in their husbands' property. This amount is often defined as from one-third to one-half of the husband's real property. The parties cannot sign away the wife's dower right by contract. In states that have passed community property laws, the wife has a half-interest in all property the couple acquires during the marriage. What couples can do, legally, is thus somewhat limited. They are permitted to agree that each partner will retain ownership and control of property owned before the marriage, and they may make similar agreements concerning property acquired after marriage by gift or inheritance.

As a general rule, couples may make agreements that do not interfere with the rights and obligations of the partners under either common law or statute law. All other agreements are legally void. We have spelled out here some of the most obvious situations, but readers should remember that there is a large grey area in which the legal force of marital agreements is uncertain. With the passage of time, too, and as women's rights become more of an issue, some courts are making more liberal decisions than they formerly did. With the ratification of an equal rights amendment to the Constitution, this process will be speeded up markedly.

THE USES OF MARRIAGE CONTRACTS

Given all of the legal restrictions on the use of marriage contracts, we might legitimately ask whether they are worth considering. If our answer is yes, we should examine how they may be used most constructively.

It is already apparent that marriage contracts generally are unable to provide a legal basis for regulating a relationship or for solving disputes.

If the partners are so uncertain about themselves and each other that they need the protection of a contract, the contract is likely to be of no help. In fact, it will probably become an additional source of conflict. Good marriages are built upon love, trust, and unselfishness, not on precise statements of rights and duties.

On the other hand, as was emphasized in Chapter 6, it is difficult for most couples to anticipate what marriage will be like and what roles they will play in it. Working out the details of a marriage contract in such situations can be used as much for testing out the relationship as for making specific agreements. Defining their duties and expectations may help couples overcome some of the artificiality of courtship and allow them to approach marriage with a firmer sense of reality.

Discussion of the terms of a marriage contract can give each partner insight into his or her own personal problems in relation to marriage. If these problems are few and minor, each partner may approach the marriage with more confidence. And if numerous or serious problems are discovered, the whole relationship may be re-evaluated. The contract writing may help the couple discover whether they really share the same basic values and if so, how they may implement those values together. If they discover they are both ready for compromise and mutual support, their prospects are more favorable. And if the discussion develops into a contest, there is reason to be wary of marriage.

As a guide for couples who might want to write marriage contracts, we have prepared a series of questions to consider, listed in the accompanying box. They cover matters of property rights, names, division of labor, finances, domicile, sex relationships, family planning, and child rearing. But individual couples may want to consider other areas as well, such as in-law relationships and religious participation.

INITIAL MARITAL ADJUSTMENTS

Willard Waller, an early student of the family, defined the honeymoon as "that period while illusion lasts." He was not talking about the wedding trip, obviously. Rather, he was referring to the fact that no matter how maturely and rationally the couple have managed their courtship, even if they have already lived together, there is an inevitable time of "settling down," a period of adjustment and reality testing.

DISILLUSIONMENT

It doesn't work exactly the same way in all marriages or occur at the same rate. Nevertheless, sooner or later, each partner must face the fact that the spouse cannot meet all of his or her needs all of the time. Anything may set the process off. One partner, for example, may be too tired to go out in the evening when the other wants to do something special; or one rolls over and goes to sleep when the other wants to make love.

QUESTIONS FOR COUPLES WHO WANT TO
WRITE MARRIAGE CONTRACTS

Property Rights
1. Should each partner retain title to, and control over, property owned at the time of marriage?
2. Should each partner retain property acquired after marriage through gift or inheritance?
3. Should each partner waive the right to any interest in the other's estate?

Names
1. Should the wife take the husband's family name; or the husband, the wife's family name?
2. Should they each retain their own surnames?
3. Should they each adopt a hyphenated combination of their family names? In which order should the names appear?
4. What surname should their children use?

Division of Labor
1. Are both spouses free to hold full-time paid employment?
2. Are both *expected* to hold full-time paid employment?
3. What arrangement should be made for the performance of housekeeping duties (cleaning, cooking, dishes, laundry, shopping)? Should the wife do them? the husband? Should they be shared equally? Divided according to some other formula?

Finances
1. Should the husband (or the wife) pay all of the expenses of the marriage?
2. Should they pool their incomes and pay all expenses out of their common funds? If so, how are surplus funds to be divided and used?
3. Should the spouses each pay 50 percent of the expenses?
4. Should the spouses retain their own income and with each paying a prorated share of the expenses?

Now there is nothing extraordinary about these things. They happen all the time. In a new marriage, though, each partner is already discovering that the other has formerly unnoticed faults, such as not picking up dirty underwear, leaving toothpaste smeared on the washbowl, belching, or any of a thousand other annoying things. In these circumstances, symptoms such as being tired or not feeling like making love can get blown all out of proportion.

Each slight, real or imagined, confirms a person's fears that the relationship is not as good as it was thought to be; maybe getting married was a mistake. More threatening yet is the implication of personal

(CONTD)

Domicile
1. Should the location of their dwelling be determined by the husband's (the wife's) job?
2. Should the couple follow the job that provides the most income? the one that yields the greatest personal satisfaction?
3. Should they make alternate moves, making one move for the one partner's job and the next for the other partner's job?
4. Should they agree to live apart, each following his or her own job?

Sex
1. Should either partner have the right to request sexual intercourse? Should sex be engaged in only when both partners are interested?
2. Should there be separate beds? separate bedrooms?
3. Should each partner have the right to seek sexual satisfaction with other partners?

Family Planning
1. Should the marriage be childless, or should it produce children? How many children?
2. Should abortion be used to terminate accidental or unwanted pregnancies? Should either partner have the right to demand abortion?
3. Should children be had by birth or by adoption?
4. Should contraception be used? What kind? Whose responsibility is it?

Child rearing
1. How are the demands of occupation and child care to be reconciled? paid child care? each parent responsible for it during certain hours?
2. How is the financial responsibility of child rearing assigned? equally? prorated according to income? Some other division of expenses?
3. How are children to be educated? public schools? private schools? boarding schools? religious training?
4. How are the children to be disciplined? by whom? Who has the final say?

---

rejection in these slights and rebuffs. Before marriage, each partner spoke of love and showed it in many ways. Now they find themselves being taken for granted. If the partner were truly in love, he or she would not behave like this. If the partner is not overwhelmingly in love, then it must be because of something wrong with oneself.

The disillusionment encountered in early marriage is directly proportional to the unreality that goes into it. Couples who really come to know each other before marriage may experience little or no disillusionment; those who marry in the full throes of romantic passion may find this phase ego-shattering. But as long as the couple learns reasonably well

how to cope with conflict, it will pass. And it is important to emphasize that it is the disillusionment that passes, not the symptoms that give rise to it.

Twenty years later, for example, that same wife who was offended by her husband's being too tired to go out will look at him sleeping on the sofa and smile affectionately. At times, of course, she will be angry because she is prevented from doing something she wants to do. But the anger is no longer blown out of proportion, because it no longer implies rejection of her. She has long since learned that at times he is just plain tired.

LEARNING TO HANDLE CONFLICT

In the abstract, everyone knows that married couples fight occasionally. Most people think that quarreling or fighting is an indication of personal failure, however; they try to hide it from friends and even from other family members. Until recently, also, physical violence was also a taboo subject for research. But very recent research shows that there is a surprising amount of violence between husbands and wives.

Physical Violence

One team of researchers tried to estimate the extent of physical violence between the parents of college students by having the students complete anonymous questionnaires. The students were asked about conflicts between the parents that occurred during the last year the students were in high school. Of the 385 parental couples, 16 percent were reported to have used physical violence against one another during that one year (Straus, 1975). This figure is remarkable for two reasons. First, these were couples who had been married for nearly 20 years or more. Second, this procedure obviously underestimates the actual amount of conflict. Yet, in 16 percent of the families, conflict was severe enough or open enough for adolescent children to be aware of it and to remember it.

A second study involved unstructured informal interviews with a non-random sample of 80 married couples. Fifty-five percent of them discussed at least one incident of conjugal violence (Gelles, 1975). Thus, it seems likely that most couples do some actual physical fighting, and that some fight occasionally even after 20 years of marriage. Unfortunately, there has not yet been research that can tell us the full meaning of these figures. Some physical fighting may actually do less damage to the partners, and to the relationship, than seemingly more innocuous quarrels. On the other hand, some physical conflict may reflect total frustration over the couple's inability to find ways to resolve disputes. Few people would argue with the statement that most couples need all the help they can get in learning how to handle conflict.

**Types of
Quarrels**

Marital quarrels take many forms. One useful way to analyze them is to classify them into three basic types, according to when and how they develop and what functions they serve. The three types are described as acute, progressive, and habituated.

Acute quarrels grow out of the couple's need to establish a successful *modus operandi;* such quarrels occur frequently in new marriages. Even if the couple has done the kind of careful analysis that goes into drawing up a marriage contract, there still are dozens of details to be worked out in daily living. Who should take out the garbage and pick up the soft drink bottles? Should it be done every evening after dinner, whenever it is convenient, or only when the mess gets too great to live with? Who goes to the store to pick up emergency items? How does one cope with a too-helpful mother-in-law? How much money is it reasonable to spend on cigarettes, cosmetics, hobbies, and so on?

There are special problems of adjustment connected with in-laws, sex, contraception and family planning, and money. These topics will all be treated in detail in subsequent chapters. The point here is more general: new marriages are, in many ways, undefined situations, and couples literally have to learn how to live together. As they do, there are bound to be quarrels and disagreements.

Moreover, as the term "acute," implies, these quarrels are likely to be sharp and loud. Precisely because the spouses are in love and do not want to hurt one another, they are likely to suppress their irritations at first and vent them only when the pressure becomes unbearable. Say the wife, for example, has to be at school or at work at an early hour. She may think it only reasonable that her husband clean up the swamp that he makes of the bathroom with his morning shower. But for weeks, she stifles the impulse to tell him so, only to blow up some morning when she is running late or things are not going well. When she finally does attack his slovenliness, he is likely to be hurt. He may retaliate by denouncing whatever aspects of her performance have been bothering him: her cooking, perhaps. They argue and shout and marvel at each other's depravity.

Some couples can be calm and rational enough to focus upon the immediate issues then and there. The husband cleans up the bathroom after himself, and the wife doesn't give him half-cooked eggs anymore. But anger gets the better of many couples, and they stalk off to the day's work without kissing good-bye. Later, away from each other, they calm down and realize that adjustments have to be made. That night they work it out.

Quarrels become *progressive* only when couples fail to focus upon the issues and resolve them. Each conflict that is unresolved becomes part of the next one, and the whole thing quickly becomes a vicious cycle. The wife brings up the dirty bathroom issue again when they fight about his being too lazy to get up and go to church on Sunday. Later, both these issues are brought into the picture when conflict develops over his paying too much attention to other women at parties.

Eventually, most of the objective issues become lost and personalities become the focus of the struggle. Each partner is in love and is hurt by the other's attacks. How better to fight back than to attack the partner at points of weakness? We are all vulnerable.

All of us have rationalizations for our failures and small fictions that we maintain to protect our self-concepts. Ordinarily, people who are close to us actively support us in these little deceptions or, at least, acquiesce in them passively. Consider the situation in college, for example, when a student fails an examination badly. He or she simply failed to study, but when the exams are returned, the student denounces the dullness of the course and the unfairness and ambiguity of the questions. The friend to whom the student complains probably knows better, but the friend either actively supports the excuses or maintains a discreet silence. To do otherwise would be to risk losing a friend.

When marital conflict becomes progressive, however, the partners may actively challenge each other's weaknesses, and with devastating effect. A wife who realizes that her husband is indecisive on the job may help him reach his decisions at home, and she may congratulate him when he later boasts of having put important decisions into effect—that is, it happens this way normally. But when a conflict becomes progressive, she is likely to tell him that everyone knows how weak and indecisive he is, that he would never have gotten this far without her help, and that she is the strong one of the pair.

Eventually, the particular quarrel ends. But permanent damage has been done to the relationship. Never again will the wife be able to assist her husband so effectively and unobtrusively, because both of them remember that quarrel; the pretense has been unmasked.

When a wife attacks her husband in this fashion, he probably will attack her in turn. Perhaps she isn't very good in bed. Or maybe she constantly is critical of other people. Whatever the details, this kind of quarreling can soon destroy a relationship. And even when it does not lead to separation, it can leave the marriage a hollow shell.

Most couples learn quickly enough to focus on the issues, rather than on personalities, so that there is little progressive character to their quarrels. And many of them devise techniques for taking the hostility out of the things that must be said. Some of these devices are as simple as waiting until the partner is in a good mood to raise a touchy issue. Some couples find that the period of greatest security for both is in bed, following a satisfactory episode of love-making. Other couples dally over coffee at the dinner table, and work out their relationship there. No technique will work by itself, of course, and many different ones are

successful when employed in a context of love and consideration for
one's mate.

Habituated conflict is most of what remains after couples have
worked out their basic adjustments and learned to avoid progressive
conflict. For most couples, there remain certain areas where agreement
will never come, and where accommodation is the best that can be
achieved. Some couples will never agree on in-law relationships, for
instance; others, on spending and saving money; and still others, on
religious matters. Couples learn to avoid these areas most of the time,
and not to invest them with a great deal of emotion. Periodically, circumstances may force these problems into the open, disagreements
occur, and then the issue submerges until the next time. In the best of
relationships, there is little such conflict; in other cases, there is a good
deal of it.

**THE ROLE
OF INSIGHT**

The amount of insight the partners develop into one another's
behavior may be the most important single factor influencing the quality
of their relationship. Insight, of course, is the capacity to comprehend the

underlying motivations for the partner's behavior and for one's own. It also means being able to anticipate the consequences of given courses of action. Insight enables people to plan constructively for their own welfare and that of others.

Insightful people realize that attacks by the partner usually are motivated out of hurt or fear: retaliation for injury done, or fear of rejection. Understanding this fact, they respond in ways that will lessen the hurt or fear rather than increase them. Allaying the partner's anxieties makes it easier for the partner to respond in kind. A new kind of cycle begins, the opposite of progressive conflict. Constructive overtures from the one partner call forth constructive responses from the other partner, and so on.

Little is known about why some people are more insightful than others. However, both common sense and research evidence (Thomas, Franks, and Calonico, 1972) indicate that the possession of power and insight are inversely related. Children, for example, often compensate for their powerlessness by shrewdly understanding and manipulating adults. When women were more powerless than they are today, their insight into many factors was sometimes labeled "feminine intuition."

The general trend toward more equality in heterosexual relationships may be encouraging a more equal distribution of insight in marriage. This development is most important, but it is not automatically beneficial. Insight itself is ethically neutral; it may be used to further sharing and love in a relationship or it may be used in exploitative manipulation.

POWER RELATIONSHIPS

One of the issues to be worked out in new marriages is the distribution of power between the husband and wife. Power involves relatively straightforward questions such as who makes the decisions about where to live, shopping, saving, buying a new car, and so on. But it also embraces more subtle ones, such as who dominates the marriage and controls the relationship, no matter which partner appears to make individual decisions.

The differential distribution of power is not peculiar to marriage relationships, of course; it probably is a feature of all relationships. Small children contest with one another to see who is the strongest, who can run the fastest, who can count the highest, who is the best-looking, and so on. The winners of these contests have increased influence in the group.

Among adolescent males, these contests sometimes involve fist-fights. In the long run, however, the winners are more likely to be those who use their brains rather than their fists. Adults may be more polite and discreet about such competition. Nevertheless, when people meet, they are likely to inquire politely into one another's backgrounds, occupations, and group affiliations. Such information cues each participant in on how to behave toward the others. The give-and-take gradually sets up an informal dominance–submission hierarchy; some people tend to lead while others follow.

So it should come as no surprise that the same thing happens in marriage. Actually, of course, the process starts long before marriage. Even from the very first meeting, one partner or the other may tend to dominate through some combination of social and personality characteristics. Often, marriage simply makes the power relationship that already exists within the couple more visible and systematic.

Under some circumstances, power may create no problems for either partner. This is often true when one partner clearly comes from a more advantaged background and is also the more aggressive and competent of the two. He or she may be happy guiding the relationship, and the other may be quite content to be the follower. If the dominant one happens to be the man, then the relationship also will be in accord with the long tradition of male domination in marriage. If it is the woman, the power relationship may receive little support from others, but it may still be quite satisfying to the two people involved.

Actually, there are three basic power patterns, rather than two: male domination, female domination, and equality. For several decades now, we have been moving hesitantly in the direction of favoring equalitarian relationships over male dominated ones; for many young couples today, dominance within marriage has become a major issue. The object of the Equal Rights Amendment to the Constitution is to forbid discrimination of any kind, by either the federal government or the states, on the grounds of sex (Friedan, 1973). The amendment is a symbol for many young women who are determined to avoid domination in marriage. For them, it is both an ideological issue and a personal one.

POWER IN MARRIAGE

Early studies consistently showed that most husbands exercise more influence in family decision-making than their wives do. Our interest now is in whether more recent studies would show the same thing. To try to find out, one group of researchers interviewed a sample of 776 husbands and wives in Los Angeles. The subjects were selected to resemble the urban population of the United States as a whole (Centers, Raven and Rodrigues, 1971). The researchers also studied a broad range of family decisions, including those traditionally made by men and those traditionally made by women. The finding was that the husbands' and the wives' power were almost exactly equal.

The respondents' answers were also used to classify them into four general power patterns: (1) husband-dominant; (2) syncratic (equal and shared decisions); (3) autonomic (equal and more independent decisions); and (4) wife-dominant. The results are shown in Table 7-3.

The vast majority of marriages, in the view of both men and women,

**TABLE 7-3
MARRIAGE AUTHORITY
TYPES, BY SEX OF
RESPONDENT**[a]

AUTHORITY TYPE	MEN'S REPORTS	WOMEN'S REPORTS
Husband-dominant	10%	9%
Syncratic	16	20
Autonomic	70	67
Wife-dominant	4	4
Totals	100%	100%

[a]747 Los Angeles residents

Source: Adapted from Richard Centers, Bertram H. Raven, and Aroldo Rodrigues, "Conjugal Power Structure: A Re-Examination," *American Sociological Review,* 36 (April 1971), p. 271.

were *autonomic* ones, in which the husband and wife have approximately equal say, and each spouse also has large areas of relatively independent decision-making. The next most common type, the *syncratic,* represents equal and shared decision making. Only one marriage out of ten was male-dominated, and only one out of 25 was female-dominated.

This same study asked the subjects whether they rated themselves "very satisfied," "fairly satisfied," or "not at all satisfied" with their marriages. The four marriage authority types answered as follows, in decreasing order of "very satisfactory" answers:

**POWER AND
MARITAL
SATISFACTION**

TYPE	PERCENT "VERY SATISFACTORY"
Autonomic	79
Husband-dominant	73
Syncratic	70
Wife-dominant	20

Consistent with contemporary values, autonomic decision-making was most highly correlated with marital success. Somewhat surprisingly, though, husband-dominated marriages were rated almost as satisfactory. This result apparently reflects a persistent need among some men and women for the husband to take charge and manage things. The syncratic marriages also ranked very high in satisfaction. The only category in which there was not high satisfaction was the wife-dominant.

Other studies have shown that shared power is associated with good health of the partners (Pratt, 1972); that the wife's power is associated with her employment (Bahr, Bowerman and Gekas, 1974); and that couples consistently dominated by one partner lack flexibility in coping with crises (Bahr and Rollins, 1971).

SUMMARY

Women's roles have changed greatly in recent years. More and more women anticipate combining marriage with full participation in the world of work. Such women are likely to have mothers who work and who enjoy their work; they are also likely to have been influenced more by professional people than by peers and family members, and to have already had work experience.

About half of college women today want careers, marriage, and children. One-fourth to one-third more want families but not careers, and about one-fifth are not certain what they want. Few want careers without marriage or want to remain childless.

Men have much more traditional expectations than women do, and this fact sets the stage for marital conflict. As many as three-fourths of college men expect their wives to subordinate work to the demands of home and family. Another one-sixth of men give some lip-service to supporting their wives' working, but fewer than one in ten is prepared to make substantial changes in his own role to accommodate it.

The counterculture of the late 1960s and early 1970s sought to resolve these problems in new ways. Couples experimented with marriages that de-emphasized money and possessions, including possession of the partner; they encouraged the development of alternative roles for men and women. Many couples achieved their goals of greater role flexibility and personal freedom. Most couples found that other problems were created, however, which caused them to shift back gradually to more conventional roles.

Another approach to working out roles in marriage employs marriage contracts. The prospective spouses sign agreements on a number of issues, including names, property rights, residence, work and housekeeping roles, sex, family planning, and child rearing. Most such contracts have no force under the law and cannot be enforced. But they can be very useful in aiding couples to think through, and agree upon, matters that are important to them. Attempts to use a marriage contract to coerce the partner, on the other hand, may make the contract just one more source of problems.

All new marriages face a period of adjustment, in which reality intrudes upon illusion and a myriad of details must be worked out. This period engenders more conflict in some cases than in others, but all couples need to learn ways of resolving conflicts successfully. Acute conflict arises out of the many undefined situations in a new marriage. It subsides as agreements are reached but may reappear whenever there are major changes in circumstances, such as moving to a new city, having a baby, and so on. Progressive conflict develops whenever acute conflicts are not solved and instead accumulate; it can destroy a marriage quickly. Habituated conflict is that which remains after a fairly steady level of adjustment has been reached. Some couples experience more of it than others do.

Insight, or the ability to understand the other's motivations and to anticipate the consequences of actions, is a major influence in learning to live together. But insight can be used either to support or to sabotage a relationship. There is no substitute for the partners' being determined to work out their problems.

The working out of power relationships is a feature of virtually all relationships, marriage included. Research shows a trend toward equalitarian relationships, both syncratic and autonomic. In the syncratic type, most decision-making is shared. In the autonomic type, each partner has a wide area of relatively independent decision making. This pattern is the most common and seems also to be most associated with perceived marital happiness.

FOR ADDITIONAL READING

Kammeyer, Kenneth, C. W., ed., *Confronting the Issues: Sex Roles, Marriage, and the Family* (Boston: Allyn and Bacon, 1975). Section 5 contains several articles on different approaches to marital fighting.

Koller, Marvin R., *Families: A Multigenerational Approach* (New York: McGraw-Hill, 1974). The chapter on "Husbands and Wives" analyzes adjustments in new marriages.

Lopata, Helena Znaniecki, *Occupation: Housewife* (New York: Oxford University Press, 1971). A report on research into the many roles of a group of Chicago women.

Scanzoni, John H., *Opportunity and the Family* (New York: Macmillan, 1970). A scholarly analysis of the relationship between occupational roles and family roles.

Steinmetz, Suzanne K., and Murray A. Straus, eds., *Violence in the Family* (New York: Dodd, Mead, 1974). Thirty-eight selections dealing with various aspects of marital and family violence.

STUDY QUESTIONS

1. According to current research, what are the orientations toward work, marriage, and family of young women today?

2. What, according to research, are young men's perceptions of the proper roles for women in work? in marriage?

3. In view of the answers to Questions 1 and 2, what advice would you give to young women approaching marriage? to young men?

4. How do counterculture marriages differ from most others? What does research show about the course of such marriages?

5. Marriage is a legal status rather than a legal contract. What is the significance of this fact? Include as many areas of marital interaction as you can.

6. Do you recommend that couples consider drawing up marriage contracts? Why or why not?

7. Analyze your own relationship with your spouse, boyfriend, or girl-friend. What are the major sources of conflict? How do you handle them? How could you handle them better?

8. Both husband-dominated and wife-dominated marriages are relatively uncommon. They report very different frequencies of marital happiness. How can you account for the difference?

Chapter 8
In-Law
Relationships

In-law relationships often start long before marriage. By the time most couples marry, a pattern of interaction already exists. Both parental families may be solidly behind the marriage, and the husband- and wife-to-be may call the other's parents "Mom" and "Dad" with meaning and affection. On the other hand, the relationship may be stiff, strained, and formal; or all concerned may be apprehensive and hostile.

THE PREMARITAL PERIOD

One may know the other person's parents even before romantic interest develops. This is usually the case if that person lives in the neighborhood, belongs to the same church, or the like. And even if the two people become involved while they are away at college, they may make ritual visits to one another's homes at Thanksgiving, Christmas, spring break, or other holidays, for the specific purpose of meeting the families. If the distance is great, however, meeting may not occur until the wedding is set, or even after. If the proposed partner comes from a radically different background, meeting the families sometimes is avoided for as long as possible. Sooner or later, however, the question of parental approval or disapproval must be faced.

SEEKING PARENTAL APPROVAL

There are people who are so alienated from their families that they meet, marry, and go on living without any contact with their parents. But most people want to remain close to their families and want their parents to approve of their intended spouses. Whether the parents are likely to react with approval depends upon many factors.

Similarity of Background

The likelihood that good relationships will develop quickly between a young couple and the parents on both sides depends in part upon how alike or how different they are. A prospective spouse who comes from a similar financial and occupational background will be welcomed more quickly than one whose parents rank significantly higher or lower. To most parents, whether or not they themselves are active in church, religious background is also important. Nationality and religion often are linked, but nationality may be a factor in its own right. Family background also is of concern to most parents. The parents of only one or two children are likely to react with alarm if their offspring wants to marry someone with six or eight siblings. Similarly, there may be some opposition if the intended spouse's parents have been divorced.

One may react to all of these parental concerns by declaring that they represent bigotry, and that the approval of such parents is not worth seeking. But there is more to it than simple narrow-mindedness. Granted that most people are somewhat parochial in their views, many parents are genuinely concerned about their offspring's welfare. They worry that choosing the wrong partner may doom their son or daughter to a less comfortable or rewarding life than he or she deserves. They worry, too, about their prospective grandchildren: how many of them there will be; whether they will be cared for properly; whether they will receive proper religious training, and so on. They fear that marriage to someone of a very different background will lead to marital unhappiness or, perhaps, divorce.

This is not to say that in-law relationships, where there are great differences in background, are sure to be bad. But parental approval is likely to come less easily and quickly in those cases, and the young people will have to work harder at achieving it. It is also true that there is a greater risk in such cases that the couple will never secure complete approval and acceptance. In short, one price that may have to be paid for choosing someone very different is the sacrifice of some closeness to one's own family.

By the time their children reach marriageable age, many parents have 20 or so years of hard work behind them, and they have labored hard to achieve their present station in life. But their offspring are generally familiar only with their present level of living; they tend to be relatively unaware of their parents' efforts and of the parents' hope that their children will have things better than they did.

Parents know that the standard of living of their daughter will be closely linked to that of her husband. When the daughter brings home a young man who plans to work in a relatively low-paying field, who does not do well in school, who seems none-too-ambitious, or who lacks social graces, parents are likely to reveal their concern. These misgivings may put the daughter on the defensive. To her, their view may seem narrow and unfair: they are overlooking his good qualities. She may point out that, today, women earn their share of the family income and that the parents need not worry.

**Life
Chances**

The parents, on the other hand, know how often unanticipated pregnancies occur. They are likely to believe that their daughter will be cheated of some of life's greatest joys if she has to hold a job all her life. The point is not who is right, the parents or the daughter. The point is that in-law relationships are likely to get off to an easier start if the parents see their prospective son-in-law as someone strong and competent. A major obstacle is removed if he seems well able to take care of their daughter and her future children.

The prospective daughter-in-law is likely to be viewed somewhat differently by a young man's parents. Parents ordinarily do not expect their son's wife to support him. In fact, a capable young woman with firm career plans may provoke quite negative reactions. The parents may see her as unfeminine and fear that their son will not have a satisfying home and family life with her. In their view, the son is likely to be neglected, and so are the grandchildren—if, indeed, there are to be any.

If the young woman is not occupationally ambitious, however, the parents may have other worries. If their son is headed for a professional or managerial career, the parents know that his advancement will be furthered by a supportive, capable, and socially gracious wife. If the prospective daughter-in-law is unambitious, reticent, or slovenly, they may view her as a potential millstone around their son's neck.

Young people often are concentrating on a different range of life's problems from those that their parents face, and, sometimes, they reject some of their parents' values as well. The parents, in turn, find it difficult to communicate to their offspring the bases for their concerns. The ways accommodation may be reached will be dealt with shortly. For now, the point is that parents' initial reactions are likely to be more favorable if the prospective son-in-law or daughter-in-law fits their image of a helpful spouse.

Living Together

Perhaps nothing has caused more trouble in recent years between parents and their offspring than parental knowledge that the young people are living together. The same obviously applies when the couple is sleeping together, even if they maintain separate residences. More young people do sleep and live together now, and they do so more openly.

Many parents, when they first learn of their children's sexual relations, precipitate a crisis. There may be angry and tearful telephone calls, face-to-face confrontations, and threats to cut off aid if the child does not desist.

This society is still masculine-biased, and the man's parents are less often an open source of trouble than the woman's. Parents may acknowledge their son's need for sex, however reluctantly. Many of them do not show too much concern until they think that marriage might follow. But then, suddenly, they may attack the young woman for being immoral: the type of young woman who would live with a man is not the kind of woman they want as their son's wife, or as the mother of their grandchildren! There is a real generation gap in this area. Knowledge that the couple is living together is likely to prejudice in-law relationships, at least in the beginning.

The situation usually is even more difficult with the woman's parents. First of all, women have traditionally been conditioned to be more dependent than men are. As a result, a young woman is likely to be more vulnerable to her parents' condemnation, and her concern for her parents' approval may make the young man feel angry or resentful toward them. Of course, they probably also have extremely negative feelings toward him. He is the seducer of their daughter, the unprincipled exploiter who is ruining her reputation, the recipient of sexual favors without responsibility.

Young people are not likely to stop living together simply because it prejudices their relationships with their parents. At the same time, though, they must realize that they are violating the parents' standards and expectations. There is a price to be paid for so doing. Couples who live together in defiance of their parents must expect problems, and they must be prepared to work them out.

THREATS TO THE PARENTS

These bases for parental objection are all, essentially, external to the parents themselves. Living together and differences in background and personal prospects are all primarily features of the relationship of the young couple. But parents also react in response to things that are internal; to problems that they themselves have as people and as parents.

Unresolved Dependency

It would be nice if all parents were mature, perceptive people who could react totally unselfishly to their grown offspring's needs. Unfortunately, that is not always the case. Ideally, parents love and care for their children and receive love from them in turn. At first, children are totally dependent upon the parents, but gradually they become more and more independent. As children and adolescents seek independence, parents gradually relinquish control.

Some parents, however, have a strong need to keep their children dependent upon them beyond the appropriate point. This tendency may become evident when the young person first begins dating or goes away to college. But a crisis often develops when the young person brings home a prospective marriage partner. There may be objective reasons enough for the parents to be concerned, of course. But, beyond those normal reservations, one parent, or even both, may show a level of concern that reveals at least part of the problem to be the parents' own.

They may focus upon specific objections to the particular relationship, but their real fear is of the loss of the child's love and dependence through marriage.

**Recognition
of Aging**

Although parents themselves may not realize it, the prospective marriage of their offspring often signals the approach of old age. They cannot help but compare their own state to the fresh vigor and beauty of the young couple; inevitably, they are somewhat dismayed by their own physical decline. This may be as true for parents who still appear youthful as for those who have more obviously aged. At bottom, of course, is the specter of infirmity and death. It is an idea unpleasant enough that most parents confront it only fleetingly, if at all. But avoiding the topic consciously doesn't prevent the accumulation of unconscious fears. These fears may be diverted into apparently rational objections to the son or daughter's choice of spouse.

Mothers may be somewhat more susceptible to this problem than fathers are. Youthful beauty is emphasized more in women than in men, and the mother is more likely to suffer in comparison with her daughter or daughter-in-law to be. Moreover, middle-aged men, at least at professional and managerial levels, have rewarding occupational roles; their professions bring them power and prestige that compensate for the facts of physical aging. Not only are women's statuses more closely tied to physical attractiveness, but their occupational roles also are less likely to offer them compensations.

**Loss of
Parental Roles**

Another factor is closely related to the preceding one; again, it often affects mothers more profoundly than fathers. This problem is the loss of the parental role. To the extent to which parents have invested time and effort in their roles as parents, the impending marriage of their child will leave a vacuum to be filled, hours that formerly were occupied with everything from preparing meals and laundering clothes to listening to problems.

For several reasons, fathers are often less deeply affected by this problem than mothers are. For one thing, the father usually has spent fewer hours in the parental role to begin with. Also, his job keeps him busy for most of his waking hours; what empty time is created by the forthcoming marriage can be filled with job-related matters or with hobbies. A mother who has a full-time job may be in a similar position. Even a mother who works just part-time can often convert her job to a full-time one as a way of filling up the empty hours. It probably is the mother who does not work outside the home, and who has made child rearing a central focus of her life, who is most vulnerable. When her son or daughter marries, she will be left with nothing to do for many hours each day. Furthermore, her concept of herself, which hinges on her role as a mother, will depend upon events that are largely in the past. Small wonder that some mothers experience something approaching panic when their offspring begin to talk seriously about marriage.

Strangely enough, there are virtually no data on how often parents accept their sons' and daughters' chosen partners easily and quickly. Nor is there any hard information on the nature and frequency of the problems that are encountered. As we have just seen, there are ample reasons, in both the young couple and the parents, for tensions and strains to develop. Moreover, problems always seem to get more attention than trouble-free situations. In this section, we turn our attention to ways in which couples can and do cope with initial parental resistances.

**WAYS OF
HANDLING
PROBLEMS**

It is natural enough, when people give us a hard time, to restrict our interaction with them as much as possible. So, when a person encounters displeasure from in-laws—even when it is only a hint of displeasure—the easiest course seems to be simply to stay away from them, thereby avoiding contacts that might lead to open conflict. As often as not, however, this strategy has the opposite effect. Instead of decreasing the chance of conflict, it increases it. The reason is that all concerned are at least somewhat aware of what is happening, and they resent or fear the lack of openness on the part of the others.

**Increasing
Contacts**

Now, not all initial suspicions or dislikes will be lessened by more frequent and intimate contacts. In some cases, for example, differences in backgrounds may be so great that more contact will only confirm the parents' original objections. Their disapproval may be grounded in fact. But even so, their objections are likely to be less qualified if they do not know the person well than if they do. After all, there must be some good reasons why their son or daughter is attracted to this person, and continued contacts are likely to make those qualities evident.

In most cases, close association will do much to lessen the in-laws' objections. It will reveal that basic attitudes are similar even where backgrounds are quite different. It will force all the parties to interact in personal terms, rather than in terms of stereotypes. And, by demonstrating that they can all get along together, it will help to diminish the fears of the parents that they will lose their child's love. The parents will be reassured that they can have a continued relationship with their offspring and the new partner. In short, withdrawal may seem to be the easiest way to cope with parental antagonism, but continued close association may be far more effective in the long run.

Some young people's difficulties in coping with parental resistance are partly a function of their own lack of solidarity as a couple. Each partner has loved his or her own parents for many years and has been

**Developing
Couple Solidarity**

dependent upon them. Each has been accustomed to placing obligations to the parents before obligations to other people. Consequently, each partner is unprepared to handle tension between his or her own parents and the other partner. No matter which side the young person takes in a disagreement, someone will interpret it as betrayal.

Even the fairest-minded parents are likely, from time to time, to take unwitting advantage of their hold over their child. But by reinforcing their own solidarity with their offspring they demonstrate, indirectly, the weakness of the relationship between the young lovers. What will counteract this tendency is the most open and frank discussion between the young people, concerning both the nature of the problem and the best way to handle it. A commitment has to be made by both partners to work together on it. When this solidarity between the partners is put into practice, it communicates to the parents that the situation has permanently changed. The parents can no longer deal with their son or daughter in isolation, but must now deal with the couple as a unit. Once this fact is recognized, parental resistance will either weaken or be redirected in ways the couple can cope with much more effectively.

Developing Understanding

Finally, some young people all too readily become defensive when they are challenged by parents. If they are very immature, they may assert, defiantly, that they are old enough to do as they wish, and that the parents should not interfere. If they are somewhat more mature, they may listen to the parents' arguments, carefully weigh the evidence, and then decide that the arguments are unsound. This procedure has an aura of fairness to it, and certainly parents should be expected to behave as maturely as their young adult offspring. The problem is that it places the two couples in an adversary relationship. Ultimately, this situation is likely to aggravate the conflict between them. And in most cases, it need not happen.

At first appearance, it seems quite unreasonable to suggest that young people should act *more* maturely than, perhaps, their parents do. Therein, though, lies one key to getting off to a good start with in-laws. It may be that the parents' emphasis upon similarity of background is exaggerated and out of touch with the times. It may be that the parents' need to keep their offspring dependent upon them is unhealthy. But those facts don't make the problems go away. These people still are one's parents or in-laws, and any extra effort devoted to allaying their fears will benefit all concerned.

Young people may feel besieged by their parents and inadequate to cope with them. They often do not realize that theirs is actually a position of great strength, from which they can afford to be tolerant and patient. After all, if all else fails, the young couple have every right to do what they want.

What, then, will they lose by going out of their way to understand why the parents feel as they do, by offering the parents reassurance and support, and by deferring to their wishes whenever possible? These small sacrifices often make no real difference in the couple's plans, but consideration for the parents' feelings may go a long way toward winning the parents over. Even when it does make a difference—for example, delaying the marriage for a while—the couple may decide that the inconvenience is worthwhile in order to begin the marriage with a greater degree of parental approval.

INITIAL MARITAL ADJUSTMENTS

It may come as a surprise to some readers that many couples not only maintain a high level of contact with their parents after the wedding ceremony, but also see a good bit of them during the honeymoon. Taking the honeymoon trip jointly with vacationing parents may enable the couple to stay or prolong their stay at a resort they could not otherwise afford. Occasionally, one set of parents may not even have met their son- or daughter-in-law before the wedding. The wedding trip can sometimes be used to visit them and get acquainted (Ryder, Kafka, and Olson, 1971).

PARENTAL SUPPORT

Parents often provide substantial financial support to young married couples. Frequently they are in the prime of their lives, having attained some financial comfort, and facing declining expenditures for the maintenance of their own home. Thus they are in a position to aid their adult children. The young couple, at the same time, is enabled to enjoy a few of life's luxuries more quickly and easily with parental support.

Wise parents structure their support of the young marriage so that it does not imply dependence of the young couple upon them. They do not want the young couple to feel any special obligations in return. This consideration usually prohibits, for example, giving a monthly check, which would be too obvious. About the only time direct support is possible is when a couple marries while still in college. In that case the parents may say, "We won't support you, but we want you to finish your education. Therefore, we will continue to pay your school expenses, just as we would have otherwise." Then the parents can send a monthly check. But this money is earmarked for education, not for support of the marriage.

In other circumstances, the parents may decide that they should refurnish some of the rooms in their homes. The furniture to be replaced may be only a few years old and in excellent condition, but the parents face a "problem" of how best to dispose of it. Most furniture companies really don't take trade-ins, they explain, and second-hand stores give far less than it is worth. "Could you kids possibly use some of it?" "Well, if it would be doing you a favor, perhaps we could." So, the young couple ends up with a large gift and everyone is pleased.

For a special event, such as graduation from college, the parents may be able to give a new automobile or, perhaps, a down payment on a house. Parents may also be able to provide an "extra" lawn mower, garden tools, and the like. When they come for a weekend visit, the parents may load down their car with groceries. The mother will report that she "just happened to find this ham on sale, and you will have to help eat it." Of course, father takes them out to eat each evening, so when the parents leave, the ham and other groceries remain behind.

Some parents maintain vacation homes that the young couple is encouraged to use or share. In other instances, joint vacation trips are suggested, strictly "Dutch treat," of course. But on the trip, the father manages, unobtrusively, to pick up most of the checks.

This parental support does not come totally without obligations, of course, but these obligations are more often social than financial. What the parents most often seek is continued access to their offspring, and particularly to their grandchildren. When grandchildren are born, the grandparents are entitled to help with a layette and to make a gift to the child, perhaps for its future education. The parents, in turn, are obligated to let the grandparents visit and, when distance permits, to baby-sit. Opportunity for grandchildren to visit in the grandparents' home may be part of the implicit bargain.

If this description sounds idyllic, we should point out that things are not always so rosy. There are parents whose gifts come with unacceptable strings attached—parents who want not only to share, but to control. There also are young married people who take advantage of their parents' generosity but who are unwilling to give of themselves in return.

There are cases, too, in which the roles are suddenly reversed. Through bad luck or illness, parents become physically or financially dependent upon the young couple. These days, social security, private pension plans, and Medicare enable most parents to stay relatively independent financially. But sometimes, prolonged illness makes help essential. It may involve assisting with medical expenses; it may mean nursing home care; it may even mean having a parent move in to receive continuous care. Fortunately, however, such crises, when they do occur, usually do not come until later in life, after the couple themselves have reached middle age. By this time, they are better able both emotionally and financially to provide the care their parents need.

On balance, young people have a great deal to gain, both in the quality of their relationship and financially, by working to develop good relationships with the parents on both sides. So far, however, we haven't distinguished between those two sides. Now we need to do so.

The initial adjustments between young married couples and their parents must be analyzed from two separate viewpoints: that of the young couple, and that of the parents.

**The
Young
Couple**

Most couples agree that neither set of parents should be favored over the other. At the same time, though, each partner is likely to have a special affection for his or her own parents and habitual ways of interacting with them that do not extend equally to the in-laws. Consequently, though neither partner intends it, an implicit contest often develops, with each spouse trying to protect the relationship with his or her own parents.

The young husband and wife try simultaneously to be fair to each other and to preserve the relationship with the parents. An elaborate ritual may develop to assure that the two sets of parents are treated equally. If the couple goes to her parents' home for dinner one Sunday, then the next Sunday they must go to his. If Thanksgiving is spent with one set of parents, then Christmas must be spent with the other. There may even have to be two Christmas gift exchanges, one on Christmas Eve with one set of parents and one on Christmas day with the other. The details vary, but some form of this ritual is common.

Building and maintaining such a schedule consumes both time and energy. Besides, each partner is likely to fudge a little in favor of his or her own parents: "After all, they are nicer people," or, "We have more in common with them," and so on. Sooner or later this favoritism precipitates a marital fight, as the other partner seeks to reimpose the norms of equal treatment. The schedule is adjusted, and the ritual continues.

Assuming that other things go well for the couple and their affection deepens, they begin to weary of the ritual. They may eventually ask, "Why do we have to eat every Sunday dinner with our parents? Wouldn't it be nice to stay at home once in a while?" So they begin, as discreetly as possible, trying to withdraw somewhat. One set of parents or both may resist a little at first. But the parents face pressures of their own, and some withdrawal to a less frequent and intense level of interaction occurs.

**The
Parents**

The months just before and after the wedding often see the two sets of parents engaged in a minor and usually unacknowledged contest to see which of them will have priority in the affection and time of the young couple. Both sets of parents wish to continue to be close to their offspring, of course. But at the same time, like their children, they know that the young couple should not favor either pair. With some minor reluctance, they usually cooperate with the young couple in working out a schedule of visits and other joint activities.

Those parents who have more than one married child face another set of constraints: they must also treat each of their children equally. If they invite one child and spouse for dinner one Sunday, then they must invite the other the next Sunday; or at least, some equivalent arrangement must be worked out. If they visit one of their offspring, or make a gift to that couple, then they must do an equal favor for the other. Although the children may not realize it, the parents may also long for relief from too much contact and too many obligations. Like their offspring, they may be ambivalent about the withdrawal when it actually begins, but they usually cooperate in it.

THE INFLUENCE OF PARENTHOOD

In the usual course of events, pregnancy and childbearing alter relationships between young couples and their parents markedly. The baby serves as an increasingly obvious symbol of the solidarity of the young marriage. But even the pregnancy itself helps to redefine roles and obligations. If the young couple wishes not to make an expected visit to the parents, they can simply say, "Her doctor says she shouldn't travel." There is no way that parents can effectively challenge such an argument.

Obligations to the child take precedence over responsibilities to parents. This acknowledged fact is symbolized by the acceptance, by all parties, of the wish that the baby should have its first Christmas at home. Whereas formerly the young couple adjusted their schedule to meet the needs of their parents and in-laws, now it is the parents and in-laws who must be fitted in, whenever they can be, to the circle of the expanding young family.

These forces work to reduce the frequency of interaction with in-laws, and they further diminish the position of authority the parents have long held. At the same time, though, the birth of a baby opens up the new role of grandparents for the older couples to fill. If nothing else, the birth of a grandchild may end whatever lingering ambivalence remains toward a son-in-law or daughter-in-law. After all, one can't continue to oppose that person without jeopardizing one's relationship with the grandchild, and few people are willing to do that. Relationships between the new parents and the grandparents are likely to become more tolerant and more genuinely accepting.

Grandparents, of course, are entitled to shower generosity, affection, and tenderness on their grandchild. The grandparents can provide gifts to their grandchild which the new parents could not accept for themselves. The grandparents can baby-sit, relieving the young parents and indulging themselves. Their right to visit the grandchild incidentally allows them to visit its parents.

If the premarital situation tended to threaten the mothers' roles more than the fathers', the situation is reversed with the birth of a grandchild. The grandmother has immediate entreé into the young family's home to

care for the new mother while she recovers from childbirth. The grand-mother also is a repository of wisdom, information, and skill in caring for babies. Her role in relation to her daughter or daughter-in-law is helpful and supportive. When the time arrives for baby-sitting, it is the grand-mother whose services are sought. The grandfather is accepted readily enough, but he is not really thought to be of much help.

Grandfathers are still expected to derive their basic satisfaction from their achievements in the world of work and in their relationships with their wives. However, the grandfather role opens new opportunities for them, too. Their identification with the achievements of their sons or sons-in-law increases. Traces of rivalry between them tend to diminish. Most directly, grandfathers are allowed to display an openness of affec-tion and tenderness toward their grandchildren that is excluded from virtually every other aspect of the masculine role.

Most couples seek parental approval of their forthcoming marriages. Whether they get it, or how easily they get it, depends upon factors that concern both the young couple and the parents.

SUMMARY

Parents are more likely to be apprehensive and resistant when the prospective spouse comes from a different religious, ethnic, or socioeconomic background. The parents may be biased against these traits in the abstract, of course, but they are also aware that they represent larger cultural differences, which may pose difficulties for the proposed marriage. When the intended spouse's economic background is poorer, they may also fear for the young couple's standard of living.

Special tensions are often created when the parents know that the couple are living together or sleeping together. Although this fact may upset the parents on both sides, the woman's parents are more likely to voice strong objections, leading to special problems of adjustment with them.

There may be problems with one or more of the parents initially, due to factors in the parents' own personalities and relatively independent of the young couple. When parents have not been able to accept the growing emotional independence of their offspring, for example, they may now make a last-ditch effort to hold on to their child. Similarly, the proposed marriage symbolizes the approach of old age to the parents; this realization often threatens the mothers more than the fathers.

A special crisis confronts mothers who have devoted much of themselves to child rearing. The proposed marriage will not only take away their child, but it will leave vacant many hours that once were spent in the care of her children.

The more young people are aware of the sources of tension with their parents, the better position they are in to resolve the tensions successfully. Generally, it is helpful to spend more, rather than less, time with the resistant parents. It also pays to work out solutions to problems within the couple first, and then with the parents. If they only realize it, young couples have most of the advantages and can afford to be tolerant and patient.

Good relationships worked out before marriage set the stage for good in-law relationships in marriage. Many parents provide substantial financial support, as well as emotional support, to the young couple, requesting in return only continued access to the lives of their children and grandchildren.

It usually takes some time and some quarreling for the young couple to work out ways of treating both sets of parents equally. Often, just about the time they get the relationships worked out, the first child comes along. The birth of a baby causes the new parents to put the child's needs first and to withdraw slightly from their relationships with the grandparents. The in-laws face comparable problems; they are forced to treat all of their children's marriages equally, and often welcome the slight withdrawal that grandparenthood affords.

Grandparenthood usually increases the solidarity between the two older generations, who share an interest in the newest generation. It also affords especially satisfying opportunities to the grandmothers, whose wisdom, experience, and assistance are sought and appreciated. Grandfathers, too, are permitted a tenderness toward their grandchildren that is without parallel in the array of masculine roles.

Adams, Bert N., *The American Family: A Sociological Interpretation* (Chicago: Markham, 1975). Good analysis of in-law relationships within the context of the kin network.

Duvall, Evelyn Millis, *Family Development* (Philadelphia: Lippincott, 1971). Covers variations in in-law relationships over the entire family life cycle.

Hill, Reuben, et al., *Family Development in Three Generations* (Cambridge, Mass.: Schenkman, 1970). A report of a longitudinal study of three generations of the same families.

Klatzky, Sheila R., *Patterns of Contact With Relatives* (Washington, D.C.: American Sociological Association, 1971). A technical monograph reporting research on the relationship of social variables and kin contacts.

Rosenberg, George S., and Donald F. Anspach, *Working Class Kinship* (Lexington, Mass.: D. C. Heath, 1973). A comprehensive analysis of kinship interaction. For the serious student.

FOR ADDITIONAL READING

STUDY QUESTIONS

1. Criticize the following proposition: couples should begin working on in-law relationships from the day of their marriage.

2. A young man and woman from markedly different social backgrounds plan to marry. Contrast the ways in which their parents are likely to view these differences with the ways in which the young couple views them. Make the best case you can for the view of each generation.

3. Some parents oppose proposed marriages because they are seeking to hold onto their children. How would you recommend that a young couple deal with such a situation? What are the likely outcomes of your recommendations?

4. Do you think that young couples generally have the advantage over parents who resist a proposed marriage? Why or why not?

5. What informal rules govern the provision of financial support from parents to their married children? What obligations does each generation incur?

6. Describe the process that young couples go through in achieving a stable relationship with both sets of parents. How is the situation faced by the parents comparable to that confronted by their married offspring?

7. How does childbearing tend to alter the relationship between married couples and their parents?

8. What special satisfactions do the roles of grandmother and grandfather provide? Which of the two roles is more rewarding? Why?

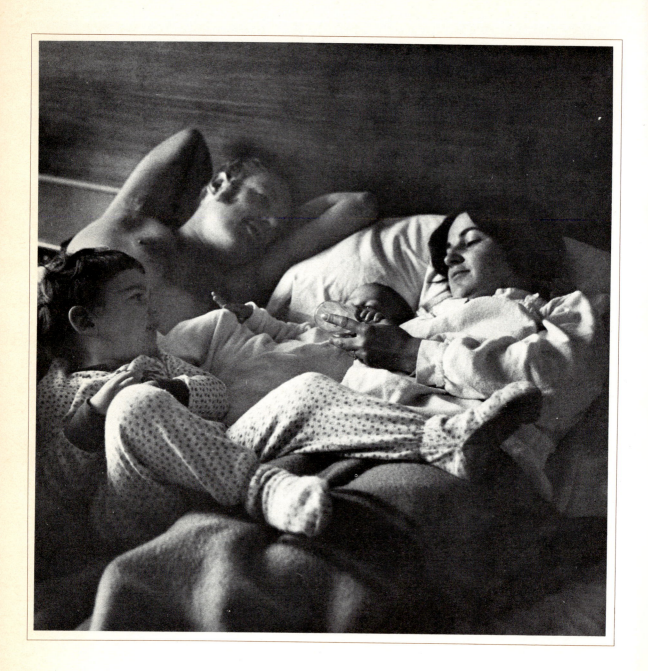

Chapter 9
Sexual Adjustment

Like relationships with in-laws and many other aspects of life, sexual adjustment is well under way by the time most people marry. This is not simply a function of how far advanced their sexual play has become. When a couple are already having intercourse, the existence of some kind of adjustment is clear enough. But even those people who have confined their activities to some level of petting also have tentatively established attitudes toward each other and ways of interacting. What marriage does is to legitimize the relationship and produce the expectation of regular sexual intercourse.

THE REPRODUCTIVE SYSTEMS

Sexual adjustment involves both physical and social factors. Before moving on to the social aspects of the sexual relationship, it is important to look at the physical foundations of sex.

*THE MALE
REPRODUCTIVE
SYSTEM*

The male reproductive system is diagramed in Figure 9-1. The male sexual organ, the penis, is some three to four inches long in the flaccid state and roughly six inches long in erection. Although there are differences from man to man in size of the penis, these differences tend to be exaggerated. Nor is there any consistent relationship between the size of the penis and the sexual pleasure received either by the man or by his partner. Sexual satisfaction is far more closely related to the love and consideration of the partners for one another than it is to the size and shape of the sexual organs.

The penis is composed chiefly of spongy tissue. This tissue fills with blood during sexual excitement, causing the penis to become erect and rigid. Ordinarily, the penis remains erect as long as sexual stimulation continues and until orgasm and ejaculation occur. But erection may be lost prematurely because of distraction from sexual play, too-vigorous play that causes pain, or various emotional states, such as anxiety, guilt, or shame. Consistent loss of erection or failure to achieve erection is called impotence, and it indicates the need for medical attention or psychological counseling.

Below the base of the penis hangs a loose pouch of skin, the *scrotum,* which contains the *testes* or *testicles.* These organs are egg-shaped and about one-and-a-half inches long and an inch in diameter. They are very sensitive to the touch, a source of sexual pleasure when caressed, and of excruciating pain when mishandled.

The testicles contain large numbers of tiny tubules which, after puberty, continuously produce the male sex cells, *sperm.* Tremendous numbers of sperm are produced; a normal ejaculation contains more than 200 million of them. In normal, healthy men, the supply of sperm is

Figure 9-1   The male reproductive organs in cross section.

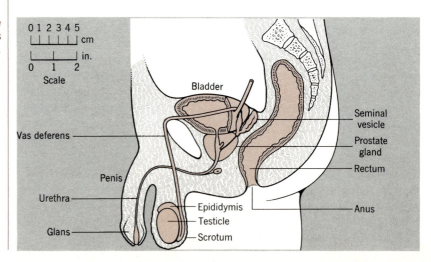

completely replaced in some 30 to 40 hours following ejaculation (McCary, 1967).

The sperm gradually are transported from the tubules to the *epididymis,* a swelling on the testicle that contains some 20 feet of a compactly wound tube; there the sperm are stored while they mature, awaiting ejaculation. The sperm are then moved to the *vas deferens.* This vessel, a tube about 18 inches long, carries the sperm to the *seminal vesicles,* small sacs whose function is not completely understood. They may be only a further storage place for sperm, or they may produce a secretion that helps the sperm to gain motility by stimulating the whipping movement of their tails.

From the seminal vesicles, the sperm travel through the *prostate gland,* which provides much of the seminal fluid. The alkalinity of this prostatic fluid provides a hospitable environment for the sperm and protects them against the acidity of the vagina. Finally, *Cowper's glands,* two pea-sized structures located just below the prostate, secrete a further alkaline fluid that lubricates the urethra for the passage of the sperm during ejaculation.

The female sexual organs are primarily internal, and consist of the *ovaries,* the *Fallopian tubes,* the *uterus,* and the *vagina* (see Figure 9-2).

The ovaries, the female counterpart of the testes, produce the female sex cells: *ova,* or eggs. They also secrete hormones that stimulate sexual desire and prepare the uterine walls to receive the fertilized ovum. At puberty, there are approximately 10,000 *follicles,* small cavities, on each ovum; each follicle contains a very immature ovum. Following puberty, one follicle ordinarily ripens into an ovum at about the middle of each

THE FEMALE REPRODUCTIVE SYSTEM

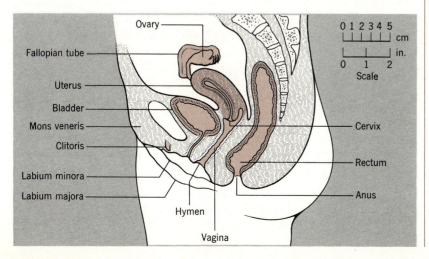

Figure 9-2 The internal female reproductive organs.

menstrual cycle; this process continues for approximately the next 35 years.

At ovulation, the mature ovum is expelled from the ovary into the bodily cavity, where, somehow, it normally finds its way into one of the Fallopian tubes. Usually only one ovum is released during each menstrual cycle, and the two ovaries usually alternate. But sometimes two or more ova are released, and one ovary may produce ripe ova for several cycles in a row. Following the discharge of an ovum, the follicle produces progesterone, a hormone that inhibits ovulation during pregnancy and helps to prepare the uterine lining to receive the fertilized ovum.

Fertilization usually occurs in the Fallopian tube while the ovum is being transported to the uterus. The fertilized ovum enters the uterus and becomes implanted in the uterine wall.

The uterus is a pear-shaped, thick-walled, muscular organ about three inches long, some two-and-one-half inches wide at the top and an inch wide at the lower end, or *cervix.* It is laced with muscles interwoven in basket fashion that enable it to stretch during pregnancy and to expel the baby at birth. These muscles also contract at orgasm and at about the time of ovulation to aid the movement of the ovum.

Human societies have often had taboos about sexual intercourse during menstruation. But recent research has shown that orgasm during menstruation often causes menstrual fluid to spurt from the cervix, alleviating menstrual cramping. Since most women experience some sexual desire during menstruation, many physicians now encourage sex during menstruation, both for the better sexual adjustment of the couple and for the welfare of the woman (Masters and Johnson, 1966).

About one-third to one-half an inch of the cervix extends into the upper end of the vagina, a muscular tube about three to three-and-a-half inches long that receives the penis during sexual intercourse. The vagina has both longitudinal muscles and circular ones, including a sphincter that surrounds the external opening. It also contains many blood vessels and some erectile tissue, which help to open and close the vaginal channel. The vagina contains very few nerve endings.

In sexual arousal, the vagina secretes a lubricating fluid through its walls in a little understood manner that can be likened to sweating. This lubrication aids the penis to enter the vagina easily and makes sexual intercourse more pleasurable. Mucous secretions from the uterus may also be present in the vagina during sexual excitement.

At the entrance to the vagina is a fold of tissue, the *hymen,* or maidenhead, which partly obstructs the opening. Some people regard an intact hymen, which must be ruptured or stretched in sexual intercourse on the wedding night, as proof that the woman is a virgin. This indication is quite misleading, however, because the hymen often is ruptured or stretched during strenuous exercise, masturbation, accidents, or the use of menstrual tampons. Increasing numbers of women also are having their physicians cut or stretch the hymen during the premarital physical examination to remove that possible source of discomfort on the wedding night.

Even with the hymen eliminated, a minority of women experience some pain or discomfort during their first sexual intercourse. This discomfort results from the involuntary contraction of the woman's vaginal muscles because of fear or anxiety. Physiologically, there is no reason why a virgin woman cannot accommodate her partner's penis comfortably from the beginning. Certainly, loving couples who have been anticipating their first sexual union should have little difficulty.

The external genitalia, collectively called the *vulva,* are composed of the *mons veneris,* the *labia majora* (large, or outer, lips), the *labia minora* (small, or inner, lips), the *vestibule,* and the *clitoris.*

The *mons veneris* is the area above the vaginal opening, covered with pubic hair and with fatty tissue over the pubic bone. The area is liberally supplied with nerve endings, stimulation of which contributes to sexual pleasure.

The *labia majora* are fatty folds of skin that enclose the vaginal opening. Their inner sides are free of hair and contain glands, secretions from which assist in lubrication. The *labia minora* are enclosed within the labia majora and are richly supplied with blood vessels and nerve endings. They tend to flare outward during sexual excitement, exposing the *vestibule.*

The vestibule is the region enclosed by the labia minora, containing both the vaginal opening and the urethra, through which urine is passed. The whole area is richly supplied with nerve endings, and stimulation of it by the partner adds greatly to sexual pleasure.

The *clitoris,* which is the most sexually excitable area of all, is a small penis-like structure, generally less than an inch long, at the top of the vestibule and projecting between the labia minora at their upper junction. Most of the clitoris is covered by the labia, and only the *glans* (head) is exposed. In sexual excitement, the clitoris becomes engorged with blood and expands to as much as twice its usual size.

The clitoris may be stimulated in several ways: directly, in intercourse, by the man's pubic bone rubbing against it; indirectly, through the pulling and tugging of the labia minora as the penis moves in and out; or manually. The clitoris is so sensitive that occasional direct stimulation of it accompanied by considerable stimulation around it may afford most women the maximum pleasure. When women masturbate, for example, they often stimulate the area around the clitoris more than the clitoris itself (Masters and Johnson, 1966).

STAGES OF EROTIC RESPONSE

In both men and women, sexual arousal and response develop through a series of four definable stages, or phases. They have been labeled and described in detail by Masters and Johnson. The four stages are termed excitement, plateau, orgasm, and resolution.

MALE SEXUAL RESPONSE

In men, the primary erogenous zone, or locus of sexual excitement, is the penis. Stimulation of the penis almost always produces an erection. Also very sensitive to stimulation in most men are the perineum (the area between the anus and the testes) and the scrotum. The nipples and the anus itself also are richly supplied with nerve endings and are erogenous zones for about half of all men. Secondary erogenous zones include the mouth, ears, neck, and thighs.

The Excitement Stage

In younger men, sexual arousal occurs frequently, without any physical stimulation at all. The sight of an attractive woman, daydreaming, suggestive pictures, telling or hearing sexual jokes, a movie—almost anything may produce a *cerebral* erection, one whose source is psychological. Most young men can be aroused quickly and easily. As men move into their thirties and forties, however, such psychological arousal occurs less and less frequently. But virtually all men continue to respond to stimulation of the penis with *reflex* erections throughout most of their lives. As many as two-thirds of all men still achieve erections beyond age 70.

Early in sexual arousal, the penis erects and the testes draw up toward the body. There is an increase in heart rate and blood pressure, and, in over half of all men, the nipples become erect. Some muscular tension becomes apparent. Younger men may move through the excitement stage quickly, particularly with vigorous stimulation. By pacing themselves, however, a couple may prolong this stage almost indefinitely, with the man partially losing and regaining his erection frequently.

The Plateau Stage

Once intense sexual arousal is achieved, the man may be able to continue it for some time, keeping his level of arousal just below that required to precipitate orgasm and ejaculation. This restraint is much easier to practice in petting than in intercourse. Few definite changes occur during this stage. The glans enlarges still more, the whole penis may become even more rigid, and its color may deepen. Muscular tension also becomes more pronounced, and involuntary contractions of the muscles of the face, neck, or abdomen may appear.

The Orgasmic Stage

Once the plateau stage is reached, continuing the stimulation almost always produces orgasm. There is a point at which the man loses control. The urethra becomes distended, and involuntary contractions of the muscles at the base of the penis and around the anus produce the ejaculation. These contractions occur at about 0.8-second intervals, and usually number three or four. The duration of the major contractions is usually three or four seconds, although slighter contractions may continue longer.

Severe involuntary muscular tension pervades the man's whole body at this moment. The rate of his heartbeat may double, and his blood pressure rises even higher than it was during the plateau stage. The rate of breathing also increases markedly, with almost a gasping for air. The senses of sight and hearing are temporarily impaired.

Psychologically, the experience is one of intense pleasure and relief. The intensity of the reaction is a function of the level and duration of stimulation achieved before orgasm begins. It may involve elements of both ecstasy and agony in some cases.

The Resolution Stage

Almost immediately following orgasm, the penis begins to lose its erection. The higher the level and the longer the duration of pre-orgasm excitement, the more slowly this process may occur. Nearly full erection can occasionally be maintained for some minutes. But virtually all men must go through a period without erection before they can again respond to the excitement stage. This so-called *refractory period* may be only a few minutes for some young men, although it is at least an hour for most. Second and third refractory periods become successively longer. The length of the refractory period also increases with the age of the man. The male response cycle is diagramed in Figure 9-3.

In addition to loss of erection, the man's whole functioning returns to pre-excitement levels. His heartbeat, blood pressure, breathing, and muscle tone all return to normal.

Particularly when the sex relationship is also a loving one, the resolution stage is characterized by a stage of profound well-being, contentment, and lassitude. The relaxation often is so complete that some men are inclined to drop off into a brief but deep sleep. Some women who are unsure of their partners, or who do not understand this

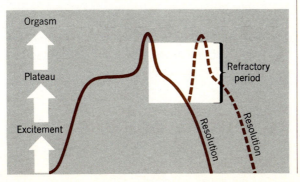

Figure 9-3   The male sexual response cycle. Following the first climax, succeeding orgasms can take place only after a refractory period. (Source: Masters and Johnson [1966], p. 5).

phenomenon, assume that it reflects lack of interest in them by the man; they may react with disappointment or anger. But more secure women are likely to react to their mates' temporary exhaustion with pleasure and satisfaction.

FEMALE SEXUAL RESPONSE

Among women, the clitoris is the primary erogenous organ, but erogenous zones are more plentiful and widespread in women than in men. The entire vulva and the mons veneris are richly supplied with nerve endings, as are the nipples and the entire breasts. The thighs are also highly susceptible to stimulation. As in men, secondary erogenous zones include the mouth, ears and neck. Literally, the whole body may be involved in sexual arousal.

The Excitement Stage

Some erection of the nipples occurs early in sexual arousal. Eventually, the pigmented area around the nipples (the *areola*) also becomes engorged, partially concealing the continued erection of the nipples, which persists through the orgasmic stage. As excitement mounts, the entire breasts become swollen, increasing in size by as much as 20 to 25 percent.

The clitoris responds by undergoing tumescence, or erection. However, its small size and the fact that most of it is covered makes this response visible in only a minority of cases. The vagina begins to lubricate itself, becoming coated with fluid, and it begins to dilate and lengthen. It also deepens in color from its usual deep red to an uneven deep purple. The uterus also experiences some muscular contractions and gradually becomes congested and expanded. It lifts upward, helping to produce a ballooning effect in the upper two-thirds of the vagina.

The labia minora begin to enlarge, becoming thicker and helping to lengthen the vaginal barrel. The labia majora also undergo change, varying with the woman's childbearing status. In women who have not borne a child, the lips thin out, flatten, and flare away from the vagina. In women who have had children, they become engorged, increasing in size two or three times.

Some women become sexually excited in response to a wide range of psychological stimuli, just as most young men do. In fact, more women than men may become stimulated to the point of orgasm by psychological stimuli. Other women, however, require tactile stimulation in order to become aroused. And until the woman is aroused and lubrication occurs, sexual intercourse for her is likely to be unpleasant or even painful.

The Plateau Stage

Most reactions during the plateau stage simply are extensions of those noted during excitement. The breasts continue to swell, and muscle tension increases markedly as the woman approaches orgasm.

As in men, there is an increase in heartbeat, a rise in blood pressure, and an increase in the respiratory rate.

The most pronounced reaction during the plateau stage occurs in the clitoris, which withdraws from its normal overhanging position and pulls back deeply beneath the hood formed by the labia minora. Just before orgasm, the length of the clitoris may decrease almost by half. The walls of the outer third of the vagina become congested with blood, causing the vagina to tighten somewhat around the inserted penis. The labia minora change in color from pink to bright or dark red. This color change is the surest sign of impending orgasm.

The Orgasmic Stage

The onset of orgasm is accompanied by strong involuntary contractions of the muscles of the outer third of the vagina, the uterus, perineum, rectum, and the lower abdomen. In lesser degree, muscles over the entire body may be involved. There are at least three or four strong contractions of the vagina, coming about 0.8 seconds apart, and there may be ten or more. The contractions decrease in force and come at greater intervals after the first few. The strength of the contractions also varies with the degree of sexual excitement and with how long the stimulation lasts.

The heartbeat continues to elevate during orgasm, usually even more so in masturbation than in intercourse. Blood pressure also rises, although not as drastically as in men. Increases in the rate of breathing are proportional to the degree of sexual excitement and the duration of stimulation.

Until recently, a controversy raged over whether there are not two different types of female orgasm. Some psychologists, influenced by the writings of Sigmund Freud, believed that the most satisfying kind of orgasm is experienced in the vagina as a result of its stimulation by the penis. Emotionally mature women were believed to be able to achieve this "superior" kind of vaginal orgasm. In contrast, clitoral orgasm, achieved through stimulation of the clitoris and the perineum, was thought to be inherently less satisfying to the woman, and an ability to have only clitoral orgasms was believed to reflect the woman's inability to fully accept her sexuality.

Recent research, however, particularly that of Masters and Johnson, has disproved the idea that there are two different kinds of orgasm. The vagina and the cervix have been found to be virtually devoid of nerve endings, whereas the clitoris is richly supplied with them. Some women do reach orgasm without apparent direct stimulation of the clitoris, but there are no measurable physiological differences between so-called vaginal and clitoral orgasms. There is absolutely no basis for regarding one or the other means of stimulation as superior.

**The
Resolution
Stage**

Muscular tension decreases rapidly during the resolution stage, completely disappearing within about five minutes unless sexual stimulation is resumed. The breasts also resume their normal size and shape at about the same rate. The areolae detumesce before the nipples do, however, giving the false impression of a new erection of the nipples. Heart rate, blood pressure, and rate of breathing also quickly return to normal. A minority of women perspire lightly over most or all of their bodies at this time. The perspiration is unrelated to the amount of physical exertion, but is roughly proportional to the strength of the orgasm.

The clitoris returns to its usual overhanging position almost immediately as vaginal contractions cease. But complete detumescence may require anywhere from five minutes to a half-hour. The vagina returns to its normal size and collapsed state in from five to 15 minutes. The uterus may be somewhat slower to return to normal. The labia minora reassume their light pink color almost instantly, but the labia majora require longer to reassume their normal size and position. Particularly in women who have had children, detumescence of the labia majora may not be complete for one or two hours.

There is no counterpart in women to the male refractory period, and if stimulation of the woman is resumed during the resolution stage, she ordinarily will not drop below the plateau stage. Some women quickly proceed to a second and third orgasm, or even more. Women report that these subsequent orgasms often are more intense than the first ones, and they are discontinued only when the woman cannot stand the intensity of the experience any longer (Figure 9-4).

Figure 9-4 The female sexual response cycle. A, B, and C represent various patterns of arousal. (Source: Masters and Johnson [1966], p. 5).

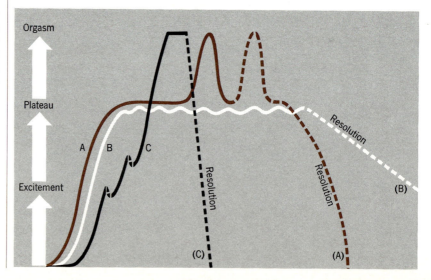

Although attitudes toward sex today are less puritanical than they once were, many couples still are unduly preoccupied with what is "normal" or "typical" sex behavior. Their anxieties are of two sorts. One is the fear of *abnormality*—the fear that aspects of one's sex behaviors or desires are unacceptable. The other is fear of *inadequacy*—anxiety that one may not measure up as a sexual partner. Neither of these considerations is really relevant to sexual adjustment in marriage. A tremendous variety of sexual patterns can and does further the solidarity of loving couples.

Recent studies show that married couples today have sexual intercourse more frequently than they used to. As part of the 1970 National Fertility Study, for example, over 5000 married women under 45 were asked how many times they had had intercourse during the preceding four weeks. The results were then compared with those from a similar sample of women questioned in 1965 (Westoff, 1974). The women questioned in 1970 reported a 14-percent higher frequency of intercourse than those questioned in 1965. Moreover, the difference held at all age levels, with older women in 1970 reporting more frequent intercourse than younger women had in 1965.

Increases in the frequency of intercourse were related to educational levels and to the use of contraception. Women with at least some college education reported having intercourse an average of 8.7 times in four weeks, compared to only 7.4 times for those who had not completed high school. Women on the pill reported the highest frequency of all, 10.0 times over the four-week period. Two forces seem to be operating here. First, reliable contraception frees couples to have sex more frequently. Second, social attitudes now favor more frequent sex, even when contraception is not used.

A related study was made in 1972. Nearly 2400 married women from 38 states reported on their frequencies of sexual intercourse per month. The results are listed in Table 9-1 by age of the woman. Wives between 26 and 30 years of age reported having intercourse just under ten times

INITIAL SEXUAL ADJUSTMENTS

FREQUENCY OF MARITAL INTERCOURSE

WIVES' AGES	AVERAGE MONTHLY FREQUENCY
26–30	9.4
31–40	7.4
41–50	6.1
50+	4.1

Source: Robert R. Bell and Phyllis L. Bell, "Sexual Satisfaction Among Married Women," *Medical Aspects of Human Sexuality* (Dec. 1972), p. 141.

TABLE 9-1 FREQUENCY OF SEXUAL INTERCOURSE, BY AGES OF WIVES (N = 2372)

a month. The frequencies dropped gradually with age, but still were over four times a month for wives past age 50 (Bell and Bell, 1972).

Certainly as significant as any average frequencies of sexual intercourse, however, is the wide variability that was found. Some young and newlywed couples have intercourse daily, or even more often than that; others have it once a week or less. There is no magic frequency that is satisfactory for everyone, and the important thing is that the couple establish the pattern that is most satisfactory to them.

SEXUAL SATISFACTION

One apparent consequence of the liberalization of sexual attitudes in recent years is an increase in the proportion of married women who always or almost always achieve orgasm. Research shows gains of ten to 20 percent over the past generation. A survey of 2,026 people in 24 urban areas was conducted by the Research Guild, Inc., in 1973. It found that 53 percent of the women reported always or almost always achieving orgasm. This finding tallies with the 1972 study of 2372 married women already mentioned, which found 59 percent to have orgasm "always" or "most of the time."

The sexual problem reported most frequently by young married couples is the husband's tendency to climax too quickly; this problem is often coupled with difficulty in bringing the wife to orgasm. Time and practice help most couples to cope with this difficulty. Couples learn to pace the husband's arousal, keeping him in the plateau stage until the wife can be aroused to a comparable level. Also, as they become more experienced in sex and more comfortable with it, many women find that they become aroused as quickly and easily as their husbands. Again in the 1972 survey, two-thirds of the married women reported that they were satisfied with their frequency of marital intercourse. But 30 percent said it occurred *too infrequently* (Bell and Bell, 1972).

Many women indicate, also, that too much emphasis has been placed upon the female orgasm and upon the desirability of the partner's reaching orgasm simultaneously. They do not deny that simultaneous orgasms are highly pleasing to both partners, but they insist that the closeness and sharing involved in sexual intercourse provide great satisfaction by themselves; not all women need to have orgasm all of the time to be highly satisfied with themselves, their husbands, and their sex relationships. Again, it appears to be true that there are many different forms of good sexual adjustment in marriage.

EXTRAMARITAL RELATIONSHIPS

People, when they marry, do not cease to exist as separate individuals. No matter how much they are in love, or how committed they are to one another, they continue to have contacts with members of the opposite sex. These contacts provide both the opportunity and the temptation to become involved. Even when social contacts take place almost exclusively on a couple-to-couple basis, each partner is likely to share some interests or attitudes with another's spouse. In the world of work, both men and women often are thrown into contact with attractive persons of the opposite sex, under conditions that encourage some sharing of themselves. These contacts may lead to cross-sex friendships, and they may lead to sexual involvement.

CROSS-SEX FRIENDSHIPS

Perhaps more as a function of the women's liberation movement than anything else, the friendships that a person has with people outside the marriage have become an issue for many husbands and wives. Until recently, the rules were quite clear. While one was growing up, and until a marital choice was made, one was expected to have many friends of the opposite sex for two reasons: to learn more about them, and to learn more about oneself. Once the commitment to marry was made, however, the situation changed completely. Each partner now was supposed to either convert those friendships into ones that could be shared with the intended spouse, or discard them in favor of new pair friendships.

There was an assumption, further, that cross-sex friendships continued after marriage, or formed while married, posed a grave threat to the marriage. They were believed to carry a strong risk of emotional and sexual involvement. Since virtually all men worked outside the home, and only a minority of women did so, the odds of forming such a cross-sex friendship were much greater for the husband than for the wife. According to the stereotype, the wife was supposed to keep a watchful and wary eye on her husband's secretaries and female co-workers, to head off any relationship that might lead to trouble.

More and more women are working outside the home now, however, and more couples are openly facing the fact that not all of any person's needs can be met by a husband or wife alone. The issue of cross-sex friendships has therefore taken on new form. Many couples today, and women particularly, are asking whether it is not both possible and desirable for both partners to share with friends those personal interests that are not shared with the spouse (Saline, 1975).

The problem, of course, is whether cross-sex friendships are possible without an erotic component that leads inevitably to sexual involvement. On the one hand, it is argued that people are more than simply bodies; they are quite capable of keeping their relationships platonic if they wish to do so. On the other hand, others argue that excluding sex from a man–woman relationship is itself a form of excessive emphasis upon sex. Despite the intentions of the friends, sexual interest will surface as soon as empathy is established.

Whether cross-sex friendships are desirable or not is not really the issue. Conditions of modern life thrust them upon more and more people. The real issue is how such friendships may be managed. The key to the

solution is for both friends to be quite aware of the nature of their relationship, and to be completely frank with each other about the boundaries of that relationship. As one marriage counselor put it, "The time to cool any relationship is when you start having bedroom fantasies with your friend in the starring role. That's a signal that you're drifting from your spouse." (Saline, 1975)

AFFAIRS

Undoubtedly there are people who never are tempted to have an extramarital affair. Probably it also is true that more people make such claims than are entitled to. People reared with values of lifelong fidelity, to whom the phrase "extramarital sex" has shameful connotations, may deny not only to others but to themselves as well that occasionally they long to stray from the marital fold.

Marriage, however, cannot continue in a state of perpetual excitement. Eventually one knows most of what there is to know about one's mate, including what he or she is like in bed. No matter how uninhibited the spouse may be, no matter how ingenious he or she is in creating new situations and inventing new sexual techniques, the repertoire is limited and eventually becomes familiar. The relationship may be richly sensual, and the partners may stimulate one another to exhaustion, but the mystery of the unknown and the titillating uncertainty of courtship must inevitably disappear.

Then too, there is the fact that no matter how similar the partners may be in values, attitudes, preferences, and leisure interests, each person has a portion of the self to which the spouse cannot relate fully. Each person has needs that the partner cannot fulfill. These needs provide the basis for extramarital friendships.

Finally, if we are candid about it, we must admit that the vast majority of men and women experience sexual stirrings when their mates are not around; most people recognize occasional strong sexual feelings for someone else. Both men and women yearn for new romantic thrills, feel lust, and are tempted to have an affair.

More than a generation ago, the Kinsey researchers estimated that about one-fourth of all wives and about half of all husbands have sexual intercourse, at some time, with someone other than their mates. There are no recent data as comprehensive as the Kinsey data, but several studies do indicate two things. First, men still have more opportunities, on the average, for affairs than women do. One study of 100 middle-class, middle-aged couples found that 68 percent of the husbands, as compared to only 28 percent of the wives, had had the opportunity (Cannon and Long, 1971; Johnson, 1970). Second, women are catching up. The 1973 survey by the Research Guild reported an increase from ten percent to 24 percent in the proportion of married women under age 25 who had had extramarital coitus. The comparable current rate for young men was 32 percent.

The studies also show that persons who have had affairs rate their satisfaction with their marital sex relationships lower than do people who have not had affairs. We should not overlook the possibility that those who have had affairs may be distorting their marital sexual adjustments in an unknowing effort to justify their behavior. Nevertheless, there is probably something more to these figures. It may be that while most people experience sexual yearnings, those who are less satisfied at home are more likely to act on them.

There is no simple answer to the question of what effects extramarital affairs have upon marriage. It depends upon whether the affair is continued. It also depends upon whether the spouse becomes aware of the affair, and upon whether the emotional involvement gets out of hand.

Some affairs may not endure beyond a single act of coupling. The experience may be disappointing, circumstances may not permit a repetition, one or both participants may feel guilt and remorse, or the couple may simply decide that they do not wish to jeopardize their marriages by continuing. Such short-lived affairs are likely to have no discernible effects upon the participants' marriages unless guilt persists, or unless one of the spouses learns of the affair.

In other cases, the affair may continue for some time without the spouses' awareness. In these cases, again, no specific outcomes may be predicted. Sometimes the participant grows away from his or her spouse, but sometimes he or she compensates by becoming more considerate and attentive.

In perhaps half of all prolonged affairs, however, the spouse eventually becomes aware of it. In these instances the results are almost always destructive. For the spouse, it is hard to escape feelings of both betrayal and inadequacy. The errant mate has violated the marital vows and held the spouse up to shame and ridicule. Can he or she ever be trusted again? Moreover, there obviously must be something wrong with the marriage and with oneself as a sexual partner. Feelings of anger, hurt, guilt, and shame are very likely to provoke a major marital crisis.

The laws and public opinion generally hold that the aggrieved spouse is entitled to a divorce, and divorce or estrangement may indeed be the outcome. But even when the marriage survives, one can expect a legacy of distrust, hostility, and anxiety.

Awareness of oneself and one's relationships is probably the best means for protecting against an unplanned affair, just as it is for coping with cross-sex friendships. In this case, however, there are even stronger rewards for being aware of the spouse's feelings and for openly discussing the matter. For a perceptive spouse is likely to be aware of developing relationships that are likely to lead his or her partner into sexual involvement. Keeping any resulting anxiety hidden may almost amount to entering an unwitting conspiracy in support of the budding affair. If, however, the spouse openly tells the partner that he or she is aware of the situation, it reinforces the solidarity of the marital relationship, and it also serves as a major deterrent to further involvement (Edwards, 1973).

SWINGING

We have seen much evidence of a general loosening of sexual standards in recent years. Given the high incidence of extramarital affairs and their frequently destructive effect, some couples have responded by becoming advocates of "swinging." Swingers believe that norms of sexual fidelity in marriage are hypocritical, and that all physical sex expression is good. Furthermore, they hold that the joint participation of husband and wife in sexual activities with other people is not only pleasurable, but actually can contribute to the stability of the marriage and the closeness of the couple.

NUMBERS AND MODE OF OPERATION

Estimates of the numbers of couples who have tried swinging or who are actively involved in it vary widely. One estimate puts the total number at an unbelievable eight million couples (Breedlove and Breedlove,

1964). An anthropologist who studied some of them estimates that there are, in all, some 8000 swinging couples within a 200-mile radius of Chicago (Bartell, 1971). The safest estimate comes from another social scientist who has studied swingers: "There are more swingers than non-swingers believe, but not as many as swingers think." (Bell, 1971)

There is no one mode of operation among swingers. Sometimes, two couples who are friends gradually move from discussions of sex and swinging in the abstract to a decision to try it. They may trade partners for a night or two, or on a fairly regular basis. Sometimes the decision is essentially forced upon one man and woman by the other two, who want to go to bed together. In either case, the swinging may remain quite private between the two couples.

In other instances, the swinging may, in effect, "go public." The couples not only switch partners, but have themselves a mini-orgy, undressing early in the evening, spending most of the time together nude and occasionally indulging in various kinds of sexual play and sexual relationships. If the couples retire to bedrooms for privacy, they are known as "closet swingers." Closet swinging is often an early stage, occurring among inexperienced swingers who later will "come out" and have their sexual play in the same room where the others are congregated.

Emphasis upon nudity and having sex relationships in the same room tends to be associated with expansion of the group, so that more people can participate, more partners are available, and some sexual play may occur almost continuously. Couples are the preferred unit for recruitment into the group. Occasional unaccompanied women are welcome, but limits are usually placed upon the number of unaccompanied men who may be accepted.

Groups tend to be larger and more fluid in metropolitan areas, where there is a larger population base to draw from, and where anonymity is easier to maintain. There also are more individual couples in major urban areas who seek to make contacts through the dozens of magazines that run ads for swingers. The couple make contact with another couple by mail or by telephone and arrange to spend a social evening together. They meet at one of the homes, size one another up, and, if impressions are favorable all around, eventually get around to swinging. If the impressions are not favorable, the evening is merely social and the association is not continued. Most such swinging relationships, even when successful, apparently are not continued more than a time or two, and the couples may spend much of their leisure time developing new contacts.

So far as we know, no swingers' group has yet become organized enough to draw up a set of by-laws. Nevertheless, through swingers' magazines and by consensus, an informal set of rules governing what is

THE RULES OF SWINGING

The 1969 movie *Bob and
Carol and Ted and Alice*
offered a wry look
at swinging.

and is not acceptable in swinging has emerged. There are essentially four basic rules.

First, swingers formally disavow any kind of double standard between the sexes. What is permissible for one spouse is also acceptable for the other. Particularly, the husband cannot impose any limits on his wife's participation. This requirement is important because, after each ejaculation, men are prevented from further sexual arousal until after the refractory period has elapsed. Wives, however, can have more continuous sexual play with a greater number of partners.

Second, the sex must be kept purely physical and impersonal. Sexual stimulation is the beginning and end goal. For any person to develop an emotional or personal interest in one of the others would threaten the group and some of the marriages within it. Explicitly, no private "dates" outside the swinging situation are allowed.

Third, no member of the group should be pressured into accepting sexual activity that he or she does not want. No one is obliged to engage in sex with a person he or she finds unattractive. Neither is he or she obliged to accept activities such as oral or anal sex. This rule seems intended basically to protect women from intimidation.

Fourth, and virtually the reverse of rule number three, each person is free to engage in any and all kinds of sexual activities without any disapproval from the others. Oral, anal, and homosexual activities are included. The explicit approval of homosexual contacts again appears to be aimed at women. Homosexual contacts among men at swingers' parties are virtually unknown, but women appear to be less afraid of them than men are. In fact, the women are encouraged by some of the men, who find their own sexual pleasure enhanced through watching.

SWINGING AND MARITAL ADJUSTMENT

Several sympathetic analyses have been published in which the authors seek to provide a rationale for swinging. One argument is that the frequency with which affairs occur testifies to the likelihood that some kind of extramarital sex will happen. These people maintain that swinging is not only less disruptive than clandestine affairs, but that it also can actually increase the commitment of husbands and wives to one another (Denfeld and Gordon, 1970). The disruptive forces in most affairs are believed to be the betrayal of the partner, the participant's emotional involvement with the paramour, and the jealousy of the spouse (Cole and Spanier, 1974). Advocates believe that none of these complications is likely to occur in swinging.

Scholarly discussions of the quality of swingers' marriages, compared to those of non-swingers, however, show considerable ambivalence. On the one hand, it is argued that swingers' marriages may be stronger than other marriages. But the supporting data are few and suggestive at best. On the other hand, it is acknowledged that many swingers are seeking to revitalize or revive relationships that have lost their attractiveness. Some of these marriages may be heading for dissolution whether or not swinging occurs.

DROPOUTS FROM SWINGING

One of the few studies of swinging that did not involve participant observation was a questionnaire study of 965 marriage counselors. About half of them reported having been sought out by couples who had been swingers but who had since given it up. By definition, these were people for whom swinging had created or augmented problems. Therefore, the findings of this study cannot be used to answer the question of whether swinging is harmful or beneficial. It can, however, help us understand those situations in which swinging fails (Denfeld, 1974).

The counselors reported nine different problem areas encountered by their clients, which are listed in Table 9-2. Jealousy was reported most often. Men acknowledged it more frequently than women did, usually envying their wives' popularity, their apparent pleasure in sex with others, and their endurance. When women reported jealousy they were more likely to emphasize their fears of losing their husbands.

Somewhat surprisingly, guilt feelings were the next most common problem. Apparently, some swingers are not as emancipated from conventional morality as the literature on swinging would lead us to believe. Both jealousy and guilt feelings probably are related to "threats to the marriage," the third most commonly cited problem. Sixty-eight couples

**TABLE 9-2
PROBLEMS
REPORTED BY
EX-SWINGERS**

PROBLEM	NUMBER OF COUPLES
Jealousy	109
Guilt	68
Threat to the marriage	68
Outside emotional attachments	53
Boredom and loss of interest	49
Disappointment	32
Divorce or separation	29
Wife's inability to take it	29
Fear of discovery	15

Source: Duane Denfeld, "Dropouts From Swinging," *The Family Coordinator* 23 (Jan. 1974), pp. 46–47.

reported that fights and quarrels became more frequent after they started swinging, and that swinging had weakened rather than strengthened their marriages.

The swingers' rule against emotional involvement and outside dating was violated in 53 cases. Sometimes this breach led the couples to seek marriage couseling; in other cases it led to separation or divorce. Twenty-nine of the couples independently reported separation or divorce as a cause for dropping out of swinging.

The categories of "boredom and loss of interest" and "disappointment" also overlap. Some couples simply found that swinging did not provide the excitement that they had anticipated. In part, this disappointment seemed to stem from the absence of personal involvement inherent in swinging; physical sex without emotional involvement was just not that satisfying. At another level, some couples reported that their marriages had not improved as expected.

Far greater in the emotional intensity with which it was reported than in the frequency of occurrence was the "wife's inability to take it."

In 54 percent of all of these couples, dropping out of swinging was initiated by the wives. In 34 percent of the cases the husbands took the first step, and in 12 percent it was a mutual decision. Many of the wives reported that they were repelled and disgusted by swinging and threatened their husbands with divorce if it was not stopped.

Finally, in 15 cases, swinging was discontinued because of the fear of the consequences of discovery. Some couples were concerned that their friends or neighbors either knew or would find out. Other couples decided to quit because of the inquisitiveness of children, particularly teenagers. In those few cases in which the children actually found out, serious conflict resulted.

*SEXISM IN
SWINGING*

Swinging has been highly touted as requiring absolute equality of husbands and wives, and it is claimed that it thereby contributes to marital solidarity. Thus, one of the most startling challenges to swinging has come from a study of 25 women swingers, which concluded that the old sexual double standard operates in swinging, just as it does in other areas of life (Henshel, 1973). This study sought answers to three questions: (1) Which spouse first becomes aware of the possibility of swinging? (2) Which spouse first suggests swinging? (3) How is the final decision to swing actually made?

The results were quite clear. Three times as many husbands as wives learned of swinging first, and in only about one-third of the cases was it a matter of joint discovery. When it came to the suggestion that the couple participate, the situation was even more unbalanced. Only one-fifth of the couples arrived at the idea jointly; 68 percent of the suggestions were made by the husbands, and only 12 percent by the wives. And when the final decision was made to swing, 28 percent of the decisions were made by the couple jointly, and 64 percent were made by the husbands. Only eight percent were made by the wives. The woman sociologist who did the study concluded that swinging is a male institution and not part of any sexual revolution.

SUMMARY

The male reproductive system is composed essentially of the penis, testicles, seminal vesicles, and prostate gland. The semen is composed of the sperm cells produced in the testicles plus secretions produced by the seminal vesicles and prostate gland. Variations in penis size from man to man are minimal and have little to do with the sexual satisfaction of either men or women.

The primary female reproductive organs are the ovaries, Fallopian tubes, uterus, and vagina. Ordinarily, the ovaries release one mature ovum during each menstrual cycle; the ovum then travels through one of the Fallopian tubes, where conception may occur. Implantation of the fertilized ovum takes place in the uterine wall. The vagina receives the penis in sexual intercourse. At its entrance is the hymen, a membrane which is an inconclusive indicator of virginity and which may be eliminated by a physician before marriage. The entire vulva is highly erogenous, but the clitoris, located at the upper junction of the labia minora, is the primary locus of sexual sensation.

In both sexes, there are four stages in the sexual response cycle: excitement, plateau, orgasm, and resolution. Excitement produces penile erection in the male, and erection of the nipples and clitoris and lubrication and dilation of the vagina in the female. A potentially stable level of arousal is attained at the plateau stage. Once this stage is reached, continued stimulation will induce orgasm. Orgasm brings intense pleasure and the release of muscular tension. In the resolution stage, the male loses his erection and the female's genitals return to normal size, shape, and coloration. There is a refractory period in the male during which intercourse cannot be continued. Many women, however, can return almost immediately to the plateau stage and experience repeated orgasms.

The frequency with which couples have sexual intercourse varies widely, and whatever satisfies a particular couple should be considered normal. Whatever the frequency, many young men tend to reach orgasm quickly, while up to half of all women occasionally have difficulty achieving orgasm. Time and practice and loving care tend to reduce both problems, and most couples achieve patterns of adjustment that are satisfactory to them.

Extramarital sexual involvements do occur, however, becoming more likely as husbands and wives endorse the idea of having cross-sex friendships, and as more women work outside the home. Most men and most women occasionally yearn for a rekindling of romance and sexual excitement through a new sexual partner, and some act upon that impulse. Short-lived affairs that are not discovered by the spouse may have no discernible effects upon the marriage. The longer and more involved the affair, however, the more likely the partner is to know, and the more devastating are the consequences. Guilt, shame, and feelings of betrayal may be so great as to destroy the marriage.

Some couples have turned to swinging for the sexual variety it provides, and as a less harmful arrangement than having affairs. By operating under explicit rules, swinging seeks to be strictly equalitarian, to prevent emotional involvements, and to strengthen marriages. Research has not yet revealed, however, whether swingers' marriages are stronger or more problem-ridden than others. Studies of former swingers do reveal unanticipated involvements, jealousies, repulsions, boredom, and fear of discovery. Other research indicates that most swinging is initiated by males and is not as equalitarian as it is reputed to be.

FOR ADDITIONAL READING

Bartell, Gilbert D., *Group Sex: A Scientist's Eyewitness Report on The American Way of Swinging* (New York: Peter H. Wyden, 1971). An anthropologist's report on swinging in the Chicago area.

Libby, Roger W., and Robert N. Whitehurst, eds., *Renovating Marriage* (Danville, Cal.: Consensus Publishers, 1973). Sympathetic exploration of new sexual life styles in marriage.

Masters, William, and Virginia Johnson, *The Pleasure Bond* (Boston: Little, Brown, 1975). Endorses sex as one aspect of long-term commitment to one's partner rather than as acrobatics or short-term pampering of oneself.

Morrison, Eleanor S., and Vera Borosage, eds., *Human Sexuality: Contemporary Perspectives* (Palo Alto, Cal.: National Press Books, 1973). Excellent sections on heterosexual interaction, homosexuality, and "The Question of Relationship."

Weinberg, Martin S., and Colin J. Williams, *Male Homosexuals: Their Problems and Adaptations* (New York: Oxford University Press, 1974). Report of research, from the Institute for Sex Research, on the adjustment patterns of male homosexuals in the United States, the Netherlands, and Denmark.

STUDY QUESTIONS

1. Compare the four stages of the sexual response cycle in men and women. What are their implications for sexual adjustment in marriage?

2. What problems of sexual adjustment are encountered most commonly by young married couples? What alternative solutions are available to them?

3. Many young men and women worry about their adequacy as sexual partners. How can a knowledge of sexual anatomy help to reduce those fears?

4. On the average, married couples today have intercourse more frequently than they used to. Why do you think this is so?

5. How do you feel about married persons having close friends of the opposite sex? How can it strengthen marriage? How can it weaken it?

6. What factors influence the effects of extramarital sex relationships on a marriage? Can all affairs be viewed in the same terms?

7. What various forms does swinging take? Make the best argument you can that it has a beneficial effect upon marriage.

8. What does research show about the problems some couples encounter in swinging? What is your view on the emancipation that swinging affords to women?

Chapter 10
Financial
Adjustment

Nobody ever has enough money. Newlyweds find out quickly enough that they need almost everything: a place to live and furniture and equipment to put in it, an automobile or automobiles, life insurance, health insurance, fire insurance, liability insurance, and auto insurance, new clothing, a savings program, and so on. It doesn't take long for them to discover, either, that their income is grossly inadequate whether it is based upon one salary or two.

Someday, however, they reason, they will have accumulated all the things it takes to keep a family comfortable; then there will be money to spare. As we will see in a moment, in one sense that is true. But in another sense it is not. People's wants expand with their ability to afford things. Absolute income levels have little to do either with how adequate the income seems or with problems of money management. When one makes $10,000 a year, it seems as though $15,000 would surely be enough. But by the time one is receiving $20,000, the magic figure of ''enough'' has increased to $30,000, and so on. There may be a few of us who achieve financial contentment, but most of us live out our lives trying to balance income with outgo, wishing we had just a little more money.

FINANCES OVER THE LIFE CYCLE

As we have already suggested, most peoples' financial situations do change over time. Incomes vary, most often increasing as the couple gets older and frequently changing as the wife and mother moves in and out of paid employment. A family's need for income varies, too. Children are born and grow up, physical energy wanes, grandparents become dependent and, eventually the couple themselves grow old. To discuss all of these variations adequately would require a book as large as this one. For that kind of detail, we can only refer students to a good textbook on personal and family finance (Cohen and Hanson, 1972; Troelstrup, 1970).

EARLY MARRIAGE

Most young couples start pretty nearly from scratch and must buy almost everything. How difficult this task is for them, however, varies widely. If they marry while they are still in school, they may find it rather easy to live in the genteel poverty afforded by part-time employment and ''educational assistance'' checks from parents. Most of their friends are in similar circumstances, and they all know the situation will change when they graduate.

The most difficult situation financially may occur when only the husband works and he is just getting started on his career. His income is probably the lowest it will ever be, and the demands on it are almost overwhelming.

In a large and growing number of cases, both the husband and the wife hold jobs. Although neither one earns more than a husband whose wife does not work, together they often achieve a feeling of relative affluence. The couple may live on one partner's income and save all or part of the other, or they may acquire furniture and possessions fairly rapidly and with some comfort.

CHILDBEARING AND CHILD REARING

Some couples have limited goals for the wife's working after marriage: long enough to save for the down payment on a house, for example, or, more vaguely, ''until she gets pregnant.'' In other instances, both partners are committed to occupational careers. In either event, the first pregnancy signals the beginning of 20 or more years of large and generally increasing expenses.

Even when both husband and wife are committed to occupational careers, childbearing often interrupts the wife's career. If there are medical complications, as there are in a substantial minority of cases, she may lose time from work. She may even have to take a leave of absence, generally without pay, or just quit work for a while. The proportion of wives who are in the labor force is lower for women with children under six years of age than for any other group. Consequently, childbearing and early child rearing often mean not only added expenses, but lowered income as well.

The addition of a child often means needing a larger and more expensive home, baby and children's furniture, clothing, and the money to meet large medical expenses. If the couple's financial adjustment up to this point has been shaky, the added strains of childbearing may test it severely. Marriages in which both partners have worked sometimes face the greatest problems of adjustment with the arrival of the baby. For the first time they may confront the problem of inadequate income. Perhaps what they thought was a very successful adjustment was based upon assumptions that cannot continue. For most couples, these years are ones of heavy demand and insufficient income. Few people are able to save much money during this period.

Firm figures on the costs of child rearing are not likely to be very meaningful, but a major life insurance company estimates that it takes about three times the father's annual salary to provide for a child to the age of 18. Therefore, if we assume the father earns a moderate salary of $15,000 a year, the formula predicts a total cost of $45,000 for one child or $90,000 for two—very substantial sums of money.

Moreover, a child's costs often are just beginning at age 18, with the college years being the most expensive of all. Expenses generally are lower for students attending public colleges and universities, particularly when they live at home. Still, $2,000 a year per child is probably an absolute minimum cost for the college years. Average costs may be nearly twice that figure, and total costs at many private colleges may run as high as $6,000 or $7,000 per student per year.

Though marriage is not a function of the college years as such, most students do marry then or soon after. This period often entails considerable expense to the parents. The costs of large weddings, large graduation gifts such as an automobile or a trip abroad, and other kinds of assistance to married children often take a large share of the parents' income.

At least at middle-class levels, the parental incomes often are adequate to these demands. If the husband and wife both have careers, the wife's career is likely to have substantially recovered from the setbacks of her childbearing years; meanwhile, the husband's career will probably have brought substantial salary increases. Some parental couples even manage systematic saving and investment programs during these years. At the other extreme, however, some parents have to

*HIGH-SCHOOL
AND COLLEGE
YEARS*

mortgage their homes to pay for their children's college educations, to say nothing of doing without luxuries, or even necessities, themselves.

THE POST-PARENTAL YEARS

Recent decades have seen substantial improvements in the financial situations of many aging couples. Chief reasons are the spread of social security, Medicare, and corporate retirement plans, and improvements in their benefits. As a result of such programs, more old people maintain their own homes today than ever before. Fewer old couples have to move in with their children or even substantially depend upon them.

Most people in the post-parental years are not yet aged, however. Typically, they are 50 years of age or under when their last child leaves home. If their incomes have been relatively adequate and their prior financial planning has been successful, these years often are relatively prosperous and comfortable. The couple's home may now be paid for, substantially reducing their cash outflow each month. The drop in their child-related expenditures is sizeable, of course. Perhaps for the first time, the couple has a significant surplus of money in relation to their habitual patterns of expenditure. Some couples seize this opportunity to take long-delayed vacations and even to do some world traveling.

These are also the years of investment for retirement and old age. Savings accounts build up, and money may be invested in stocks and bonds, either through mutual funds or directly through brokers. More prosperous couples may prefer municipal bonds, the interest upon which is exempt from federal income tax. Other couples prefer to invest in real estate on either a small or a large scale. The investment possibilities are almost endless.

Of necessity, this sketch of the family's financial life cycle has been brief. But it is useful to have the general characteristics of the several stages in mind as we turn to the root causes of many financial problems in marriage. The two most important are inadequate income and differences in values.

MONEY AND HAPPINESS

People have questioned for years whether personal and marital happiness increase directly with the size of one's income. The reasoning goes that higher incomes are both a sign of one's self-worth (assuming that income is a measure of competence) and also a means of purchasing more of the goods and services that bring satisfaction and happiness. Early fragmentary studies of marital success sought to relate marital happiness to differences in income. These studies yielded generally inconclusive or negative findings. Most researchers concluded that how people felt about their incomes, and how they used them, probably were more important than the size of the income itself. There the matter rested until recently.

A report of the U.S. Census Bureau in 1971, however, showed that marital stability, at least, does seem to increase with family income. It examined the segment of the population from 35 to 54 years of age and found that about 72 percent of the household heads who earned less than $5000 per year had been married only once. But among those earning $15,000 or more, 83 percent were in their first marriages. Thus, on a national scale, if money does not buy marital happiness, it at least seems to serve as a deterrent to divorce.

To get to the question more directly, an economist reported, in 1973, an analysis of data from 30 separate surveys, done in 19 countries, on the relationship between size of income and reported happiness. In all countries, more money typically was associated with higher happiness ratings. One of these surveys was done in the United States in December 1970. It showed that a little more than one-fourth of those people with under $3000 annual income reported that they were "very happy"; in the over-$15,000 category, the proportion reporting they were "very happy" was almost twice as large (Easterlin, 1973).

It probably is significant that the low incomes upon which all of these comparisons are based are very low—from $3000 to $5000. Common sense would tell us that incomes in this range are likely to pose serious psychological and material problems for their recipients. It also appears likely that the differences discovered would be reduced substantially if the comparisons were made between more typical middle-class income levels, such as $10,000 and $15,000 or $20,000.

Up to some minimum point, however—a point that is difficult to define precisely and is constantly changing—the absolute size of one's income probably is an important factor in both happiness and financial adjustment. But above that point, simple lack of money is less of a factor, and differences in values and money management become increasingly important.

FINANCIAL VALUES

There is no sharp dividing line between financial values and other values. People's values all relate directly to what they want out of life and how they achieve their goals. In a fundamental sense, financial adjustment is almost synonymous with marital adjustment. But couples may or may not know much about each other's basic values, and how those values are expressed in the use of money, before they marry.

Similarity or difference in values quickly becomes evident in the style of life that couples adopt. A basic concern is whether the wife should hold paid employment. If the answer is yes, there remains the question of what the relationship should be between the demands of her job and the demands of his. We will devote a whole chapter to this situation later in this book. For now, it is enough to say that opportunities for both partners to develop their careers may well come in conflict with the husband's ability to proceed unhampered in the development of his. Our corporate system often forces couples to make choices between one partner's career and the other's.

Statistics show, for example, that some 300,000 to 500,000 employees are transferred by their companies each year. A 1969 survey examined the personnel policies of 60 large companies. Fourteen of them reported moving their managerial employees, on the average, every two years. Sixteen companies moved them every three years, and ten every five years. Eleven companies moved their employees every year[1]! Such moves often are essential to the career development of young executives, at least if they stay with the same companies.

Some young couples accept the prospect of such moves rather easily, although each move would disrupt the wife's career and uproot the whole family (Barrett and Noble, 1973; Butler, McAllister, and Kaiser, 1973; Jones, 1973; Landis and Stoetzer, 1966). These families place the

[1] Atlas Van Lines, Traffic Managers' Survey, 1969.

development of the husband's career first. When this pattern is followed successfully, increases in the husband's income ease the financial situation of the whole family. Other couples, with different values, find the strains of frequent moving to be very great, however (Seidenberg, 1975). Some wives oppose the pattern because of its interference with their careers (Long, 1974).

The corporate style of life also involves regulation of the couple's consumption patterns in ways that one partner or both may find onerous. The couple may feel pressure, for example, to gauge their possessions to their status level in the company. They are careful to drive a slightly better car, wear slightly more expensive clothes, and live in a somewhat better neighborhood than the husband's immediate subordinates; at the same time, they must be equally careful not to duplicate those of his corporate superiors.

Additional strains may be placed upon the marriage when some expense-account living is involved. There is a widely recognized pattern here: the husband lives lavishly while travelling at company expense, and the couple patronizes expensive restaurants and clubs when entertaining clients or company guests; but the rest of the time, they must live quite frugally in an effort to keep up appearances and still make ends meet. This double life not only causes tensions to develop between spouses, but it may tempt them into trying to live beyond their means through the unwise use of credit. This practice, of course, may cause disaster later on.

Differences in financial values may also cause problems at the personal level. One spouse may view savings and systematic investment as means of ensuring security, while the other's philosophy is to enjoy the fruits of one's income as fully as possible. Conflict is bound to result. Such differences must be worked out just as other differences are, and there is no one pattern that is satisfactory for all couples. Many different kinds of adjustment can work well.

Beyond these considerations, and regardless of the type of adjustment the couple makes, there are basic problems of sound money management to be confronted. The wise use of money can help to make almost any adjustment pattern work; its unwise use can cause serious and lasting problems. We cannot cover all facets of money management here. We will, however, analyze some of the more common and important ones.

MONEY MANAGEMENT

We shall analyze problems of money management roughly in the order in which most couples confront them. The overall question of how much money there is, and how to use it, comes first. A place to live is second. Then, as soon as major purchases begin, credit enters the picture. Life insurance assumes increased importance as soon as a baby arrives and, later on, opportunities to invest systematically increase. Taxes, of course, are always with us; we will treat them here in the context of minimizing the tax bite and maximizing the investment potential.

***PLANNING AND
BUDGETING***

There are people who can account for every nickel or dollar they spend, and who even seem to thrive on keeping records in meticulous detail. Most of us, however, find detailed bookkeeping an overwhelming bore and quite impractical. Instead, a successful budget is most often a flexible financial plan that establishes priorities and helps people get the most for their money.

**The
General
Plan**

Some people can do broad financial planning in their heads and don't need to develop written budgets at all. If you can do that, fine. But there probably are more people who find out the hard way that they must be more systematic. Sitting down and establishing one's spending priorities is a nuisance at best, and often it is terribly frustrating. There just isn't enough money to do everything one wants to do. But painful as it may be to make choices, it is better than finding one day that you can't meet the payments on the car and furniture, that you have to borrow money at exorbitant interest rates, and, eventually, that your life style must include dodging the bill collectors.

Many couples find that the best starting point in developing a workable budget is to estimate their annual income. If there is just one salary involved, or even two, that is a relatively simple matter. If there is also income from investments, temporary part-time work, or other sources, that money also needs to be figured in. The next step is to make an estimate of annual expenses, by separate categories.

If the estimates of income and outgo are close together, there is no real problem. If, however, the estimated expenses exceed the estimated income, then some hard decisions must be made. This is the point at which some couples throw up their hands in dismay and give up budgeting as impractical. They are also the ones who are sorry later on, when each partner blames the other for their financial problems, or when they face the garnishment of wages to satisfy unpaid debts.

**Budgeting
Techniques**

Once a general budget has been worked out on an annual basis, it needs to be translated into a plan for spending over each month or each pay period: so much for rent or the house payment, so much for food, clothing, transportation, and so on. Most young couples today pay their bills by check. If they bank all their income and make all major payments by check, the monthly bank statement provides them with the equivalent of a bookkeeping system. They can use their cancelled checks to make

sure that they are living within their income and that their expenditures have been as planned.

For couples who prefer to pay by cash rather than by check, a good system consists of setting up a series of envelopes corresponding to the several budget items and dividing up each paycheck among them. Each bill can then be paid from the proper envelope as it becomes due. If some envelopes run out of money, it indicates the need to readjust the budget. Couples using this system need to guard against the possibility of theft.

The details of income and spending vary widely from couple to couple, as do their financial values. Some couples place great emphasis upon maintaining external appearances through elaborate wardrobes, new cars, and the like. Others prefer to drive a six-year-old car and to save systematically, or to travel, or to do any number of other things. Some have large medical bills, aged parents to support, and so on.

Many different patterns will work for different people as long as the

**Model
Expenditure
Patterns**

TABLE 10-1 SUGGESTED EXPENDITURE PATTERNS BY INCOME AND FAMILY SIZE

MONTHLY INCOME[a]	NUMBER	SAVINGS	FOOD	HOUSING[b]	CLOTHING	TRANSPORTATION[c]	PERSONAL, MEDICAL, AND OTHER[d]
$ 315	2	$ 7	$ 84	$ 95	$ 23	$ 39	$ 67
	4	5	100	95	34	36	45
375	2	10	95	110	35	50	75
	4	5	110	115	45	45	55
425	2	15	105	125	35	55	90
	4	10	125	130	45	50	65
475	2	20	110	140	40	65	100
	4	15	130	145	55	60	70
525	2	25	125	160	45	70	100
	4	20	140	165	65	65	70
600	2	35	135	180	55	85	110
	4	30	150	185	70	80	85
650	2	45	140	190	65	85	125
	4	40	155	200	75	80	100
750	2	50	165	210	75	100	150
	4	40	180	225	85	95	125
$ 850	2	$ 80	$175	$225	$ 85	$115	$170
	4	55	195	250	95	115	140
950	2	100	190	240	95	135	190
	4	75	210	265	105	135	160
1050	2	130	210	250	100	150	210
	4	100	230	270	110	150	190

[a] After taxes.
[b] Includes shelter, fuel, furnishings, appliances, and equipment.
[c] Includes automobile purchase and operation, and public transportation.
[d] Includes advancement, recreation, gifts, education, and other expenses.

Source: American Bankers Association, *Personal Money Management,* as reprinted in Jerome B. Cohen and Arthur W. Hanson, *Personal Finance: Principles and Case Problems* (Homewood, Ill.: Irwin, 1972), p. 68.

couple plans the spending and saving, and as long as they agree on how it is done. Assuming these basic adjustments have been made, there are guides concerning how much of one's income may safely and reasonably be allocated to different expenses, at different income levels, and with different family sizes. One such set of suggestions, prepared by the American Bankers Association, is presented in Table 10-1. The income figures shown represent after-tax net income.

Several things are evident from the table. First, costs for the basics—food, clothing, and shelter—are higher in larger families. As a corollary of that fact, less money is available for transportation, medical care, personal needs, and savings when children or other family members are present. At the lower-income levels, housing is the largest expenditure, followed closely by food; there is little left over for savings. At higher income levels, housing and food still entail the greater costs, but now there is more money left over for savings and for personal uses.

Not all couples, of course, will develop budgets that fit these models. Differences in circumstances and values will cause them to spend relatively more in some categories and, of necessity, less in others.

HOUSING

Housing needs often change markedly over the life cycle. What makes sense for a couple at one time may not be appropriate at another. As a general rule, young married couples do not have other people living with them, so they do not need large amounts of space in their housing. Both husband and wife are likely to hold jobs and to spend relatively little time at home. Thus it is easy to see why most couples start out in apartments. Efficiency apartments or one- or two-bedroom flats often will do nicely. Since the couple needs relatively little space, the total cost is not great. They can also afford a newer apartment, with more of the conveniences, than they could otherwise manage. An added advantage is the fact that someone else is responsible for maintenance, leaving the young couple free to use their leisure time as they wish.

For many couples, increases in income, the birth of babies, and alterations in life style change the whole picture. Increases in income permit them to seek increased comfort and spaciousness and make possible the use of housing as an investment. Babies result in the need for more space, and they also mean that the couple will spend more time at home. Since the parents are concerned for the baby's uninterrupted sleep, the very things that once attracted them to apartment complexes—lots of "action," poolside parties, and the like—may become sources of annoyance. This is the period in life when many people want a private house to live in and confront the question of whether to buy.

Let us deal with three basic questions about housing. First, how much should people spend on it? Second, what are the advantages and disadvantages of renting? Finally, what are those of buying?

**The Cost
of Housing**

Recommended amounts of income to be spent on housing are stated somewhat differently, depending upon whether one is renting or buying. In renting, a common rule is to limit the monthly rental to no more than one week's take-home pay. Thus, if a couple is bringing home a combined $1200 a month, they can afford a maximum $300 rental. Lower incomes require lower rentals, and so on.

In buying, the rules generally are stated in terms of either the total cost of the house or apartment or the maximum mortgage that should be carried. The most common rule on total cost is that it should not exceed two-and-a-half times one's total annual income. If the mortgage alone is considered, the comparable rule is that it should not exceed twice one's total annual income.

Until recently, there was systematic discrimination against women's incomes by most lending agencies. In considering mortgage loans, savings and loan companies and other lending institutions generally refused to include a wife's earnings in the total family income. Their grounds were that she might become pregnant and have to quit work, or that the pressure of family responsibilities might force her to leave paid employment. Similarly, single or divorced women and widows were customarily denied mortgage loans.

The blatantly discriminatory character of such policies became an issue during the late 1960s under challenge from the women's liberation movement. Women reported instances of being humiliated by loan officers who inquired into their contraceptive practices and childbearing plans. The women's movement asserted that women had good records as credit risks. Further, they argued that the discriminatory policies of lending institutions violated their constitutional rights. In the early 1970s, some states passed legislation forbidding sex discrimination in lending. And in 1974, an amendment to the federal Consumer Credit Protection Act forbade any credit discrimination on the basis of either sex or marital status.[2] Consequently, women and families may not encounter as many problems from now on.

For young couples who are "on the way up," the recommended limit of two to two-and-a-half times their annual income invested in housing is somewhat conservative. The reason is that the mortgage will be paid off more in terms of future income levels than in terms of present ones. Thus, the couple may "gamble" on their ability to pay more in the future and secure housing adjusted to their future needs. Then again, they may buy conservatively and find their mortgage obligations increasingly easy to meet, though their housing standards will reflect their past rather than their present circumstances. General standards are helpful, but they do not determine the wisdom, or lack of it, with which they are applied to the individual case.

[2] *Family Planning/Population Reporter* 3 (Dec. 1974), p. 112.

Any simple listing of the advantages and disadvantages of renting compared with buying is likely to involve oversimplification in at least two respects. First, the two life styles may attract different personality types. Renters may value their freedom from the responsibilities of home ownership and the easy physical mobility that renting permits. Second, there is the life-cycle variable. That is, many couples prefer to rent before they have children, shift to home ownership during the family years, and then go back to renting again during their aging years.

Beyond these considerations, the advantages of renting are several. Living in the central city, close to the husband's job, the wife's job, or both, may be more feasible in rented apartments than in single-family housing. An in-town location cuts down on both transportation costs and the inconveniences of commuting, and it puts all the advantages of the city at the couple's doorstep. Renting also allows a couple to avoid long-term commitments. They can move and adjust their housing to changing needs at the end of every lease period. They are also relatively free from the nuisance of maintenance and repairs, which generally are the landlord's responsibility. And finally, the capital that would have to be used for a down payment on home ownership is available to them for other forms of investment. Renters may be able to invest more quickly in stocks or bonds, and they may be able to plan their investments for capital growth, income, or a combination of the two.

The disadvantages of renting are almost the reverse of the advantages. Renters have no build-up of equity; each month's rent is gone forever. A related problem is the fact there are no income tax breaks for rental payments like those given to mortgage payments. In the short run, renting often is less costly than owning, but in the long run, it is almost always more expensive. There are also restrictions on life style that accompany renting: pet ownership is often forbidden or strictly regulated, and the noise of parties or even the stereo set may be closely controlled. And finally, the couple is always vulnerable to increases in the rent. At the end of every lease period, renters face the possibility of big rent hikes.

People who buy homes may be, disproportionately, those who emphasize family stability, child rearing, and the security that comes with having a place of one's own. Their rewards, as they see them, are likely to be both financial and psychological.

The long-term trend in the economy is inflationary, and home ownership is one way of keeping up with it, at least in part. Not only does part of each mortgage payment increase one's equity in the property, but the sales price of the property tends to increase along with the general price level. Over time, the value of one's investment usually increases considerably. Moreover, the portion of the mortgage payment that goes for interest and taxes receives very favorable income-tax treatment,

Renting

Buying

lowering one's tax liability. And finally, once the mortgage has been secured, housing costs are relatively fixed. There may be some increases in taxes, insurance, and utility rates, but nothing like the increases that regularly confront renters.

For many of the same reasons, lending institutions are now pressing for the establishment of variable-interest-rate mortgages. In principle, the interest rates on these mortgages would fluctuate up and down with other interest rates; this device in theory would help ensure a plentiful supply of mortgage money at all times. In practice, however, it would limit drastically the current financial advantages of home ownership; interest rates would go up far more often than they would go down. Young couples would do well to avoid such variable-interest mortgages in favor of traditional fixed-interest-rate mortgages.

The disadvantages of buying a home are implicit in the discussion of the advantages. The required downpayment on a home may consume virtually all of the couple's capital at a time in their lives when they have very little available. Thus, indirectly, the couple is also denied the opportunity to make alternative investments. Home ownership also tends to restrict one's geographical mobility, and it often is associated with high transportation costs. Desirable single-family housing may be located far from one's place of work. Houses can be sold, of course, but selling is a complex process. Finally, home ownership carries heavy responsibilities. Painting, repairs, and lawn care are only a few of the continuing obligations of the home owner.

THE USE OF CREDIT

The use of credit is by now only a little less certain than death and taxes! Two-thirds of all new car purchases are made on credit. One household of every two has some installment debt. Over half of all retail purchases are made on credit, and six million people carry general-purpose credit cards. In addition, there are 100 million retail credit cards in circulation, 90 million gasoline credit cards, and 60 million bank credit cards. Sooner or later, virtually everyone uses credit. Some use it more wisely than others.

How Much Debt?

With credit literally being thrust upon them ("Buy Now, Pay Later!"), some couples find themselves overextended and unable to meet their monthly bills. How much credit can a couple use, and how much debt can people afford to carry?

Various standards are used to gauge the maximum debt that people should carry. Although the standards vary in how they are figured, they all produce approximately the same results. Two of the simplest ones are as follows. First, total debts should not be more than 20 percent of annual take-home income. Thus a take-home income of $10,000 permits carrying a debt load of up to $2000.

Second, total debts should not be more than can be paid off with 10 percent of one's income over a period of 12 to 24 months. Thus, with a take-home pay of $1000 a month, debts that must be paid off in one year should not exceed $1200. If two years are available for repayment, up to $2400 is allowable. Couples who observe such standards are not likely to find themselves hounded by bill collectors.

Advantages and Limitations of Credit

Since virtually everyone is forced to use credit sooner or later, most couples find life easier and more comfortable when they have an established credit rating. Even such basic things as utilities connections (electricity, gas, and telephone) often are arranged more easily and at lower cost by people whose credit is established. Beyond these basics, most major purchases, such as a new car, require time payments. The size and cost of those payments can be lower for people with established credit than they are for others.

The wise use of credit, through charge accounts and credit cards, also provides users with the equivalent of interest-free loans. As long as the charges are paid in the allotted time (commonly 30 days), there are no interest charges. Thus, if the credit-card company bills on the first of the month, charges made during the last week of the month are likely to appear not on the next statement but on the following one. In effect, this provision gives the user almost two month's free use of that money.

The temptation to overspend, of course, is a major problem for some people. But beyond this obvious risk, the use of credit can be quite expensive. Charge accounts that are not paid within the prescribed billing period typically carry interest rates of one-and-a-half percent a month—which translates to a whopping 18 percent a year. Wise money management includes the use of 30-day charge accounts, but *not* their use for making time payments.

Another disadvantage of the credit system is its heavy dependence upon credit bureaus. These companies are local clearinghouses through which business people exchange information on their credit experience with particular individuals. In principle, it is an excellent system for keeping track of the promptness with which people pay their bills. In practice, however, many credit bureaus are poorly run, error-prone, and inclined to collect malicious gossip.

The situation got so bad that, in 1971, Congress passed the Fair Credit Reporting Act, which empowered consumers to demand to know what information credit bureaus have assembled upon them. It also gave them the right to demand that improper or erroneous information be expunged from the file. Any responsible consumer who is denied credit or has difficulty with a credit investigation would be well advised to investigate the credit bureau through an attorney.

**Charge
Accounts**

Business establishments that offer charge accounts usually include the cost of maintaining their credit operations in the sales prices of their merchandise. Thus, even patrons who pay in cash help pay the cost of credit. If one intends to shop at such a store, it makes sense to take advantage of the 30-day charge privilege.

Many establishments offer, in addition, so-called "revolving credit." Under this arrangement, customers are permitted to keep adding purchases to their accounts and to pay the balance over an extended period, commonly ten months. The exorbitant interest on such accounts, roughly 18 percent a year, argues against their use.

**Credit
Cards**

Companies such as American Express, Diners' Club and Carte Blanche offer, to persons above certain income levels, general-purpose credit cards that can be used to charge an incredibly wide variety of goods and services at an equally wide range of businesses. Such companies charge an annual fee, usually $15, for the use of the card; they also charge participating merchants a fee, which is usually five to seven percent of the amount of the charge. Such cards are very convenient for people who travel a lot, who eat in restaurants frequently, and who keep track of their expenses either for tax purposes or for employer reimbursement. These general-purpose credit card companies are quite strict about demanding on-time payment from cardholders, and they withdraw them from habitually delinquent payers.

Over the past several years, bank credit cards such as Bank-Americard and Master Charge have become very popular. They work like the general purpose credit cards except that they are used more for local retail purchases, and less for travel and entertainment. The banks also encourage spreading the payments over a period of months because of the high interest rates that are charged on unpaid balances.

**Installment
Purchases**

So-called consumer durables, such as automobiles, major appliances, TV sets, and furniture, often are purchased on time-payment plans. The merchandise is paid for in a series of monthly installments, and the seller holds title to the property until the payments are completed.

The advantages in such arrangements lie all with the seller. If the purchaser falls behind in the payments, the merchandise may be repossessed, and the seller's claims are satisfied before the buyer gets anything. Some unscrupulous merchants have been known to "work the game" so that the careless buyer not only loses the property but is compelled to make additional payments as well. Installment sales contracts typically are long and complicated, and few people read them carefully before signing. With known reputable dealers, the buyer may not suffer. But, in many instances, such careless consumers are asking for trouble.

Installment buying also tends to be expensive. Since the passage of the Consumer Credit Protection Act of 1968, installment sales outlets are required to state clearly and specifically the various finance charges. There is no limit, however, on the amount they can charge. Interest in installment plans tends to be higher than can be arranged by borrowing the money directly. It may be further inflated by such devices as requiring the purchase of credit life insurance.

Borrowing Money

It is often cheaper to borrow money directly than it is to get it indirectly through installment contracts or credit. The costs and risks of direct borrowing vary with the source of the loan.

One of the cheapest ways to borrow is on life insurance. After a few years of premium payments, most insurance policies have a "cash value" or "loan value." This amount may be borrowed in part or in full at only five or six percent interest; repayment terms can be arranged to suit the borrower. In a pinch, the loan does not need to be repaid at all. If the borrower dies while all or part of the loan is outstanding, that amount is deducted from the amount collected by the beneficiary. The loss of some insurance coverage is the greatest risk in borrowing on life insurance.

Most commercial banks have personal loan departments that make loans at an average of 12- to 14-percent interest. Rates for unsecured loans or loans on a revolving credit basis may run higher. The banks can make such loans because they make sure that their clients are good credit risks, and the money that they lend is their own depositors' money, upon which they pay correspondingly lower interest rates.

Credit unions, which are cooperative savings associations, are another good source of funds. Some 24 million people in the United States are members of them. As soon as one joins, one becomes eligible to borrow up to $2500 or more at interest rates that range downward from 12 percent. Credit unions can offer low rates because they have little in the way of overhead expenses and because there is minimal risk involved in lending to their own members.

There are people who either don't have life insurance or who don't want to borrow on it, or who fear that they are not good enough credit risks for commercial banks. They are the chief patrons of consumer finance companies, the so-called small loan companies. Some consumer finance companies operate nationally and are quite reputable. Because they make unsecured loans and lend to people who are poor credit risks, however, they are permitted to charge very high interest rates. This high interest is partially concealed by advertising it on a monthly basis, usually about two-and-a-half to three percent. This figures out, of course, to a frightening 30 to 36 percent a year.

Some consumer finance companies make larger, secured loans, and on these they may charge lower interest rates. Their interest rates are almost always higher than those available at commercial banks, however. Use of a consumer finance company almost always signals poor financial planning or a financial situation bordering on the desperate. If this is true of the larger, reputable small loan companies, it goes without saying that companies that solicit loans by mail should be avoided at all cost.

BUYING LIFE INSURANCE

Most people begin to think about buying life insurance about the time they marry. They recognize that providing as much income protection as possible for their dependents is a part of adult responsibility.

Some people also look upon life insurance as a form of saving or investment. They are encouraged in this belief by insurance agents, who earn larger commissions on the more expensive, savings-oriented policies. The dollars that most people can invest in insurance, however, are quite limited. Most people can get both more insurance protection and more efficient savings by keeping their goals quite separate: protection against loss of income on the one hand and investment on the other.

In deciding how much and what kind of insurance to buy, couples need to assess a variety of factors: their ages, the number and ages of their children, their present and estimated future incomes, and their debts. Ideally, the proceeds from insurance should be adequate to pay off the deceased partner's debts, to cover burial expenses, and to provide income support for the surviving spouse, who will be faced with everything from child care expenses to the cost of college educations.

Obviously, people should get the most protection possible for their insurance dollars. To do so, they will need to make choices among several general types of policies.

Term Insurance

Some term insurance, under the label of *group insurance,* commonly is available to people from their employers. Group insurance is written upon large numbers of employees, and generally without medical examination. It affords more protection per premium dollar than any other kind of insurance. Such insurance is available only in fixed dollar amounts, however, and it must be dropped or converted to some other type of insurance upon leaving the particular employer. While it will not be adequate to meet most couples' total insurance needs, group insurance is almost always too good a buy to pass up.

Regular *term insurance* is just like automobile insurance in that it is written for a specified length of time, such as one year or ten years, for a given premium. At the end of the period, it expires. If the insured person dies during the period covered, the beneficiary receives the face value of the policy. If the insured lives, neither the insured or the beneficiary gets anything.

Term insurance is purely for protection, and there is no savings feature involved. As a result, it costs less than any other kind of insurance. Its main disadvantage is that it must be renewed at the end of each contract period at steadily increasing premium rates, because the chances of dying are greater as one grows older. Consequently, most insurance authorities recommend the following course: Young couples with small children should buy relatively large amounts of term insurance. They should reduce the amount of coverage as they grow older, combining it with a smaller amount of more permanent insurance to cover the aging years.

A useful variant on regular term insurance is the *decreasing term* policy. Such policies are written for longer periods—20 to 40 years. Premium payments over the life of the policy stay constant. The maximum protection is provided during the first years, and the amount of protection gradually decreases to zero at the end of the contract period. Again, such policies ordinarily should be held in combination with more permanent insurance.

Straight Life Insurance

Straight life or *whole life* policies involve the payment of a fixed premium for the insured's entire life. When that person dies, the beneficiary receives the face amount of the policy. If the insured lives to be 100, the face value of the policy is paid directly to the holder.

There are two principal advantages to straight life policies. First, the premium payments do not rise with increasing age. Second, such policies accumulate a "cash value," or "loan value," which may be withdrawn to meet financial emergencies. This process was described in the section on borrowing money.

The disadvantages of straight life policies also essentially are two. For young adults, whose need for protection is greatest, they are about twice as expensive as term insurance. Second, they are poor investments, especially in an inflationary economy. The dollars received when a claim is settled many years later are likely to have much less purchasing power than did the dollars paid in.

Limited Payment Policies

A variation of straight life insurance is the *limited payment* policy. In these plans, the premiums are paid over a limited period—20 or 30 years, or by age 65, for example—rather than over the insured's entire lifetime. The annual premiums in these policies are even higher than those in straight life policies of the same face value. As a result, they are even more difficult for most young people to afford. They probably are useful only to people whose incomes are highest during the young adult years, such as entertainers or professional athletes, or to people whose incomes after age 65 are likely to be too low to permit them to continue paying premiums.

**Endowment
Policies**

Endowment policies emphasize savings more than protection. The insured pays premiums for a prescribed period, just as is done under limited payment policies. In the event of the holder's death during that period, the face value of the policy is paid. But if the insured person outlives the premium payment period, he or she is paid the face value of the policy directly. Such policies have great appeal for many people, because they feel it is the only way that they, personally, can profit from carrying life insurance. What they ignore, of course, is that if they collect on the policy themselves, they leave their survivors without that insurance protection.

Per dollar of protection, endowment policies are the most expensive of all and thus are poor buys for young people with limited incomes. Using them for savings purposes may mean leaving one's family with inadequate protection. Moreover, compared to some other kinds of investments, the rate of return on endowment policies is quite low and subject to erosion through inflation.

INVESTMENTS AND TAX PLANNING

Most people recognize the need to include savings as one aspect of their financial planning and budgeting. Money placed systematically in a savings account provides protection in case of emergency. It also permits the eventual purchase of large items, such as automobiles and furniture, without incurring finance charges, or at least without having them exceed reasonable limits.

Few couples can save much money in the early years of marriage. One of the best ways to do so is to make a modest down payment on a house or apartment, and thus to begin building equity in a home. Over the years, this equity usually becomes substantial. It is also important, however, to begin a program of systematic investment as early as possible.

Investment differs from saving in being oriented toward capital growth rather than simply capital accumulation. The principle is that money breeds money through the provision of interest and dividends. Take as an example even one of the most conservative investment situations: putting one's money into a savings bank. At six percent interest, a monthly investment of $100 will, through compound interest, multiply to such an extent that after just 12 years, $100 can then be withdrawn from the account each month forever without the principal's ever being touched.

The basic trick in this example, of course, is to establish a program of monthly savings and continue it. Actually, this scheme is not quite as good as it sounds because, over the 12-year period, inflation is likely to reduce the purchasing power of the $100 considerably. To ensure maximum rewards, there are three major factors that should be considered in determining how to invest money. They are growth, yield, and safety.

Growth refers to the degree to which the value of the assets keeps pace with, or exceeds, the growth of the economy. Assets that are fixed in value, such as bonds and insurance policies, do not grow at all; common stocks and other forms of securities may have the potential for very rapid growth. *Yield* refers essentially to the effective interest rate paid on the assets. Frequently, these two characteristics of investments stand in reciprocal relationship to one another. That is, investments with high growth potential often provide low current income, and vice versa. *Safety,* of course, refers to the protection against losing all or part of one's original investment. Unfortunately, safer investments frequently offer both low yields and little growth potential.

There is no magic way of finding investments that optimize these three criteria. Financial advisers often recommend dividing one's investments, with some money to be kept in savings accounts where it will be safe (insured), available, and drawing moderate interest. Certificates of deposit, which tie up the money for periods of time, provide somewhat higher interest without any sacrifice of safety and little loss of availability.

Some money should also be invested in assets such as common stocks or real estate, in which large gains in value are possible. For people who lack the time or inclination to learn the workings of the stock market, mutual funds or investment companies permit purchasing shares of professionally selected and managed portfolios. Real estate investments can be of the "mom-and-pop" variety, in which one buys a house or two in addition to one's own dwelling, or they can be large-scale, such as the purchase of an apartment complex or of open land destined for residential development.

An important word of caution here: investments that promise capital growth can also produce capital losses. Although the long-term trend in the economy is inflationary, there are deflationary periods in which the unwise investor, or the one who is stretched too thin, may lose heavily. There also are always unscrupulous "investment counselors," who are only too ready to part the uninformed investor from his or her money.

Given the complexities and the hazards of investing, one of the things that makes investment attractive is the favorable treatment that investment income is accorded under the federal income tax laws. The breaks start with home ownership. Home owners are permitted to deduct both the cost of interest payments on their mortgages and their real estate taxes as expenses on their income tax forms. This provision often affords them deductions larger than the standard deduction. Further tax savings can be realized by bunching tax and interest payments in alternate years: paying them in January for the preceding year and again in December for the current year. In the "bunching" year one itemizes deductions, and in the alternate year one uses the standard deduction.

For those who invest in rental property, the same advantages accrue. And, in addition, expenses of operating and maintaining the property can be deducted from the rental income. A further major advantage is that "depreciation" of the property can also be charged as an expense. If one sells the property later at more than its "depreciated" value, one pays only capital gains tax rates on the difference; these rates are usually lower than straight income tax rates.

Favorable tax treatment also is accorded to securities income. The first $100 in dividend income ($200 for a married couple) is exempt from income tax, and the remainder is taxed at the lower capital gains rates. When stocks are held for more than six months (as they almost always are) and then sold at a profit, the lower capital gains tax rates also apply to the profit.

For those investors who get into the higher tax brackets, 33 percent to 50 percent or more, municipal bonds issued by governmental agencies are a valuable investment. Such bonds have their interest exempted from income tax altogether. Thus, a person in the 50-percent bracket who buys five percent municipal bonds receives an effective interest rate of ten percent.

As surely must be apparent, the issues of managing and investing money wisely are many and complex. One chapter cannot begin to do them justice. It is to be hoped that this discussion has created an awareness of some of the more basic issues and problems. For further information, we recommend either taking a course in personal and family finance or studying a good textbook on the subject, such as Cohen and Hanson or Troelstrup. More details will be found in the reading list at the end of this chapter.

THE COMMUNAL ALTERNATIVE

The counter cultural wave of the late 1960s and early 1970s rejected the goal of financial affluence and emphasized ''natural'' living. It also encouraged some people to try communal living as an alternative to the other forms of adjustment already described in this chapter. We have enough knowledge by now of commune living to permit some comments on this pattern.

The ideal of most communes is to become self-sufficient economic units, with members of both sexes performing productive work within the commune itself. Private property generally is disallowed; instead, the possessions and income of all members are pooled for collective use. In practice, this system seldom works well. Communes teach that work should be enjoyed and integrated into the larger rhythm of life, but this principle does not ensure that the work will be done. As one investigator put it, ''Canning may be bucolic fun, but it requires lots of hard work. Meanwhile the cellar is full of rotting vegetables.'' (Pitts, 1973)

Very few communes have adequate financial bases. They usually depend upon a variety of outside sources for support. Some members receive checks from their parents. Divorced women often contribute alimony and child support payments. Dependence on food stamps and surplus commodities is also common. Occasionally a wealthy benefactor provides support.

Whatever the details, most communes exist in poverty or on the edge of it. At first, and when everyone is healthy, their communal ideals protect the members against the stark realities of deprivation. But when accumulated capital runs out, clothes wear out, winter comes, and the children (or adults) become ill, the lack of money often becomes an overwhelming problem (Kephart, 1974).

Few communes last very long, and the tenure of most individual members within them is even shorter. Sooner or later, virtually all commune members return to face the problems of financial adjustment with which most of this chapter has dealt.

SUMMARY

Financial adjustment problems vary over the life cycle. Young married couples generally must start almost from scratch and purchase virtually everything required to run a household. On one income, this is difficult; on two incomes it is easier. Pregnancy and childbirth cause additional expenses and often restrict the wife's income, at least for a while. Expenses mount as the children grow up; fortunately, income often increases at the same time. With the departure of children, expenses are reduced markedly while income often remains high. These are years when systematic investment often is possible. Retirement and old age bring reduced income. How well people live in the retirement years often is determined by how well they managed earlier.

Up to a minimum point (which is difficult to locate precisely), the amount of one's income may be very closely linked to marital happiness. Beyond that critical income level, absolute size of income is less significant, and financial values and financial management become paramount.

Financial values include the earning roles of the two marital partners; they also include their choice of careers, because jobs have a controlling influence on their life style. At professional and managerial levels, the demands of the job on one's life style may be very great. Promotions frequently require moving the family over long distances, disrupting the other partner's job, and so on. Moreover, the expectations of one's colleagues may closely limit the family's consumption patterns.

Financial values are also important at the personal level. Some couples are "savers" and some couples are "spenders." Either pattern, within limits, can work. When the husband and wife differ in their basic attitudes toward money and spending, however, major adjustments may be necessary.

Many people confuse financial planning and budgeting with detailed bookkeeping. But a budget need be no more than a flexible plan that establishes priorities and helps people get the most for their money. Housing is a major budget item, and the nature of the need for it frequently changes over the life cycle. A major decision is whether to rent or buy, and there are advantages and disadvantages both ways.

Virtually everyone uses credit, and many people are tempted to use it unwisely. Charge accounts and credit cards can be used to excellent advantage if one avoids being lured into time payments and the high interest that they entail. Installment purchases tend to be still more costly, and most people would be well advised to borrow the money directly instead.

Loans on life insurance policies are easily secured, carry low interest rates, and do not even have to be repaid. The disadvantage is that such borrowing reduces the amount of one's insurance coverage. Credit unions and commercial banks also make personal loans at fairly reasonable costs. Consumer finance companies generally should be avoided because of their excessively high interest charges.

Particularly as children are born, people need life insurance protection. Group and term insurance plans generally afford the best buys and may be combined with some straight life insurance to provide long-term protection. Limited payment policies are appropriate in some special circumstances, and endowment policies should be looked upon more as investments than as protection.

Investment is aimed at the growth of capital, through the principle of compound interest. The qualities of growth, yield, and safety are desirable ones in investments, and some balance among the three is usually desirable. The income-tax advantages afforded by investments also are a major consideration.

Although some people opt temporarily for a communal life style, which denies the need for financial planning, it is almost never a permanent solution.

FOR ADDITIONAL READING

Cohen, Jerome B., and Arthur W. Hanson, *Personal Finance: Principles and Case Problems* (Homewood, Ill.: Richard D. Irwin, 1972). A highly recommended, detailed treatment of the areas covered in this chapter.

Hill, Reuben, et al., *Family Development in Three Generations* (Cambridge, Mass.: Schenkman, 1970). Report of long-range research, emphasizing family consumption patterns.

Landis, Judson T., and Mary G. Landis, *Building a Successful Marriage* (Englewood Cliffs, N.J.: Prentice-Hall, 1973). See the chapter on buying life insurance.

Seidenberg, Robert, *Corporate Wives—Corporate Casualties?* (New York: Doubleday, 1975). A perceptive psychiatrist's analysis of the strains the modern corporate system imposes upon wives.

Smith, Carlton, and Richard P. Pratt, *The Time–Life Book of Family Finance* (New York: Time–Life Books, 1969). A recommended supplement to this chapter.

Troelstrup, Arch W., *The Consumer in American Society: Personal and Family Finance* (New York: McGraw-Hill, 1970). A basic textbook on financial planning.

STUDY
QUESTIONS

1. Do all couples experience the same stages in the financial family life cycle? See how many variations you can describe.

2. In families you know, do you think there is an association between amount of income and happiness? Why or why not?

3. What does the phrase "financial life style" mean to you? Describe the financial life styles of families you know. What style do you want for yourself?

4. What role did budgeting play in the family in which you grew up? How do you expect to use it in your own life?

5. Which pattern do you believe to be wiser and more satisfying in the long run, buying a home or renting? Why?

6. How can people assure themselves that they will use credit wisely? Does direct borrowing fit into the picture? How?

7. What kind of life insurance program would you recommend for a childless couple when both partners work? For a similar couple who have two children?

8. How does investment differ from savings? What combination of investments would you like to build for yourself? Justify the total package and the individual investments that compose it.

Chapter 11
Family Planning

Lapel buttons and bumper stickers reading "None Is Fun" and "Stop at Two" symbolize a rapidly spreading attitude in the United States. Increasing numbers of people have come to favor limiting childbearing. There are few areas in which recent years have seen more rapid change.

For the first time on a national scale, people are arguing that having children is not necessarily a good thing. At the collective level, they point out that our growing population already is despoiling the natural environment and exhausting scarce resources. At the individual level, they are asking a formerly heretical question: whether having children contributes to happiness and personal growth, or whether it induces frustration, financial hardship, and deterioration of the marital relationship.

THE DEMOGRAPHIC BACKGROUND

The emphasis in this book is on personal adjustment patterns more than on broad social trends. The two are often closely linked, however. In this case, we can tell much about the decisions of individual couples to have children or not to have them by looking at changes in birth rates and childbearing expectations.

*THE NEW LOW
FERTILITY PATTERN*

For about the last 20 years, the U.S. birth rate has been dropping irregularly. New birth control technology is obviously a major factor, but it is not the whole story. The birth rate first started down in 1957, and the birth-control pill was not introduced commercially until 1960.

The drop in the birth rate was slow at first, but it accelerated in the last half of the 1960s. By 1970 there were over three million *fewer* preschool children in the United States than there had been in 1960 (Grier, 1971). In 1972, the American fertility rate dropped below the replacement level for the first time. This figure is defined as the birth rate which, if continued, would lead eventually to zero population growth. It is currently calculated at 2.10 children per family. (It is slightly above 2.0 because some people do not marry or have children.)

What lies behind these figures is a virtual revolution in our attitudes toward childbearing, supported by a vastly improved birth control technology. In the not very distant past, there was simply no way a married woman could plan to remain childless. She could not even avoid having unwanted births; birth control methods simply were not that reliable. Women were forced to organize their role expectations around motherhood.

The desire to limit childbearing was there, however. The development of the pill encouraged for the first time the hope that birth control could be 100-percent effective. It also meant that sexual intercourse could be kept separate from considerations of childbearing. The pill was the chief instrument in bringing about the revolution, but it also stimulated the use of other birth control methods, particularly the intrauterine device. It also helped to popularize sterilization and abortion as birth control techniques (Bumpass, 1973).

*CHILDBEARING
EXPECTATIONS*

The development of greater confidence in birth control measures has been accompanied by a decrease in the number of children that women say they want and expect to have. The trend from 1967 through 1974 is shown in Table 11-1. By 1974, 58 percent of married women between the ages of 18 and 39 said that they expected to have no more than two children. Seventeen percent of the youngest women, ages 18 to 19, said that they expected either to remain childless or to have only one child.[1]

Although it is hard to show by research, the drop in the number of children desired or expected appears to be related to women's redefinition of their marital roles. In Chapter 7 we saw that most young women say they want occupational careers, marriage, and children. But those data did not relate work plans to the number of children desired. Some researchers have argued that such a relationship exists (Scanzoni,

[1] *Family Planning Perspectives* 7 (Jan.–Feb. 1975), p. 5.

YEAR OF STUDY	AVERAGE NUMBER OF CHILDREN EXPECTED
1967	3.1
1973	2.6
1974	2.5

Source: U.S. Bureau of the Census, "Prospects for American Fertility: June 1974," Series P-20, No. 269, Sept. 1974 (Washington, D.C.: U.S. Government Printing Office).

**TABLE 11-1
NUMBER OF CHILDREN
EXPECTED BY MARRIED
WOMEN, 18–39 YEARS OLD**

1972). One still unpublished long-term study of 15,000 women college graduates reported that women with high career commitments want fewer children than those with low career commitments do (Rossi, 1970).

CHILDREN AND MARITAL ADJUSTMENT

Researchers have been fascinated for decades by the problem of possible relationships between the success of a couple's marriage and the number of children they have. Early studies, up until about 1960, generally showed either no relationship or a negative one. That is, the parents of more than three or four children often reported that they wished they had not had so many and said that children were a problem to them.

Then, during the 1960s and 1970s, a number of studies showed that the actual number of children was not the most important factor in marital happiness. What mattered even more was the agreement between the number of children desired and the number of children people actually had. Couples who wanted large families, and had them, tended to report themselves as happy and satisfied. People with small families also were happy if they had desired few children. The unhappiest couples were those who had more children than they wanted (Figley, 1973; Heath, Roper and King, 1974; and Nye, Carlson and Garrett, 1970).

Other studies have shown that children are a source of deep satisfaction in many marriages, but that they also often interfere with marital adjustment. One study of 38 highly satisfied couples and 34 unsatisfied couples after at least 13 years of marriage, for example, reported that more than 85 percent of the husbands and wives of both groups regarded their children as one of their greatest sources of satisfaction. The generally happy couples reported satisfaction with the companionship aspects of their marriages also; the unhappy couples said that their children were their only major sources of satisfaction (Luckey and Bain, 1970).

A second study queried 112 couples in the Washington, D.C. area after they had been married three or four months, and again one to two years later, to determine the impact of childbearing on their marital relationships. The only significant finding was that the wives with children felt that their husbands paid too little attention to them (Ryder, 1973).

CHILDLESS MARRIAGES

Only about five percent of married couples remain voluntarily childless. Until recently, this five percent tended to be defined as deviant—abnormal, self-centered, or immature. Now, however, research indicates that the childless state may not be all that bad. Couples who are deliberately childless are organizing to promote what they believe to be a superior way of life, at least for some people.

CHILDLESSNESS AND MARITAL HAPPINESS

A major study of 5163 persons in California sought to discover sources of dissatisfaction in marriage. It reported that childless marriages produce more satisfaction than those with children. Moreover, the couples *currently* raising children reported the least satisfaction of all (Renne, 1970). Since this study was of currently married persons, we should not leap to the conclusion that childless marriages are happier than those with children. In fact, it is known that childless marriages are more likely to end in divorce. The conclusion that legitimately may be drawn from this study is that the partners in *surviving* childless marriages report more marital happiness.

Although she acknowledges that childless marriages are more divorce-prone, one noted scholar again emphasizes that surviving childless marriages are happier than those with children (Bernard, 1972). She bases her conclusion on the findings of a nationwide study that examined a representative sample of the population. It found that childless husbands and wives viewed marriage as less restrictive, and presenting fewer problems, than did husbands and wives with children (Veroff and Feld, 1970).

These statistical studies all are comparisons of childless marriages with those having children. Unfortunately, they have not yet been supplemented by much study of the actual workings of childless marriages. Preliminary data from one promising study have been published, however.

DECIDING TO BE CHILDLESS

A study done in Toronto and London, Ontario, involved in-depth interviews with 52 voluntarily childless wives (Veevers, 1973). All of the wives had been married for at least five years, and all of them were now past childbearing age, either having been sterilized for contraceptive purposes or having reached menopause. These women were classified into two groups: those who had decided even before marriage not to have children, and those who had drifted into childlessness as a result of a series of decisions to postpone having children. The researcher tells us little about the first group but elaborates upon the second.

Most of the second group of couples moved through four stages. First, they decided to postpone parenthood for a definite period of time; at this stage, they did not appear to differ from other newly married couples. Next, however, they shifted to an indefinite period of postponement: until they "could afford it," or they "felt ready" for it. In the third stage, their emphasis shifted to the positive advantages of remaining childless: more money, more opportunities, fewer restrictions. Now the couples confronted openly the possibility of remaining permanently childless. The fourth stage consisted of making the explicit and irreversible decision not to have children.

The researcher portrays these wives as being not without doubts and conflicts. All of the wives reported being somewhat stigmatized; they often had to justify their situations to other family members and to outsiders. They cope with these pressures well, however, by depending upon the support of their husbands, who are also actively committed to a childless way of life. Many of the wives have given some thought, apparently as a way of hedging their bets, to the possibility of adoption should they one day decide they want children. All in all, one gains the impression of a group of wives relatively satisfied with their own situations, but under some presure from a generally disapproving society.

There is another group of married couples who believe childlessness is a superior way of life and who actively promote it as a philosophical ideal. They seek such a life style for themselves, and although they do not necessarily seek to convert others to their beliefs, they do question the automatic assumption that people must have children. They argue that parenthood should be the result of a very carefully considered decision, weighing all of the advantages and disadvantages.

**DEDICATED
NON-PARENTS**

It is impossible to tell how many such dedicated childless couples exist at present. Some of them got together in 1971 to found a national organization called the National Organization for Non-Parents (NON). Within a year or so, NON had acquired about 600 members; about one-fourth of those members were people who have children. NON publishes a bimonthly newsletter,[2] and its stated goal is to promote "the emergence of childfree life styles in the hope of achieving a more spacious and humane world for themselves and the children of tomorrow."

NON members contrast the advantages of their life style with what they believe to be the disadvantages of parenthood. Without children, they say, they have more free time and more money. They can devote themselves to one another more fully and avoid the loss of sexuality and love-making that so often accompanies having children. They are free to continue their educations, to travel, and to continue the process of self-development. These advantages are contrasted to the financial costs of parenthood and the accompanying strains on the marital relationship.

[2] *NON,* 8 Sudbrook Lane, Baltimore, MD 21208.

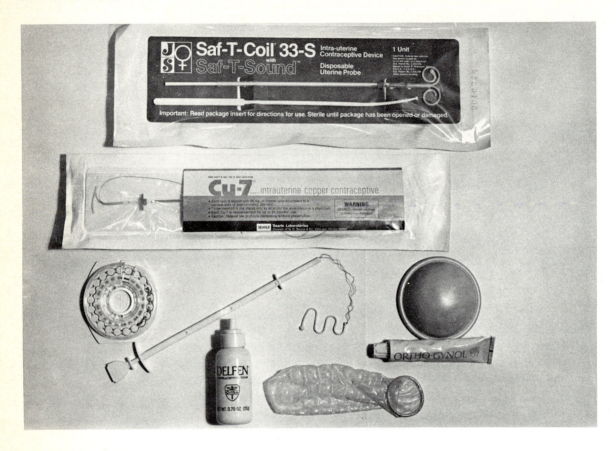

NON members, in short, have decided that they don't want to spend at least 20 years of their lives in a child-oriented existence (Katz, 1975).

Contraceptives do not take sides in the issue of whether people should have children or not. Properly used, they permit couples to remain childless if they wish to do so. Contraception also serves those who simply wish to delay childbearing and those who want to space the births of their children. Finally, one type of contraceptive—the pill—can even be used for a while to create a rebound effect and increase the likelihood that infertile couples will be able to produce a child.

A large number of contraceptive methods and techniques are available, and the development of new ones has been changing the situation rapidly. By the mid-1970s the most popular methods had come to be the pill and the intrauterine device (IUD). But several older methods also are still in common use.

THE PILL

Although it was not marketed commercially until 1960, some ten million American women currently use the pill—more than use any other contraceptive method. Actually, there are several brands of "the pill," marketed by different pharmaceutical companies and employing slightly different principles. But all of them use combinations of the female sex hormone, estrogen, and a synthetic version of the pregnancy hormone, progesterone.

So-called "combination" pills contain both hormones. They are taken one each day for 21 days, beginning with the fifth day after the start of the menstrual flow. Three or four days after the last pill is taken, menstruation occurs again and the whole cycle starts over.

The "sequential" method employs two different kinds of pills. For the first 15 days of each cycle, the pills contain estrogen only. The next five pills contain both estrogen and progesterone. Manufacturers of the sequential pills admit that they are slightly less effective than the combination pills, but claim that they more closely approximate the natural hormonal cycle of the female body. The biggest disadvantage of the sequential pills is the mounting evidence that they may encourage uterine cancer, particularly in younger women. Efforts are underway to withdraw the sequential pills from the market. They should be used only with informed medical advice.

Currently, the most popular system is one that provides a pill for each day of a full four-week cycle. A combination pill is taken for the first 21 days. The pills for the fourth week contain only inert ingredients or supplementary iron. During that week, a menstrual-like bleeding occurs; then the cycle starts over again. This system has the advantage of providing a pill for every day, so the woman is spared the trouble of stopping and remembering when to start again (Connell, 1975).

The pill must be prescribed by a physician, who should select the most appropriate one for the particular woman and instruct her carefully in its use. Taken as prescribed, birth control pills are almost failure-free. When the woman forgets to take them regularly, however, they become very unreliable. Forgetful women who borrow pills from one another are running a strong risk of unplanned pregnancy.

The birth control pill works by altering the hormonal functioning of the woman's body. Ever since the pill was introduced there have been recurring questions concerning its safety. The pill does have some known unfavorable side effects (as well as some favorable ones), and it simply has not been in use long enough for us to rule out completely the possibility of unrecognized long-term harmful effects. On balance, however, most scientists believe that the advantages in using the pill far outweigh the risks.

The pill has several minor, unpleasant side effects. In some women, it causes a combination of headaches, nausea, breast tenderness, and retention of body fluids. As newer pills, containing smaller quantities of chemicals, are marketed, these side effects appear to be diminishing. The side effects are troublesome enough, however, that about 20 percent of all women who try it discontinue the use of the pill within a year (Brody, 1975).

The most serious side effect is an increased tendency to develop blood clots in the legs and lungs, with the resulting possibilities of stroke or heart attack. These dangers are greatest for women over 40. The estimates are that of one million women using the pill for one year, some 13 would die of these complications. In addition, 5000 of those million women would become pregnant, and one of them would die of complications of pregnancy and childbirth. Thus, in all, 14 women would die. This figure seems very frightening until it is compared with the alternatives. If the diaphragm were used by a comparable one million women, for instance, no deaths would result directly from its use. There would be 120,000 pregnancies, however, and these pregnancies would result in 27 maternal deaths. And if these one million women used no contraception at all, there would be at least 150 deaths among them from complications of pregnancy and delivery. Thus, the risks of oral contraception are small compared to the alternatives. Still, there is some hazard in using the pill, and it should be used only under close, continuing medical supervision. Signs of possible complications should be reported to the physician immediately.

There are also some beneficial side effects from using the pill. Many users report that their menstrual cycles become more regular and that they experience less premenstrual tension and less menstrual cramping. A study of 452 women in the San Francisco area also showed that pill users have lower rates of benign breast disease than do nonusers. This apparently protective effect increases with increased duration of pill use.[3]

THE IUD

Starting from a very low rate of use during the early 1960s, the intrauterine device has now become the second most popular contraceptive in America.[4] IUDs are small metal or plastic objects of various shapes (loop, spiral, coil, ring, or bow) which are inserted by a physician through the vagina into the neck of the uterus. Once inserted, the IUD remains in place indefinitely, providing almost as secure protection against pregnancy as does the pill. It should be checked by the physician at least twice a year to make sure that it has not become dislodged and that no complications have developed.

Strangely, we don't know exactly how or why the IUD works. Probably it irritates the lining of the uterus, interfering with the implantation of the fertilized ovum. It is also possible that it may prevent conception directly by causing the ovum to move through the Fallopian tube too rapidly. But, whatever the reason, it does work, and it is relatively safe. Of one million women using the IUD for one year, two would die from

---

[3] *Family Planning Perspectives* 7 (Jan.–Feb. 1975), pp. 8–9.
[4] *Family Planning Digest* 1 (Nov. 1972), p. 10.

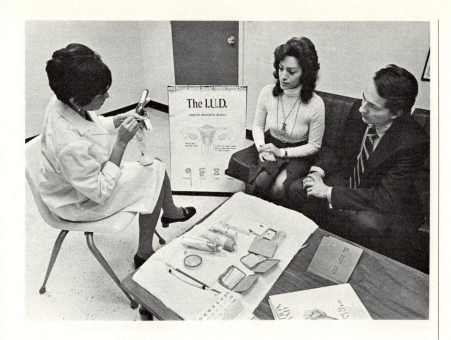

complications caused by the IUD. About 30,000 would become pregnant, and seven of them would die from complications of pregnancy and childbirth.

For many physicians who take their patients off the pill because of complications, the IUD is the alternative of choice. It is not often prescribed for women who have not borne a child, however, because it is likely to cause too much discomfort.

Like the pill, the IUD has both advantages and disadvantages. It is generally trouble-free, effective, and safe, and it does not interfere with the spontaneity of making love. On the other hand, it sometimes is expelled from the uterus without the woman's knowledge. In some women it causes pain and bleeding, and it can aggravate relatively common genital infections (Mishell, 1975). All these problems are reasons for having its use closely monitored by a competent physician.

THE CONDOM

The third most commonly used form of contraception among married people is that of the condom, also known as the sheath, or "rubber" (Westoff, 1972). It is an elastic covering that fits over the erect penis; at ejaculation, it catches the semen and prevents it from being deposited in the vagina. The condom is the only fairly reliable contraceptive used by the man rather than the woman. Used alone, it provides less secure protection than the pill or the IUD. But used in combination with a spermicidal jelly or cream, inserted by the woman into the upper vagina, it is highly effective.

The advantages of condoms are several. First, they do not require medical prescription and are widely available in drugstores or even by mail. Second, they permit shifting the responsibility for preventing conception at least partly to the man. Third, they dull the male response slightly, helping some men cope with the problem of premature ejaculation. Finally, the fact that they are used directly in connection with sexual intercourse avoids the problem of "forgetting" associated with the pill.

The condom, naturally, also has disadvantages. Since it must be placed on the erect penis, it may interfere with love-making at a crucial moment. Second, some men and some women object to it because it prevents direct contact of the penis with the vagina. Third, a condom may sometimes tear or slip off the penis following ejaculation, nullifying its protection. Finally, there is a slight chance that an imperfection in the condom will permit some sperm to pass through a small hole. This last problem can be avoided by testing the condom before use, either by blowing air into it or by filling it with water.

One final comment. Condoms today are available in a variety of shapes and colors, and with or without lubricants. They also vary widely in price. People with strong esthetic preferences may find the higher prices justifiable. All condoms in the United States are manufactured to rigid government standards, however. Price differences do not reflect differences in quality or in interference with sexual pleasure. Wise consumers can save considerable money over the years by using less expensive brands.

RHYTHM

The use of the rhythm method has declined in recent years as much as, or more than, any other system of birth control; today it is used by only about one out of every 20 couples. Its one major advantage is that its use is not forbidden by the Roman Catholic Church. Yet, even so, the National Fertility Study of 1970 showed that more than two-thirds of Catholic women are using methods other than rhythm[5] (Bouvier, 1972). A Gallup poll in March 1975 also reported that 83 percent of Roman Catholic women approve of the use of other methods of contraception.

In principle, the rhythm method is very simple. Conception can occur for only a short period following ovulation. If intercourse is avoided for a few days before and after ovulation, conception will not occur. In the so-called "normal" 28-day menstrual cycle, ovulation is believed to occur at about the mid-point of the cycle. In longer or shorter cycles it occurs about 14 days *before* the onset of the *next* menstrual flow. After keeping records of the length of several successive cycles, couples should be able to predict the approximate date of ovulation in future cycles.

[5] *Family Planning Digest* 2 (March 1973), pp. 7–8.

In practice, however, the rhythm method is not that easy. Some women have quite irregular cycles, making prediction of ovulation unreliable. Colds or other minor illnesses can disrupt the cycle temporarily. Also, sperm are capable of living in the uterus for several days, so the period of enforced abstinence from intercourse should really begin several days early and stretch out for more than a week. Add to that week the days of heavy menstrual flow, and the period when couples can have intercourse unencumbered may be reduced to half the month or less. This abstinence encourages couples to take chances and makes the use of rhythm even more unreliable.

A refinement of the rhythm method, designed to increase its reliability, requires keeping careful records of the woman's basal body temperature. In theory, her temperature remains at a fairly even level for the first part of the menstrual cycle, takes a slight drop just before ovulation, and then rises to a higher level for the post-ovulatory phase. By keeping careful track of it, the woman can determine the time of ovulation much more precisely, and the required period of abstinence can be shortened.

The temperature method is an improvement but, again, there are problems. The woman's temperature variation over the cycle may be less than one degree, and the normal daily variation is almost that great. This fact means that her temperature must be taken under carefully controlled and constant conditions: immediately upon awakening in the morning is usually best, even before rising, eating, drinking, or smoking anything. Sometimes, though, the expected temperature drop before ovulation does not appear. Also, minor illnesses, or even a late night out, may play havoc with the method.

In sum, the rhythm method is unreliable and is a great deal of trouble to its users. Except for people whose religious beliefs will not let them use any other method, it has little to recommend it (Mastroianni, 1974).

THE DIAPHRAGM

Before the introduction of the pill, the diaphragm was medically the most widely recommended contraceptive. Circular in shape and made of rubber, it is designed to be inserted into the upper vagina, blocking the entrance to the cervix. It can be inserted well in advance of anticipated sexual intercourse. It should be left in place for several hours afterward, until the slightly acid nature of the vagina, and the spermicidal jelly which is spread around the rim of the diaphragm, have immobilized the sperm. Many users of the diaphragm routinely insert it before retiring in the evening and remove it again in the morning.

Like the pill and the IUD, the diaphragm requires medical prescription. It must be fitted by a physician, who also instructs the woman in how to insert it properly. Physicians often encourage sexually inexperienced brides to use the condom and a spermicidal jelly until regular intercourse has stretched the vagina appropriately, at which time the diaphragm can be fitted. A diaphragm should also be refitted periodically, and must be refitted after the woman has a baby.

Use of the diaphragm dropped sharply during the 1960s because of the greater convenience and reliability of the pill and the IUD. Unless the woman shows consistent foresight, love play often has to be stopped while the woman goes into the bathroom to insert the diaphragm. But the most devastating blow to the popularity of the diaphragm was the research of Masters and Johnson. They discovered that the upper vagina balloons out with sexual excitement; hence, the diaphragm is not the effective barrier to sperm that it was thought to be. There still are medical situations in which use of the diaphragm is appropriate, but they are relatively few.

JELLIES, CREAMS, AND FOAMS

A variety of birth-control products are designed to immobilize the sperm. Spermicidal jellies, creams, and foams, as well as suppositories and tablets that are designed to melt in the vagina, can be purchased in any drugstore. The foams, jellies, and creams come with applicators designed to ensure good distribution of the spermicidal chemicals. In principle, they work well as long as they are inserted at least 15 minutes before intercourse. But this process often interferes with love play, and research has shown that, used by themselves, they do not provide adequate protection against conception. Most physicians recommend them for use only in combination with a diaphragm or condom. The condom and a spermicide together provide almost sure protection against pregnancy.

THE DOUCHE

According to the 1970 National Fertility Study, only about three percent of married couples depend upon douching for contraception (Westoff, 1972). The douche differs from all other contraceptive methods in being applied after sexual intercourse. The woman fills a syringe with water, perhaps adding a spermicidal agent, and uses it to flush the semen from the vagina. It is an extremely unreliable contraceptive technique, however, because no matter how soon after intercourse it is used, large numbers of sperm have moved up into the uterus where they cannot be reached.

Some women who douche do so as much under the impression that it is desirable for purposes of cleanliness as for contraception. They are encouraged in this belief by the purveyors of commercial products for "feminine hygiene," who imply that the female genitals need regular internal cleansing to keep them free of offensive odors. In normal, healthy women, this simply is not true. In fact, douches may do as much harm as good and should be used only under a physician's direction.

A very few married couples use the technique of withdrawal, which requires the man to remove the penis from the vagina just before ejaculation. This technique interferes seriously with the sexual satisfaction of both partners, which fact alone would account for its low rate of use.

Withdrawal is also very unreliable. The natural urge of the man at sexual climax is not to withdraw from the vagina, but to thrust deeply into it. Thus, many "accidents" occur, as the man delays withdrawal for just an instant too long. And even when he is very proficient in the technique, there are risks. Though the man is generally unaware of them, the few drops of fluid that are expelled from the penis before ejaculation often contain sperm.

Contraceptive technology today is highly developed. When used properly, it permits couples to avoid, delay, and plan conceptions with some precision. New contraceptive developments looming on the horizon, such as a "one-a-month" pill and male chemical contraceptives, promise to make it even more versatile. The more complex the technology becomes, however, the more important it is that it be used under careful medical supervision. The proper choice of a method at any time depends upon the particular woman, her medical history, and her sexual and reproductive experience.

WITHDRAWAL

STERILIZATION

Sterilization differs from other ways of preventing conception by being, for all practical purposes, irreversible. Couples depending upon any of the conventional contraceptive methods do so with the knowledge that they can discontinue them and have a child if they wish. Not so with those who choose sterilization. Not only can the sterilized person not have a child with the present partner, but he or she also cannot have a child with any future partner. Given the relatively early ages at which most persons seek sterilization, coupled with high divorce rates and the possibility of early widowhood, this permanence becomes an important consideration.

SALPINGECTOMY

Theoretically, either the male or the female partner may be sterilized. The operation to sterilize the female is called a *salpingectomy*. In this procedure, the physician removes a section from each of the Fallopian tubes and ties off the ends of the severed tubes so that neither the sperm nor the ova may pass through. Thereafter, the woman need not fear becoming pregnant.

The salpingectomy does not interfere with the woman's sex life in any way. Her ovaries function normally, and she ovulates and menstruates; the ovum simply cannot reach the uterus. If anything, women are likely to report that sterilization improves their sex lives by eliminating the fear of pregnancy.

There are disadvantages to the salpingectomy. The cost—an average of $500 or more—is considerable. And though technically it is possible to reconnect the Fallopian tubes *in some cases,* the practical irreversibility of the operation should not be discounted. It is little comfort to the woman seeking reversal to know the statistical probabilities of success. Moreover, the attempt to restore fertility, which carries no guarantee of success, is much more costly than the original operation.

As of today, the salpingectomy also is major surgery, involving the opening of the abdominal wall. For this reason, it usually is performed when other abdominal surgery, such as a cesarean section, is under way. Several days of hospitalization are required, and the total recovery period lasts three or four weeks.

Because of these difficulties, simpler techniques are being developed. One employs an approach through the vagina. Another experimental technique, called a *laparoscopy,* requires only a tiny incision below the navel. The laparoscope is a long, thin optical instrument that is inserted through the navel to permit the surgeon to see into the abdomen. Then, forceps carrying high-intensity radio waves are inserted through the incision to burn out sections of the Fallopian tubes. Afterward, the tiny incision is stitched and covered with a Band-Aid.

Current estimates are that at least 250,000 women in the United States are sterilized each year (Presser and Bumpass, 1972). That number appears not to be increasing significantly, however, whereas the number of men having vasectomies is increasing rapidly.

VASECTOMY

Surgical sterilization of the male, *vasectomy,* requires the physician to make only a small incision in the scrotum. The next step is to cut and tie, or cauterize (burn), sections of the tubes that carry the sperm from the testicles to the urethra. The whole procedure can be done in 15 to 20 minutes in the doctor's office, under local anesthesia, and at half the cost of a salpingectomy, or less. As in a salpingectomy, there is no interference with the person's hormonal functioning or sex life. The sperm are a microscopic component of semen and are simply absorbed into the surrounding tissues. The man must continue to use contraception for several weeks after the operation, until a microscopic examination of the semen shows that all sperm have been exhausted from the reproductive system. After that, there is no further danger of inducing pregnancy.

Much publicity has been given recently to the possibility of restoring the male's fertility after vasectomy. Estimates have been published of a 50- to 80-percent possibility of reconnecting the *vasa deferentia* successfully. Still more recently, however, it has been discovered that the male body, following vasectomy, often develops antibodies that attack and destroy the unused sperm. After the *vasa deferentia* are reconnected, these antibodies may continue to function. Thus, there is only a ten- to 25-percent chance that fertility actually will be restored (Westoff, 1974).

Sterilization as a means of contraception mushroomed in popularity between 1965 and 1970, increasing by a full 50 percent. In fact, it actually surpassed the use of the IUD. An estimated six million people in the United States have already undergone voluntary sterilization, and the number is increasing by over a million a year.

Paradoxically, many people seem to have become more dissatisfied with contraceptives even as those devices have been becoming more reliable. Many people object to the fact that conventional contraceptives are inconvenient, uncomfortable, messy, and burdened with unpleasant and possibly harmful side effects. In addition, they fear contraceptive failure—and with some reason. The 1970 National Fertility Study showed that women using the pill have had an annual contraceptive failure rate (due largely to improper use) of six percent. Those using IUD's have had a failure rate of 12 percent, and other methods ranged still higher (Ryder, 1973).

Sterilization is most popular among older couples who have already had all the children they want. Among couples in which the wife is between 30 and 44, sterilization is even more common than the use of the pill; fully one-fourth of all such couples have had one of the operations. The numbers of vasectomies and salpingectomies are about equal (Westoff, 1972).

CONTRACEPTIVE USE OF STERILIZATION

Just as there are unresolved questions about possibly harmful long-term effects of the pill, so are there unanswered questions about the effects of sterilization. Probably because salpingectomy is often associated with cesarean sections, abortions, and hysterectomies, there have been few studies of its aftereffects when used for contraceptive purposes only. What studies exist are generally of poor quality, and their findings tend to reflect the pre-existing biases of those who have conducted them. Psychiatrists tend to report profound psychological disturbances following sterilization, whereas other physicians report few and minimal complications. Now that the simplicity of laparoscopy appears to be increasing the number of female sterilizations, we badly need reliable data on this problem.

The rapidly increasing numbers of vasectomies in recent years, and the fact that most vasectomies are done specifically for contraception, have led to a series of studies that are somewhat more trustworthy than those done on women. Again, there has been a debate between psychiatrists and nonpsychiatrists over possible psychological complications. Even some of the psychiatric studies of vasectomy, however, have minimized the long-term psychological effects (Westoff, 1974). And most

SIDE EFFECTS OF STERILIZATION

of the nonpsychiatric studies have reported satisfaction with the procedure from both the husband and wife, with many couples reporting beneficial effects upon their sex lives (Freund and Davis, 1973; Roberto, 1973).

Other studies, focusing on possible physical complications, were sparked by the discovery of sperm-destroying antibodies in sterilized men. Some physicians have warned that these antibodies may contribute to the formation of blood clots and to other complications. At the same time, it has been found that not all vasectomized men develop the antibodies, and that some men have the antibodies *before* they have a vasectomy. Since vasectomy has been in use on a limited scale for at least 50 years, the chances that future research will show major complications are considered slim (Westoff, 1974).

COUNSELING FOR STERILIZATION

Because the surgery is largely irreversible, physicians have been reluctant to approve sterilization without careful counseling of the couple beforehand. In fact, up until 1969, the American College of Obstetricians and Gynecologists suggested that salpingectomies be performed only on women who were at least 25 years old with five living children, 30 years old with four living children, or 35 years old with at least three living children (Presser and Bumpass, 1972). Although these standards have now been dropped, many physicians still are hesitant to perform sterilizations before making sure that the couple have considered the potential effects on their lives of divorce, death of the spouse, or death of existing children. These risks can now be somewhat hedged if the man, before undergoing vasectomy, deposits some of his semen to be held frozen in a sperm bank (Holden, 1972).

In addition, physicians frequently attempt to make sure that the couple agree on the desirability of the sterilization, that their marital adjustment is stable, and that neither has major emotional problems that might be aggravated by the sterilization. Finally, the couple are warned about the possibility of physical complications (Uhlman, 1975).

Over the past few years, a major ethical and legal issue has emerged concerning the physician's attempt to make sure that both husband and wife agree that the surgery should be done. The doctor's interest in the solidarity of the marital unit occasionally runs head-on into the one partner's insistence upon the right to do whatever he or she wants with his or her own body, regardless of the wishes of the other partner. In a showdown, the courts are likely to support the view that each person has the right to control his or her own destiny, but judicial intervention is likely to be accompanied by bitter conflict between the partners.

ABORTION

Until a few years ago, people had little opportunity to choose whether a particular pregnancy should be aborted. The laws in most states permitted abortion only when physicians certified that continuation of the pregnancy would jeopardize the woman's life, and illegal abortions carried harsh penalties. Questions of the more general welfare of the woman and the unborn child were considered irrelevant.

Under these conditions, "abortion mills" flourished, run by incompetent physicians, quacks, and an occasional conscientious physician willing to risk prison to alleviate human suffering. Exact numbers could not be known, but estimates of the annual number of illegal abortions ranged from 250,000 to one-and-a-half million. The quality of the medical care was usually poor, and the whole experience was degrading, if not dangerous, for many women.

The first signs of change came during the 1960s. Statistics were published showing abortion-related mortality rates to be much higher in the United States than in countries with more lenient abortion laws. The pro-abortion campaign gained momentum following the thalidomide scandal, in which many horribly deformed babies were born to women who had taken the drug. Many people questioned the ethics of forcing women to go full-term when there was a high risk of appalling defects. The Rh blood factor and maternal rubella (measles) were other cases in which public awareness developed that the hazards of pregnancy often face the unborn child rather than the mother.

In the late 1960s, several states passed liberalized abortion laws, generally permitting abortions whenever continuation of the pregnancy posed a threat either to the woman or to the baby. In some cases, states eliminated the necessity to show any cause at all, so long as the abortion was performed before the fetus was mature enough to be able to live outside the woman's body. But many states held to the old laws.

Then, in January 1973, the situation was clarified significantly. The United States Supreme Court, ruling on the constitutionality of the Texas and Georgia abortion laws, held that during the first 13 weeks of pregnancy, the decision to have an abortion must be left entirely to a woman and her physician. After the first 13 weeks, the states could impose regulations on abortion "reasonably related to maternal health," and during the last three months they could forbid them altogether.[6]

In the wake of that decision, about 800,000 legal abortions were performed in 1973, and an estimated 900,000 were done in 1974. Abortion became the most common surgical procedure in the United States after tonsillectomies (Weinstock, Tietze, Jaffe, and Dryfoos, 1975). The death rate associated with these abortions has been extremely low, approximately 3.0 per 100,000.[7] Legal abortion also has reduced the number of illegitimate births substantially.[8]

[6] *Family Planning/Population Reporter* 2 (Feb. 1973), pp. 1–2.
[7] *Family Planning Perspectives* 7 (March–April 1975), p. 54.
[8] *Family Planning Perspectives* 7 (Jan.–Feb. 1975), p. 11.

Public opinion polls show that a slight majority of the U.S. population is in favor of permitting abortions during the first three months of pregnancy, but that opinion is deeply divided.[9] Men are more favorable to abortion than women are, young people are more favorable than older people, and better educated people are more favorable than those with less education. The most consistent opposition comes from Roman Catholics, a majority of whom are opposed.

The controversy over whether abortion should be permitted has resulted in a flurry of legislative activity since the Supreme Court decision of 1973. In the ensuing 21 months, 31 state legislatures enacted 57 new laws regulating abortions.[10] Although not all of these laws were aimed at getting around the Supreme Court decision, many of them are.

In addition, a group that calls itself Right to Life has been instrumental in having three constitutional amendments proposed. One would define the word "person" as used in the Fifth and Fourteenth Amendments to apply to unborn offspring at every stage of biological development. The second states that, "Neither the United States nor any state shall deprive any human being, from the moment of conception, of life without due process of law. . . ." The third proposed amendment would simply turn the whole abortion question back to the states (Pilpel, 1975).

Although we cannot predict the future, at present our reality includes the possibility of avoiding unwanted births through abortion. To be

[9] Harris Poll, April 1973; Gallup Poll, April 1974.
[10] *Family Planning/Population Reporter* 3 (Oct. 1974), p. 88.

medically safe, abortion should be done as early in the pregnancy as possible, generally before the twelfth week. Needless to say, it should also be done only by well-trained physicians working in a medical setting in which the woman has full confidence.

Some couples practice contraception only to discover, when they are ready to have a child, that they are unable to achieve a pregnancy. In other cases, the woman is unable to carry the child long enough for it to be born alive. Although we hear less about these problems than about contraception, they plague as many as ten to 15 percent of all couples.

There is no precise rule stating when medical help should be sought. But some help probably is needed if the woman does not become pregnant in a year of trying. Very often, the infertility is due to a combination of factors in both partners, so both of them must undergo careful examination.

Sperm can be studied outside the body, so attention may be concentrated first upon the man. The physician examines the contents of a complete ejaculate that the man brings to the laboratory. The total volume of semen is checked, and then a specimen is examined under the microscope to determine the number of sperm, their normality, and their mobility. Most frequently, male fertility is not an all-or-none matter; rather, it ranges from high to low. If it is determined to be low, the physician prescribes a program of treatment to increase it. If the man's fertility cannot be increased significantly, the physician may try artificial insemination, implanting the husband's semen in the woman's uterus.

If the man's fertility can be raised to satisfactory levels, attention shifts to the woman, though her role may be studied concurrently with that of the man. Generally, she is instructed to keep a temperature chart to determine if and when ovulation occurs. With that information, the couple may be instructed when to have intercourse to maximize the chances of conception. The woman's Fallopian tubes are also checked, and gas is forced through them to make sure they are open. Then, the cervix is examined to make certain that mucus is not obstructing the entry of the sperm.

Some physicians believe that emotional factors, including tension, help to produce many infertility problems. As just one possibility, they cite the presence of small sphincter muscles around the lower ends of the Fallopian tubes, which, under tension, may tend to close off the tubes. It is known that some women conceive while diagnostic studies are still under way, and before treatment begins. These cases support the likely role of emotional factors in infertility.

The most dramatic advances in recent years have occurred with the development of fertility drugs, which are used when studies show that the woman does ovulate. There are two kinds of fertility drugs: a synthetic

HELP WITH INFERTILITY

hormone-like drug that stimulates the pituitary gland, which in turn produces hormones that ripen the ovum; and a hormonal extract from the urine of postmenopausal women that stimulates the ovaries directly. Both work, but both should be used with great care.

The biggest problem with the use of fertility drugs is their tendency to produce multiple births: triplets, quadruplets, and even quintuplets. Severe medical complications often result in these cases from the fact that the babies often are born prematurely after having been too crowded in the uterus. In addition, few couples are prepared, emotionally or otherwise, to cope with four or five children born at once. Most medical experts believe that great care should be used to prevent such multiple conceptions. Some, in fact, believe that if more than three foetuses are counted, the woman should be aborted to avoid even more serious problems. Side effects, in the form of ovarian cysts, present another possible hazard. If not treated properly, they can rupture and possibly cause death.

Fertility drugs have been a boon to many childless couples. Used carefully, by physicians who are well trained in their use, they also are relatively safe. They should never be used casually, however, or without sound medical advice.

SUMMARY

The trend toward smaller families began about 20 years ago. It reflected both the desire of people to have fewer children and an improving birth control technology that made it possible to do so. Childless marriage came to be viewed, for the first time, as possibly a good thing for substantial numbers of people. Studies showed that childless marriages are somewhat more likely to end in divorce, but that surviving childless marriages often are happier than those with children.

Most couples who remain childless apparently do not plan to do so from the beginning, but rather, they gradually drift into it. First, they decide to postpone parenthood for a while. Then, the postponement becomes indefinite. Eventually, they realize that they like being childless and, finally, they make the decision to stay that way. They prefer being free to travel, study, and enjoy themselves to being tied down by child-rearing for most of their young adult lives.

Contraceptives can be used to avoid childbearing, to space the births of children, and even to increase the likelihood of conception. A large number of methods and techniques is available.

More women use the pill than any other birth control method. It is almost completely effective, but it must be prescribed by a physician and must be used carefully. Although, all things considered, it is safer than any other method, it does produce side effects serious enough to cause about one woman in five to stop using it within a year. The pill also has some beneficial side effects, such as regularizing the menstrual cycle, lessening pre-menstrual tension, and lessening the risk of benign breast disease.

The IUD has come into widespread use in recent years and is frequently prescribed for many women who cannot use the pill. Although it has some side effects, it is generally safe and effective. The condom also is in common use and, when used in combination with a spermicidal foam or cream, is quite effective. Its big disadvantage is its interference with sex play.

Because of its inherent unreliability, and the growing acceptance of mechanical contraception by many Roman Catholics, the use of the rhythm method has been declining rapidly. Although the principle underlying the method is sound enough, it is difficult to use reliably by either the calendar or the temperature method. It also interferes substantially with the couple's sex life.

Use of the diaphragm has fallen off rapidly since the introduction of the pill and in the face of research challenging its reliability. Spermicidal foams, jellies, and creams can be used reliably in conjunction with the condom, but not alone. Douching should not be used for contraceptive purposes. Withdrawal is both unreliable and frustrating.

Contraceptive sterilization is now the technique of choice among middle-aged couples, surpassing even the pill. About equal numbers of male operations (vasectomies) and female operations (salpingectomies) are performed. The biggest disadvantage is the lack of any assurance that the operations can be reversed. Surgical technique is not adequate in some cases, and sperm-destroying antibodies persist in others.

The U.S. Supreme Court ruled in 1973 that a state cannot interfere with a woman's right to abort a pregnancy during the first 13 weeks. Abortion thus became available as a means of avoiding unwanted births. Although a majority of people support the policy, many remain deeply opposed to it and controversy rages.

Medical assistance permits about half of the ten to 15 percent of all couples with fertility problems to produce a child. In cases in which the woman does not ovulate, new fertility drugs have been very helpful. They must be managed very carefully, however, to prevent unwanted multiple births.

FOR
ADDITIONAL
READING

Crawley, Lawrence, *et al., Reproduction, Sex, and Preparation for Marriage* (Englewood Cliffs, N.J.: Prentice-Hall, 1973). Contains a detailed treatment of sex, family planning, and reproduction.

McCary, James L., *Freedom and Growth in Marriage* (Santa Barbara, Cal.: Hamilton, 1975). See the chapters on "Adjustment in Marriage" and "Becoming Parents."

Sarvis, Betty, and Hyman Rodman, *The Abortion Controversy* (New York: Columbia University Press, 1973). A sane and comprehensive analysis of an explosive topic.

Wells, J. Gipson, ed., *Current Issues in Marriage and the Family* (New York: Macmillan, 1975). Excellent articles on whether to have children or not.

Yankelovich, Daniel, *The New Morality: A Profile of American Youth in the 70's* (New York: McGraw-Hill, 1974). Presents recent data on attitudes toward having children. An up-to-date supplement to this chapter.

STUDY
QUESTIONS

1. Birth rates started dropping before the pill was introduced. Keeping this fact in mind, what do you think is the relationship between today's small families and the availability of modern contraception?

2. What statistical relationships exist between number of children, number of children desired, and marital happiness?

3. Are all of the marriages that remain childless alike? What differences exist? What are your own views on the matter?

4. Evaluate each of the major types of contraception available. Consider safety, reliability, side effects, and esthetics. What advice would you give to couples contemplating the use of contraception?

5. Describe the male and female sterilization operations. In what situations is each likely to be performed? Consider the couple's ages, financial circumstances, medical histories, and family size.

6. How many people in the United States use sterilization for contraceptive purposes? Who are these people? What complications may they encounter?

7. What is the current status of abortion legislation in the United States? What factors should be considered by a couple who contemplate using abortion to prevent an unwanted birth?

8. How do physicians go about helping couples with an infertility problem? Under what conditions are fertility drugs helpful?

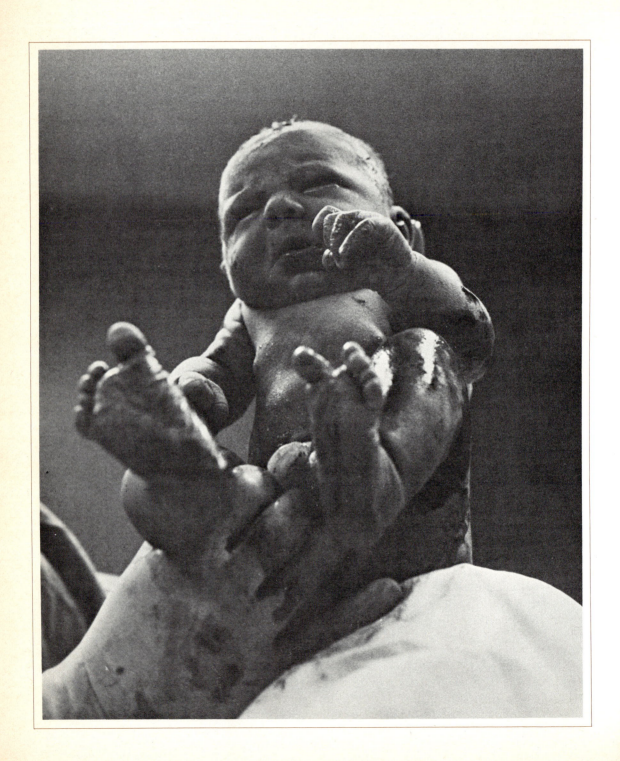

Chapter 12
Having Children

Surprisingly to many of their elders, a majority of young people today reject the idea that childbearing is a moral obligation. At the same time, however, about three-fourths of them look forward to having children as a personal choice, believing that a fulfilling marital partnership provides a sound basis for rearing children in an environment of love and affection (Yankelovich, 1974). They use family planning to limit and space their children and to provide a healthy child-rearing climate.

PREGNANCY

The usual first sign of pregnancy is a missed menstrual period. This indication is not wholly reliable, of course, because many emotional and physical conditions can delay a woman's period. Sometimes, they can even cause her to miss one altogether. With the missing of a period, however, couples begin to look for other signs of pregnancy.

DIAGNOSIS OF PREGNANCY

In some women, "morning sickness," a tendency to nausea particularly upon awakening, develops almost immediately after conception. But in other women, it doesn't appear at all. A tendency for the breasts to swell and to become more sensitive to the touch is another presumptive sign of pregnancy. Increased frequency of urination still another.

Some combination of these signs typically sends the woman to her doctor to confirm her suspicion that she is pregnant. If there is a strong need to know for sure, the physician may perform one or more pregnancy tests when the woman's period is at least ten days late. The tests depend upon the build-up of hormones in the pregnant woman's body, so the longer the tests are delayed, the more accurate are the results. A combination of tests provides results of between 95- and 98-percent reliability.

Two kinds of tests are in common use today. One that can be performed in minutes involves the examination of a specimen of the woman's urine, mixed with testing agents, under a microscope. Slower, but more reliable, is a second procedure that requires mixing the urine specimen with testing agents in a test tube and waiting for precipitation to occur. This test takes about two hours. If there is enough need to perform one of the tests, it is generally recommended to do both, to guard against the possibility of error.

In most circumstances, the tests are not really required, and the physician uses the same presumptive signs to test for pregnancy that the woman herself uses, supplemented by a pelvic examination. From discernible changes in the condition of the cervix, the physician confirms that the woman is pregnant and plans with her for both the management of the pregnancy and the birth.

PREDICTING THE DATE OF BIRTH

One of the first things the prospective parents usually want to know is when they may expect their baby. Technically, pregnancy lasts for about 266 days. In practice, there is a very simple rule of thumb for predicting when the baby is due. The woman begins with the date on which her last menstrual flow began, adds one week, and subtracts three months. This formula gives the approximate date in the following year when the baby will be due. Not all babies are that punctual, of course, and the baby may be born either before or after the expected date.

THE FIRST TRIMESTER

For convenience, analysis of pregnancy usually is done by *trimesters,* or by thirds. The first trimester lasts from the moment of conception until the end of the third month.

The first thing the physician does is to take a complete medical history, if he doesn't already have it, to determine whether any special management of the pregnancy will be necessary. Weight gain and adequate nutrition are two prime considerations. If the woman is already too heavy, the physician may want her to gain no weight at all during the pregnancy. Since, eventually, the baby and the placenta combined will weigh about 15 pounds, holding her present weight would mean an actual weight loss during the pregnancy. If, on the other hand, the woman is too thin, the physician may want her to gain more than the usual 15 pounds, so that she will be heavier after the birth. In either case, he is likely to provide guidelines, at least, for a nutritious diet.

About one pregnant woman in five experiences some light menstrual-type bleeding, called ''spotting,'' during the first trimester. The physician usually takes spotting as a sign of possible impending spontaneous abortion and decides whether to restrict the woman's activity in order to minimize its likelihood. There may be no curtailment at all, or there may be restrictions ranging all the way to complete bed rest, depending upon the woman's general medical condition, her past reproductive history, and specific signs in this situation.

Unless there is spotting, no limits are likely to be placed upon the couple's sexual activity. A full, healthy sex life is quite compatible with pregnancy. The partners need to be quite conscious of their adjustment during this period, however, because it may change, for either the better or the worse.

Pregnancy may well interfere somewhat with sexual activity initially. If the woman is bothered by nausea, she may just not feel like making love. Many women also experience considerable fatigue and drowsiness during the first trimester, causing them to be temporarily less interested in sex. If the husband interprets these reactions as rejection, he may be hurt and become hostile. On the other hand, where deep affection is present, an increased tenderness and consideration for the partner may develop; this feeling may suffuse the couple's sex life as well as all their other interaction. Not all women are plagued with nausea and fatigue, and their sex lives during this period may reach new levels of passion.

The physician will also check the woman's Rh blood type. About one person in six is Rh-negative; the rest are Rh-positive. Complications can occur if the woman is Rh-negative and the baby's father is Rh-positive, in which case, the woman may be carrying an Rh-positive baby. The reason for caution is that there may be some very slight mingling of the baby's blood with the mother's. This exposure causes the mother's blood to develop antibodies against the alien blood group. If these antibodies then get back into the baby's bloodstream, they may cause a severe or even fatal anemia.

Unless the woman has had a blood transfusion or has been pregnant with an Rh-positive baby before, there is little risk; the danger increases, however, with each succeeding pregnancy. Fortunately, the physician can now make tests to determine whether the antibodies are present in the mother's blood and in what quantities, and a vaccine that neutralizes them can be administered. In extreme cases, the physician can be prepared to transfuse the baby's blood at birth to prevent damage. These tests and precautions extend into the second and third trimesters of pregnancy.

During the first two weeks of life, the fertilized ovum is called a *zygote.* For the next six weeks, it is called an *embryo,* and from the end of the eighth week until birth, it is a *fetus.* Development during the first trimester, which embraces the zygotic and embryonic stages and part of the fetal period, is complex.

It takes about two weeks for the fertilized ovum to travel through the Fallopian tube and to become firmly embedded in the uterine wall. Tiny blood vessels then gradually extend from the embryo to the uterine wall. In time, these become elaborated into the *placenta,* a mass of spongy tissue permeated with blood vessels, through which nutrients pass to the child and waste products from the baby are discharged through the mother's body. The connection between the placenta and the fetus gradually develops into the *umbilical cord,* a rubbery tube containing arteries and veins.

Some of the first cells in the developing baby form into the *amnion,* a sac or membrane filled with a watery fluid (the *amniotic fluid*), which provides a protective environment within which the fetus grows and develops. By the end of the third month, the fetus is about three inches long, and most of its body organs have begun to develop.

THE SECOND TRIMESTER

As the woman moves into the second trimester, most of the problems of pregnancy diminish markedly. The danger of spontaneous abortion is largely past, and any tendencies toward nausea are likely to have disappeared. The fatigue and lassitude of early pregnancy often are replaced by a general sense of well-being and physical health. Many women report that they feel better during this period than at any other time in their lives.

This well-being often is reflected in the couple's sex life. The woman often is eager and easily aroused, and levels of sexual satisfaction tend to be high for both partners. The woman's abdomen is growing large enough so that the popular man-above position for sexual intercourse may become uncomfortable for her, but there are no other restrictions on the couple's sexual activity.

About midway through the fourth month, the physician can hear the fetal heartbeat with the aid of a stethoscope. This development provides final confirmation that the woman is pregnant and that the baby is alive. The woman also feels the first signs of life at about this time, as the baby begins to move within the uterus. These "kicks" by the baby become more frequent and more pronounced as the baby grows larger.

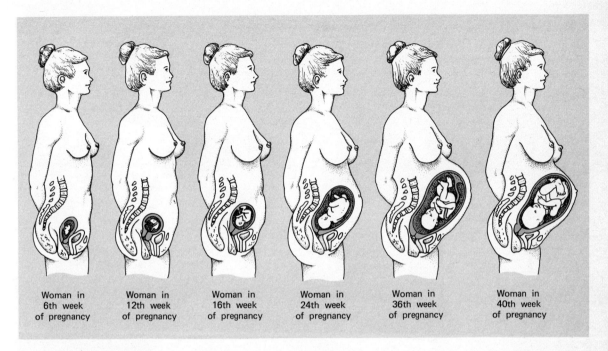

| Woman in 6th week of pregnancy | Woman in 12th week of pregnancy | Woman in 16th week of pregnancy | Woman in 24th week of pregnancy | Woman in 36th week of pregnancy | Woman in 40th week of pregnancy |

Figure 12-1 Development of the fetus during pregnancy.

By the fifth month, the baby is some ten to 12 inches long, but it still weighs under a pound. A month later, it has reached over a foot in length and weighs up to one and one-half pounds. Although it still could not survive outside the mother's body, it can move its arms and legs and open and close its eyes. The stages of fetal growth are depicted in Figure 12-1.

THE THIRD TRIMESTER

During the final three months, the baby increases in size rapidly. It weighs around three pounds during the seventh month and five pounds during the eighth month, reaching an average of seven-and-a-half pounds by the usual time of delivery. Generally, babies have a good chance to survive if they are born any time after the seventh month. Technically, they are considered premature, and receive special treatment, until they reach a weight of five pounds.

Although the woman usually continues to feel well during this last trimester, she often becomes physically uncomfortable. The baby is become large and heavy, straining her muscles and balance and forcing her abdominal organs out of their normal position. As the baby moves into position for birth, the woman often feels what she describes as ''pressure'' in the lower abdomen. This sensation is caused by the baby's head moving to the cervix and by preliminary contractions of the uterus.

Sexual activity is likely to be curtailed again during this trimester. The

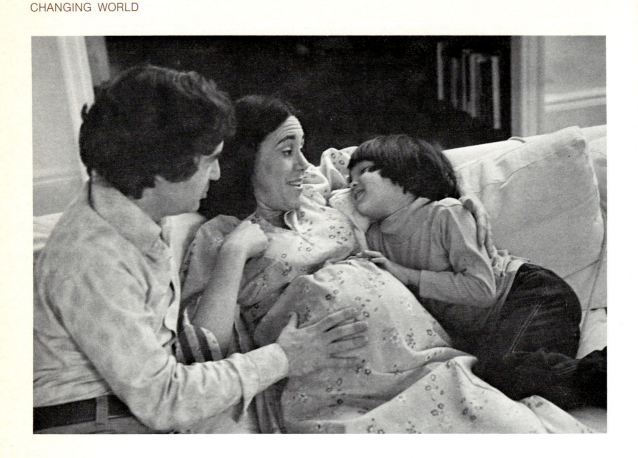

woman experiences a new kind of fatigue, resulting both from the weight of the pregnancy and from the fact that it now often interferes with her rest at night. Sexual intercourse also becomes increasingly uncomfortable for her. Many physicians recommend that intercourse be discontinued approximately six weeks before the baby is expected, not because of any possibility of injury but to prevent the introduction of germs into the birth canal.

By the time labor begins, most women are more than ready for it. They yearn to be relieved of physical discomfort and to regain their pre-pregnancy figures. They are anxious about the pain that delivery will cause and eager to make sure that the baby is normal and healthy. Inevitably, there is curiosity about whether it will be a boy or a girl.

CHILDBIRTH

During the last weeks of pregnancy, the baby ordinarily moves into the head-downward position for delivery. Since the baby's head is the largest part of its body, once the head has emerged from the vagina the rest of the delivery usually follows easily. About 95 percent of all deliveries involve this so-called *normal presentation.* Most of the remaining five percent are *breech presentations* in which the buttocks move into the cervix first. Breech deliveries are more difficult. If the physician discovers a tendency to breech presentation during the final weeks, he may try to turn the baby manually to a normal position.

In a few cases, there may be a *transverse presentation,* in which the baby lies crosswise in the uterus. If this condition persists, the physician must deliver the baby surgically, through the abdominal wall, in a cesarean section. Certain other conditions in the mother, such as a too-small or a misshapen pelvis, may require a cesarean operation. Some women think that they might prefer this form of delivery because they would be under anesthesia, feeling no pain. A cesarean is major surgery, however, and should be resorted to only if the physician deems it necessary.

LABOR

Women having their first child, and many of their husbands, worry about how they will know when labor begins and when it is time to go to the hospital. They have good reason. Uterine contractions, which are the essence of labor, actually occur throughout most of the pregnancy, and they become more frequent and pronounced during the last weeks. Occasionally, over-anxious couples go to the hospital during one of these periods of contractions before true labor begins.

There are three signs of the onset of true labor. One is the regularity and frequency of contractions. As labor begins, the contractions tend to be strong and to come about 15 or 20 minutes apart. Then, gradually, they become stronger and closer together: 15 minutes, then ten minutes, then five. When they reach five-minute intervals it is time to call the doctor.

The second sign of labor is the appearance of the "show," a small plug of blood-stained mucus that has been blocking the cervix and preventing infection from entering. The expulsion of this plug from the vagina indicates that birth is imminent. The third sign is the "breaking of the bag of waters." The "bag of waters" is actually the amnion, the fluid-filled membrane that surrounds the fetus during its development. The rupture of this membrane and the gush of the amniotic fluid from the vagina again indicate that birth is near.

Physicians divide labor into three stages, which are diagramed in Figure 12-2. The first stage lasts from the beginning of labor until the time when the cervix dilates to permit the passage of the baby's head. The length of this stage varies widely, but most commonly it lasts somewhere between six and 18 hours in first births. It is substantially shorter in second births, and still shorter in later ones. Most of the babies born in taxis and ambulances on the way to the hospital are second or third births.

Figure 12-2   The three
stages of labor. (Adapted
from Jones, Shainberg, and
Byer [1969], p. 117.)

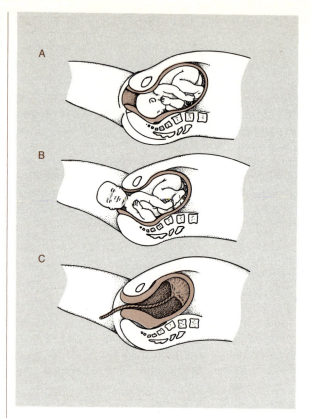

The second stage lasts from the time the cervix is completely opened until the moment the baby is born; this stage seldom takes much more than about 20 minutes. Because of the risk that the mother's tissues will be torn as the baby's head emerges, many physicians prefer to make a small incision, called an episiotomy, at the upper end of the perineum to enlarge the opening. After the birth, the incision is quickly and easily repaired. This method minimizes discomfort to the woman.

As the third stage begins, the physician removes any mucus that may have been lodged in the baby's mouth and throat, so that it can breathe unhindered, and places the baby upon the mother's abdomen. He then squeezes the umbilical cord between his fingers until it stops pulsating and clamps it off near the baby's abdomen. Then he places a second clamp a few inches further away and cuts the cord between the two clamps. To avoid irritation, the tiny piece of cord that remains is usually taped to the infant's abdomen. Eventually, it dries out and falls off, leaving the navel.

The key event of the third stage of labor is the expulsion of the placenta, or afterbirth, and whatever else remains in the uterus. This stage again seldom lasts much more than about 20 minutes. As it proceeds the woman is given injections to stimulate contraction of the uterus, to stimulate milk production if she wishes to nurse the baby, or to restrict milk production if she does not.

The medical profession manages childbirth very well these days, and most births occur without complications. A growing number of people, however, object to what they believe is excessive medical intrusion into what should be a very natural biological experience for both the mother and her baby. Women object to being given so much anesthetic that they are only semiconscious during delivery; they also are concerned that anesthetics may affect the baby during and after delivery. They believe that childbirth need not be difficult if the woman is properly prepared for it, emotionally and physically.

NATURAL CHILDBIRTH

The term "natural childbirth" covers a variety of specific techniques. Generally, however, the preparation includes both classes and exercises. The classes are designed to allay the woman's anxiety and to inform her about childbirth. They are usually coupled with exercises designed to tone up her muscles and with instruction in how to cooperate with the physician during birth. In some cases, prospective fathers also participate, sharing the woman's experiences and becoming active participants in the preparation for the birth.

In a few of the most modern hospitals, the father may be allowed to be present during delivery, or at least to watch it from an adjoining glass-walled room. But most hospitals are simply not equipped for his presence. Some physicians also believe that they have enough to do in caring for the mother without having to attend to the father, too.

In natural childbirth, the mother usually receives no general anesthetic and is fully awake, and she actively works with the physician in aiding the birth. There may even be mirrors positioned so that she can watch what is happening. She may or may not be given a local anesthetic in preparation for emergence of the baby's head from the vagina. Many women report that they derive great emotional satisfaction from active participation in childbirth, and they also maintain that their recovery is easier and faster.

A relatively few hospitals have so-called *rooming-in* facilities, which permit the newborn baby to be cared for by the mother in her own room instead of by hospital personnel in a nursery. The father generally is permitted easy access to the room, and both parents are actively involved in caring for the baby almost from the hour of its birth. Both parents and medical personnel tend to be enthusiastic about such arrangements. Unfortunately, few hospitals have them.

ROOMING-IN

In most instances, mothers feed their babies on a hospital-determined schedule, and fathers see their babies only through glass walls for the first few days. The usual hospital stay for maternity is now only three or four days. Then the parents take their new baby home.

ADJUSTING TO THE BABY

Homecoming with the new baby is likely to be exciting. After all, the parents have been waiting over nine months for this day. When the baby is safely asleep in its crib, the new parents can finally relax, at peace with themselves and the world.

But their peace doesn't last. An older woman, usually the wife's mother or the husband's mother, may be around to help during the first few days, but soon she goes home. With her departure, the partners suddenly confront their new roles as parents. Newborn babies demand attention—feeding and changing—at all hours of the day and night. The mother gets tired and the father gets tired. When the baby screams at two or three in the morning, each feigns sleep and hopes that the other will get up. But somebody has to get up, and not only this time, but the next and the next. No matter how considerate the new parents try to be, elation over having a new baby gives way at times to fatigue and frustration. Each of the parents faces problems.

THE NEW MOTHER'S LETDOWN

Not all new mothers experience an emotional letdown during the first few weeks, but many do. The excitement and suspense of pregnancy suddenly are over, and the fantasies of idyllic parenthood have been replaced by a seemingly endless succession of dirty diapers. The mother's schedule is completely subject to the whims of an increasingly tyrannical infant. The husband doesn't do his share and is quarrelsome and remote as well. Some new mothers find that they break into tears without apparent provocation and wish that they had never had a baby. That wish, in turn, makes them feel guilty and only increases their misery.

These symptoms are so common that they need not be considered abnormal. It helps, of course, if the husband is understanding and sympathetic. And it helps, too, if the parents are blessed with a relatively happy baby. In those few cases in which the new mother's distress is severe, and her sadness turns into deep emotional depression, psychiatric help should be sought. But most women find that their melancholy disappears after a while as mysteriously as it arrived, and parenthood comes to offer much brighter prospects.

THE NEW FATHER'S NEGLECT

Some fathers also undergo a psychological crisis after the new baby comes home. Its arrival brings a drastic shift in the father's status. His needs and expectations no longer get first priority from his wife. His meals must wait while the baby's needs are attended to. Social activities are interfered with, and vacation plans must be built around taking the baby along or, at least, arranging for its care.

More subtly, but also more devastatingly, the father is replaced somewhat in the mother's attention and affection (Dodson, 1974). Whereas once he was her first concern, she now lavishes affection on the baby and leaves her husband feeling somewhat unimportant and unloved. Any reasonably mature man is likely to be somewhat aware of what is happening, and to realize that his wife loves him no less. But acknowledging the fact is not always enough to do away with feelings of neglect and resentment against the new arrival who is the source of the problem.

More often than most people will admit, the problems of the husband and father are complicated by strong feelings of sexual deprivation. Intercourse usually is discontinued six weeks before the baby's birth, and most physicians recommend that it not be resumed until six weeks after. Most men accept the early restrictions readily enough and do not suffer too many feelings of deprivation while they wait for the baby's arrival. Afterward, however, the excitement and suspense are gone—and it has been a long time! The wife, in the meantime, is very alert to the baby's needs and seems almost oblivious to her husband's.

Couples can have sex without vaginal penetration, of course, and most couples do. Feedings at two in the morning take their toll, however, and the wife, particularly, is often just too tired to be very interested in sex. Although the husband usually does not experience the sort of depression his wife does, he may develop a strong feeling of being unneeded, unappreciated, and unloved.

THE TRANSITION TO PARENTHOOD

A generation ago, several researchers studied the crisis aspects of new parenthood. Not until the late 1960s and early 1970s, however, were there any studies of large representative samples of new parents. A recent one, including almost 300 Minneapolis couples whose babies ranged from six to 56 weeks of age, focused upon both the problems and the gratifications of new parenthood (Russell, 1974).

In the Minneapolis study, both husbands and wives reported that the baby's arrival precipitated a slight-to-moderate crisis. Wives were worried about their physical appearance and bothered by fatigue and general nervousness. The husbands were troubled by in-laws' interference with the baby's care, and by the baby's interference with their sleep and their plans. The complaints are listed in Table 12-1.

For both parents, there was a negative relationship between their general level of marital adjustment and the amount of crisis reported. That is, the more satisfied they were, the less of a crisis they reported. Probably the cause-and-effect situation works both ways. Couples who are more satisfied with their marriages find that their babies are less disruptive, and those whose babies cause fewer problems rate their marriages higher. This reasoning is supported by the fact that fathers

**TABLE 12-1
CRISIS SYMPTOMS
REPORTED BY NEW
PARENTS**

MOTHERS	FATHERS
1. Worry about personal appearance	1. Interrupted sleep
2. Fatigue	2. In-laws' suggestions about baby
3. Interrupted sleep	3. Money problems
4. Worry about loss of figure	4. Interference with plans
5. Feeling edgy or upset	5. Additional work required

Source: Candyce Smith Russell, "Transition to Parenthood: Problems and Gratification," *Journal of Marriage and the Family* 36 (May 1974), pp. 296–97.

who said that their babies cried too much, or had feeding problems, or
were ill, also reported parenthood to involve more crisis.

On the whole, both mothers and fathers reported more gratifications
than problems in parenthood. The gratifications included pride in the
baby's development, fewer periods of boredom, more things to talk to the
spouse about, feelings of fulfillment, and enjoying the baby's company.
Most couples also reported that their marriages had either improved
since the baby's birth (42 percent), or remained unchanged (43.5
percent). Only 5.5 percent of the husbands and 7.5 percent of the wives
believed that their marriages had worsened (Russell, 1974).

RELATING TO YOUNG CHILDREN

There is no sharp line between infancy and childhood. Basically,
infants are helpless, but they become increasingly active with each
passing week. They learn to eat as well as to suckle; they grasp, they roll
over, and then they begin to crawl. As soon as they can walk, the active
exploration that defines childhood has begun.

TODDLERS

Toddlers explore their homes and adjacent areas with seemingly
insatiable curiosity and boundless energy. For most parents, these years
are an exciting and rewarding period. The parents get to watch young
skills develop and to share vicariously in the child's pleasure in its
achievements. The child responds to the parents' pleasure, in turn, and
expands the areas it explores.

Toddlerhood is a demanding period for parents, too. The child who
experiments with toys, brothers and sisters, and pets can also reach for
hot stoves, electrical outlets, medicines, chemicals, tools, and other
things that can hurt or kill. Toddlers require very close and continuing
supervision.

If the mother does not work outside the home during this period,
most of the burden falls upon her. Although she does not experience the
overwhelming physical fatigue that marked late pregnancy and the first
weeks of the infant's life, her days are long and demanding. Relief is
available only during the hours when the father is home. If the father is
sensitive to the situation, he will consciously try to take as much of the

burden as possible. If he does, things can work out reasonably well for both parents. A less sensitive father may, however, insist upon keeping his leisure hours for himself, playing with the child only when he feels like it. In that case, the wife is likely to develop resentment at the unbalance of duties.

In some ways, the burden of these years may be lighter for both parents if the wife also works outside the home. The child's care is then transferred to a sitter, a day-care center, or some other child-care facility for eight or nine active hours a day. If the two parents divide the child's care between them for the remaining four to six hours, each of them gets to participate actively in the child's development without being tied constantly to its care. Of course, if the burden at home is not shared equally, the combined demands of work, child care, and home maintenance can be overwhelming for the wife.

A problem for many parents during toddlerhood is protecting the home and its contents. Grimy or sticky fingers can destroy painted walls

or wallpaper, and such large flat spaces provide excellent places for the child to try out new crayons. The most persistent problem probably is breakage—of lamps, china, ashtrays, bric-a-brac, anything that will break and is valuable. Most wise parents handle this problem by simply moving such items out of the child's reach until the initial period of exploration is over.

Finally, there is some need for discipline. There are "no-no's" in even the most childproof house. Parents worry over possible damage that may be done to the child's developing self-concept by constantly forbidding various activities. There is some cause for concern, but the possibility may be minimized by helping the child to understand the reasons for the prohibitions as early as possible. It is one thing to say "no" to the child a hundred times a day, and another to calmly tell it that it can't touch the stove "because it is hot," or that it can't run across the street "because the cars go fast." Restrictions that the child can understand are not likely to cause damage.

In most circumstances, there also are better ways than punishment for teaching children—which is really what the term *discipline* means: to make a "disciple" of the child (Dodson, 1974). At this early age, distraction is a very useful technique, because the child's attention is easily diverted to less dangerous activities. And finally, the old psychological principle that reward is more effective than punishment applies. Too-frequent punishment may jeopardize the child's trust in its parents, but praise for its accomplishments, and frequent demonstrations of love, make the child eager to continue to please them.

PRESCHOOLERS

Toddlerhood merges into the preschool years. This period is hard to define precisely. It begins when children establish identities separate from those of their parents; when they come to see themselves as independent people capable of making demands upon parents and others, rather than simply conforming to the expectations of others. Many children reach this stage by the age of two. Though some children enter nursery school as early as age three, we are talking here, roughly, about the ages of from two to five.

Developing a firm sense of identity is not easy for most children, and their lack of ease with themselves and with their parents shows itself in frequent unhappiness. They grow frustrated with things in general and with many things in particular. The delightful toddler turns into the "terrible two." No matter what the parents want, the child objects. When the parents give in, the child objects to that, too. Most parents find that the child tries their patience severely. They face a strong temptation either to clamp down and enforce rules and regulations rigidly, or else to give up on discipline completely and let the child have its way. Neither course of action will help the child.

Children at this stage need to be helped to distinguish between their feelings and their actions. They have to learn that it is all right to have hostile feelings, but that it is *not* all right to engage in hostile actions. Left to themselves, preschoolers will grab one another's toys, hit, kick, bite, and shout, "I hate you!" at parents who interfere. If the parents are shocked and disapproving, the child feels that he or she is "bad" for harboring such emotions. But children can't help having negative feelings. Rage is as natural an emotion as love. Children who are made to feel guilty over anger run the risk of becoming emotionally impaired adults.

Ideally, the parents should show that they accept the child's feelings but, at the same time, convey to the child that it is not always right to act on those impulses: "I know that you want that toy, but you can't take other people's things," or "I know that you are angry, but you can't hit your parents no matter how angry you are." The distinction is a subtle one, and it requires mature, self-confident parents to be able to accept children's negative emotions while still putting reasonable limits upon their behavior.

Fortunately, for parents and children both, most children learn the distinction between emotions and behavior, and they gradually learn to restrict their behavior. As they do, they become more comfortable with themselves and with others. There is less need for anger, and hence less anger. Long before the preschool period is over, most children become much more pleasant people again.

As two-year-olds, children get acquainted with one another, and parents often assume they are playing together. Child development experts point out, however, that they are engaging in "parallel play" rather than truly playing together. They may play side by side, but each child is engaged in his or her own activities, and there is little or no cooperation between them. This pattern changes drastically at age three or four, however, as children learn to engage in joint and cooperative play. Such cooperation is reflected in the child's relationship with its parents, too; there is a new era of sharing and cooperation at home that restores most parents' faith in parenthood.

SUCCESSFUL PARENTHOOD

A comprehensive analysis of parenthood, covering the nuances of child development at various stages, and the corresponding roles of parents, would require at least two books as large as this one. Two suitable books are listed at the end of this chapter (Hurlock, 1970; LeMasters, 1974).

Some aspects of child development were analyzed in Chapters 2 to 5, in the context of preparation for adult heterosexual relationships; others have been treated briefly here. But one topic remains untouched:

concepts of successful parenthood. These ideas, like so many we have examined, are currently being reshaped.

PARENTAL
LOVE

The days when getting married necessarily meant having children are nearly gone. So, too, is the idea that having children is an obligation to society or to the future. Modern contraception permits couples to decide whether they will have children. And if the answer is yes, contraception permits them to space their children with some accuracy.

For these reasons, couples who choose to be parents today are likely to be people who have made deep emotional commitments to one another, and whose relationships involve long-range planning. It stands to reason that such people are more able to love their children freely and enthusiastically than people to whom parenthood was either accidental or inevitable. Not all people choose to be parents now. Qualitatively, parenthood probably is better for it.

Modern parents are frequently deeply committed to one another and make plans to have children out of mutual love and hope for their unborn offspring. Such people also are likely to view parenthood in positive terms; as providing opportunities for personal growth and development, rather than as saddling them with 20 or more years of responsibility. Such parents emphasize that they are persons as well as parents, and that their rights and their feelings are as important as those of their children. They are sensitive to their children's needs and to their own needs as well.

The emphasis in such families is likely to be upon open and honest communication—between the parents, between parents and children, and among the children. Such people try to listen to one another and then to act in ways that promote the benefit of all. Life in such families is not without problems, of course. Life is seldom without problems, and families bound together by affection and trust may even have troubles not shared by many more traditional families. But these troubles are more likely to be basic ''people'' problems—specific grievances with specific individuals—than they are to be generational ones. That is, there is less risk of the kind of a conflict that stems from the parents' simply not understanding the children, or vice versa. The generation gap is replaced to some degree by the more basic ''communication gap'' that plagues all human interaction (Rogers, 1974).

PARENTS AS PEOPLE

SUMMARY

A missed menstrual period, coupled with other signs, is taken as an indication of pregnancy. These signs send the woman to her physician, who usually confirms the diagnosis on the basis of a pelvic examination; hormone tests, which are highly accurate, can be used if needed. The physician helps the woman plan for the management of her pregnancy and determines when the baby is due. Ensuring adequate nutrition and appropriate weight gain are early considerations.

About one-fifth of pregnant women show some ''spotting'' or vaginal bleeding during the first trimester. The physician will watch this condition closely and may prescribe rest or medication to prevent spontaneous abortion. Otherwise, there are likely to be few restrictions on the woman's activities at this time. Her blood type is checked for possible Rh-factor complications, and precautionary measures are taken if necessary.

Feelings of pervasive well-being often characterize the second trimester, and the couple's love life generally recovers from the fatigue and nausea of early pregnancy. The infant's heartbeat can be heard during the fourth month, and other signs of life appear at this time.

The growth of the infant is the main feature of the third trimester, and the infant can be born alive after the seventh month. The woman becomes increasingly uncomfortable as the time for delivery nears, and sexual intercourse is usually discontinued during the last six weeks.

Uterine contractions, increasingly frequent and severe, signal the onset of labor. Expulsion of a mucous plug ("show") from the vagina, and the breaking of the "bag of waters" are other signs. Labor is divided into three stages: from the onset until the complete dilation of the cervix; from dilation to the birth of the baby; and from birth until the expulsion of the placenta. In first births, the whole process usually takes from eight to 18 hours. The time is shorter for each subsequent birth.

Some couples prepare for natural childbirth by learning about pregnancy and delivery, preparing themselves emotionally, and practicing birth-assisting exercises. The woman is fully awake during natural childbirth, and no general anesthetics are used. A few hospitals have rooming-in facilities that permit the parents to care for their baby almost from birth.

Major adjustments are required after the baby comes home. Fatigue plagues both parents, the mother may suffer some emotional depression, and the father may feel neglected. Fortunately, these symptoms do not ordinarily last long. Research shows that the transition to parenthood gives most couples more gratification than problems.

The transition from infancy to toddlerhood is exciting for the parents, but also demanding. The child is into everything and must be supervised constantly. The joys are greater, and the demands less onerous, if the parents cooperate in that supervision. Valuables can be protected from damage by being placed out of reach. The few necessary prohibitions on the child's behavior should be interpreted to help the child understand the reasons for them.

The preschool years present new joys and new problems. The child has to establish its identity as a person. It must also learn the difference between having negative feelings, which is acceptable, and engaging in antisocial behavior. Gradually it learns to adjust to other children and to adults.

Parenthood is more of an option today than a necessity. As a result, more babies are born out of love and desire. The parents of such children are likely to emphasize personal growth and development, for themselves as well as for their children. These families are not without problems, but life in them often is rich and rewarding.

FOR ADDITIONAL READING

Dodson, Fitzhugh, *How to Father* (New York: New American Library, 1974). A practical guide to the father's role as a parent.

Foster, Henry H., Jr., *A Bill of Rights for Children* (Springfield, Ill.: Charles C. Thomas, 1974). Principles and guidelines for fairer treatment of children under the law.

Hurlock, Elizabeth, *Child Growth and Development* (New York: McGraw-Hill, 1970). Systematic analysis of child development stages and problems. A good supplement to this chapter.

LeMasters, Ersel E., *Parents in Modern America* (Homewood, Ill.: The Dorsey Press, 1974). A comprehensive analysis of what happens to fathers and mothers in child rearing.

Wilkes, Paul, *Trying Out the American Dream: A Year in the Life of an American Family* (Philadelphia: Lippincott, 1975). A perceptive account of the joys, satisfactions, trials, and disappointments of the five members of one family.

STUDY QUESTIONS

1. What are the common presumptive signs of pregnancy which send the woman to her physician? How does the physician confirm the diagnosis?

2. Trace the usual course of pregnancy from the first trimester through the third. Emphasize the effects upon the couple's life and adjustment.

3. What are the three stages of labor? When does each stage begin and end? How long do they last?

4. What is natural childbirth? What is "rooming-in"? How common is each?

5. Describe some of the typical adjustment problems faced by new mothers and fathers after the baby comes home. What techniques would you recommend for coping with them?

6. According to research, what balance of satisfactions and problems do new parents encounter?

7. Describe the stages through which toddlers and preschool children pass. How can parents help make these stages easier?

8. What is implied by the phrase, "parents as people?" What kind of family life does it promote?

Chapter 13
Dual Careers

Today's young-adult generation differs from its predecessors in a very significant way. Many young men and women today have grown up with mothers who worked outside the home, at least part of the time, and many of these mothers have enjoyed their combined work and family roles (Almquist and Angrist, 1972). Young people today have also been indoctrinated with the ideal of equality between the sexes and believe in the right of women to full participation in the occupational world. It should be no surprise, then, that about half of today's young college women are making plans to combine occupational careers with marriage and having children.

TRADITIONAL VS DUAL-CAREER MARRIAGES

The simple fact that the wife works outside the home does not make a dual-career marriage. Most women are working when they marry and continue to do so for a time. They hold jobs until they can accumulate a downpayment on a house or a given level of savings, or until they become pregnant. But then, typically, they drop out of full-time work until all their children have been born. Later on, when the children are at least partly grown, they may return to full-time work. But that common pattern is not what is meant by dual careers.

A dual-career marriage is one in which both the husband and the wife pursue individual careers with approximately equal vigor and commitment. Their jobs afford them major satisfaction, pay relatively well, and offer opportunities for advancement. But at the same time, these couples remain committed to marriage and the family. They seek a life that offers the best of the worlds of work and family living.

Nobody knows how many dual-career marriages there are. Obviously, they occur mainly among people with some higher education or technical skills. They include many different types of workers: executives and managers in business; officials and administrators in government, social agencies, and organizations of all sorts; college professors and school teachers; professional people such as architects, attorneys, doctors, and social workers; scientists and technicians; artists and musicians; and still others. Although we don't know how many dual-career marriages there are, they are increasingly conspicuous, and their numbers appear to be growing rapidly.

SUCCESS IN FAMILY PLANNING

Some childless marriages emphasize the equal development of the man's career and the woman's. But those marriages, discussed in Chapter 11, do so at the expense of the child-rearing dimension of family living. Dual-career marriages as we define them here do have children. Typically, however, these couples do not have many children: one or two, and seldom more.

Theoretically, it is possible that these couples just happen to be of low fecundity; that is, that they have difficulty having children. This fact would, of course, make it easier for both partners to have careers. It is more likely, however, that their careers are so important to them that they practice birth control successfully. Research shows that women who have a high level of commitment to their jobs use birth control more effectively, and have fewer children, than other women do (Safilios-Rothschild, 1972).

MARITAL SUCCESS

No statistical studies have yet been made of the success of dual-career marriages. Therefore, we cannot say for sure whether there are differences in marital success between dual-career couples and traditional ones, couples for whom the demands of the wife's employment yield to those of the husband's. One approximation to an answer has been made, however. A study in the late 1960s compared three kinds of marriages: those in which the woman worked of necessity outside the home, those in which she worked by choice, and those in which she did not work (Orden and Bradburn, 1968). Marriage adjustment scores were higher among the women who chose to work than among those who had to work. There was no difference in adjustment between those who chose to work and those who chose not to. Indirectly, then, this evidence suggests that the level of adjustment in dual-career marriages is relatively high.

Studies of dual-career marriages to date have dealt intensively with small numbers of couples. One study compared 20 dual-career couples with seven traditional ones; the dual-career wives all had PhD's in the humanities, social sciences or physical sciences (Holmstrom, 1972). A second study provided detailed case studies of five dual-career couples (Rapoport and Rapoport, 1971), and a third compared 14 dual-career couples with another group of traditional couples with similar backgrounds (Bebbington, 1973). What follows is a composite portrait of dual-career couples based upon these three studies.

THE NATURE OF DUAL-CAREER MARRIAGES

Most dual-career couples marry relatively late: at least after the woman graduates from college, and sometimes after she has completed post-graduate or professional training. The fact that marriage may not occur before the mid-twenties, or even the thirties, contributes to the low birth rate among such couples.

AGE AT MARRIAGE

Some women decide, long before they marry, that they want careers as well as marriage. In these cases, their prospective husbands probably accept the idea of dual careers as well. But in other cases, although both partners know of the woman's high commitment to work, the actual decision to have dual careers may not be made until some time after marriage.

THE DUAL-CAREER DECISION

The decision to have dual careers often is made in successive stages, in a process comparable to the way some couples decide to remain childless. It begins with the woman's high work commitment before marriage and the man's acquiescence in it. A second step is taken when the woman continues her employment after marriage. The crucial decision probably is made at the time of the birth of the first child. Since most women quit working, at least temporarily, at this point, the fact that a woman continues with her job after the birth of a child usually means that she has decided to continue working indefinitely. A positive decision to have a permanent career may be made at that time, or it may be deferred until still later.

People live where their jobs are. When only one marital partner works, the choices boil down to whether to choose a house or an apartment and what section of the community to live in. But among dual-career couples the situation is much more complicated.

DECIDING WHERE TO LIVE

When the couples are college graduates who are launching their careers simultaneously, they face the problem of finding acceptable jobs in the same geographic area. Sometimes this task is not too difficult. But other times it is nearly impossible, and in that case the couple must decide right away which partner's career should take precedence. Increasingly, couples seem to be making that decision on practical grounds. They move to the location of the best job offered to either partner: the one that pays the highest salary, that offers the best possibilities of advancement, or that affords the greatest intangible satisfactions.

Often, the husband launches his career before the wife starts on hers. Her first choice of job is thus limited to the geographical area in which the husband is already working. This fact may prevent her from taking the best job available, and it sets the stage for problems in deciding about subsequent moves.

The American population as a whole is exceedingly mobile. Some 18 to 20 percent of our population changes place of residence each year (Packard, 1972). Dual-career couples, being generally highly educated and well trained, might logically be expected to be even more mobile than the average. Whether they actually are, however, we do not know. But we do know that decisions of whether to move, and where, sooner or later become an issue in many dual-career marriages.

Advancement for management personnel—whether in the business and industrial world, or in scientific, or academic jobs—often requires a change in geographic location. When either partner is offered a promotion, accepting it may mean some disruption of the other partner's career. Impressionistic evidence suggests that couples more often follow the demands of the husband's career, and that it is the wife's career that usually suffers. She packs up and moves with him, hoping that she can find an equally good job in the new location.

Logically, of course, the couple might decide to give priority to the wife's career, and some couples do. This happens particularly when the wife works for a large organization while the husband is a self-employed or professional person; he can follow her more easily than she can follow him.

Some couples even alternate their decisions to move. If the husband's career dictates one move, then the wife's career determines the next one, and so on. This system is fairer to each partner, but the career advancement of both is likely to suffer somewhat.

One major study has been made of how families' mobility patterns are affected when wives work (Long, 1974). It is based on the U.S. census bureau's sample surveys for the period 1966 through 1971. This study showed that married men whose wives work are less likely to move to another county or another state than are married men whose wives do

*"I'm afraid I have to leave the firm, sir. My wife's
company is transferring her out of state."*

DRAWING BY VON RIEGEN; © 1975 THE NEW YORKER MAGAZINE, INC.

not work. This fact suggests that, statistically, the wife's having a career
sometimes interferes with the husband's ability to move in pursuit of job
advancement.

At the same time, families in which the wife works are more likely to
move from one location to another *within* a county than are families in
which the wife does not work. Most of these moves probably are to
larger, more luxurious quarters and to better neighborhoods. This evidence indicates that one effect of dual careers is to raise the family's
standard of living within a given geographic area.

Finally, the study showed that when dual-career couples do make
long-distance moves, there is some chance that the wife will drop out of
the labor force, at least temporarily. For those wives who continue to
work, a move often brings a drop in their earnings. These statistical data
confirm that dual careers entail career sacrifices for both partners.

COMPETITIVENESS
AND SHARING

Given the fact that some career sacrifices are almost inevitable in dual-career marriages, the question naturally arises whether both partners tend to resent these restrictions. And one may wonder whether strong competition might develop between the two careers. Generally, however, the evidence indicates that disruptive competition does not occur (Holmstrom, 1972).

Most husbands and wives in dual-career marriages report that, rather than feeling competitive with one another, they take pride and satisfaction in each other's accomplishments. The ways in which they handle the job situation vary widely.

Many couples discuss their work with one another, in either technical or laymen's terms. They also discuss problems that they face, particularly in their relationships with other people on the job, and how best to deal with them. When the husband identifies with his wife's career, his satisfaction in her accomplishments appears to be a strong source of solidarity in many marriages.

Other couples, however, compartmentalize their lives effectively, keeping their family lives and their work quite separate. This practice may be more common when the two fields are so different that little effective communication about their work is possible. It also may be a deliberate tactic when there is overt or potential competition between the two.

Finally, some dual-career couples share their work to some degree. When both partners have been trained in the same field or in complementary ones, they may work together at least part of the time. Husband–wife teams of attorneys or physicians would be an example of the first situation; an accountant–attorney team is an example of the second.

Successful dual-career couples, disproportionately, are people who either are not competitive with one another or who have learned how to handle their competitiveness and minimize its disruptive effects. Where competition remains strong, the likelihood of disruption of one of the careers, or of the marriage, is great.

WORK
OVERLOAD

One of the most striking things about dual-career couples is how incredibly busy they are. With both partners following demanding occupations, there just doesn't seem to be enough time to get everything done.

Mornings, before work, are frantic. Everyone has to get ready for work or school. Breakfast must be prepared and eaten and the dishes cleared away. Since both partners typically have management or supervisory responsibilities, their work days are often longer than eight hours. And when they finally do get home from work, both partners need time to relax and unwind. But there is still dinner to be prepared and cleaned away, shopping and laundry to be done, and at least occasional cleaning of the home. There is, in short, more work to be done than time in which to do it.

Most of the burden of this extra work load tends to fall upon the wife. The International Labor Organization of the United Nations reports that employed mothers usually have less than two-thirds the free time that their husbands enjoy. Working wives frequently labor between 70 and 80 hours a week on the job and in the home.[1] And even when the husband and children help out, as they often do, it still is the wife who suffers the fullest impact of the two roles. To avoid collapse under impossible pressures, dual-career couples must alter their housekeeping, child-rearing, and leisure patterns.

DIVISION OF LABOR

One of the most crucial factors in making dual-career marriages work is the attitude of the husband and his psychological investment in his wife's career. If his attitudes are traditional, and he resists doing housework and household chores, the load on his wife and children is correspondingly increased. Such traditional men appear to be in the minority in dual-career marriages, however.

[1] *The New York Times* (Jan. 12, 1975), p. E7.

Most dual-career wives and husbands report that they share most of the household duties. In some instances, couples rigidly define their duties. If the wife cooks one week, the husband cooks the next. Or if she cooks, he cleans up and does the dishes. If one does the laundry, the other does the cleaning, and so on. Other couples are more flexible about the division of labor: the one who arrives home first does the cooking, and both of them pitch in to clean up afterward. There even are cases in which the husband is self-employed or a professional man who can reduce his schedule or do a good part of his work at home, while his wife has to put in full days in the office. Some of these husbands assume most of the housework.

In each of these forms of adjustment, there are both satisfactions and costs. Marriages between traditional men and non-traditional women may be fraught with tension. The man can come to resent his wife's inattention to household matters, while the wife equally resents the unfairness of the situation. But when there is effective cooperation between the two, both partners may feel a deep satisfaction when they finally are able to rest in the evening after having shared the day's duties (Roache, 1975). There also are annoyances in the best of marriages. Children who are fussy or ill can strain the patience of both partners, just as they frustrate chiefly the wife in more traditional marriages. And when the refrigerator breaks down or the sink clogs up, someone must stay home—for ages, it seems—until the repairman arrives.

CHILDREN'S DUTIES

Children in dual-career families are likely to be pressed into service as soon as they are old enough. The child may be assigned certain responsibilities, such as doing the dishes or starting the preparation of the evening meal before the parents get home. The children usually must clean their own rooms, care for pets, and so on.

Children in these families are not angels, of course, and they may complain about having more duties than their friends do; they may even shirk their duties occasionally. But, on the whole, one gets the impression of young people being taught responsibility and cooperation from an early age. The children probably derive satisfaction and an enhanced sense of self-worth from this experience. The parents also treat their children as contributing members of the family and take pride in their achievements.

PAID HOUSEHOLD HELP

Having enough income, and managing it well, is less of a problem for most dual-career families than it is for other families. Typically, both partners earn salaries in the five-figure range. Like almost all couples, they may feel they never have enough income to satisfy all of their wants. But they often do have enough to be able to make choices on how to use it after the basic necessities of food, shelter, and clothing are secured.

Many dual-career families invest some of their income in paid household help to lighten the burden on themselves. While the children are young, babysitters or governesses may be employed to relieve the parents of most of the burdens of child care. There may also be a cleaning lady who comes once or twice a week or every day. In addition to sweeping, dusting, washing dishes, and doing the laundry, the help may also do heavy cleaning, such as floors and windows.

Those families that are fortunate enough to secure competent and reliable household help find that life is much more pleasurable. There is a second person in the home to perform most of the traditional tasks of the housewife. The paid help may enable the couple to have the benefits of dual careers without most of the work overload that usually accompanies them. In the best of situations, the paid household help may almost become nominal members of the family, doing babysitting or house- or apartment-sitting on weekends, or even living with the family.

In many cases, however, the situation is not nearly so idyllic. Most people do not want to do housework for a living, and help is increasingly difficult to get. Sometimes, too, the standards of the available help are not the same as those of the dual-career family. A drop in the quality of the household environment may be one price that has to be paid for dual careers.

To escape these worries, some families do most of the routine household work themselves but employ a variety of professionals for the heavy jobs, such as carpet and furniture cleaning, window washing, floor cleaning, laundering, and the like. They also eat many of their meals in restaurants, and bring many pre-prepared meals into the home. All of these devices help to minimize the heavy work burden that is almost the inevitable cost of dual careers.

PLANNED LEISURE

The leisure that comes naturally to most traditional families often must be carefully planned for by dual-career families. At the most routine level, dual-career couples often deny themselves spur-of-the-moment evening visits with other couples. There is simply too much work to be done, and, by the time it is finished, they are too tired to want to be sociable. Dual-career couples often look forward to weekends when they don't have to get up and go to work. These days may be the only time they don't have to be on a schedule. Some couples almost literally "hide out" on the weekends, sleeping late and restoring their energy for the busy week ahead.

Other couples achieve both escape and restoration by having regular weekend activities that they share. They may have a weekend home or cottage in the country. They may share a passion for boating, swimming, skiing, tennis, painting, or any number of other activities. The point is not so much that dual-career couples have certain leisure pursuits, as that they have so little leisure time that they must plan for it carefully.

Some dual-career couples also plan more lengthy vacations, and plan them more frequently, than most other couples do. Recognizing the strains that both of their careers place upon them, they may plan a week of vacation during each quarter of the year. Often, they will spend time at a resort where their every physical need is catered to, and where they can finally rest. Or, if they travel they will at least do different kinds of things from their normal routines. Other couples try to get away for a whole month during the year, feeling that one long vacation is more restorative than several shorter ones.

SOCIAL ACTIVITIES

Among many traditional couples, in which only the husband has a job of some responsibility, social life and business life often become somewhat merged. The couple entertains business friends in their home, and the wife consciously plays the role of hostess to advance the husband's career. This pattern seldom is found among dual-career couples. In the first place, the demands of the wife's career ordinarily are too great to permit her the luxury of devoting long hours to entertaining people at home. In the second place, most dual-career couples hold ideals of equality that make the hostess role seem demeaning for the woman.

For the most part, dual-career couples avoid lavish entertaining at home. They have neither the time nor the inclination for it. When they are required to entertain formally, they are likely to do it at restaurants or other commercial establishments catering to such needs. They can thus transfer the entire burden of preparation and cleanup to someone else. This device is another example of how dual-career couples use money to achieve what more traditional couples accomplish through their own labor.

Dual-career couples do sometimes entertain business acquaintances in advancement of their careers. But they are as likely to be promoting the wife's career as the husband's. In some circumstances, moreover, when the partners follow quite separate careers and do not know each other's colleagues, either partner may conduct business entertainment without the other partner's presence. On the average, entertainment among dual-career couples is less frequent and less lavish than it is among traditional couples.

Most dual-career couples do appear to have a small circle of friends with whom they associate informally on a fairly regular basis. Typically, these people are other dual-career couples, who share the same values and problems.

In one other respect, dual-career couples frequently differ from traditional ones. Among traditional couples, friendships are heavily influenced by the husband's occupation. But dual-career couples more often draw their joint friends from among the wife's associates. After all, it is the wife's career that makes dual-career couples unconventional; it is her way of life that subjects them to some criticism and disapproval from outsiders. Drawing friends from among the wife's colleagues helps to avoid such disapproval, and it also provides the couple with support and approval of their life style.

Many dual-career couples recognize that the relative infrequency of their contacts with parents and other family is a price they pay for success. Whatever the career forces that cause them to be in a certain location, family ties play little or no role in their decision. They often live far away from relatives. As a consequence, and because they are simply so busy, dual-career couples see other family members only occasionally, and usually only as a result of major effort.

Relationships with the couple's parents, especially after children come along, are the most troubling. The couples' parents sense that their adult children have grown far away from the circumstances of their upbringing. Except for emotional ties, the two generations seem to have little in common anymore. The parents take pride in their children's achievements, but they regret that they see them so seldom and are unable to share in their lives.

The full impact of this situation hits many career couples as their children grow up. They suddenly realize that their children are virtually strangers to their grandparents. Some grandchildren experience this

RELATIONSHIPS WITH KIN

situation as deprivation, although others consider it to be perfectly natural. If the dual-career partners were not formerly close to their parents, they may sense no loss, either. But where affection persists, nostalgic longing for closer family relationships is common.

Dual-career families have to plan visits with grandparents as they plan everything else, carefully and far in advance. Standards of equal treatment for both sides of the family often break down, and some favoritism develops. Continued kinship ties come to be based upon true affection and compatibility in basic values.

DISRUPTION OF DUAL-CAREER MARRIAGES

Dual-career marriages on a large scale are too new to allow us to tell much about their durability. The logical possibilities are varied. First, they may be very stable; husbands and wives may find in them the egalitarian relationships that so many people seek today. At the other extreme, however, dual-career marriages may place so many demands upon the partners that many arrangements break under the pressure, and either divorce occurs or the wife returns to the homemaker role. Then again, the reality may be something in between. As in most other marriages, the partners may have to keep altering their adjustments, never taking anything for granted.

Only one study, of 20 dual-career couples and seven traditional ones, has yet reported on the break-up of dual-career arrangements (Holmstrom, 1972). Even that study was able to follow the couples for only a short time and described just the events of the previous several years.

Four of the dual-career wives in the study had gone through divorces. In addition, two of the traditional wives had been divorced from earlier husbands, with whom they had tried to combine marriage and a personal career. The sample was a small and select one, of course, and these numbers will not permit us to draw any conclusions about whether dual-career marriages are more or less prone to divorce than others. What we are interested in primarily is what led to the divorces. There were two major kinds of problems.

Some women reported that, with the passage of time, they became increasingly unable to tolerate their relationships with their husbands. As they tended to gain in competence and self-confidence, they wanted ever more egalitarian marriage relationships, while the husbands sought to preserve their positions of greater dominance. This struggle went on until the final break. Most of the divorces occurred by mutual agreement, and the wives did not feel betrayed or rejected. In two cases, in fact, the wives left their husbands to go with other men.

The second major problem was the extreme commitment of one or both of the spouses to their careers, leaving insufficient time and energy for marriage and family relationships. In some cases, both partners were so committed to their careers that they just decided to give up on the marriage; there was no compelling reason to continue it. In other instances, the one partner yearned for an intimacy in the marriage that the other was unable to provide. Sometimes these problems were complicated by a difference in the emphasis they were willing to place on child rearing. Again, the break-up of these marriages was not characterized by excessive hostility or bitterness. The couples had tried, but they simply hadn't been able to make marriage work.

The two women now in traditional marriages whose dual-career marriages had ended in divorce chose another solution. Both of these women now concentrated on marriage and child rearing, having essentially given up their careers. They played subordinate and supportive roles to their new husbands and seemed to derive real satisfaction from doing so.

SUMMARY

Dual-career marriages are not simply those in which women hold full-time jobs outside the home; rather, they are marriages in which the woman views her occupation as a major source of satisfaction. Up to one-half of young women today wish to make major commitments to both work and marriage.

Dual-career couples are relatively prosperous. They usually use family planning to make sure that they have only one or two children, and they are about as happy and successful in their marriages as other couples are. There are differences between them and traditional couples, however. Dual-career couples often marry later and recognize from the start that the woman has a strong commitment to work.

Deciding where they will live may be a problem from the start, or it may appear only later, when one of the partners is transferred or gets an opportunity for a better job in some distant city. However they manage a decision to move, at least one partner's career must suffer. Research has shown that men whose wives work make fewer long-distance moves than other men do; they make more short-distance moves, however. This evidence suggests that loss of job mobility is compensated for, in part, by higher living standards in the same geographical area.

One key to success in a dual-career marriage is a husband who identifies with his wife's career goals, and who derives satisfaction from her accomplishments, rather than feeling threatened by them. Many couples share their successes and problems on the job, but others exclude job-related matters from the home. Still other couples, mainly professional, do at least some of their work together.

The most common and pervasive problem for dual-career couples is the lack of time and energy to get everything done. Two full-time careers, plus management of a home and family, place enormous demands on both partners. Couples solve this problem in various ways. First, they cooperate flexibly to see that the household and family chores get done. Children tend to assume various responsibilities from an early age, and many families also have paid household help. Families plan carefully to make the best of the limited leisure time they have, and they often forego many of the kinds of routine social activities that more traditional couples participate in. They are likely to associate with other dual-career couples who support them in their life style.

Relationships with families on both sides pose other problems. Parents often are too far away for regular visits, and, besides, there isn't enough time for them. The problem becomes acute as the grandchildren grow up. All three generations often feel that something is lacking in their lives.

Dual careers impose special strains on the family but also offer special rewards. Data are not yet available on how durable these marriages are. We do know that in some cases the strains are too great, and divorce occurs. Divorce appears most likely if the husband is not sufficiently equalitarian, or if either partner overemphasizes career advancement at the expense of family relationships. In other instances, wives sometimes give up or limit their careers in the interests of enjoying their homes and children. The fact that some dual-career marriages do not last, however, does not deny the likelihood that they constitute a new and spreading life style.

FOR ADDITIONAL READING

Epstein, Cynthia Fuchs, *Woman's Place: Options and Limits in Professional Careers* (Berkeley and Los Angeles: University of California Press, 1970). Analyzes the roles and role conflicts of women in the professions.

Hoffman, Lois Wladis, F. Ivan Nye, *et al., Working Mothers: An Evaluative Review of the Consequences for Wife, Husband, and Child* (San Francisco: Jossey-Bass, 1974). A readable evaluation of the findings of research.

Holmstrom, Lynda Lytle, *The Two-Career Family* (Cambridge, Mass.: Schenkman, 1972). The most comprehensive study of dual-career families available.

Lopata, Helena Znaniecki, *Occupation: Housewife* (New York: Oxford University Press, 1971). An analysis of traditional wife roles, to contrast with those discussed in this chapter.

Petras, John W., ed., *Sex:Male/Gender:Masculine, Readings in Male Sexuality* (Port Washington, New York: Alfred, 1975). Valuable sections on "Male Liberation" and "The New Masculinity."

STUDY
QUESTIONS

1. What is the crucial factor in determining whether a given marriage is a dual-career marriage? What distinguishes a dual-career marriage from other marriages in which the wife works?

2. When and how do couples decide that theirs are to be dual-career marriages? Is there any one pattern?

3. What role does geographical mobility play in dual-career marriages? How would you handle the problem?

4. Does job competition seem to be a major factor in most dual-career marriages? How do you explain this?

5. What is meant by the phrase "work overload?" How does it apply to dual-career families?

6. What are some of the ways in which dual-career families deal with the problem of work overload? Discuss the roles of husbands, of children, and of household help.

7. What kinds of relationships do dual-career couples typically have with their parents? View the problem from the perspectives of grandparents, parents, and children.

8. Are dual-career marriages more or less susceptible to disruption than other marriages? How do you know? Does disruption necessarily mean divorce?

Chapter 14
Divorce

Nobody wants a divorce. To be divorced is a sign of failure; it makes things awkward socially; it is lonely; and for a while, at least, it hurts. Yet divorce has become so common that most people realize it might happen to them. They wonder what makes divorce happen, how to avoid it, and how to handle it wisely if, one day, it proves inevitable.

DIVORCE IN AMERICA

For more than a decade now, the number of divorces in the United States has been climbing rapidly. It increased from less than one-half million in 1965 to over one million a decade later. Part of this numerical increase is due simply to population growth, but that explanation does not account for most of it. The divorce *rate,* the number of divorces per 1000 population, has also almost doubled over the ten-year period. In other words, both the number of divorces and the probability of divorce have been increasing rapidly.

PROBABILITY OF DIVORCE

Most people want to know more than the number of divorces and the divorce rate. They also want to know the likelihood that any given marriage will end in divorce.

Such a figure is not very useful, however, because some groups have much higher probabilities of divorce than others do. Divorce rates among black people, those who marry young, and the poor are significantly higher than among those who marry late, have more education, and are wealthier. Nevertheless, stripping away these complications, U.S. divorce rates have now climbed so that, on the average, one marriage out of every three will end in divorce (England and Kunz, 1975; Glick, 1975).

WHEN DIVORCE OCCURS

Although some people refer to divorce as the death of a marriage, it is more properly the funeral ceremony. Considerable time usually passes between the couple's decision that they cannot live together, or do not want to, and the time their divorce becomes final. More couples who are destined to become divorced separate during the first year of marriage than during any later year. They don't always file for divorce right away; instead, they may continue to test out the possibility of reconciliation and making the marriage work. By the time they do file for divorce, the case is heard, and the divorce becomes final, they have typically been married for about three years.

Although the first year of marriage is the most hazardous, some couples separate and begin divorce proceedings later on, even after the twentieth or thirtieth year of marriage. But, as might be expected, the proportion of couples seeking divorce drops each year. On the average, because some people divorce after many years of marriage, marriages last about seven-and-a-half years before divorce occurs (Glick and Norton, 1971).

WHO SEEKS THE DIVORCE?

Traditionally in the United States, divorce was as male-dominated as marriage itself. In about three-fourths of all cases, the wives rather than the husbands filed the divorce petitions. But they often did so only after the husbands, who were the ones who really wanted the divorces, badgered them into it. There was sometimes a chivalrous aspect to such proceedings, because most states required that one partner be charged with an offense and be adjudged guilty. When both spouses wanted the divorce, or even when the wife alone wanted it, she often was permitted to file the charges so that her ''good name'' would not be besmirched. But overall, wives were more often the reluctant partners than the aggressive seekers of divorce.

No other area of man–woman relationships has changed more drastically in recent years. It is too early for the trend to show up in official divorce statistics; and, besides, the traditional pattern of allowing the wife to file for divorce would obscure the change. But it seems quite certain

that more women are becoming more aggressive than ever before in ending unsatisfactory marriages.

This change shows up most vividly in the reports of commercial agencies that specialize in locating missing persons, particularly runaway spouses. During the late 1960s, there were some four cases of husbands deserting their wives for every one of the reverse. By 1970, the change was evident: agencies now reported almost as many runaway wives as husbands (Culhane, 1973; Bruning, 1974). By 1975, the number of runaway wives was actually greater than the number of runaway husbands.[1]

Not all of these wives were seeking divorce, of course. Some of them left trails so obvious (by using their old credit cards, or checks, for instance) that the investigative agencies concluded that they wanted to be found and returned to their husbands. But these women were communicating to their husbands, in a very dramatic way, their dissatisfaction

[1] *The New York Times,* Feb. 23, 1975.

with their marriages and with their lives in general. And other women did follow through by getting divorces, or covered their tracks so well that they could not be found.

The signs of change are obvious and plentiful. Not only are women entering marriage today with new expectations about what their married lives should be like, but they are showing new determination to end marriages that don't measure up.

CAUSES OF DIVORCE

It is impossible to establish the causes of divorce in any absolute sense. Husband and wife often report different sources of dissatisfaction with the same marriage. Their attorneys may see the cause of divorce as being different still, and a priest or minister likely would ascribe the divorce to yet other causes. Which of them is right? Or are they all correct?

There is little to be gained by trying to argue such questions. Rather than seek the ultimate causes of divorce, we shall try to identify the factors that seem to make some groups more divorce-prone than others, and to see what divorcing persons themselves say are their chief complaints.

UNHAPPY MARRIAGE AS A SOCIAL PROBLEM

In Chapter 11 we cited a study of 5163 married persons in California, which showed that childless marriages are more satisfactory than other marriages (Renne, 1970). This study is relevant again here. The researcher classified the respondents into those satisfied and dissatisfied with their marriages on the basis of answers to several questions. They included, "Do you ever regret your marriage?" "Have you seriously considered separation or divorce recently?" and "All in all, how happy has your marriage been for you?" Approximately 20 percent of the respondents were judged to be dissatisfied.

The major portion of the study was directed toward finding what subgroups in the population were more dissatisfied than others. The respondents' sex, race, socioeconomic status, physical health, emotional health and, of course, childlessness were all considered.

As is consistent with the recent increase in the number of runaway wives, more wives than husbands were found to be dissatisfied. Apparently, a large proportion of dissatisfied wives do not run away.

Black people were also much more likely (two-fold) than white people were to report dissatisfaction. People with lower incomes and less education were also more likely to be dissatisfied. These characteristics all tend to be interrelated, of course. The racial differences almost disappear, but not quite, when comparisons are made only between college-educated persons or between those earning $10,000 a year or more. In this cluster of factors, then, low socioeconomic status is more important than race.

People who reported themselves to be in either "fair" or "poor" physical health also were more likely to be maritally dissatisfied. There are two possible explanations: illness interferes with marital adjustment, or poor marital adjustment influences people to report more ill health. These data do not permit us to say which factor is more important. There is also the possibility that unhappy marriage leads to psychosomatic illnesses that eventually become chronic.

Various symptoms of emotional ill-health also were related to marital dissatisfaction: loneliness, depression, boredom, general dissatisfaction, uneasiness, and a feeling that life is meaningless. Heavy drinking of alcohol also was associated with marital dissatisfaction. Again, as in the case of physical health, we are unable to separate cause from effect.

When all of these findings are viewed together, they point to marital unhappiness as something of a social problem that most often affects people who have other kinds of problems. Thus, racial discrimination, poverty, physical and mental ill-health, and heavy drinking all provide conditions that lead to dissatisfaction and dissatisfaction may lead, in turn to divorce.

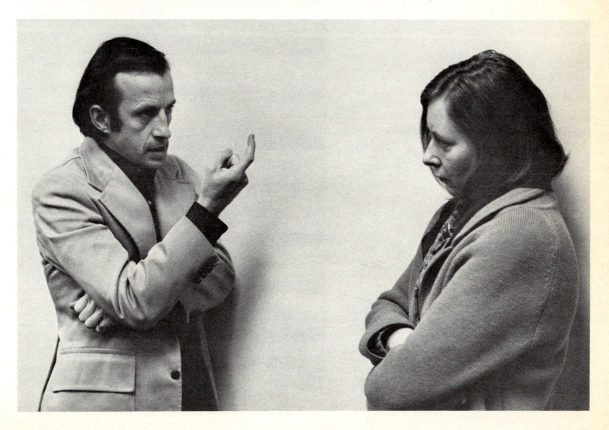

COMPLAINTS
LEADING TO
DIVORCE

A study of 600 couples applying for divorce in Cleveland, Ohio, reported the complaints that brought them to the divorce court (Levinger, 1966). Some of the results are shown in Figure 14-1.

Again we find that wives' complaints outnumber those of husbands by a wide margin. Mental cruelty, neglect of home and children, physical abuse, financial problems, and drinking all were frequently reported by wives. Only three grievances—making excessive demands, in-law trouble, and sexual incompatibility—were reported more often by husbands

Figure 14-1 Complaints of 600 divorcing couples about their marriages. (Adapted from Levinger [1966].)

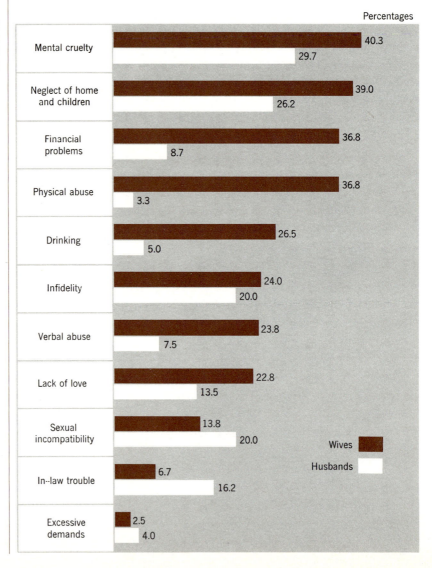

Percentages

	Wives	Husbands
Mental cruelty	40.3	29.7
Neglect of home and children	39.0	26.2
Financial problems	36.8	8.7
Physical abuse	36.8	3.3
Drinking	26.5	5.0
Infidelity	24.0	20.0
Verbal abuse	23.8	7.5
Lack of love	22.8	13.5
Sexual incompatibility	13.8	20.0
In-law trouble	6.7	16.2
Excessive demands	2.5	4.0

than by wives. This study, like the preceding one, also found that problems differed in frequency according to the couples' socioeconomic status.

The most common complaint, from both husbands and wives, was "mental cruelty." While this finding seems obvious enough, mental cruelty is almost impossible to define. What it likely means, among other things, is that most couples go through a prolonged period of fighting and quarreling before they finally decide to divorce. There often is physical fighting involved; 37 percent of the wives complain of physical abuse by their husbands. The difference between husbands and wives is larger for this complaint than for any other; only a little over three percent of the husbands complained of physical abuse. We do not know, however, whether so few wives actually hit their husbands, or whether the husbands are less likely to report hitting as a problem. Other studies have shown that up to one-third of families in which violence is used report some hitting by the wife (Gelles, 1972).

The neglect of home and children was the second most frequent complaint of both wives and husbands. This finding is consistent with the stereotyped image of the irresponsible husband. It is not consistent, however, with the stereotyped image of the responsible, dutiful, family-oriented wife. This finding may mean that the image of the wife has been wrong all along, or it may mean that the situation has changed drastically over the past decade or so. Probably both interpretations have some merit. It appears likely, also, that marital discord may lead both men and women to neglect their domestic responsibilities.

Wives also frequently report financial problems and excessive drinking. Husbands often complain of sexual incompatibility, sexual infidelity, and in-law problems. Wives are less likely to complain of sexual incompatibility, but they are slightly more likely to complain of infidelity.

We should remind ourselves again that these stated grievances are not necessarily the causes of divorce; those reasons may be more deep-rooted. They are, however, the things that divorcing couples complain of when they discuss their marriages.

DIVORCE LAWS

As one writer phrased it decades ago, American divorce law is characterized by either a charming individuality or a vicious lack of uniformity, depending upon your point of view. Each of the 50 states and the District of Columbia has its own divorce laws, and the laws of no two jurisdictions are exactly alike. A partial summary of divorce laws is presented in Table 14-1. Obviously, we do not intend it to be memorized; nor should it be taken as an authoritative legal guide. The divorce laws of most states are fiendishly complex and subject to change. Anyone contemplating divorce should secure legal advice.

TABLE 14-1 GROUNDS FOR DIVORCE IN THE UNITED STATES[a]

STATE	Cruelty	Desertion	Non-support	Alcohol	Felony	Impotency	Pregnancy at Marriage	Drug addiction	Fraudulent contract	OTHER CAUSES	RESIDENCE TIME
Alabama	X	X	X	X	X	X	X	X	...	D,H,J,K,AA	1 year
Alaska	X	X	...	X	X	X	...	X	...	B,D,H	1 year
Arizona	...	...	...	...	...	...	...	...	...	BB	90 days
Arkansas	X	X	X	X	X	X	...	...	...	B,H,K,O	3 months
California	...	...	...	...	...	...	...	...	...	H,CC	6 months
Colorado	...	...	...	...	...	...	...	...	...	BB	90 days
Connecticut	X	X	...	X	X	...	...	...	X	D,H,BB	3 years
Delaware	X	X	X	X	X	...	...	...	...	D,H,K,O,Q	2 years
Dist. of Columbia	...	X	...	...	X	...	...	...	...	K	1 year
Florida	...	...	...	...	...	...	...	...	...	H,BB	6 months
Georgia	X	X	...	X	X	X	X	X	X	H,I,L,BB	6 months
Hawaii	...	...	...	...	...	...	...	...	...	BB	1 year
Idaho	X	X	X	X	X	...	...	...	...	H,K	6 weeks
Illinois	X	X	...	X	X	X	...	X	...		1 year
Indiana	...	...	...	...	X	X	...	...	...	H,BB	6 months
Iowa	...	...	...	...	...	...	...	...	...	AA	1 year
Kansas	X	X	...	X	X	X	X	...	X	D,H,N	6 months
Kentucky	...	...	...	...	...	...	...	...	...	BB	180 days
Louisiana	...	...	...	...	X	...	...	...	...	K	1 year
Maine	X	X	X	X	...	X	...	X	...	K,CC	6 months
Maryland	X	X	...	...	X	X	...	...	...	H,K	1 year
Massachusetts	B	X	X	X	X	X	...	X	...	V	2 years
Michigan	...	...	...	...	...	...	...	...	...	AA	1 year
Minnesota	...	X	...	X	X	X	...	...	...	H,K,Y	1 year
Mississippi	X	X	...	X	X	X	X	X	...	H,I,O	1 year
Missouri	...	...	...	...	...	...	...	...	...	BB	1 year
Montana	X	X	X	X	X	...	...	...	...	H,CC	1 year
Nebraska	...	...	...	...	...	...	...	...	...	BB	1 year
Nevada	X	X	X	X	X	X	...	...	...	H,K	6 weeks
New Hampshire	X	X	X	X	X	X	...	...	...	C,R,S,T,CC	1 year
New Jersey	X	X	...	X	X	...	...	X	...	H,K,W	1 year
New Mexico	X	X	...	...	...	...	...	...	...	D	6 months
New York	X	X	...	...	X	...	...	...	...	K	1 year
North Carolina	...	...	...	...	...	X	X	...	...	H,J,K	6 months
North Dakota	X	X	X	X	...	...	...	...	...	H,CC	1 year
Ohio	X	X	...	X	X	X	...	...	X	M,N,O	1 year
Oklahoma	X	X	...	X	X	X	X	...	X	D,H,M,N	6 months
Oregon	...	...	...	...	...	...	...	...	...	CC	6 months
Pennsylvania	X	X	...	...	X	X	...	...	X	B,H,I,K,O	1 year
Rhode Island	X	X	X	X	X	X	...	X	...	C,K	2 years
South Carolina	X	X	...	X	X	...	...	X	...	K	1 year
South Dakota	X	X	X	X	X	...	...			H	1 year
Tennessee	X	X	X	X	X	X	X	...	...	A,O,P	6 months
Texas	X	X	...	...	X	...	...	...	...	D,H,K,DD	1 year
Utah	X	X	X	X	X	X	...	...	...	H,K	3 months
Vermont	X	X	...	...	X	...	...	...	...	H,K	6 months
Virginia	...	X	...	...	X	X	X	...	...	B,F,K	1 year
Washington	...	...	...	...	...	...	...	...	X	B,H,K,CC	6 months
West Virginia	X	X	...	X	X	...	...	X	...	H,K	2 years-Z
Wisconsin	X	X	X	X	X	...	...			H,K	6 months
Wyoming	X	X	X	X	X	X	X	...	...	B,G,H	60 days

Adultery is either grounds for divorce or evidence of irreconcilable differences and a breakdown of the marriage in all states. (A) Violence. (B) Indignities. (C) Joining religious order disbelieving in marriage. (D) Incompatibility. (E) Any gross misbehavior or wickedness. (F) Wife being a prostitute. (G) Husband being a vagrant. (H) Insanity. (I) Consanguinity. (J) Crime against nature. (K) Separation for a term specified by law. (L) Mental incapacity at time of marriage. (M) Procurement of out-of-state divorce. (N) Gross neglect of duty. (O) Bigamy. (P) Attempted homicide. (Q) Plaintiff under age at time of marriage. (R) Treatment which injures health or endangers reason. (S) Wife out of state for 10 years. (T) Wife in state 2 years; husband never in state and has intent to become citizen of foreign country. (U) Seven years absence. (V) Life sentence dissolves marriage. (W) Deviate sexual conduct. (Y) Course of conduct detrimental to the marriage relationship of party seeking divorce. (Z) No minimum residence required in adultery cases. (AA) Breakdown of marriage with no reasonable likelihood of preservation. (BB) Marriage irretrievably broken. (CC) Irreconcilable differences. (DD) Incompatibility without regard to fault.

[a]State laws are subject to change, and there are many local variations and areas for judicial discretion. Persons contemplating divorce should secure legal advice.

Source: Adapted from a table compiled by William E. Mariano, Council on Marriage Relations, Inc., for *The World Almanac and Book of Facts,* 1975 (New York: Newspaper Enterprise Association, 1975), p. 962.

The year 1969 brought the beginning of a period of drastic change in divorce law and procedure, amounting virtually to a revolution: the movement toward no-fault divorce. That revolution is still in its early stages, but it appears likely to affect most states and most courts within the next decade or two. In the meantime, most people in most states who seek divorces will find themselves contending with traditional laws and practices.

TRADITIONAL DIVORCE LAW

Most state governments traditionally have looked upon divorce as a necessary evil at best; they have thus attempted to make it difficult to secure. First, they have limited the legal grounds upon which divorce can be obtained. Louisiana, for example, grants divorces on only three grounds, and New Mexico on four; several other states permit only a few additional grounds.

The Traditional Philosophy

Second, the legal grounds for divorce generally consist of quite serious offenses, such as adultery, bigamy, cruelty, conviction of a felony, fraud, habitual drunkenness, insanity, incest, and nonsupport.

Third, in order for a divorce to be awarded, not only must one spouse be proven guilty of one of the specified offenses, but the other spouse must also be innocent of any of them. Moreover, an additional fiction must be maintained, that only one spouse wants the divorce and the other opposes it. If the partners agree that they should seek a divorce, that is termed *collusion,* and the judge is obligated to deny the divorce.

Traditionally, the law pits divorcing wives and husbands against one another in a legal contest to determine which shall be judged guilty and which shall be held blameless. It persists in doing so despite the fact that any reasonable person knows that the vast majority of embattled husbands and wives have both committed acts that are grounds for divorce.

The Adversary System

We have already referred to marital quarreling and fighting. Many instances of it could easily be construed as cruelty, mental cruelty, defamation, gross misbehavior, incompatibility, violent temper, or willful neglect, all of which are legal grounds for divorce in some states. By the time things reach the divorce courts, each spouse often has been driven to other hurtful acts. Some of these can be classified as desertion, force, impotence, indignities, or neglect of marital duty, still other legal grounds for divorce.

In spite of these realities, which often cause both spouses to accept the inevitability of divorce, the adversary system requires that in all divorce proceedings there be a plaintiff (the party who brings charges against the other) and a defendant (the accused). In turn, this necessity requires that the wife and husband each have a lawyer. These rules set the stage for transforming the marital battle into a legal one.

Fairly typically, couples have reached at least some tentative agreements between themselves concerning the terms of the divorce. One will stay in the house or apartment, and the other will move. The furniture and the automobiles will be divided in a certain manner. Even tentative amounts for alimony and child support payments may be agreed upon.

There are wise and compassionate attorneys who, even if they cannot transform divorce into a healing process, at least seek to minimize its hurtful aspects. These humanitarian urges, however, run head on into the attorney's ethical obligation to get the best settlement possible for the client. Even if one partner's attorney favors accepting the couple's compromises, the other often opposes them. Rarely, both attorneys take a humanitarian view. But even so, the necessity of working out the details usually results in increased bitterness and hostility between the spouses. Most likely, this process is complicated by the partners' feelings of hurt and rejection, and by the further breakdown of communication between them at this time.

Fairly typically, the wife's attorney advises her that she should seek a more generous property settlement than the husband is offering, with the implication that he owes it to her. Similarly, when there are children, her attorney reminds her that more than a simple monthly support payment is involved. There is the matter of hospitalization insurance and medical bills, to say nothing of life insurance in case the husband should die. Special educational expenses may be involved as well. In any case, the husband's obligations are often defined as lasting through the period of the children's college educations. The attorney may also suggest that there be periodic increases in the support payments to compensate for inflation, or that the court review the situation at regular intervals so that the level of the children's support keeps pace with increases in their father's income.

Either gradually or suddenly, the husband learns that the divorce is going to cost him a lot more than he expected. Intellectually, he may understand the need to provide for his children's welfare. At the same time, though, he is hurt by what appears to be his wife's new vindictiveness and her attorney's insatiable greed. But his anxiety over having his future income mortgaged away often turns to rage when he learns that not only must he pay his own attorney's fee and the court costs, but he must pay his wife's attorney as well.

Somewhere in this process, the couple is likely to try to talk about the situation again to see if they cannot settle things more reasonably. But by this time they are usually in no position to do so. The husband asserts belligerently that his wife has betrayed their agreements and is listening to unsound advice from a greedy lawyer. These charges merely strengthen her conviction that her attorney is right, and that she must protect herself and her children against this man, whose cruel streak and irresponsibility are becoming only too evident.

Finally, there is the fact that evidence must be presented in court. It has to be proven that one partner has committed misdeeds serious enough to entitle the other partner to a divorce. In most instances, the attorneys settle for using a relatively nonjudgmental legal ground, such as cruelty or desertion, rather than grounds that carry more stigma, such as adultery. Nevertheless, the partner who is the plaintiff must be coached to say in court that the other partner has committed acts serious enough, and repeatedly enough, to convince the judge that the divorce should be granted. The other partner usually is warned by his or her attorney of what must happen in court. Still, the experience hurts. Both partners find it personally degrading and are further embittered by it.

The details vary from divorce to divorce, and the husband and wife become angry and hurt in different ways. But no matter how mature and rational they try to be, the adversary nature of the whole legal process works against their cooperating and remaining on friendly terms with one another. Often, by the time the divorce is awarded, enough hostility has been generated to guarantee that the former spouses will remain enemies for a long time to come.

In 1969, California became the first state to pass legislation that eliminated the adversary philosophy underlying traditional divorce law. It was replaced with a new "no-fault" concept, which holds that marriages should be terminated when they are no longer viable, and without any imputation of guilt or wrongdoing on the part of either spouse. The California law actually eliminated the term "divorce" and substituted "dissolution of marriage" for it. Dissolution was to be granted whenever "irreconcilable differences have caused the irremediable breakdown of the marriage." The law also provided for approximately equal division of the couple's property. It based alimony upon the length of the marriage and the earning ability of the man and the woman.

Some people feared that this new law would lead to a flood of divorces and further weaken the family, but the fear proved groundless. Over the following three years, the divorce rate in California increased less than the national average. At the same time, the number of Californians who traveled to adjoining Nevada for divorces declined substantially.

No-fault appears to be an idea whose time has come. In the six years after the California law was passed, Arizona, Colorado, Delaware, Florida, Iowa, Kentucky, Michigan, Minnesota, Missouri, Nebraska, Oregon, and Washington all followed suit, going to completely no-fault divorce systems. Of these, all except Michigan adopted the term "dissolution"

THE MOVEMENT TOWARD NO-FAULT

instead of "divorce." Other states added no-fault legal grounds for divorce to their existing grounds. Most other state legislatures are considering making changes in their laws.

NO-FAULT IN PRACTICE

The California law is still very young, and the others are even more recent. But early experience shows the new laws to be working better in some ways than in others and better in some states than others.

In some cases, no-fault seems to be working very well indeed. The need for the spouses to have separate attorneys has been eliminated. There have even been instances in which couples have filed their own legal papers, dispensing with attorneys altogether. Attorneys counsel people against doing so, and their arguments are not altogether selfish. Nevertheless, the dollar costs of securing a divorce can now be reduced markedly.

More important still is the fact that the adversary process can be eliminated. The couple can work together with a single attorney to develop and formalize their compromises about the distribution of property, child support, custody, and visitation rights and privileges. This system doesn't necessarily make the money go any further than it did before, but it helps to minimize the spouses' feelings that they are being victimized.

Finally, much of the guilt and recrimination associated with traditional divorces can now be eliminated. Divorce occurs simply because the marriage has failed, and not because one of the spouses has committed some horrible misdeeds. No-fault divorce is not painless—far from it—but it does minimize unwarranted bitterness.

PROBLEMS OF NO-FAULT

In some other respects, however, no-fault divorce is not working so well. The above list of advantages must be qualified. Some problems exist in various circumstances.

First, there is a gap between the passage of laws and the realization of the legislature's intent. Some judges are older people, accustomed to administering harshly-worded divorce laws, and imbued with a firm sense of the morality and immorality of divorce. Thus, although the written law may now state that the irreversible breakdown of the marriage is the only criterion on which the divorce decision can be made, some individual judges still insist upon hearing detailed testimony cataloguing the specific acts by one of the spouses that have destroyed the marriage. This attitude makes the divorce process unnecessarily painful, and it perpetuates the idea that one of the partners is to blame and should be punished.

Problems arise, as well, in states that have preserved the old fault grounds for divorce and merely added some no-fault provision to them. In such states, couples may have the alternative of seeking divorce on grounds of cruelty, adultery, and so on, or of claiming marital breakdown.

If they agree on marital breakdown, fine. But if one partner wishes to be vindictive, he or she can file using one of the traditional grounds. The other's right to the no-fault divorce is thus effectively nullified. With or without the encouragement of attorneys, one partner may also threaten to use fault grounds in order to win a more favorable no-fault settlement.

The movement toward no-fault divorce appears to have wide public support and enough momentum to assure that divorce will be more common and more humane in the future. Great improvement already is evident. But we must also acknowledge that the "revolution" is still in a very early stage. It will be years, and perhaps decades, before the change is complete.

Marriages that end in divorce are not all alike. Some couples in their late teens or early twenties live together for only a short time before discovering that their marriage was a mistake. They have not become emotionally very dependent upon one another, and there are no children involved. The divorce trauma for them is likely to be much less severe than it is for couples who have lived together for a long time and who have children. Some marriages are wracked with bitter conflict, but in others there is only a gradual and almost indiscernible growing apart. Allowance must be made for these variations when considering the divorce experiences that people have.

Divorce hurts. It may hurt only a little but, more often, it hurts a lot. One way to convey the nature of that hurt is to contrast divorce with the opposite process, being married. Being married is a reassuring, self-enhancing experience. One has been chosen as being something special and desirable. Other people actively or benignly approve of the situation, and both the man and the woman feel good about themselves. The world seems a friendly place, and one's position in it seems secure (Bohannon, 1970).

Divorce's effect is just the opposite. Instead of being chosen, one is rejected. Even the person who seeks the divorce most actively seldom escapes the feeling of having failed in the marriage. One not only rejects the partner but also, sooner or later, experiences rejection in turn.

Moreover, other people disapprove of divorce. Members of one's own family, even if they openly agree that the divorce is inevitable, are likely to be saddened by it. In-laws are even more likely to express disappointment, blame, and anger. Friends and acquaintances may take sides, or they may try to be scrupulously objective. But either way, the divorcing person almost inevitably suffers disapproval. Although it may be directed specifically at the divorce action, it seems to become generalized to the person. Divorce usually introduces severe threats to the person's self-esteem.

THE PERSONAL EXPERIENCE OF DIVORCE

EMOTIONAL TRAUMA

Another way to appreciate the emotional trauma of divorce is to compare it to bereavement. The loss of a marriage partner through divorce is not unlike losing someone through death. No matter how much one has come to dislike some things about the spouse, there is a deep sense of loss and a particularly nagging form of grief. But when someone dies, there are public rituals: the displaying of the body, the funeral, the wake, and so on. The function of all these rituals is to encourage the open grieving that alleviates pain and to provide an environment of group support. There are no grieving rituals and no public support in the case of divorce. The divorcing person must suffer alone and in silence. Yet the

"I SAW THEM ON THE DATING GAME AND THE NEWLYWED GAME, AND NOW...DIVORCE COURT."

DRAWN FOR *BROADCASTING* BY SIDNEY HARRIS

grief must take its natural course before the person can put it behind and go on to reorganize his or her life.

Ultimately, the trauma passes. Divorced people find that they can live without the former partners. The new house or apartment becomes "home," and the routine problems of meal preparation, laundry, cleaning, and so on are solved. Most importantly, divorced persons gradually come to feel "whole" again. They recover from the attacks on their self-esteem, they come truly to believe that the divorce was for the best, and they begin to look to the future rather than to dwell in the past (Krantzler, 1975).

Just as divorce is an ego-shattering experience, so also is it a step on the road to maturity and self fulfillment for many people. If divorcees are people who failed to make or sustain good marriages, they are also people who would not settle for bad ones. They are people who are continuing the search for richer, more satisfying lives (Bohannon, 1970).

CHILD CUSTODY AND SUPPORT

Love for their children and concern for their welfare cause many couples to delay filing for divorce as long as possible. Obviously, after divorce, the children cannot continue to live with both parents; one parent loses the right to participate fully in their upbringing, to share their joys and their sorrows. Moreover, there is almost always a problem of money. Most families have barely enough income to support one household, and not enough to support two without suffering a drop in their standard of living.

Custody

Which parent should have legal custody of children is specified by the court. If the parents and their lawyers agree on a custody arrangement, the judge may merely ratify that agreement. If they cannot agree, the judge awards custody on the basis of what appears to be in the best interests of the child or children.

It is commonly believed that the courts usually favor the mother in awarding custody because of several assumptions—that children need their mothers more than their fathers, that mothers are more concerned with the child-rearing role than fathers are, and that the necessity to earn a living interferes with the father's ability to be a good parent. It is true that many courts do favor the mother in awarding custody. And this likelihood may lead the woman and her attorney to attempt to coerce a generous financial settlement and a higher level of child support. If the man does not accept the terms suggested, the woman and her attorney may then threaten drastic restriction of the father's rights to see and visit with his children. The chances are that they could not enforce their threats through the courts. Nevertheless, many fathers yield. Not only do they fear bias on the part of the court, but they also wish to avoid a nasty court battle.

Most courts take the position that young children of both sexes need to be with their mothers more than with their fathers. As children approach adolescence, however, some courts hold that boys need masculine role models to help them make the transition to adulthood. With older boys they give some preference to the father, particularly if the boys indicate a wish to go with their father.

It is too early to tell whether the new no-fault legislation is changing custody patterns. But by eliminating the implication that one parent is unfit, the concept of no-fault at least opens the way for both parents to be treated equally in all custody cases. If no-fault works as intended, minimizing hostility between the divorcing spouses, then both parents may be able to continue to play large roles in their children's upbringing, regardless of which parent has physical custody.

Support

Both law and legal practice are quite traditional where child support is concerned. The father is responsible for the financial support of his children even though he may be divorced from their mother. As in the custody arrangement, the spouses and their attorneys may decide on the amount of support to be paid, and the judge may merely ratify that agreement. The judge can, however, either raise or lower the amount, and sometimes does. Most judges appear more likely to raise it than to lower it.

The amount of the support payments depends on both the ability of the father to pay and the estimated needs of the children. The only trouble is that it is quite easy, in most cases, to demonstrate that there simply isn't enough money.

Initially, all parties concerned are likely to agree that the children should be maintained at their present standard of living, and it is also easy to demonstrate that caring for the children will interfere with the mother's ability to earn a living for a while. Clearly, then, it will cost more than it did in the past just to maintain the children's current living standard. When the arithmetic has been done, it usually is quite obvious that the father's living standard will have to drop substantially. This, of course, is when the trouble starts. Both parents seek to protect themselves in the struggle, and eventually a compromise is reached that each party believes favors the other.

No comprehensive data are available on the dollar amounts of child support payments over the country, but they vary widely from region to region and even among judges in the same locations. In 1975, the results of a two-year national study of the costs of child rearing were published. These figures are now being used in Seattle, Washington, as a basis from which to begin negotiations.[2] The study showed that the costs of child

[2] *The New York Times,* March 8, 1975.

rearing are much higher than was believed, and its adoption in Seattle resulted in a substantial increase in support payments.

Before the study was published, the schedule in use by the Seattle courts provided that a parent with a net income of $1000 a month should pay $130 for the support of one child, $245 for two children, and $345 for three children. After the study, the amounts were raised to $240 for one child, $350 for two children, and $420 for three children. Thus, a parent paying support for three children might pay nearly half of his or her income for child support.

FRIENDS AND THE COMMUNITY

When they contemplate divorce, few people realize that they will be divorcing not only a mate but also a set of friends and almost a whole way of life. They should not be surprised, however, because the same sort of thing happens each time one undergoes a major change in life circumstances. Childhood friendships, for example, despite determined efforts to preserve them, seldom survive a move to a new neighborhood or another city. There is loneliness for a while until one makes new friends. Similarly, few high-school friendships survive the transition into college. Entry into the world of work requires still another new set of friends, and the most drastic change of all comes with marriage. Each spouse may keep a very few friends from pre-marriage days, and some of these friends become friends of the couple. But most old friends simply fade away, while new pair friendships are formed.

Still, few people are prepared for the lack of support they get from friends after the separation occurs, or when it is announced that a divorce is forthcoming. Suddenly, neither the husband nor the wife is invited out any more. And when one of them seizes the initiative and proposes a social event or just an evening of visiting, there is a certain awkwardness or hesitation in the friends' response. The friends' reactions discourage further overtures.

There are exceptions. An occasional friend from before the marriage rises to the occasion and provides badly needed companionship and emotional support. Now and then, there are even friends of the couple who carefully avoid taking sides, and who entertain separately the friends they used to entertain jointly. Finally, there are people whose interest develops precisely because of the separation. There are always a few men who would like to comfort the estranged wife, particularly in bed, and an occasional woman to whom the estranged husband has been ''off limits'' is now free to pursue her interest in him.

But these are exceptions. Most potential divorced people, and most recently divorced ones, are lonely. Their old friends avoid them because they disapprove, or they take sides, or they just don't know how to cope with the situation. Not surprisingly, the divorced persons become bitter about the situation and conclude that most of their so-called friends were shallow friends indeed.

A special case of the friendship situation concerns the families of the former spouses. Logically, one could make a case that each partner will experience a closing of ranks with his or her kin, while the former spouse is excluded by them. To see just what does happen, a pair of researchers interviewed 42 women and 62 men who had been divorced, generally for less than four years (Spicer and Hampe, 1975).

Visits to one's own relatives, or being visited by them, remained at about the same level for most divorced persons as it had been during the marriage. In about one-fifth of the cases, however, visits became more frequent after the divorce. This evidence suggests that there was some closing of ranks in support of the divorced person. Men and women divorcees interacted with their parents with about equal frequency. Women, however, interacted more frequently with brothers and sisters and other relatives than before.

As expected, most divorced men and women saw their former in-laws less frequently, if at all. There were exceptions, however. Women saw their former in-laws more frequently than men did, particularly when they had children. Apparently, the role of grandparent legitimizes continued contact after divorce, and it promotes relationships of some affection between the man's parents and their former daughter-in-law. Although the men were less likely to see their former in-laws, most of them reported that they felt no hostility toward their former spouse's parents.

Like the pain of divorce itself, the loneliness passes. Some divorced persons, cut loose from their former obligations, develop new interests and make new friends in the process. Others continue former interests and just make new friends. Eventually, most of both groups come to believe that their new friends are superior to their former friends. The bitterness that they felt toward the former friends is replaced by a more or less tolerant understanding.

Nobody likes divorce. It is a painful and ego-damaging experience. For many people, however, the temporary suffering of divorce is preferable to perpetuating a marital mistake or continuing a marriage that no longer affords real satisfaction. If it is painful, it is also a learning experience, and divorce can be a step on the way to a richer, more meaningful life.

SUMMARY

People marrying today face about one chance in three that their marriages will sooner or later end in divorce. In most cases it is sooner, the first year of marriage being the most likely time of separation. On the average, however, marriages last seven-and-a-half years before divorce.

Women have become much more aggressive in confronting their marital dissatisfactions and more likely to want to end unsatisfying marriages. One symptom of this trend is the growing number of women who desert their husbands and children.

The root causes of divorce are difficult to pinpoint. Studies confirm the fact that there are more dissatisfied wives than husbands; they also report that black people, poor people, and people who are in poor physical or emotional health are more likely to report marital unhappiness. Divorcing couples emphasize mental cruelty, neglect of home and children, financial problems, and physical abuse as sources of complaint. Only in the areas of sexual incompatibility, in-law problems, and making excessive demands are husbands more likely to complain than wives.

Traditionally, in the United States, divorce was defined as a necessary evil and was made difficult to secure. One partner had to bring charges against the other, based on legal grounds, and had to prove that person guilty in court. This requirement led to hostility between the spouses and their attorneys which, in turn, caused divorce to be unnecessarily painful and destructive.

In the six years after 1969, 13 states enacted no-fault divorce laws, and 11 additional states added no-fault grounds to their existing legal grounds for divorce. No-fault is directed at finding out whether a marriage is irretrievably broken rather than which partner is guilty; its aim is to end the marriage as painlessly as possible. Substantial improvements in divorce procedure have been made in many states, but some judges and some attorneys are slow to change.

Most people going through divorces experience painful feelings of failure and rejection. In addition, there is a profound sense of loss, not unlike that felt when someone dies. The grief of divorce must be suffered alone, however, and is the more difficult for that reason. Most people recover from these feelings after a while and go on to become more mature persons, determined to make the most constructive use of their lives.

One parent loses custody of the children at divorce. The courts generally favor the mother, at least when the children are small, but some courts favor granting custody of teenaged boys to the father when the boys themselves wish it. The question of the amount of child support is very difficult because, in most divorces, there simply isn't enough money to permit all family members to continue their past standard of living.

Finally, divorced persons must face the loss of old friends and the need to make new ones; few couple friendships survive divorce. Some loneliness is typical and some bitterness toward apparently false friends is common. These feelings pass, too, and the divorcee's new friends eventually seem superior to the old ones.

FOR
ADDITIONAL
READING

Bohannon, Paul, ed., *Divorce and After* (New York: Anchor Books, 1971). A judicious selection of readings on divorce and adjustment to divorce.

Fisher, Esther Oshiver, *Divorce: The New Freedom* (New York: Harper and Row, 1975). A practising counselor's guide to those who are seeking divorce or are adjusting to it.

Krantzler, Mel, *Creative Divorce: A New Opportunity for Personal Growth* (New York: New American Library, 1973). Sensitive analysis of the emotional trauma of divorce and of ways to use it constructively.

Rheinstein, Max, *Marriage Stability, Divorce and the Law* (Chicago: University of Chicago Press, 1972). Scholarly analysis of worldwide trends, by a noted attorney.

Wheeler, Michael, *No-Fault Divorce* (Boston: Beacon Press, 1974). Comprehensive discussion of the many ramifications of the new no-fault divorce concept.

STUDY
QUESTIONS

1. What is the likelihood that marriages today will end in divorce? Do these figures apply to all divorces? Which ones are least risky?

2. Which spouse do you think is more often dissatisfied in marriage? Cite as much evidence as you can to support your position.

3. What do you think are the basic causes of divorce? Are they the same complaints that divorcing persons express about their marriages? Why or why not?

4. How does no-fault divorce differ from traditional divorce? Do you think it is a good or a bad thing? Why?

5. A popular book is entitled *Creative Divorce*. In terms of the content of this chapter, what do you think the author intends his title to mean?

6. The grief that accompanies divorce ordinarily is suffered in private. Can you think of ways in which others might share in that grief and help to minimize it?

7. Do you think that no-fault divorce eventually will have some influence on the award of custody of children? Will the effects be good or bad? Why?

8. How would you recommend that persons undergoing divorce deal with their friends? Consider personal friends, joint friends, old friends, and new friends.

Chapter 15
Parents
Without Partners

In about three out of every five divorces today, there are minor children in the home. In some instances, both parents remarry promptly. When that happens, neither the parents nor the children have the experience of living for long in a one-parent family. Speedy remarriage is not typical, however. Although most divorced persons eventually remarry, parents with custody of their children are slower to remarry than either non-parents or parents who do not have custody. For many of them, there are months or years of living without a spouse and co-parent. Some mothers and some fathers completely raise their children without remarrying.

THE NUMBERS INVOLVED

At any one time in the United States, over three-and-a-half million families with children have only one parent present (Brandwein, Brown and Fox, 1974). In about 85 percent of all cases, these parents without partners are women. In view of the publicity given to mother-headed or fatherless families, this fact may not surprise anyone. When we stop to think, however, that these figures mean there are also at least a half-million father-headed or motherless families in the United States, we may begin to see the situation in a new light.

Not all of these one-parent families have been created by divorce. Perhaps one case out of three arises from the death of one parent. In some cases, the parents were not married to begin with. Most often, however, one-parent families are created by divorce.

Over seven million children live in one-parent families. Some, of course, live in them for only a few months until the parent remarries. But others spend much or all of their youth living with parents without partners.

THE CHILDREN'S DIVORCE

The emotional pain suffered by the man and woman in the course of divorce is bad enough, but they are not the only ones who suffer. Their children suffer, too, and mother and father suffer with them. If the home has been an openly unhappy one, no one may have to tell the children that something is wrong; they may know it only too well and yearn for the relief that divorce can bring. In other situations, the children may be vaguely uneasy without really knowing why. The news that a divorce is likely may precipitate an emotional crisis for them. Finally, some children manage not to know much about the relationship between their parents until the fateful day when one parent, or maybe both, sits them down to tell them what is happening.

CHILDREN'S REACTIONS

In addition to the differences among children and among families, the ages of the children are a factor in determining how they react to the prospect of a parental divorce. At the risk of some oversimplification, we can describe typical reactions among infants, preschool children, school-aged children, and adolescents.

Infants

Babies, of course, cannot know what is happening and cannot be told of it. Neither is there any reason to expect specific reactions from them. Yet they do react to the feelings of their parents; great anxiety, prolonged anger, or deep sorrow, particularly in the mother, may produce general symptoms of upset in the baby. Eating and bowel functioning may be affected, with resulting fussiness. The baby's responses to various stimuli may be interfered with, and crawling and walking may be delayed (Krantzler, 1975).

The baby's upset lasts only as long as the parent's does, however, and, as soon as the emotional crisis is past, the child's normal development resumes. The effects are no more long-term than those that follow the many kinds of physical and emotional upsets that all babies experience. By the time the child is old enough to understand even in a rudimentary way what divorce means, its parents may have become so accustomed to single-parent living that, to the child, its way of life may seem totally normal and unexceptional.

Typically, young children do not take divorce nearly so easily. Unlike babies, they do know that they have two parents, and they have a sense that, somehow, their security is tied up with those parents. Much of this "knowing" is more emotional than intellectual. It is experienced by the child through a mixture of fantasies and fears as it attempts to understand the powerful forces in the adult world that seem either to afford it protection or to threaten to destroy it.

Thus, when the child is told that one of its parents will no longer be with it, it may be filled with both foreboding and guilt. This feeling may be intensified as the child becomes aware that one of its parents indeed is gone. What has really happened to the absent parent? Is he or she dead? If the one parent has disappeared so easily, will the other parent disappear too? In that case, what will happen to the child?

Even in less troubled circumstances, the rage that young children occasionally feel toward their parents is frightening. These urges to hurt (or kill) the parent are repressed, however, because to act on them would bring calamity. But when that parent disappears through divorce, the child's emotions may tell it that its wish for the parent to be harmed has somehow come true. The child feels responsible for what has happened.

The preschooler's emotional upset is likely to be much more apparent and pervasive than that of the infant. Regression to more immature forms of behavior may appear in many areas. The toilet-trained child suddenly loses control of its bowels; bed-wetting may become a nightly occurrence. Nightmares in which the child is threatened by formless monsters may make it scream and awaken in terror. Daytime hours may find the child clinging fearfully to the remaining parent, afraid to go out and play, or subject to violent temper tantrums without provocation.

Even the most understanding parent's patience is likely to be sorely tried by such behavior. Moreover, most divorcing parents are sufficiently upset themselves that they are less than normally understanding. The temptation is strong to scold and punish a child who persists in disapproved behavior. Punishment is likely only to make matters worse, however, because the child is merely acting out fears and anxieties that it cannot put into words. When the crisis passes, so will the misbehavior.

There are some things that the parents can do to minimize the crisis. For one thing, the child should have the opportunity to visit with, or be visited by, the absent parent frequently. Such contact will at least stop the child's fantasies about that parent's being dead and allay any guilt feelings the child has developed about the fantasied death. It also helps the child learn that the divorce doesn't mean the end of the relationship

Preschoolers

with the other parent. Obviously, the better the parents handle the situation, the easier it will be for the child to accept it. In any case, the child needs to be helped to keep its hold on reality.

**School-Aged
Children**

Children beyond the age of five or six generally can understand something of what is happening to their parents. They may be aware of quarreling or, at least, may sense that their parents have problems. When the separation occurs, they know that the other parent has gone away somewhere, and they also know that he or she will be back to see them again.

What children of this age need more than anything else is a careful explanation, adjusted to their age levels and guided by their questions, of just what is happening. It is better if the explanation comes from the parents jointly, but the most important thing is that the explanation be honest. The parents should not evade the fact that they can no longer live together; but at the same time, the parents should also reassure the children that they are still loved, that both parents will cooperate to take care of them, and that the children will continue to see the parent who moves out of the home.

No matter how well the parents handle the situation, they should be alert for indications that the children are having difficulty adjusting. One source of pain for the children may be their schoolmates, who can be very cruel at these ages, taunting them with the fact that "you don't have a daddy (mommy) any more." Teachers and parents can help minimize this problem. And if the parent who has custody must move to another house or apartment anyway, it sometimes helps to move to another school district where the other children will not know of the divorce.

School-aged children are also prone to take sides, at least temporarily, in the conflict between their parents. They may become intensely hostile to the parent whom they believe to be responsible for the divorce. They may also knowingly or unknowingly engage in maneuvers that are intended to get the parents back together again. These tactics can range from ostracizing the "guilty" parent to becoming especially dependent upon that parent; they can include doing poorly in school, or misbehaving so outrageously that the parents are tempted to attempt reconciliation solely to cope with the child.

Probably the thing that is most helpful to school-aged children, as well as to younger and older ones, is for the parents to reorganize their lives as efficiently and calmly as possible. When they are settled in their new living quarters, new routines have been established, both parents have become comfortable with the situation, and the absent parent's involvement with them is predictable, most children settle down. They begin to look forward instead of backward.

Adolescents

Adolescence is frequently a turbulent period, whether or not the teenagers must cope with a divorce. Divorce, however, often complicates things. Spared the fantasies and fears of younger children, teenagers are likely to begin to see their parents not only as parents but also as people with all the strengths and weaknesses of other people. If the parents are unwise enough to involve the teenagers in their struggles, it may be an extremely painful experience. The children may take sides and become very bitter toward the parent they think is to blame. And when they do so, it complicates adjustments for all concerned and delays the time required for satisfactory compromises to be reached.

Perhaps more often, however, after the first acute distress has moderated, most teenagers acquire a degree of objectivity about their parents and try to understand what has happened (Spears, 1973). They seek answers to numerous questions: What caused the break-up? In what ways was the father responsible? In what ways, the mother? Is one of them, or are both of them, bad people? What do I think of adultery?

What do I really think of each of my parents? Am I like them? What role did I play, if any, in the break-up?

The answers may not come easily, but they do come. And as they do, many teenagers manage to achieve some emotional withdrawal from their parents' problems. Basically they conclude, ''I am not my parents,'' ''I am sorry for what happened to them,'' ''I love them and I would like to help them, but I cannot solve their problems.'' In so doing, teenagers get their own hold on reality and become prepared to deal with their now separated parents both as parents and as people.

MOTHERS WITHOUT PARTNERS

In the vast majority of divorces, custody of the children is awarded to the mother, who faces the need to build a new life for herself and for them. Circumstances vary, of course. There may be only one child, or there may be two or three. The children may range from babies to teenagers. The woman may or may not have a career. She may be used to handling money and paying the bills, or she may not. Whatever the variations, there is a common range of problems that faces mothers without partners.

WORK AND MONEY

Although there are divorced women fortunate enough to have enough money without working, they are relatively few. Typically, divorced mothers can't make ends meet on child support payments, although many try to do so for a while. When the bills pile up, there may be tearful or angry scenes with the ex-husband, who is berated for failing to support his children adequately. He is likely to be having financial problems of his own, however, and the woman seldom gets any relief from him. Sooner or later, she faces the inevitable: she has to get a job.

This initial period, before the mother gets a job, often lasts from several months to two or three years. Although she may not recognize it at the time, it serves a useful function. It enables the family to become comfortable in its new household routines, and it gives the younger children time to do some growing up, so that they do not present as great a problem of child care when the mother finally begins to work outside the home.

Getting a job is an anxiety-producing experience for most people of both sexes, and divorced women are no exception. But they do eventually get jobs. Some of these are challenging occupations that offer substantial rewards, and some of them are just ordinary jobs that provide a paycheck.

Getting a job typically has two effects for the divorced woman. First, it bolsters her self-esteem and her self-confidence. After perhaps years out of the labor force, she once again is able to show her worth. She has met the world on its own terms and established her competence and independence. Her bolstered feelings of self-confidence affect her social life as well. She need not apologize to people for her divorced status or hold back in relationships with them. In short, she has a new lease on life.

The second effect of getting a job is to bring her standard of living, and that of her children, back up to the level where it was before the divorce. Although she will continue to have all of the money management problems that other families have, the financial pain of the divorce is behind her.

Tied up with all of these developments is the achievement of mastery over the details of household financial management. She has learned to arrange for utilities—electricity, gas and telephone—and to deal with appliance repairmen, furniture movers and the like. She has established credit in her own name, made major purchases, and arranged both life- and health-insurance protection. Finally, she has even confronted the formidable forms of the Internal Revenue Service and found that she can cope with them as well as anybody else.

The details vary from family to family, of course. But the mother who is head of a household is likely to become more capable and more self-assured in the world of work and money than she was before her divorce. When eventually she remarries, as she probably will, she can be as complete a financial partner as she wishes to be.

BEING FATHER AND MOTHER

If divorced women are likely to look first to their ex-husbands to solve their financial problems, they may be even more likely to expect them to assist with the disciplining and upbringing of the children. Fortunately, in this case, many fathers want to continue close relationships with their children. To the extent to which the relationship between the ex-spouses permits it, they may continue to be fathers in fact as well as in name. The divorced woman quickly learns, however, that no matter how cooperative her ex-husband is, most of the crucial incidents of parenthood occur when he is not around.

The crises, of course, range from the common physical accidents and illnesses of childhood through the academic problems of school-aged children to the social and heterosexual crises of adolescence. Mothers without partners are likely, at such times, silently to curse their ex-husbands, and to curse themselves for ever getting into such a predicament. But they manage well enough. Each crisis passes and is forgotten until the next one occurs.

Most of the business of being a parent is not so dramatic as handling crises. It lies, instead, in the competent management of everyday living. Mothers without partners face challenges in at least four areas of child rearing.

Setting Limits

It doesn't take long for children of any age to discover that their father's authority is no longer around to enforce their mother's demands upon their behavior. So they begin to test her. Younger children may whine or throw temper tantrums in behalf of staying up beyond their usual bedtimes. Slightly older brothers and sisters may avoid doing their homework and household chores. Teenagers may openly defy authority both at home and at school, and they may seek approval from their friends by challenging their mothers.

The temptation is strong for divorced mothers to give in to their children's threats and pleas. The woman's ego usually has been damaged enough by the divorce and the loss of her husband, without having her children turn on her, too. Some mothers make mistakes initially and give in when they should stand firm. It doesn't take long, however, for most mothers to realize the nature of their children's misbehavior. It is both an attempt to see how much they can get away with and a plea for reassurance that their mothers are still in control of the situation. When the mother conquers her own anxieties and sets reasonable but firm limits on her children's behavior, there is an almost audible sigh of relief as everyone settles down again to a cooperative pattern of living.

Giving Responsibility

The work overload of mothers without partners is much like that of dual-career wives. They must rise early to get breakfast prepared and cleared away, the children ready for school, and themselves off to work. Then, after a hard day on the job, their work is just beginning. Shopping, housecleaning, laundry, dinner, cleanup, baths, and preparation for bed all must be attended to.

Most divorced mothers manage to cope with all of these demands, in part, by sharing the responsibility with their children. Even very young children can prepare their own breakfasts and clean up afterward, once they have been shown how to do so. At slightly older ages, they can learn to make their own beds and clean their own rooms. Even before they become teenagers, they can assist with the cleaning, shopping, meal preparation, and cleanup.

The situation varies with the number and ages of the children present. If there is only one child, the mother must be very careful that she doesn't solve her work overload problem by creating a work overload for her child. When there are two or three children, a reasonable sharing of responsibility may contribute to the welfare of all concerned.

Sharing Confidences

Perhaps one of the hardest things for mothers without partners is to know how much of their own inner feelings and needs to share with their children. Soon after the divorce, the mother is likely to be lonely for intimate companionship. If her children are teenagers or approaching adolescence, it is all too easy to treat them almost as adults. A teenaged daughter is cast in the role of confidant, while a teenaged boy may be

encouraged to be the "man of the house" and to assume a manly, protective role with his mother.

If these tendencies are not watched carefully, an exploitative situation can easily develop. Teenaged girls are not their mothers' equivalents in experience or understanding, and they need their mothers to be mothers more than friends. Similarly, teenaged boys need to shape their masculinity in relation to girls of comparable experience, not with mothers who respond to them as though they were dates rather than sons.

The situation is particularly delicate where the woman's feelings toward her ex-husband are concerned. Her need to talk to someone about these feelings may receive encouragement from her children, out of their natural curiosity to know what happened between the parents. But the mother may unwittingly reveal more to the children than they really want to know or are prepared to understand. The effect may be to upset them emotionally and draw them into an alliance against their father.

Divorced mothers should be as honest with their children as possible about the marriage and the problems that led to divorce. In so doing, however, they should also remember that their children are children; although they must learn to understand what has happened, they also need to maintain or build favorable images of each of their parents. Mothers should distinguish clearly between their own needs and their children's needs in talking about the divorce. The mother's own needs should be talked about with other adults.

Providing Role Models

The most helpful and reassuring thing for children and teenagers as they grow up is to see their parents confidently and competently managing their own lives. In one sense, the cards are stacked against divorced parents, because the divorce itself is a symbol of an earlier failure. But that failure need not pursue them far into their post-divorce lives. The parents can still work together to ensure that their children will have adequate adult models of both sexes as they grow up.

Divorced mothers who are concerned about the long-term welfare of their children will see to it that the father's right to visit with the children, and his right to have them with him, are as meaningful as possible. Individual cases vary enough so that it is not possible to specify the details precisely. But they certainly shouldn't be carefully limited to ritualistic visits on Sundays from 1:00 P.M. to 9:00 P.M., during which the father takes them to the movies or to some other place of commercial recreation. And it doesn't involve the use of the children as pawns in a contest to see whether the amount of child support can be effectively raised or lowered.

It does mean cooperation between the parents, both to ease the mother's burden of custody and to let the father play a meaningful role in the children's lives. There is no reason, for example, why the children should not spend occasional weekends with their father. The mother can thus be freed to travel, to be solely with other adults, or just to spend a quiet weekend at home without having to get up early or to adapt to anyone else's schedule.

Being able to spend time in the father's home, and to share with him the routines of getting up, dressing, preparing and eating meals, cleaning, and so on, can go a long way toward removing the artificiality that otherwise accompanies court-provided rights of visitation. The children get an opportunity to know their father as a person and not just as someone who takes them out and spends money on them. They see how he copes with routines and with problems, and they see how their relationships with him are affected as a result.

This principle of parental cooperation to provide the children with adequate role models can be extended in many ways. The father can be pressed into service as baby sitter during some of the mother's evenings out and during times of illness. Arrangements can be made for the children to be with him for special events, such as birthdays (his as well as theirs), holidays, and so on. The children might even spend a month or two with him during the summer, when school does not tie them to their regular home.

From the standpoint of the divorced mother, probably the most important thing is her attitude toward the children's father and their relationship with him. If she thinks it is important for the children to know him, to be with him, and to love him, then the details of the arrangement probably don't matter too much. If the children see their mother coping well with her own divorced status, still accepting their father as a worthwhile human being, and making efforts in his behalf and theirs, they are likely to grow up well prepared to assume their roles as adult men and women.

Many divorced mothers, at first, have relatively little social life. They no longer are completely comfortable around many of their old friends, most of whom function as couples, but they haven't had much opportunity to make new friends. It is a lonely time, and many divorced mothers feel rejected and unwanted. This is the time when they must guard most carefully against becoming too dependent upon their children, against confiding in them too much, and against using them as "friends."

For most divorced mothers, this period of social isolation does not last too long. Various influences operate to bring them out of it. When the woman gets a job, for example, she is usually brought into contact with both men and women with whom she is likely to develop friendships. If she was at all active in interest groups before the divorce, such as amateur theater, musical societies, or community service organizations, she is likely to take them up again afterward. Churches, sororities, and neighborhood action groups offer further opportunities. Most women find some route or routes to a renewed social life.

The title of this chapter happens also to be the name of an organization that was incorporated in 1958 to help divorced parents escape social isolation for themselves and their children, and to provide for them the equivalent of a normal family life (Bohannon, 1970). The local chapters of Parents Without Partners vary widely. Most of them emphasize the exchange of experiences and ideas and the development of understanding, help, and companionship. They accomplish these things

SOCIAL LIFE

**Parents
Without Partners**

through regularly scheduled meetings, sometimes with speakers who are knowledgeable about family life, divorce, adjustment to divorce, and child rearing, and sometimes with some of their own members as discussion leaders.

Most chapters also have social programs that are more or less highly organized. Pot-luck dinners, picnics, and other kinds of outings are frequent. Such activities give divorced mothers (and fathers) and their children the opportunity to become socially active again, to find that their situations are not at all unique, and to share feelings and experiences with others. For some divorced parents, Parents Without Partners offers a badly needed assist at a critical time. For others, who do not soon remarry or develop other consuming interests, the organization becomes a long-term connection with the larger community.

Dating

In concentrating upon the impact of divorce on husbands, wives, and children, it is easy to overlook the fact that either marital partner, or both, may develop important new man–woman relationships even before the divorce is awarded. The wife, for example, may have men friends who are important to her even before she and her husband begin having serious problems. As marital tension mounts, and she feels rejected and unloved, she may become increasingly attached to one of these men. He, in turn, may become a confidant and major source of emotional support.

When the husband and wife finally separate for good, the man may begin to see the woman regularly, taking her out to dinner and other places, and visiting with her at home. The same thing may be happening to the husband, of course, as he seeks the companionship and understanding he no longer has from his wife. Either partner or both may pursue these newly important relationships openly or, if the divorce is a bitterly contested one, discreetly.

In either situation, however, dating for the divorced mother may begin effectively before the divorce is granted. In this case, both the woman and her children become accustomed to it as part of the upheaval that accompanies divorce. And consequently, they escape the mild trauma that is often experienced by divorced women who do without male companionship for a while before and after their divorces. Women who find new male companions early often remarry soon, as well, so that they escape prolonged living as parents without partners.

Most divorced women do begin to go out with men sooner or later. If it is later, there often is a certain awkwardness and hesitancy about it. The woman has learned by this time that a considerable number of the men she encounters are interested in getting her into bed as quickly as possible. This anxiety may make it difficult for her to respond, even if she needs and wants to go to bed with someone. Besides, after being married for some years, she may also have difficulty playing the role of the single woman again. It can seem very strange at age 25 or 30, or older, to behave again with men as she did when she was in college.

If her children are already having problems adjusting, the introduction of a man or men into their lives may intensify their problems. Younger children may deal with the threat posed by the intruding male obliquely, by regressing to more immature levels of behavior, by becoming more dependent, or by throwing temper tantrums. Older children and teenagers may confront the perceived threat more directly, by showing antagonism to their mother's friends and openly disapproving of her dating. At all age levels, such reactions often cause temporary distress for the mother. They may even effectively sabotage one or more dating relationships before the mother learns to handle them. As soon as the children discover, however, that their tactics do not work and that the mother is firmly in control, their opposition fades and the mother can get on with building a new life for herself.

One problem may be that she doesn't know, herself, what kind of new life she is seeking. She may not even be sure whether she is seeking a new life. If the last years or months of her marriage were very unpleasant, she may be very hesitant to enter into any new emotional relationships and may discourage any men who show more than a casual interest in her. These reservations may lead her to break off specific relationships with particular men, and they may even result in her discontinuing dating altogether after a few such experiences. In that case, parenthood without a partner may become a semi-permanent life style.

At the other extreme, some women are anxious to escape their newly single way of living, and they consciously evaluate each new date as a prospect for marriage. If they do so too obviously, of course, they may scare off most men before they have any chance to get involved. The greater risk is that such women will be so eager for meaningful heterosexual relationships that they fail to be sufficiently critical. They may become involved too quickly.

Undoubtedly there are some divorced women for whom these approaches to dating are characteristic and lasting. More frequently, however, they probably represent temporary tendencies that are found in most divorced women as they seek to build new man–woman relationships. After a few uncomfortable experiences, most divorced women find that they can relax and be themselves in their relationships with men, that some men appeal to them more than others, and that, in turn, some men are more than casually attracted to them. Most divorced women remarry. Motherhood without a partner is usually a temporary phase.

Little has been written about the sexual frustrations encountered by women during and after their divorces. In part, this omission may be a result of pervasive sexism, which emphasizes the sexual frustrations

**Sexual
Reinvolvement**

encountered by men and ignores those of women. In part, too, it may reflect the unwillingness of many women to talk about their sexual needs.

Common sense should tell us that many women, accustomed to active sex lives in marriage, should suffer feelings of deprivation as their marital relationships deteriorate and as sexual intercourse with the husband is discontinued. In fact, although it is impossible to document it statistically, it is known that some embattled married couples continue to have intercourse irregularly right up to the time of divorce, and even after. Such encounters may alleviate the physical frustration, but they do nothing to aid the woman in finding a new sexual partner. More likely, they interfere with it.

When the woman who is being divorced has a male confidant and supporter, the relationship with him not infrequently comes to include sexual intercourse. The transitions from married woman to divorced woman to remarried woman in such instances may require only a short time.

For most other divorced women, the question of when and with whom to become sexually involved is a more practical one than whether or not to become involved. Again, comprehensive statistics are lacking, but one of the best informed popular writers on the subject believes that about four-fifths of all divorced women eventually begin to have sexual intercourse again (Hunt, 1966). The Institute for Sex Research at Indiana University has also reported tata on 632 formerly married women, some of whom had been divorced and some of whom had been widowed (Gebhard, 1970). Eighty-two percent of the divorced women had had sexual intercourse after their divorces.

For some divorced women and divorced men, there is a period of fairly casual experimentation with sex. It seems to be linked to their need to reassure themselves of their continued attractiveness to members of the opposite sex; going to bed with people is one way to demonstrate it.

Some women, having lost most of their earlier sexual inhibitions in marriage, adopt a very pragmatic view and engage in sexual activity whenever physical urges or emotional needs motivate them to do it. This pattern, however, seems to be more common among men that among women. The Gebhard study just mentioned reported that only twelve percent of the divorced women who had postmarital intercourse confined it to just one man.

The Institute study also reported that most divorced women found their sexual relationships to be quite satisfying. In fact, the women who were divorced were likelier to reach a sexual climax than they had been when they were married, and they also did so more often than other married women of the same ages. Actually, this finding should not be surprising. Married women often have intercourse whether or not they are particularly aroused at the time, whereas divorced women may do so only when they really want to.

This study also found that most divorced women begin having intercourse again within a year after the end of their marriages. If many mothers without partners remain in that status for extended periods of time, most of them do not do so without the company of men. Most of them also remarry eventually.

FATHERS WITHOUT PARTNERS

Although mothers usually get custody of the children in divorces, fathers can also be awarded custody, becoming "fathers without partners." The proportion of such cases seems to be increasing. Some states, Colorado and Minnesota for example, have laws that prohibit favoring one parent over the other in awarding custody. A 1971 study in Minneapolis showed that custody was awarded to the father in 38 percent of contested cases where there were children under seven years of age.[1]

Regardless of how much increase there is in the number of fathers without partners, there is a new openness among both men and women about the needs of some fathers to have their children and the needs of some mothers not to have them. Many fathers love their children deeply, just as many mothers do. Some fathers also are better off financially after divorce than their ex-wives are, and are thus better able to care for their children. If the father also has an occupation that permits him to do much of his work at home or to follow a flexible work schedule, the advantages in the father's having custody are obvious.

From the mother's standpoint, she almost always has to work to support herself, and she probably is less likely to have the job flexibility that some men, particularly professional men, have. An eight-to-five job, five or six days a week, can rob a woman of many of the traditional satisfactions of motherhood even when she does have custody. Moreover, many women today feel less pressure to seek custody than they used to. In some cases, they have the option of being the partner who departs from the marriage relatively unencumbered.

In many ways, the situations of fathers without partners are identical, or very similar, to those of mothers without partners. In some ways, however, they are different.

WORK AND MONEY

Most fathers without partners do not face quite the drop in living standards that confronts many mothers without partners soon after the divorce. Nevertheless, they are likely to suffer a severe financial shock. Having the children means, of course, that the father has to have a larger and more expensive house or apartment than he would need otherwise. Then, too, there is the matter of a housekeeper or paid household help. Many unsuspecting fathers find that such services are quite expensive. Furthermore, housekeepers, unlike wives, work only an eight-hour day,

[1] The New York Times, Jan. 29, 1973.

and not at all on weekends. Inevitably, this fact means a heavy work overload for the divorced father (Weigand, 1974). Like the divorced mother's, his work day begins early in the morning with the necessity of getting the children up and launched upon their day, and it continues late into the evening after the children are in bed again.

KEEPING MOTHERS INVOLVED

In situations in which the father has custody, both parents may have to work harder than usual to prevent the children from feeling that their mother has deserted them. Friends and acquaintances, also, are likely to have a more difficult time understanding a father-custody divorce than a mother-custody one; they may unwittingly say and do things that reflect their confusion. With a mixture of disbelief and disapproval, for instance, they remark that they "can't understand how a woman could give up her children" or offer sympathy and assistance to the father. But they fail to recognize that the arrangement may have been worked out with the full participation of both parents, and it may be working quite well.

If there is good reason for the father without custody to have regular entreé to his children's home and to have the children visit with him, there is equally good reason to have such arrangements when the mother does not have custody. With the father's support and encouragement, the mother can be in regular contact with her children by telephone, reassuring them of her love for them and her concern for their welfare. She can participate in decisions about their schooling, help them in the selection and upkeep of their clothing, and even work with them on vacation plans. She can relieve the father by staying with the children, or having them stay with her, when he has to be away. Occasional weekend visits can be arranged. Regardless of which parent has custody, flexible and constructive arrangements are possible when both parents wish it that way, and when they appreciate the importance of such arrangements to the children.

HOUSEHOLD MANAGEMENT

Some fathers may be better at managing the details of running a household than some mothers are. Some fathers are excellent cooks and housekeepers and are intuitively sensitive to the moods and needs of children. It is not simply sexism, however, to indicate that most fathers probably have less experience and less skill in these matters than most mothers do. The experiences of males, both in their parents' homes and in marriage, usually have not emphasized the efficient preparation of nutritious meals, housekeeping, or the care and repair of clothing. Most new fathers without partners find that they have a lot of learning to do.

Some divorced fathers quickly learn the skills of homemaking and household management and come to perform as well in these areas as most women do. Other fathers without partners adapt the running of the household to their own somewhat masculine styles. Other things being equal, for example, divorced fathers probably press their children into the sharing of household tasks more than divorced mothers do. Both sons and daughters may become proficient in cooking, sewing, cleaning, and so on.

Some fathers discover, too, that there are ways of cutting down on the burdens of housekeeping. One father, for example, solved the problem of daily bed-making by replacing fancy spreads with durable quilts that could easily be pulled up to present a reasonable appearance. That same father, aware that his cooking and meal planning were not very great, insured the adequacy of his children's nutrition through the simple expedient of eliminating commercial snack foods from the home and substituting fruits and vegetables. When other children might have been eating candy or potato chips, his children were munching on apples and celery sticks.

We should not overemphasize the differences between households headed by fathers and those headed by mothers. In both cases, there are financial shocks to be absorbed, there is too much work to be done in the time available to do it, and one parent must serve in place of two most of the time. There is loneliness, and there is the need to build new adult friendships. For most parents without partners, there is also, eventually, remarriage.

COED LIVING

We have tried, in this book, to analyze the alternative life style possibilities facing men and women at various stages of the life cycle. These include the option of permanent singlehood, communal living before marriage or after, marriage without parenthood, and others. In talking about premarital relationships, we discussed coed dormitory living on college campuses. Here, we extend that general idea to include a developing new life style for some divorced men and women.

A logical alternative for parents without partners, faced with the burdensome costs of maintaining their customary standards of living, is to get someone to share the expenses. The large costs of rent and utilities may thus be substantially reduced.

A decade ago, the suggestion of such an arrangement would have called forth images of a mother and children sharing her house or apartment with another single woman, or of a father and children perhaps taking in another man as a roomer. Not surprisingly, such arrangements were not especially popular. Neither men nor women were attracted to sharing other people's children. What has emerged recently, however, is a pattern of residential sharing, particularly by a woman with children and a single man who shares their dwelling and some of their lives.

The pattern exists particularly in large cities, where, without public censure, women can advertise in newspapers to share their homes and where such arrangements can be worked out through real estate brokers. There is no way to determine how common it is, but it is conspicuous and apparently spreading. It also has some obvious advantages in addition to cutting down on costs.[2]

Some divorced women, conditioned by earlier experiences with coed dormitory living, see no moral issue in sharing their homes with men. They may actually prefer sharing with a man to living with another woman. Beyond the wish for male companionship, some women feel safer and more secure in their homes with a male housemate, believing that his presence will serve as a deterrent to possible intruders. Moreover,

[2] *Time,* April 14, 1975, pp. 46–47.

they feel uncomfortable raising their children without a continuing masculine influence in the home: they hope that the male housemate will play at least a minor parent-substitute role.

For men, the attractions are complementary. They want to escape the loneliness and boredom of single living. In addition, they want a feminine influence in their lives, rather than the reinforced "maleness" that so often is the product of living with other men. Some men, also, yearn for relationships with children on a day-to-day basis.

Some people question, of course, whether such relationships are platonic and whether they can remain that way. But apparently some of them are, and some of them do. The arrangements usually are made quite explicit at the time the agreement is made. The man and woman have separate bedrooms, private areas into which the other may not intrude. There also is some agreement on a division of labor—which chores are hers and which are his. Each person is free to continue his or her social life without interference from the other.

The pattern is too new for its long-term features to be evident, but in many situations it seems to be working well. The woman has a man available to mow lawns, do heavy cleaning, paint, move furniture, make minor repairs, and so on. In turn, the man has a woman to do much of his cooking, laundry, mending, and other things.

It is no accident that this division of labor often is more traditional than many liberated married couples could tolerate; people who enter such arrangements are likely to be seeking the security and comfort of a fairly conventional family setting. Change is evident here too, however, because one of the most common complaints from women is that they get stuck with too much of the housework.

In part, this complaint is compensated for by the man's playing a quasi-parental role with the woman's children. Gradually, he may become a confidant in matters that children usually share with their father rather than their mother. His quiet support of the mother in disciplining the children may make the situation easier for mother and children alike. If he gets too heavy-handed, he may encounter the joint resistance of mother and children, much as in a conventional family.

Possibly the area in which minor complications most frequently arise is that of dating. In the most common situation, the woman's date frequently calls for her at her home and returns her there later. Calling for her and finding another man sitting in the living room may cause the date to wonder whether there is more to the arrangement than the sharing of expenses. And if the couple returns sooner than expected to find the housemate watching TV in his underwear, the suspicions may be brought up openly.

The man typically leaves the shared dwelling to pursue his dating activities on the outside. Nevertheless the woman or the children or both may develop more than a casual interest in whom he is seeing, what she is like, and how involved they are. If this curiosity is verbalized, another minor crisis may be precipitated.

Given the fact that most men and women living in such coed fashion are in their twenty's and thirty's, romantic attractions must occasionally develop between them. Little is yet known about that aspect of coed living. For some people, it probably is the route to remarriage.

SUMMARY

Divorce creates over half a million new one-parent families each year. Remarriage keeps reducing the number of existing one-parent families, of course, so up to four million parents and seven million children are involved at any one time. For some one-parent families, the experience lasts for only weeks or months; for others it is a quasi-permanent arrangement.

The foundations for adjustment in the one-parent family are laid in the children's reactions to the parental divorce. These reactions vary by the ages of the children, ranging from regressive behavior in young children, obstinacy and taking sides in school-aged children, to defiance and rebellion among teenagers.

Mothers without partners are about five times as common as fathers without partners. Most of them experience severe money problems at first, which are lessened partly by taking jobs outside the home. Getting a job not only helps to solve the woman's financial problems but also tends to bolster her self-confidence.

As divorce becomes more common and people are more objective about it, divorced fathers have more opportunity to continue to play active parental roles with their children. Most of the burden of parenthood, however, falls upon the mother who has custody. She must become competent and self-assured in the management of both the crises and the common events of everyday living. She must also be able to set appropriate limits on her children's behavior and give them as much responsibility as they can handle comfortably.

An especially ticklish area concerns what confidences the mother should share with her children. Teenage children may be curious about the divorce and about their parents' attitudes and feelings, and they may ask questions. Mothers, in turn, may be lonely and may need someone in whom to confide. Generally, the mother should be honest and open in replying to her children's questions. But she should share her own innermost needs and feelings with other adults.

Children achieve adulthood more easily when both parents teach them how to become adequate men and women. Flexible visitation arrangements can help. So can a sustained effort to see that the father plays a meaningful role in the children's lives, and that they play a significant role in his. The mother's attitude toward the father is a very important factor.

Most mothers without partners eventually resume active social and sexual lives. They may begin doing so even while the couple is separated and awaiting divorce; in most cases, they do so within a year of the time of divorce. There may be some hesitancy on the woman's part, and the children may be temporarily upset by it, but most divorced women not only resume dating but also remarry relatively soon.

Perhaps 15 percent of all one-parent families are headed by fathers, whose situations are comparable in most respects to those of mothers without partners. Both men and women are coming increasingly to accept some fathers' needs and abilities to have custody of their children, and some mothers' needs and rights not to have custody. Most divorced men, like most divorced women, eventually remarry.

A new variant on parent-without-partner living, at least in its frequency, is coed living. Typically, a mother and her children share their home and the expenses of running it with a male housemate selected for the purpose. Beyond cutting costs, the arrangement permits both the man and the woman to enjoy many of the benefits of family living without the special problems that marriage entails. The arrangement generally is intended to remain platonic, and often does so. But for some people it probably sets the stage for romantic involvement and, perhaps, for remarriage.

FOR
ADDITIONAL
READING

Bell, Robert R., *Studies in Marriage and the Family* (New York: Crowell, 1973). See the selection on "The World of the Formerly Married."

Fullerton, Gail Putney, *Survival in Marriage* (New York: Holt, Rinehart and Winston, 1972). The chapter on post-marital roles includes sections on "The Role of the Former Husband" and "The Role of the Former Wife."

George, Victor, and Paul Wilding, *Motherless Families* (London: Routledge and Kegan Paul, 1972). An analysis of father-headed families created by divorce, death, separation, hospitalization, and imprisonment.

McCary, James Leslie, *Freedom and Growth in Marriage* (Santa Barbara, Cal.: Hamilton, 1975). The chapter on "Special Families" includes a section on single-parent families.

Schlesinger, Benjamin, "The One-Parent Family in Canada: Some Recent Findings and Recommendations," *The Family Coordinator* 22 (July 1973), pp. 305–9. A non-technical analysis that adds perspective to the treatment in this chapter.

STUDY
QUESTIONS

1. This chapter analyzes one-parent families created by divorce. How would such families differ if they were created by death, hospitalization, or imprisonment?

2. Describe the typical reactions of children of various ages to a parental divorce. Then indicate ways in which parents may cope, constructively, with those reactions.

3. How do problems of income adequacy differ between mother-headed and father-headed families? Problems of income management?

4. How may divorced parents cope effectively with the need to provide their children with adult role models of each sex?

5. How much should divorced parents tell their children about the things that led to the marital breakup? Evaluate the possible negative effects of the course of action you recommend.

6. This chapter discusses dating and sexual reinvolvement for divorced mothers. How do you think the situation is similar, and how is it different, for divorced fathers?

7. What factors do you think should guide the award of custody of children when the parents divorce? Are there circumstances that would cause you to favor one parent or the other? Why or why not?

8. What do you think of the kind of coed living described in this chapter? Evaluate its advantages and disadvantages from the standpoint of the children.

Chapter 16
Remarriage

The stereotype of divorced people living in a prolonged state of loneliness and unhappiness is generally false. There are some divorced people who are miserable and maladjusted, of course, just as some single people and some married people are unhappy. But most divorced people—about four out of five—eventually remarry (Glick, 1975; Kuzel and Krishnan, 1973). Moreover, most of them remarry relatively quickly. One-fourth of those who remarry do so within one year of the time of divorce. One-half remarry within three years, and three-fourths remarry within nine years (Glick and Norton, 1971).

HAPPINESS IN REMARRIAGES

Many people who have been divorced worry about whether they will be able to do better in a second marriage or whether they are doomed to repeated failure. Very recent research evidence should reassure them. Of a nationwide population who had married at least 20 years earlier, only about three percent had been married three or more times

(Glick and Norton, 1971). Furthermore, the U.S. census bureau estimates that only five to ten percent of the people who get one divorce will eventually get a second one (Glick and Norton, 1973).

The absence of multiple divorces on any scale does not necessarily mean that remarriages are happy, of course; it might only mean that people who are divorced once don't want to go through the experience a second time. Recent evidence from Canada, however, offers grounds for optimism. In a study of 96 Metropolitan Toronto couples, of whom at least one partner had been married before, over 80 percent of both the husbands and the wives reported that their marriages were "very satisfactory." Roughly ten percent said they were "satisfactory," and only from five to ten percent rated them as "unsatisfactory" (Schlesinger, 1970).

Happiness in many remarriages depends upon much more than just the relationship between the husband and wife. There often are children from one or both former marriages, and there may be children born to the remarriage. The concept of marital happiness must be broadened, then, to include the relationships between the parents and their stepchildren and the relationships among the stepchildren.

STEP-KIN RELATIONSHIPS

A study of a random sample of 88 remarried Cleveland, Ohio, parents focused not only on the new spouses but also upon their relationships with the other partners' children; it also examined the relationships between the two sets of children. The results generally contradict earlier writers who emphasized the problem aspects of reconstituted families (Duberman, 1973).

This study also went beyond the analysis of remarriage following divorce. It included some remarriages that followed widowhood, and some in which the remarrying partner took a spouse who had never been married before. The results of that part of the study are presented in Table 16-1; the parent–stepchild adjustments are shown separately for fathers and mothers.

The first thing that stands out is that the largest percentages of all three types of remarriages are found in the "excellent" adjustment category. When the results for remarried fathers and remarried mothers are combined (not shown in the table), only 18 percent of the adjustments were rated as poor. Another 18 percent were rated good, and a whopping 64 percent were rated excellent.

A second conclusion is apparent from the table. Remarriage following widowhood yields a higher proportion of excellent adjustment ratings for both mothers and fathers than does remarriage following divorce. This finding seems reasonable enough, if we assume that the first marriages of the widowed persons were good ones, setting the stage for good adjustment in their remarriages.

STATUS	PARENT–CHILD RELATIONSHIP (PERCENT REPORTING)			
	POOR	GOOD	EXCELLENT	TOTAL
Fathers				
Divorce	24	22	54	100
Death	5	19	76	100
Never Married Before	15	0	85	100
Mothers				
Divorce	20	17	63	100
Death	12	12	76	100
Never Married Before	20	25	55	100

Source: Adapted from Lucile Duberman, "Step-Kin Relationships," *Journal of Marriage and the Family* 35 (May 1973), p. 289.

One set of findings is somewhat surprising, although the number of such remarriages is rather small and the results need to be confirmed in other research. The *single* men who married women with children made more "excellent" adjustments with their stepchildren than did men who were either previously widowed or previously divorced. Perhaps men who are willing to take on the responsibilities of "ready-made" families are also likely to be flexible and patient in adjusting to those families. Perhaps, also, remarried mothers and their children are especially considerate of new husbands who have not had prior marital experience.

The opposite situation prevails, however, among women who have not been married before and who marry men with children. These women make fairly high percentages of poor adjustments and lower percentages of excellent adjustments. Even here, however, it is important to emphasize that the majority of the relationships are reported to be excellent, and only one relationship in five is reported to be poor. Taken both singly and as a whole, these results indicate that the quality of life in families created through remarriage is relatively high.

FAMILY
INTEGRATION

The Cleveland study also focused upon the reported closeness or lack of it within the entire family. It then related this family integration to the quality of the parent-stepchild relationships and the relationships among the two sets of children. We will look at these two aspects separately.

The family integration scores, which were based upon reports from both the husband and wife and on independent ratings by the researcher, again showed these remarriages to be of high quality. Actual numerical scores were converted into categories of low, moderate, and high integration. Only 21 percent of the families were judged to have low integration, 34 percent were classified as being moderately integrated, and 45 percent were rated as being highly integrated.

Table 16-2 shows the association between overall family integration and the quality of the parent-stepchild relationships. Where the parent-stepchild relationships are poor, most of the families are judged to be

**TABLE 16-2
PARENT–STEPCHILD
RELATIONSHIP AND
FAMILY INTEGRATION**

PARENT–STEPCHILD RELATIONSHIP	FAMILY INTEGRATION (PERCENT REPORTING)			
	POOR	GOOD	EXCELLENT	TOTAL
Poor	63	31	6	100
Good	25	50	25	100
Excellent	9	30	61	100

Source: Adapted from Lucile Duberman, "Step-Kin Relationships," *Journal of Marriage and the Family* 35 (May 1973), p. 289.

STEPSIBLING RELATIONSHIP	FAMILY INTEGRATION (PERCENT REPORTING)			
	LOW	MODERATE	HIGH	TOTAL
Poor	35	55	10	100
Good	18	41	41	100
Excellent	0	18	82	100

Source: Adapted from Lucile Duberman, "Step-Kin Relationships," *Journal of Marriage and the Family* 35 (May 1973), p. 290.

**TABLE 16-3
STEPSIBLING
RELATIONSHIPS AND
FAMILY INTEGRATION**

poorly integrated. Where those relationships are excellent, most of the families, as a whole, are perceived to be highly integrated. The message is clear. The adjustment between each spouse and the other spouse's children is critically important to the welfare of the whole family.

Ratings of the relationships between each spouse's children and the other spouse's children also were secured from the two parents (see Table 16-3). Where the relationships among the children were poor, few families achieved more than a moderate level of integration. Where relationships among the children were excellent, on the other hand, four out of five of the families were reported to be highly integrated.

Two other factors relating to the children were found to be important. First, younger children (under 13 years of age) got along with their stepmothers better than did teenagers, as might be expected. Second, relationships among the stepchildren were better in those families in which there was at least one child born to the new marriage. The causal relationship may work either way. Better remarriages may tend to produce additional children; or shared babies may tend to increase everybody's identification with the new family.

GOING TOGETHER

Some people marry, divorce, and are ready for remarriage by their early or mid-twenties. Most people who remarry are somewhat older, however, in their late twenties, thirties, or even forties. Some widows and widowers remarry in their sixties and seventies.

Except perhaps for the very young, man–woman relationships among those who are approaching remarriage tend to be rather direct and straightforward. A man of 35 with two children, for example, is not likely to flatter, tease, and cajole a woman in an effort to make her fall in love with him. Neither is the woman likely to feign a reluctance that she really does not feel. Both of them will tend to approach interpersonal intimacy somewhat cautiously, because they know how much is at stake for both themselves and their children.

At the same time, neither person is likely to feel under much pressure to "dress up" for the other, or to go to fashionable places or do fashionable things. They may go out together formally, to restaurants or night clubs, but more of their time will probably be spent just sharing their daily routines. Meals will be eaten at her house or at his, rather than in restaurants. Evenings may be spent simply talking and playing with the children, taking walks, getting some ice cream, or engaging in other essentially domestic pastimes. Much of the time the couple spends together may be on weekends when, again, home-centered activities probably will take precedence over formal or commercial ones.

INTIMACY AND SHARING

If their first experiences convince the man and woman that they would like to know each other better, if may be only weeks before they are sharing both emotional and physical intimacy in a family-like setting. If one person cooks dinner, the other may clean up afterward. They may share doing the dishes and clean house and do the laundry together. In short, they share routines that never-married couples seldom do, at least so extensively.

They also talk not only about casual things, but also about the things that are very important to them—about the loneliness that accompanies being a parent without a partner, about needing to love and be loved, about problems with the children, about problems in making ends meet, and about dreams and hopes and fears. Either a confidence shared by one person leads to reassurance and support from the other and to reciprocal sharing of confidences, or the relationship quickly withers.

Passion flourishes, too. Men and women approaching remarriage have been accustomed to sharing their beds and knowing the lusty pleasures of sex. Physical attraction to one another may precede or follow the development of other intimacy, but it quickly becomes important in most relationships that endure. Hours are spent in bed together after the children are asleep, and physical intimacy increases the closeness that the man and woman feel to one another.

INVOLVING THE CHILDREN

How rapidly things move toward marriage may depend, as much as anything else, upon how the children react to the relationship. If they welcome it, marriage may occur quickly. If they oppose it, the parent of those children is likely to resist a marriage that seems bound to cause problems.

Involving children takes various forms. The specifics depend on their number, ages, and sexes. With young children, the prospective mate is likely to quickly assume a quasi-parental role. Cleaning up after dinner includes bathing and putting the children to bed as well as doing the dishes. There are bruised knees that require Band-Aids and bruised feelings that require comforting and reassurance. Although the use of terms like ''Mother'' and ''Dad'' may be avoided with the prospective stepparent, both the man and the woman watch to assure themselves that their children are getting a parent who can help them grow to secure adulthood.

With older children, particularly teenagers, there is more of a possibility that the new partner will be viewed as an intruder and a rival to the natural divorced parent. For the potential stepparent to try to play the role of parent with such older children may be disastrous. Instead, the man and woman may seek to gain the children's approval and support by emphasizing how good the relationship is for themselves. They try to make it clear that the new partner will not seek to replace the absent, divorced parent. There is often a self-conscious effort by all concerned to avoid the use of kinship terms; instead, the children are urged to call the new partner by his or her first name. The relationships range from ones of warmth to ones of suspicion and distrust, and, as we have already seen, the integration of the whole family group varies accordingly.

ADJUSTING IN REMARRIAGE

Most of the adjustment problems that confront first marriages confront remarriages also. But in some ways remarriages are distinct. In remarriage, there are ex-husbands and wives and the natural parents of one's stepchildren to cope with. Occasionally, too, friends and associates object to the new marriage. There are also, of course, the problems of being a stepparent and the gradual process of becoming a new family.

ADJUSTING TO EX-SPOUSES

Particularly when there are children involved, there are multiple parties to a remarriage. Although they do not live with the new family, the ex-wife and an ex-husband frequently enter the picture in their roles as parents of the children. They have rights to visit the children and to have the children visit them, and they have a continuing interest in the children's welfare.

Relationships Between Ex-Spouses

If the parents adjusted wisely during the divorce and after, and have worked out most of their old antagonisms, stable and constructive relationships may exist between the ex-spouses at the time of the remarriage. Visitation of the absent parent with the children may continue much as before. Much of the adjustment, in fact, may center around the new marriage partner, who in one sense is an intruder into this situation.

There can be problems, however. If the ex-wife still has not completely accepted the divorce, for instance, and if she continues to make demands or to depend upon her ex-husband, the new wife may feel threatened. Or it may be the ex-husband who is still hanging on, and who creates problems for his ex-wife and her new husband. The new spouse may insist that these patterns be discontinued.

Part of the problem is that there simply are no clear guidelines to tell us what kinds of relationships are appropriate and proper between ex-spouses (Bohannon, 1970). They should not still be having sexual intercourse, obviously. And it is assumed that each former partner will have found a new friend or friends for most affection and emotional support. But there are few guidelines to say what the tone of the relationship should be between the ex-partners: two adults who are no longer married to one another but who are bound together by their shared interest in their children.

Should the relationship be polite, formal, and uninvolved? That would ease the situation of the new spouse of either partner, but only in a very artificial way. This kind of adjustment ignores the fact that the ex-spouses did live together at least long enough to have children and that, formerly, they were very close to one another. Such an arrangement does work in some cases, but both the ex-spouses and the new spouses are likely to be uncomfortable with it.

Another possibility, of course, is for the ex-spouses to treat one another as what they are: people who formerly were close but no longer are, and who retain a genuine interest in one another's welfare. They can be concerned about each other without running any risk of a resumption of romantic interest between them. There are two dangers in this arrangement, however. First, one of the ex-spouses may not be quite able to maintain the proper balance between concern and separation. Second, a new spouse may perceive more potential involvement of the two ex-spouses than is really there.

Relationships Between Spouses and Ex-Spouses

Little systematic research has yet been done on the matter, but impressionistic evidence is accumulating that the sort of problems we have just described are associated primarily with the first few months or years of remarriage. Long-term adjustments involving new spouses and ex-spouses are complex, varied, and often surprising. The relationships between spouses and ex-spouses may be important sources of harmony in remarriages.

When a triangle situation preceded the divorce, relationships between the ex-spouse and the new spouse often are hostile and bitter, at least at first. When the new romantic interest developed after the divorce, the ex-spouse may feel some resentment toward the new partner; often, however, there is more curiosity than negative feeling. And even when a triangle existed, the hostility often largely disappears with time.

The new spouse and the ex-spouse often are thrown together through the simple necessity of making arrangements for the children. There must be telephone calls and, at least occasionally, one must appear at the other's home. Moreover, it often seems easier for the remarried parent to let the new spouse and the ex-spouse make the arrangements than to be involved in them directly. Increasingly, the new spouse and the ex-spouse have the opportunity to talk.

After a while, the new spouse and the ex-spouse often find that they

are able to communicate with one another quite effectively. They learn to understand and even to like one another. It should not be surprising that the new spouse and the ex-spouse often are much alike. After all, they fell in love with and married the same person; and, increasingly, they share the same children.

In some cases, the new spouse and the ex-spouse even become something like friends and confidants. They may meet over lunch or elsewhere to make general or specific plans for the children, and they may even share confidences on how to deal with the mate/ex-mate that they have in common. Far from working to the disadvantage of that person, this friendship often removes much of the strain from the relationship with the ex-spouse.

ADJUSTING TO OUTSIDERS

Whether remarriages face any special problems of adjusting to friends and acquaintances depends heavily upon whether those people perceive some kind of triangle situation. It need not be a sexual triangle, and it need not be associated with divorce. Sometimes when widows or widowers remarry, for instance, family members respond as though the remarrying partner were betraying the memory of the deceased spouse. This is particularly likely if the remarriage occurs soon after the death. It may appear, though, even if the remarriage occurs after several years. The problems facing the remarrying partners in such cases are much like those facing persons who remarry after divorce.

Some friends and associates implicitly, at least, take sides in almost any divorce situation. Those who do so openly, of course, are likely to have been dealt with as part of the adjustment to the divorce. But others may make their feelings known only when the prospect of remarriage develops, or even after the remarriage. They may object to the new partner on real or fancied grounds, or they may openly disapprove of the divorced person's remarrying anyone. Their objection may be vocal and pointed, or it may be shown only through slights to the new couple.

However it is shown, such disapproval is painful for the new couple, and it is a source of strain for them. If the disapproval comes from only one or a few people, the solution is fairly simple and obvious: ignoring those people and having as little as possible to do with them. If the disapproval is more widespread, but mild, it will tend to disappear if the new couple does not overreact to it; other people will gradually get used to the idea of them as a couple.

The most difficult situations are those in which formerly valued friends and associates strongly oppose the new marriage, especially when those people cannot easily be avoided. These people can include family members, work associates, and others. Part of the solution, again, lies in making new friends to replace the disapproving ones. In any case, the wounds often heal with the passage of time.

"What's wrong with us, Mason? Everyone we know has been divorced at least once but us!"

NEW WOMAN, FEBRUARY 1975.

In some instances, rejection from others may be painful enough for the new couple that they wish to escape it completely and quickly. Moving from the old neighborhood to a new one may help. A change of job or a transfer may solve the problem of disapproving work associates. Changes to different churches, social groups, and the like may permit the couple to establish almost a brand new social identity for themselves. New friends and co-workers are unlikely to have more than a mild curiosity about the couple's former marital lives. They will more probably treat the couple as they want to be treated: as a new family.

The terms "stepfather" and "stepmother" may be two of the most unfortunate terms in the English language. They came into existence at a time when remarriage generally followed the death of one of the natural

ADJUSTING TO STEPPARENTHOOD

parents rather than divorce. In those days there was little recognition of the possibility that love and affection might develop between the stepparent and the stepchild (Bohannon, 1970). Consequently, stereotypes developed of what stepparents are like: harsh, cold, punitive, and unloving. Many people who remarry today are shocked to realize that the term "stepparent" applies to them. The challenges that they face are many and complex.

**Being One of
a Set of Parents**

Since most remarriages today follow divorce, becoming a stepparent generally means becoming a co-parent. The stepfather acquires a set of children who already have a father, and the stepmother must confront the fact that her new children already have a mother. There are thus two things with which the new stepparents must cope: the children's emotional ties to the biological parent, and the physical presence of that parent.

At the outset, the stepparents must realize that they cannot and should not try to replace the original parent in the children's affections. The children are sure to detect any attempt to do so and are sure to resent it. The natural parent will resent it too, and with good cause. That person did not resign parenthood just because he or she can no longer live together amiably with the other parent.

Stepparents must also get used to the periodic presence of the biological parents. They usually have a legal right of visitation and, even if they do not, it usually is in everybody's interest for the divorced parent to continue to play the most meaningful role possible in the children's lives. The children are more likely to respect and love a stepparent who encourages such closeness than one who opposes it or accepts it grudgingly.

**Going Slowly
and Easily**

The temptation often is strong for new stepparents to demonstrate their affection for their stepchildren as frequently and in as many ways as possible: by caressing them, praising them, buying gifts for them, and so on. But the children may be slightly overwhelmed by this sort of pressure. Especially if the parental divorce was recent, they may have anxieties about the new stepparent: Will he or she desert me? Will he or she really take care of me? Will he or she be good to me? Can he or she be trusted? In the emotional logic of childhood, these are serious questions. They must be answered satisfactorily before love can be freely given.

In the early stages of a remarriage, it is as reasonable to expect resistance and antagonism toward the stepparent as it is to expect love and affection. The children often must test the relationship to find out if it can be depended on. They have to find out in their own way whether misbehavior and hostility will be met with understanding and patience. Only after they have gained reassurance can many children develop trust and love (Dodson, 1974).

What to call the new stepparent is a dilemma which confronts many children, and which the stepparent may make easier or more difficult. After the initial period of formality has worn off, the use of Mr. or Ms. is replaced by the use of the new partner's first name. This transition often occurs before the remarriage, and the use of first names may be continued into the remarriage, permitting all concerned to avoid the issue of using kinship terms such as Mom and Dad in the new relationships.

Providing that the first name is used with warmth and approval, it can work very well. Teenaged children, particularly, may resist the use of kinship terms, and there is no particular need to employ them. Certainly, the stepparent is wise not to press the issue. The relationships may develop more positively if they are identified as ones of friendship as well as of kinship.

There is a hazard in this arrangement too, however. If there is not a feeling of friendship on both sides, addressing the stepparent by the first name may be an indirect means of undercutting his or her authority and of interfering with the maintenance of discipline.

Eventually, the children themselves may reach the point where they wish to acknowledge their tie to the stepparent both in private and in public. They may search about for a way to do it without being awkward and without implying disloyalty to the divorced parent. The solution adopted by some parents and stepparents is to use the same kinship terms for both sets of parents, but to add a postscript for the stepparent when necessary. Thus the stepparent becomes Dad or Mom in casual conversation and address around the house, but "Dad II" or "Mom II" in correspondence, introductions, and dealings with the natural parents.

Again, such devices and techniques work well for some families, while for others they seem forced and artificial. If there is a general rule to be followed, it is that the stepparent should not force the situation, but should accept what the children find comfortable and gradually develop more intimacy with them. It takes time.

The Problem of Names

The stepparent in a new family created by remarriage is to some degree an outsider, an intruder into the existing family relationship of the spouse and children. No matter how hard everyone tries to include the stepparent, he or she simply hasn't shared most of the experiences that the other family members have known together. Feelings of being left out are natural in such a situation. But they diminish as the new family gradually develops a shared body of experiences of its own. In addition to what has already been said, two factors can aid in this process.

BECOMING A FAMILY

Sometimes the natural parent of the children may live far away and may be engrossed in creating a new family also. In that case, he or she may consent to the stepparent's adopting the children. This is particularly true when the absent parent is the father, whose child support payments

Adoption

would no longer be required following adoption. Adoption allows the stepparent to become the legal parent, to assume full responsibility for the children, and to strengthen ties with both them and the marriage partner. It thus helps to create an identity for the new family that otherwise might take years longer to develop. However, when the divorced, natural parent is nearby, takes an active interest in the children, and sees them regularly, adoption is not feasible.

New Children

When the remarried couple have children of their own, in addition to their children from the first marriages, the solidarity of the new family tends to be strengthened. The new children have a biological relationship to the other children in the family, (half-sister, half-brother) as well as a maritally-created one. Moreover, there usually is enough of an age difference between the children of the former marriages and those of the new marriage that competition is not very likely to develop among them. Finally, shared parenthood strengthens the bonds between the new husband and wife, encouraging each to think in terms of ''our'' family, rather than ''your'' family and ''my'' family.

SUMMARY

Most people remarry after divorce, and research shows that most second marriages last. Moreover, most remarried people rate their second marriages as very satisfactory. Adjustment in remarriages frequently involves children and stepchildren as well as the marrying couple. Again, research shows most stepparent–stepchild relationships to be excellent. In remarriage following widowhood, adjustment is superior, and men who have not been married previously and who marry women with children also appear to adjust well.

Overall family integration is related to the quality of parent–stepchild relationships. Good relationships with the stepchildren are associated with high family integration. A similar situation exists with relationships among the two sets of children. When the children get along well, the whole family seems to get along well. Younger children do better in this regard, and having a child born to the new marriage seems to help the adjustment.

Relationships between a man and woman approaching remarriage are likely to be free of most bargaining and coquetry. Much of the interaction is organized around the care and supervision of the children, and it also involves the sharing of daily and household routines. Sexual intimacy is usually part of the relationship and an important source of satisfaction and solidarity.

In a very important sense, the ex-husbands and ex-wives who are the parents of one's children are part of a remarriage. Usually, fairly stable adjustments between the ex-spouses have been worked out before remarriage occurs: the new spouse must become accustomed to those patterns. There is no clear set of guidelines in such situations, but neither too formal nor too intimate relationships are appropriate. Surprisingly to many remarried persons, present spouses and ex-spouses often get along fairly well, easing the burden of adjustment for all concerned.

Friends and associates who object to the new marriage sometimes pose problems, creating strain for the new couple. Developing new friendships is an obvious solution, and changing jobs or moving to a new location may solve the problem in extreme cases. Most such objection is not that serious, however, and diminishes as the new partners establish themselves as a couple.

Becoming a good stepparent requires a high level of personal maturity and a great deal of skill. It includes encouraging and supporting the relationship between the children and the divorced natural parent; one must not try to replace that parent in the children's affections. It requires patience and understanding of the children's need to test out the relationship with the stepparent. It takes time for them to become comfortable in it. Finally, it takes time for the new family member to become accepted as a parent.

It also takes time for all members to become accustomed to thinking of themselves as a family. The new identity emerges more rapidly when the stepparent can adopt the other partner's children and when the new marriage produces a child.

FOR
ADDITIONAL
READING

Bohannon, Paul, ed., *Divorce and After* (New York: Doubleday, 1970). See the chapter on "Divorce Chains, Households of Remarriage, and Multiple Divorcers."

Fullerton, Gail Putney, *Survival in Marriage* (New York: Holt, Rinehart and Winston, 1972). The chapter on "Post-Marital Roles" integrates divorce, widowhood, and remarriage.

Leslie, Gerald R., *The Family in Social Context* (New York: Oxford University Press, 1976). The chapter on remarriages includes extensive statistical and research data.

Nye, F. Ivan, and Felix M. Berardo, *The Family: Its Structure and Interaction* (New York: Macmillan, 1973). The chapter called "Sequel to Divorce" includes a section on the institutional analysis of remarriage.

Glick, Paul C., and Arthur J. Norton, "Perspectives on the Recent Upturn in Divorce and Remarriage," in Robert F. Winch and Graham B. Spanier, eds., *Selected Studies in Marriage and the Family* (New York: Holt, Rinehart and Winston, 1974), pp. 447–457. A comprehensive demographic analysis to provide a context for the treatment in this chapter.

STUDY
QUESTIONS

1. Why is the concept of family integration a more useful one than the concept of marital happiness in evaluating remarriages?

2. Would you use the term "courtship" to describe the relationships of couples contemplating remarriage? Why or why not?

3. In what way are ex-spouses significant participants in remarriages? What kind of relationships with them do you think remarried couples should seek?

4. Do you think it is a good idea for the present spouse and the ex-spouse to be friendly with one another? Why or why not?

5. Can spouses and ex-spouses have genuine concern for one another's welfare without threatening their current marriages? How should such relationships be handled?

6. How would you recommend handling friends and acquaintances who indicate polite disapproval of a remarriage? Are there different ways to do it?

7. Becoming a successful stepparent is a major challenge. Indicate how you think a person should go about it.

8. What is implied in the phrase "becoming a new family"? What criteria would you use to determine when this has been achieved?

Chapter 17
Retirement

Retirement is the withdrawal of men and women from paid employment. Some couples look forward to it eagerly, having waited years to gain the freedom to live their lives as they want, without having to go to work each day. But other couples dread retirement. It means a drastic cut in income, the loss of a meaningful status, and the uncertain effects of being thrown together all day, every day.

Retirement means one thing, too, in families in which there is only one breadwinner and another when there are two. Most people, when they think of retirement, picture a traditional family situation in which the husband works outside the home while the wife is a homemaker. This assumption is natural enough, because that situation is still the most common. But increasing numbers of wives work for pay, and many of them invest as much of themselves in their jobs as their husbands do. The problems they face are much the same as those of working men.

If the working husband and the working wife are the

same age, they may retire together. If one partner is younger, that partner may either take an "early" retirement or continue to work for a few years after the spouse retires. Most commonly, it is the wife who continues to work longer.

There are too many variations in retirement patterns to allow us to keep them all in mind all of the time. We are interested primarily in the relationship between marital and family patterns in retirement. We also assume that the emotional, social, and economic consequences of retirement are essentially the same for men and women.

THE LATER FAMILY LIFE CYCLE

To pick any one age as indicating the departure from middle age and the entrance into old age would be arbitrary. To do so would ignore major differences among people in physiological aging and in kinds and levels of social and emotional adjustment. Yet the society in which we live *is* arbitrary. It sets age 65 as the time when most people must retire from paid employment, and, in so doing, it precipitates major changes in people's lives. These changes overlap with growing old and with facing the death of one's spouse and, eventually, oneself.

Twenty-two million people in the United States already have reached the age of retirement, and the number is increasing rapidly. It will reach 29 million by the end of the century. Men who reach age 65 now live for an average of 13 more years, and women of 65 can expect to live for almost 17 more years. Men who reach age 75 can still expect to live for an average of eight more years, and women, ten (see Table 17-1).

Thirteen to 17 years of expected life after age 65 is a long time. Not unexpectedly, tremendous changes occur during those years. One way to keep things from getting too complicated is to divide the retirement years into two stages: early retirement and later retirement. The early retirement stage we shall regard as lasting from age 65 up to age 75, and later retirement from age 75 onward (Thompson and Streib, 1969).

**TABLE 17-1
EXPECTATIONS OF
LIFE BEYOND AGE 65**

| AGE | YEARS EXPECTED TO LIVE | |
	MEN	WOMEN
65	13.0	16.8
67	11.9	15.4
70	10.4	13.4
72	9.4	12.1
75	8.1	10.3

Source: Adapted from Metropolitan Life Insurance Company, *Statistical Bulletin* 56 (April 1975), p. 7.

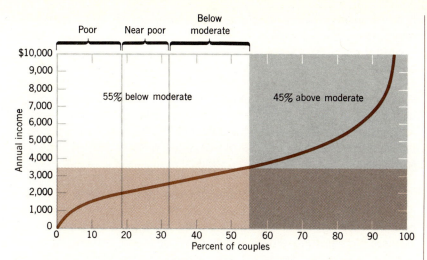

Figure 17-1 Income distribution of couples 65 and over. (Source: Social Security Administration [1971].)

How retirement affects the adjustment of a married couple depends to a large degree upon its impact upon the individual retiree. There are at least five areas in which retirement causes people to experience loss. The amounts and types of the losses vary considerably.

When people stop working, they also stop receiving paychecks. For most people this fact means a drastic drop in their total income. We would like to put the loss in quantitative terms. To be meaningful, however, because of inflation, the dollar figures must be very current ones, yet the time it takes to collect and publish income statistics means that they are almost always out of date.

Figure 17-1 presents data for the late 1960s. If we look at the curve more than at the actual income amounts, we can see that over half of all people over 65 have total incomes that provide less than a moderate standard of living, according to the criteria of the U.S. Bureau of Labor Statistics. Most of these people, technically, are not poor. Nevertheless, one of the factors that affects their adjustment to retirement is that they do not have enough money to pay for travel or a life of ease. They often worry about having enough money to live on, or enough to get by on if they should require continuing medical or nursing care.

On the other hand, almost half (45 percent) of people over 65 have incomes high enough to enjoy above-moderate standards of living. Over three-fourths of retirement-aged couples own their own homes, and over 60 percent own them free of any mortgages. These fortunate couples are, to a large degree, those who have employed financial planning wisely, as was described in Chapter 10. About 25 percent of their income is provided by investments, and a similar amount comes from their continuing to work part-time.

PERSONAL FACTORS IN ADJUSTMENT

LOSS OF FINANCES

**LOSS OF
DEMAND FOR SKILLS**

The loss of income that accompanies retirement is a problem for most people. But people also suffer other important kinds of losses. Having a job provides people with a sense of self-worth. At work they perform tasks that they and other people consider important, and they return home at night tired, perhaps, but with some sense of satisfaction. Retirement means not only not having to go to work in the morning but also being *unable* to go to work. The individual suddenly is denied a major source of self-esteem. The man or woman no longer has access to the work setting in which his or her skills were employed (Sheldon, McEwan and Ryser, 1975).

**LOSS OF
SOCIAL CONTACTS**

Work not only provides income and a sense of self worth, but it also is a source of meaningful social relationships. Roughly half of most people's waking hours are spent on the job and in contact with co-workers. Some of these people may be close friends, some just casual acquaintances, and some actively disliked. But together all of these people play a significant role in the individual's life. Retirement means no longer being able to carry on a pattern of habitual banter with a colleague, no longer being chided by a superior, and no longer being able to counsel a subordinate. The retired person is suddenly cut off from a large part of his or her social contacts.

**LOSS OF
MEANINGFUL TASKS**

Contemporary society tends to treat old people who do not work as people who no longer have much reason for living. We traditionally have defined meaningful living largely in terms of problem solving or the achievement of mastery over tasks. And much of this problem solving is done on the job, or at least during the years when earning a living is important. The loss of one's job means loss of the daily challenge of new problems, of new tasks to be accomplished. Life goes on, of course. Logically, it is possible to shift the locus of task achievement from the place of work to the home. In practice, however, home life has long since become routine for most couples. And only the development of a consuming new interest can result in challenge to the person's capabilities.

**LOSS OF A
REFERENCE GROUP**

Reference groups are groups that are important in people's lives, with which they identify, and whose values, attitudes, and beliefs they adopt. Working people, for example, are not just working people: they are newspaper people, college professors, bankers, criminal justice personnel, and so on. They think of themselves not only as citizens but also as members of their businesses or professions. This identification affects their reactions to everything from local political issues to national and international developments. Not all of this source of personal identity is lost immediately upon retirement. Nevertheless, to be an ex-civil service employee or an ex-labor mediator, or an ex-anything, is not the same as being an active member of a work group. The individual suffers the loss, sudden or gradual, of an identity that formerly had great meaning.

Planning for retirement is as important as planning for any other aspect of life, although few employers and few workers yet realize it. Financial planning, incorporating social security and corporate retirement programs, has come a long way in the past few decades. The wisdom of planning for the reorganization of people's personal and family lives, however, is just beginning to be recognized.

SLIDING INTO RETIREMENT

Ideally, people should be able to disengage gradually from work. This system worked well in early, rural America. The young man and his bride returned to the family homestead, and bit by bit he took over responsibility for the farm from his father, while his wife gradually took over the domestic duties from his mother. The aging couple could remain as active as they liked for as long as they liked, and there was none of the trauma that is associated with sudden retirement. This pattern, in modified form, still exists in some parts of the country.

GRADUAL DISENGAGEMENT

Other occupational groups, particularly the professional and the self-employed, have similar opportunities for phased withdrawal. Doctors, lawyers, accountants, architects, and many others who have private practices can taper off their professional services over a period of several years. They can continue with reduced loads well into old age, or they can plan ahead so that by the time they discontinue offering paid services, they have developed substitute interests and activities to fill their time and absorb their energies. Self-employed business people can do the same thing. Gradually the older person relinquishes responsibility and authority to younger people in preparation for a more leisurely, relaxed way of life.

Many people are not so fortunate, however. Most employers expect full-time work up to some fixed retirement age and then require the employee to discontinue work completely on a given date. These people may have to make a much greater effort to achieve some orderly disengagement. It can be done, however.

First, a smooth adjustment requires that the individual or the couple face up to the fact that retirement will come whether they plan for it or not. They must avoid the common mistake of not beginning to adjust to retirement until the final day arrives. They can, for example, think through and talk through the differences that retirement will make in their lives. They can determine whether they will have enough income to permit a life of leisure, or whether they will have to find ways to continue to earn money. In either case, they can begin to develop new activities. This may have to be done in the evenings, on weekends, holidays, and vacations, but it can be done. If a couple does find challenging activities, by the time retirement finally arrives, they may face their new lives with anticipation rather than with dread and a sense of loss.

DEVELOPMENT OF NEW INTERESTS

We have used the term "disengagement" so far to refer to withdrawal from work, but students of aging use the term in another sense. They believe that, as people grow older, they withdraw from many kinds of relationships with other people; in effect, they begin preparing themselves for their own deaths. Retirement is an obvious point for this kind of disengagement to begin. In some people, in fact, retirement and physical and social aging are so closely linked as to suggest that retirement and disengagement may help to *cause* aging. Some people retire, withdraw from most activities and relationships, and literally sit around waiting to die.

Retirement need not be the end of vital challenges, however. Many people of 65 and older are healthy and vigorous, and increasing numbers of them are gaining financial security. Although retirement does force

disengagement from regular work and work-related relationships, this isolation may be temporary. It certainly does not prevent people from developing new interests, activities, and relationships. Disengagement from work may be followed by re-engagement with life.

If full retirement must be avoided for financial reasons, people may start developing a new income-producing activity, hobby-related perhaps, or a part-time job, in the pre-retirement years. Retirement also affords the opportunity to develop or indulge in hobbies that there just wasn't enough time for earlier. Such hobbies are as varied as people themselves; gardening, woodworking, stamp collecting, furniture refurnishing, and birdwatching are a few of the more popular ones.

Some people devote themselves enthusiastically to the grandparent role. If their children and grandchildren live nearby, the older couple may be in almost daily contact with them. The grandparents may baby-sit in their children's homes, and the grandchildren may visit overnight or longer in the grandparents' home. Whatever the practical details, the grandparents' situation is an enviable one. They can enjoy their grandchildren, indulge them, love them, and comfort them without having to discipline them severely. Indeed, they may serve as allies of the grandchildren against parental misunderstanding and authority. Some retired grandparents gain great satisfaction from their families. They remain healthy and vital by almost reliving their own childhoods through their grandchildren.

Some retired people re-engage by identifying with aging itself. According to the stereotype, aging people are lonely, isolated, and discriminated against. This picture still has some basis in fact but, increasingly, people over age 65 are becoming a social group as well as a population category (Sheldon, McEwan, and Ryser, 1975). They are finding that there are many other people like themselves in their communities, and they are banding together, not only for social activities but for political ones as well. The American Association of Retired Persons and the National Retired Teachers' Association are two of the larger and better organized groups. Such groups provide cut-rate vacation tours and life- and health-insurance-plans for their members, and they also lobby local, state, and federal governments to provide better housing and welfare benefits for older people.

Still other people simply shift their interests and activities upon retirement, without making any special reference to the fact that they are growing older. They may travel, become active in politics, or do any number of other things. The important thing is that disengagement from work need not mean disengagement from life.

Although many people do not realize it, retirement affects husband–wife roles directly and significantly. For many years, the man and

REORGANIZATION OF SCHEDULES

woman have been going their own ways for much of each working day. After an hour or so together in the morning, they did not see one another again until evening. Because they had been apart, there were things for them to talk about: things that happened to them during the day, and things that there just wasn't time to talk about at breakfast.

The weekends were generally spent together, but those days had their routines, too. Whether they were spent simply relaxing at home, on special hobbies, or at a weekend retreat, both partners knew the routine and the schedule and were comfortable with them. They looked forward to occasional long weekends and vacations when the schedule could be relaxed even more. But by most Monday mornings, and by the ends of most vacations, both partners were ready to go back to work and to their regular routines. Too much "togetherness" is about as hard on the relationship as too little.

Retirement changes all of that. It tends suddenly to throw the partners together on a 24-hour-a-day, seven-day-a-week basis. Until new schedules and new routines are worked out, adjustments in the home may be as troublesome as adjustments to the loss of work.

When both partners have worked outside the home, retirement is a good time to discharge the household help that was used for routine cleaning and maintenance. The couple can assume those duties themselves. Not only does this help them save money, but it also gives the retirees something to do with their time.

There are now plenty of hours in which to do the household chores. But working couples often are the kind of people who do not derive satisfaction from such routine tasks and who avoid them as much as possible. One result, early in retirement, may be that some of the work does not get done as regularly or as competently as before. Moreover, the husband and wife may maneuver to see who is going to do the most distasteful jobs, much as a young married couple might do. After a while, however, new routines do become worked out and most couples settle into them with some relief.

In many ways, this kind of adjustment is more troublesome for more traditional couples, those in which only the husband has worked outside the home and faces retirement. The wife has had the home to herself each day, and she has long since become habituated to managing and maintaining it in her own way. Upon her husband's retirement, she finds her daily life being severely disrupted.

The husband suddenly is under foot all day every day. He sits in the living room watching TV when she wants to vacuum the carpet, and he strews ashes and newspapers about. When she is in the kitchen working, he suddenly feels the need to fix himself something to eat. Wherever she is, he is. No matter what she tries to do, he is in the way.

Not surprisingly, the wife gets short-tempered with him and wishes he were back at work again. For his part, his wife seems to be doing anything but aiding in his adjustment to retirement. She seems perpetually grouchy, and when he tries to help with some of the housework she tells him that he is only in the way. These couples may quarrel and snap at one another consistently enough to alarm their children and friends. They may wonder what has happened to the marriage, or whether it can stand the strains of retirement.

Marriages that have withstood the stresses of decades seldom succumb at this point, however. Sooner or later, the husband establishes new routines, not all of which infringe upon his wife's domain. He may develop a hobby that he can enjoy in a spare bedroom converted for that purpose; he may spend time in a basement or garage workshop or associate with a group of cronies at a neighborhood center, a local bar, or whatever. There are numerous ways he can get out from under foot.

Some husbands and wives work out a division of labor and a sharing

of tasks that brings them closer together than ever before. He does the outside work while she does the inside work, and then they go shopping together: later they take in a movie, perhaps. Again, there are many alternatives. The need to reorganize habits and schedules after retirement is pressing, and the adjustment is sometimes traumatic, but most couples manage it in a reasonably short time.

MARITAL HAPPINESS

Retirement is almost always viewed as creating adjustment problems for men and women, and most people associate love and romance with vigorous young adulthood. As a result, either people do not think much about marital happiness in the retirement years, or they assume that it is not very important. Older people do not feel that way, however.

One revealing study was based on 408 older husbands and wives whose names were secured through senior citizens' centers. It found that these people were still very much concerned with marital happiness. The largest number of them were between 65 and 69 years of age, a period that coincides with the retirement years. A portion of the findings is shown in Table 17-2.

A startling 94 percent of these presumably retired people rated their marriages either as very happy or happy. Even allowing for some tendency to give socially approved responses, it seems certain that the vast majority of them find their marriages to be deeply satisfying. This conclusion is supported by their answers to questions about whether their

**TABLE 17-2
OLDER PEOPLES'
RATINGS OF THEIR
MARRIAGES**

RATINGS	PERCENTAGES
Marital Happiness	
Very Happy	45
Happy	49
Unhappy	3
Undecided	3
Marriage Improved or Worsened Over Time	
Better	53
Worse	4
About the Same	41
Undecided	2
Happiest Period in Marriage	
Present Time	55
Middle Years	27
Young Adult Years	18

Source: Adapted from Nick Stinnett, Linda Mittelstet Carter and James E. Montgomery, "Older Persons' Perceptions of their Marriages," *Journal of Marriage and the Family* 34 (Nov. 1972), p. 667.

marriages had improved or worsened over time, and about which had been the happiest period in their marriages. Ninety-four percent said that their marriages had either improved or stayed about the same, and over half reported that their marriages were happier at present than at any earlier time.

When these older persons were asked what were the major problems during their present lives, only five percent mentioned their marriages. Unsatisfactory housing was mentioned most often (27 percent), followed by poor health (21 percent), and not enough money (20 percent). Apparently, marriages are major sources of satisfaction for most people confronting the infirmities and reduced resources of old age (Stinnett, Carter and Montgomery, 1972).

Although not directly linked to retirement, aging brings inevitable changes in family living arrangements. During early retirement, great variation develops in living arrangements. The most common situation is still married couples living independently of their children and other relatives. Almost half of the women, however, have already been widowed, and one-fifth of the men are widowers (Thompson and Streib, 1969). Living arrangements in widowhood and later retirement we shall save for the next chapter.

Aging couples differ in the degree of closeness and dependence that exists between them, in the number and importance of the things they do together, and in the closeness of their relationships with children, other relatives, and outsiders. Two social gerontologists have used these facts to divide aging couples into four basic types. They can be classified according to their closeness as a pair into high- and low-cohesion types, and they can be classified according to their broader social contacts into those having close-knit and those having loose-knit social networks (Thompson and Streib, 1969; Darnley, 1975). The resulting four types help us to understand how aging marriages function. They also allow us to predict the impact of widowhood upon the survivors. We shall look at all four combinations in turn.

In the high-family-cohesion, close-knit network type, the husband and wife are emotionally close to one another and share interests and activities. They also have meaningful ties to, and relationships with, relatives and others. The husband and wife do many things together, but not all. They are, however, appreciative and supportive of one another's independent interests. They also do many things with other people. Often these other people are the couple's adult children and other relatives, but they may be friends or members of organizations to which the couple belongs.

The last years that such couples have together are likely to be

LIVING ARRANGEMENTS AND FAMILY COHESION

HIGH FAMILY COHESION, CLOSE-KNIT NETWORK

fulfilling and rewarding. They reap the benefits of many years of effort in building the marriage relationship and relationships with others. When widowhood comes, the survivor is likely to be devastated, of course, for the loss is great. But there are other important people to share the grief, and painful as it is, readjustment occurs within a relatively short time. Memories of the relationship are treasured, but relationships with the living afford the survivor the opportunity to remain socially active and emotionally healthy.

*HIGH FAMILY
COHESION,
LOOSE-KNIT
NETWORK*

A second group of aging couples share all of the intimacy and joint interests and activities of the first group, but their relationships with others are fewer and less important. The spouses do virtually everything together but do little with their children or with others. They are not active in groups or organizations.

Their marriages are tremendously rewarding to them, but widow-hood comes as a savage blow. The grief is more devastating because it must essentially be suffered alone. When the first crisis of widowhood is past, there is little left for the widowed spouse. Adjustment occurs slowly if at all. A spiral of deterioration in social, emotional, and even physical health usually begins at this time.

LOW FAMILY COHESION, CLOSE-KNIT NETWORK

Other couples have low family cohesion but a close-knit social network. In these marriages, there often is the comfort and security that accompany long-standing habitual adjustments. The partners may get along well enough, but they are not particularly close. Each spouse has his or her own important interests that are pursued without the other. Each spouse has relationships with persons or groups outside the marriage that give most of the meaning to life.

Widowhood brings a crisis that varies in intensity with how much closeness there was in the relationship. But the trauma is less than it is in either of the high-cohesion types. The grief experienced is comparable to that which results from the death of any other person who was important in the survivor's life. The grief passes, and life goes on much as before, because the most important relationships in the person's life are still intact.

LOW FAMILY COHESION, LOOSE-KNIT NETWORK

The final group of couples, with low family cohesion and a loose-knit social network, are those for whom retirement is likely to be the most difficult. Since there is little closeness in the marriage relationship, it can neither absorb the interests nor meet the needs of either partner. Moreover, these couples also have little in the way of important relationships with anyone other than the marriage partner. Even before widowhood, life is likely to have little meaning for such people.

Widowhood produces a sense of loss and increases the loneliness of the survivor, but it is impossible to withdraw meaning from that which has no meaning already. The survivor has little to look forward to other than death. Death may be awaited with fear or resignation, or it may even be welcomed.

Unfortunately, little research has yet been done to verify the meaningfulness of these types, or to determine what proportions of the population fall into the various categories. These categories do, however, accord with the common experience of people as they observe aging couples.

SUMMARY

Most people face compulsory retirement at age 65. Some of them look forward to it with pleasure, but others dread it as signaling the end of their useful lives. In fact, men live an average of 11 years after age 65, and women average an additional 17 years.

The impact of the losses varies tremendously by economic level and from one couple to another, but some losses ordinarily accompany retirement. First, income drops, requiring some couples to readjust their styles of living and producing real hardship for others. Second, a threat to self-esteem is posed by the loss of one's occupational status. Closely related is the loss of opportunity to do work that both oneself and others regard as valuable. Meaningful social contacts are lost as one is cut off from former co-workers, and additional losses derive from enforced separation from one's occupation and occupational identification.

The strains of retirement can be eased by carefully planning for it, and by moving into it gradually. This process is easier for self-employed and professional workers, but even salaried employees can do it, using their evenings, weekends, and vacations to make plans and develop new interests. Ordinarily, the more gradual the disengagement from work, the better; the more new interests and activities one develops, the more satisfying retirement will be.

Retirement requires drastic changes in the daily schedules and habits of both men and women. When both spouses have worked outside the home, strains may be caused by the partners' being thrown together all day. They may be reluctant to embrace household tasks that they have not had to perform for many years. When the wife has played the role of homemaker, her husband's retirement and sudden presence in the home each day may severely disrupt her routines, leading to conflict.

The tensions ease as both partners reorganize their schedules and habits. Some couples come to share daily activities as they never have before, becoming emotionally closer in the process. In other cases, one or both partners develop new outside interests. In any event, fragmentary research shows that the vast majority of retirement-aged couples rate their marriages as happy or very happy. Over half say that their marriages are happier than they ever were before.

Although married-couple living still is the most common pattern during early retirement, widowhood begins to make major inroads during these years. Retirement-aged couples can be divided into groups according to how much sharing there is in the marriage and how effectively the partners are integrated into relationships with family members and non-relatives. Widowhood almost always is devastating, but the healthiest adjustments are made by persons who have had good relationships with both the spouse and others.

FOR ADDITIONAL READING

Brantl, Virginia M., and Sister Marie Raymond Brown, eds., *Readings in Gerontology* (Saint Louis: Mosby, 1973). Twelve essays cover the range from theories of aging and research on aging to problems of dealing with grief and suicide.

Jacobs, Jerry, *Fun City: An Ethnographic Study of a Retirement Com-munity* (New York: Holt, Rinehart and Winston, 1974). A fascinating account of an upper-middle-class retirement community in the southwest.

Maas, Henry S., and Joseph A. Kuypers, *From Thirty to Seventy* (San Francisco: Jossey-Bass, 1974). Comprehensive report of research on the personalities and life styles of the same persons over 40 years of adult life.

Newman, Barbara M., and Philip R. Newman, *Development Through Life: A Psychosocial Approach* (Homewood, Ill.: Dorsey, 1975). See the chapter on ''Later Adulthood.''

Sheldon, Alan, Peter J. M. McEwan, and Carol Pierson Ryser, *Retire-ment: Patterns and Predictions* (Washington, D.C.: National Institute of Mental Health, 1975). A good summary of the literature, along with a report of research.

STUDY QUESTIONS

1. What is the further life expectancy of women who reach age 65? of men? What implications do these facts have for adjustment in the retire-ment years?

2. Why do we distinguish between the early retirement period and later retirement? What family problems increase and what ones diminish over this period?

3. In what areas do retiring persons generally suffer losses? Of these, which do you think are more important? Why?

4. How can average couples prepare to ease into retirement? How far ahead should they plan? What plans should they make?

5. What special problems confront a woman who is retiring from a career? Assume first that she has a husband, and then that she does not.

6. How does retirement often create strains in the marriage relationship? What do you think is the best way to resolve these strains?

7. What does research show about the happiness of retirement-age marriages? To what factors do you attribute these findings?

8. Weigh the benefits and costs to the individual of having close rela-tionships with the spouse and others before finding oneself widowed.

Chapter 18
Widowhood

Not all widows and widowers are beyond retirement age. Some husbands and wives die while they are still in their twenties or thirties. The widowhood that occasionally occurs at these ages is like the widowhood of older people in some ways but quite different from it in others. Young widows and widowers with children find themselves propelled into one-parent family situations like those described in Chapter 15 (Schlesinger, 1971). They are likely to remarry, and to finish raising their children in their new families.

Eventually, in any case, the remarried partner faces the possibility of widowhood again in the context of old age. It is the widowhood of people in their sixties and seventies that we are concerned with here.

THE EXTENT OF WIDOWHOOD

Eventually, one partner in every surviving marriage faces widowhood. Of the more than 22 million people in the United States who are 65 years old or older, almost half of the women and one-fifth of the men have lost their marital partners. With each additional year beyond 65, the risk of having one's life partner die becomes greater.

On the average, women live almost eight years longer than men do, so obviously most of the widowed are women. There are over ten million widows in the United States, and the number increases at the rate of more than 100,000 a year. Proportionately, there are four times as many widows as widowers.

To put the figures somewhat differently, there are only 72 men over 65 years of age for every 100 women. And more than 70 percent of these aging men are still married and living with their wives. Only 35 percent of the women, however, are still married and living with their husbands.

ADJUSTMENT TO BEING WIDOWED

The amount of warning that people get of impending widowhood varies greatly. In some instances, the partner is felled swiftly with no warning at all. In other cases the terminal illness lasts only a few weeks but allows for some grief before death occurs. In still other cases death follows a lingering illness, during which there is a great burden of physical care and financial cost. The burden may be so great that the grief becomes tempered with yearning for relief from the strain, until finally the death is almost welcomed. Finally, some couples grow very old together, and die eventually of old age, without traumatic illness. Each pattern carries its peculiar problems of adjustment for the survivor. Adjustment problems also differ for women and men.

WIDOWS

Regardless of the medical circumstances, the death of a beloved life partner is a devastating blow. Life may not seem worth living, and the widow may look forward to her own early death (Bock and Webber, 1972). The sympathy and comfort offered by grown children and other family members and friends helps to ease the pain, but after the funeral is over, lives must be resumed, children must go back to their own children and jobs, and the widow is left to face her grief essentially alone.

For a while at least, she is likely to resume life in the home she shared with her husband. Her grief is complicated further by the loss of at least some of his retirement income (Chevan and Korson, 1972; Gubrium, 1974; Harvey and Bahr, 1974; Hutchison, 1975). During this period of intensive mourning, she may be convinced that life will never be full for her again. Although generally unrecognized by the widow, however, some forces are working to relieve her distress.

Before the husband died, the woman's life was likely to have been better organized and more fulfilling in some ways than his was. A good part of her days was spent in caring for the home: cleaning, cooking, doing the laundry, and so on. After her husband's death, she has these same tasks to perform. Thus, even while she is feeling that life has lost all meaning, the daily necessities help her re-instill order in her life (Cosneck, 1970). The chances are, also, that at least some of her children and grandchildren live nearby, so that she will continue to play a

significant role as grandmother, babysitting frequently and sharing her children's and grandchildren's lives in many ways.

Many new widows also discover that their plight is shared by many others. Some of the husbands of friends have died also, leaving other lonely women with whom the new widow can share everything from understanding and emotional support to lunches, dinners, and evenings on the town. Through one or two widows, the new widow often meets still others until an informal social group based upon similarity of values and life styles is established. Thus, the new widow's life gradually becomes less lonely and life begins to take on meaning once again.

WIDOWERS

The emotional devastation experienced by men who lose their wives often is complicated by extreme unreadiness for the role of widower (Berardo, 1970). Many men, for example, are almost totally dependent upon their wives for even the simplest of household chores. For many years, the wife has cooked the meals, cleaned the home, and washed, ironed, and mended her husband's clothes; the wife's death leaves him temporarily almost totally unable to fend for himself.

By continuing to prepare three meals a day after their husbands' deaths, widows not only continue to receive adequate nutrition, but the routines of meal preparation and cleaning up afterward help to reestablish order in their lives. Contrast this situation with that of widowed men. Often they don't know how to cook properly, and they begin to eat meals out of cans, to skip some meals altogether, and to eat unbalanced meals at relatively inexpensive quick-service restaurants. Their health suffers, and their incompetence in household routines encourages lack of cleanliness and order in both their clothing and the house or apartment.

The widower's situation is further complicated by the traditional definition of man's role in society. Men are supposed to be independent and able to look after themselves. The masculine stereotype makes no provision for men to be old, infirm, and unable to cope. There is also no detailed prescription for grandfatherly behavior. Neither the widower or his children is likely to think it appropriate for the grandfather to be incorporated into his children's home, so the widower is likely to continue to live alone. Furthermore, he is less likely than widows are to receive financial support from his children.

In one respect, however, widowers generally fare better than widows do. Although widowers may be more isolated from relatives and from friends of the same sex, they have more opportunities to make friends of the opposite sex. Since there are four times as many widows as widowers, older men are always in great demand (Booth and Hess, 1974). Whether at dances or other social activities for older people, at church or other organizational meetings, or just around the neighborhood, older, unattached men find their company eagerly sought after by lonely women for whom there is a shortage of male companions.

Moreover, society at large probably views the possible remarriage of widowers more favorably than that of widows. Many people assume that widows should devote themselves to their grandchildren, their homes, community service, and the memories of their husbands. But the same people often assume that an old man needs a woman to look after him.

LIVING WITH CHILDREN

Since women are widowed in far greater numbers than men are, it is not surprising that mothers more frequently than fathers move into their children's homes. Widows are far more likely to live with a daughter's family than with a son's. This doesn't mean that sons are less likely to provide support for aging parents; it just means that sons support their wives' parents, while daughters support their own parents.

This pattern probably tends to work out better for all concerned. The home and its management are still primarily feminine prerogatives, and having two women in the home can easily bring them into conflict over how the home should be run. A woman and her own mother are more likely to have the same housekeeping values and to have compatible routines than are a woman and her mother-in-law.

Even when a woman and her mother share the same home, some division of labor between them usually helps to maintain harmony. The kitchen ordinarily is the most important area, and usually it is recognized to be the domain of one woman or the other. If the wife is primarily responsible for meal preparation, then her mother may be assigned certain satellite duties, such as preparing salads, setting the table, and so on. Reversing the roles may work equally well. Particularly when the wife works outside the home, there may be a great advantage in having the widow acknowledged as the primary housekeeper. The important thing, in addition to the need for a clear division of labor, is that the widowed mother play a regular and highly valued role in the family.

There is always the possibility, of course, that the widow's entrance into the home will upset the pattern of in-law adjustment that was achieved years or even decades before. By the time a widow reaches 65 or 75, however, her daughter is usually middle-aged, and there is likely to be more closeness and understanding between them than existed when they both were younger. The division of labor in the home makes it easier for them to share activities, accomplishments, and problems without conflict (Johnson, 1973).

The husband's adjustment to the presence of his mother-in-law depends greatly upon his relationship with her earlier and upon his relationship with his wife. If the middle-aged couple are secure in their mutual affection, and if the husband has grown close to his mother-in-law over the years, he may welcome her into the home almost as he would his own mother (Wake and Sporakowski, 1972). She may assume some of his household duties as well, thus relieving the pressure upon both his wife and himself.

When the husband and the mother-in-law are not that close, other kinds of adjustments often are made. The mother-in-law may have her own room or apartment complete with radio and TV, for example, so that she can spend much of her leisure time there, leaving the living room or family room to the rest of the family during the evening hours. In other ways, the widow may seek to be unobtrusive and to recognize her son-in-law's needs as well as her own. He, too, may occasionally yield the "public space" in the dwelling to his wife and mother-in-law, retiring to a study, garage, or basement to enjoy himself with hobbies or private pursuits.

Finally, a special kind of "joking relationship" often develops between the widow and her son-in-law that both gives order to their relationship and drains off strains and antagonisms between them. The mother-in-law may consistently tease him, for example, about some little habit that really is not offensive to her, almost as a means of showing solidarity with him. She is, in effect, saying, "Thank you for welcoming me into your home." In return, he teases her about something else, communicating that, "You are welcome; we care about you." The negative part of the adjustment is revealed in the occasional teases that are not part of the regular routine. With them, each person signals to the other, "Look, we have a problem here and something should be done about it before it becomes an open source of disagreement." More often than not, the other person picks up the clue and serious conflict is avoided.

The widow in her daughter's home often has a special grandparental role to play as well. The specifics vary according to whether there are young grandchildren or middle or late teenagers. But in any case, the widowed grandmother often is granted unstated permission by all concerned to become a special confidante of her grandchildren, protecting them against minor calamities in their relationships with parents, teachers, friends, and so on. The uncomplicated affection the widow receives from the children may be one of the most important rewards of her declining years. The widow must be very careful, of course, not to become so intensely identified with her grandchildren that she comes into conflict with their parents.

Many widowed people, particularly women, live out their lives in the security and comfort of their families, remembering fondly the days before their spouses died, and projecting the satisfactions of those relationships forward through children and grandchildren. They thus avoid both the challenges and the frustrations of those who resume active, independent heterosexual lives after their first spouses have died.

SEXUALITY AND COMPANIONSHIP

Age and physical health are important factors affecting people's adjustments to widowhood. Although detailed data are not available, we suspect that many of the widows who elect to live with their children's families are older and less able to care for themselves than many widows and widowers are. But many retired widows and widowers are healthy, vigorous people who are not ready to give up either their independence or meaningful relationships with members of the opposite sex. Some of these people keep a firm hold on life well into their seventies and even their eighties.

SEX AND AGING

The effects of aging upon men's and women's sexual needs and behavior are just beginning to be learned. Until recently, people snickered at the possibility that widows and widowers might be interested in sex, and too often they still do. Other people go further and express outright disapproval. The concept of the "dirty old man" symbolizes this sort of bigotry, which defines very normal interests in sex at old age as being somehow unclean and immoral.

Given this strong cultural pressure against continuing sexuality into old age, it would not be surprising if most old people gave up sex in spite of a continuing biological need for it. But this is not, at least, the usual situation. The fragmentary research that has been done shows that both men and women continue to be sexually active into old age, but also that there are differences between them.

As we might guess, given the existing social attitudes toward sex, older men are more active than older women. Longitudinal studies at Duke University show that approximately two-thirds of men past 65 are still sexually active, and about one-fifth of all men continue sexual activity into their eighties (Lobsenz, 1974). About half of all 80- and 90-year-old men report still having a moderate degree of interest in sex. Another study of 2801 male urological patients found that 25 percent of the men in their sixties and ten percent in their seventies were still having intercourse as frequently as once a week (Rossman, 1975). The need of many older people for sexual relationships thus seems clear enough. It also seems likely that these needs would be more widespread if the society at large did not discourage them (Broderick, 1975).

Fewer older women remain sexually active. According to the Duke University studies, about one out of three women in their sixties reports being interested in sex, but only one-fifth are sexually active. These low rates of sexual activity during the sixties, do not decrease appreciably at still older ages.

Such differences between men and women will encourage some people to intensify the long-standing debate over the significance of biological sex differences between males and females. But no such differences are required to explain the situation. As women move into their sixties they are much more likely to be without available partners than men are. Many of their spouses have died, and there is a shortage of available males. That this situation drastically affects older women's sexual activity was shown by a study that reported that only twelve percent of a sample of postmarital women at age 60 were having intercourse; yet 70 percent of a comparable group of married women were doing so (Burnside, 1975).

There are other reasons as well for the lower sexual activity of older women. For one thing, after their spouses have died, many women are more reluctant to accept nonmarital sex than men are. Many older women also have been conditioned to believe that sexual activity should end with the menopause, and consequently they suppress whatever sexual urges they do feel. Finally, women generally attach more significance to physical appearance than men do; many of them are reluctant to expose their aging bodies in sexual relationships.

These differences between older men and women should not obscure the fact that both many widows and many widowers are still capable of forming, and still need to form, meaningful relationships with members of the opposite sex. For some people, these needs persist into very old age and even survive severe physical disability. Perceptive operators of nursing homes recognize, for example, that some of their patients, both married and unmarried, still need to be close to other people, to touch, to caress, and to be caressed. Sadly, virtually no such homes have facilities that allow patients to have any privacy.

NEW MAN–WOMAN RELATIONSHIPS

Not all widows and widowers recover from their mates' deaths with the health and vitality to begin to yearn for new loving relationships. But an increasing number do. Older men and women renew relationships with persons of the opposite sex whom they knew earlier in life, or they meet and make new friends.

Although these new relationships may not be as passionate as those of young adulthood, many of them are explicitly sexual, involving all of the touching, fondling, and caressing of man-woman relationships in general. The men are thus reaffirmed in their masculinity and the women in their femininity, and both re-experience feelings of being wanted and needed.

People in their sixties and seventies have little time for coquetry, and loneliness and living arrangements are problems for many of them. Consequently, mutual attraction often leads quickly to living together. In addition to their emotional and physical needs, the older man needs someone to be his cook and housekeeper, and the older woman needs a man to do heavier chores, to make repairs, and so on.

Financial problems also influence older couples to live together. Both may be on social security, and one or both may have small pensions. Most often, their individual incomes are inadequate, and they can get along better by living together in one household with two incomes. Ironically, social security often forces old people to live together without marriage. By getting married, most women would forfeit their widow's benefits, a loss that many older couples cannot afford.

Surprisingly, or perhaps not so surprisingly, some older couples encounter resistance from their grown children. The children may merely be insensitive to their parents' relationship needs, so that they ridicule or belittle them. Or they may oppose a new involvement because they fear that the new person in the parent's life may inherit money or property that the children feel is properly theirs. There have been instances in which grown children have sought psychiatric examination, or even commitment, of their parents in attempt to break up these new relationships.

As might be expected, some older couples attempt to conceal their living arrangements and their relationships from their children in order to forestall such difficulties. This necessity frequently produces guilt and resentment in the older people. They are made to feel that they are doing something wrong, and they suffer distress over their lack of acceptance by their children.

Other adult children, however, feel deeply their parent's loss of a life partner and encourage the parent to form new meaningful relationships. Some adult children resist at first but come to accept the relationship when they discover how important it is to the parent. Some of the widowed parents, too, are strongly independent of others' reactions and choose to live together without marriage, for a while at least, for the additional satisfaction that a clandestine relationship brings them.

When older couples wish to marry, but meet strong objection from grown children who fear that they may lose their inheritances, a marriage contract may be useful. Older couples generally are not very worried about such matters as where they will live or what name they will use, but they may wish to have an attorney draw up an agreement specifying that, upon death, certain money or property will go to their children rather than to the new marital partner. As long as the couple's wills are brought into conformity with the marriage contract, the contract's provisions are likely to be enforced by the courts. The need to make such arrangements may be a sad reflection on the relationships between the older couple and their children, but a contract still may be worthwhile to secure the children's acceptance of the new marriage.

REMARRIAGE

Little study has yet been done of the remarriages of people following widowhood, but one study of 100 Connecticut couples may help to broaden our understanding of them. At the time of study, all of these couples had been married for at least five years and all had remarried after being widowed. The men were at least 65 years of age, and the women were at least 60 years of age, at the time of remarriage (McKain, 1972).

The research dealt first with how the new relationships had developed. Over half of the couples, it was discovered, had known one another before they were widowed. Most commonly, they had been neighbors, had belonged to the same church, or had associated socially. In almost ten percent of the cases, the new partners were already related by marriage. Men tended to marry sisters of their first wives, and women favored brothers of their first husbands. In a few cases, the new partners had dated one another before they married their first spouses and got together again after being widowed.

The men remarried more quickly after widowhood than the women did. Most of the men remarried within a year or two of the deaths of their first wives, while the women often waited for several years. The difference probably reflects the greater demand in which widowers find themselves. It also suggests the tendency for women to complete the rearing of all of their children before remarrying.

Many couples reported encountering resistance to their remarriages. In addition to the problems with children that have already been discussed, some couples reported subtle and not so subtle disapproval from friends and neighbors. One couple out of every four stated that they had almost been deterred from remarrying by these pressures, and many couples had been discreet about their courtships and avoided much public ceremony in connection with their remarriages.

Since all of these remarriages had survived for at least five years, and since the couples had agreed to be interviewed, they cannot fairly be used to estimate the quality of all remarriages following widowhood. Yet a strikingly high percentage of these remarriages were successful. According to statements from the partners themselves, and according to the estimates of the interviewer, 74 of the 100 marriages were quite successful. Twenty of the marriages were judged to be mainly successful but to have minor problems, and only six of the marriages were judged to be unsuccessful.

Finally, the study analyzed these older persons' reasons for remarrying and the satisfactions the remarriages brought them. Almost three-fourths of the men and two-thirds of the women emphasized their needs for companionship. These included the needs for physical closeness and sex, for having someone to depend upon and to be depended upon, for having someone to make plans with, and for reaffirming one's masculinity or femininity. Smaller proportions mentioned needs to stretch their incomes, to have someone to help around the home, and to avoid the possibility of becoming a burden on their children (McKain, 1972).

The portrait of these couples that emerges is one of essentially healthy, vigorous people in generally satisfactory marriages. There was some hint that the older and more infirm couples who sought increased income, household help, and nursing care more than companionship had less satisfactory remarriages. Sooner or later, extreme old age becomes a problem.

COMMUNAL LIVING

Most of the time when people think of alternative life styles and communal living, they have relatively young people in mind. Some of the most successful communal groups in recent years, however, have been organized by older people seeking to build new lives for themselves.

The problems that lead old people into communal living are the familiar ones of old age. Their spouses have died, and their former homes have broken up. Inadequacy of income discourages the attempt to set up a new private home even if a partner is available to share it. Ill health or just lack of strength and endurance often militates against one couple's managing a household and the grounds. Finally, not all aging persons can find members of the opposite sex with whom they want to share an intimate, exclusive relationship.

If a half a dozen or more people pool their incomes, however, they may well be able to afford a house with enough bedrooms to accommodate them all in relative comfort. The several men can share the heavier maintenance tasks, and the whole group can work out a division of labor satisfactory to them all. Many duties can be shared, so that there is direct companionship as tasks are being performed. Physical care is handy for those who need it, and there is a life-restoring challenge in a group's embarking upon a bold adventure when its members are in their sixties and seventies.

Most senior-citizen communes, so far, seem to have developed in warmer sections of the country, where large numbers of older people congregate. There is no fixed pattern of age or sex, although the number of participants is limited by the number of people that an available house can accommodate. The core of the group often is one or more married couples, most often remarried couples. There may be one or more other couples who share bedrooms. In addition, unattached men and women friends may fill out the group. The pattern is too new, and the communes are too few, to have any more rigid structure than that.

Scattered reports from the members of such communes suggest that they can be a very practical and rewarding way of life. The problems of competition, unconventionality, and rejection of a work ethic that have plagued younger communes seldom appear in these groups. The longevity of older people's communes is unknown. Obviously, death is likely to take a heavy toll of members over a few years, but many older people are quite willing to settle for a way of life that affords even that much stability.

Sadly, the most troublesome problem encountered by some groups has been opposition from neighbors and self-appointed guardians of community morality. Some neighbors have brought legal or police action against old-age communes because they really don't want several old people living nearby, and because they fear that the commune will result in a drop in property values. In other instances, the preposterous claim has been made that having unmarried older people sharing the same household will encourage deterioration of community morality.

We might hazard the guess that old people's communes as a distinctive style of life may become an enduring part of the contemporary scene. They foster continued independence, they make sense economically, they offer limited physical care, and they provide companionship. All old people should be so fortunate.

We have avoided drawing a sharp line between early old age and advanced old age. The reason is that aging is so heavily influenced by social and emotional factors that chronological age alone does not provide a clear guide to life styles. Aging and infirmity are inevitable,

OLD-AGE FACILITIES

however, unless death intervenes. As the effects of aging increase, more people are forced into special facilities for older people.

RETIREMENT COMMUNITIES

The term "retirement community" accurately describes the residential setting and way of life of an estimated half a million people in the United States.[1] Large real estate corporations have built such communities, either apartment buildings or large developments of single houses, particularly in the warmer sections of the country. They appeal to the relatively affluent, often requiring investments of from $25,000 to $50,000. Typically, they also have age restrictions. People under 50 or under 65 are not permitted to buy or lease the facilities, and children may be permitted as visitors only under specified conditions and at certain times.

Some retirement communities look like many other suburban neighborhoods, with well-maintained one-family houses lining litter-free streets. The streets may be wider than usual to avoid congestion, and they may be elaborately curved with culs-de-sac and other arrangements to discourage fast-moving automobile traffic. There may also be sidewalks for bicycle use and for leisurely strolling.

Some residents buy or lease homes in such retirement communities for the age segregation that they provide. They no longer wish to cope with the noise and bustle of playing children or boisterous teenagers. The economic and physical segregation also protect them from street crime and most of the other hazards of urban life. Some communities post guards at the entrances to keep unwelcome visitors out.

Most of the residents value the other amenities that retirement communities offer. There may be swimming pools, tennis courts, golf courses, shuffleboard courts, and so on. In addition, there may be organized social programs including such activities as dancing, picnics, arts and crafts, and amateur theater. Sometimes there also are regularly scheduled free bus rides to and from shopping centers and to entertainment events outside the community.

Obviously such areas cater to couples; single people are seldom found in them. Many of the younger couples, age 50 and up, are still in their first marriages, but many of the older ones have been widowed earlier and are remarried. If they haven't bothered with a second wedding ceremony, that fact is unlikely to be known to others.

Urban apartment-house counterparts of these suburban retirement communities also are restricted to the affluent, but they are likely to contain more older people, age 70 and up, and more men and women living alone. Because there are many more aged widows than widowers, retirement apartments or condominiums often have many more women residents than men.

[1] *Time*, June 2, 1975, p. 45.

There may be special facilities that permit relatively unobtrusive adjustment to infirmity. In addition to kitchens in the apartments, there may be a central dining room for those who can't cook or don't want to. There may even be a ''hot meal service,'' delivering meals to the apartments of residents who can't get to the dining room. Some communities have nursing home units as part of the facilities; residents can move into the nursing facilities when they are no longer able to care for themselves.

Although the prospect of death and illness is downplayed in most such communities, their management is often organized both to ward off deterioration of the residents' adjustment and to be alerted to it quickly when it does occur. In one San Francisco community, for example, a night watchman hangs a card on the doorknob of each apartment about midnight each night. If the resident hasn't removed the card by late the following morning, someone checks to make sure the person is up and about and that everything is all right (Johnson, 1973).

The advanced old age of the residents does not prevent most of them from having active social lives. Social activity is likely to be confined to the building, and it often centers around a recreation room or other shared facility. Groups of residents may gather for coffee or tea at pre-arranged times, some cliques sharing one time and other cliques another. There may also be a great deal of reciprocal entertaining in the individual living quarters (Hochschild, 1973; Whitchurch, 1975).

Special patterns of care often seem to develop among the residents. Widows come to concentrate upon and care for some of the older widowers. This care may range from cleaning their apartments and preparing their meals to providing quasi-nursing care. The man and woman may be almost constant companions and, when the older man is not incapacitated, there may be a sort of sharing that is reminiscent of courtship among younger people.

This brief discussion cannot do justice to the range and variety of retirement communities over the country. They are a new and rapidly growing phenomenon. For older people who have the money to afford them, there is an increasingly wide range of choices.

NURSING HOMES

Nursing homes provide care for those who are rapidly approaching the end of life and who can no longer care for themselves. The people in them are patients as well as residents. Typically, the one room allotted to each patient has to be shared with other patients, and there is no opportunity for privacy, or to personalize or decorate one's few square feet of space. And even when the patients are able to do so, there is no provision for them to prepare their own meals or to clean their own quarters.

There is a day room or recreation room for the use of those who are not confined to bed. Television is always there, and there are card tables for cards and other games. Reading seems to be the most common way of passing the time. Some patients cling to life tenaciously and remain quite active, but ill health and the lack of challenges and variety take their toll on most residents.

Most patients are alone, their spouses having died before them. Moreover, only a minority of patients develop any real friendships within the nursing home. For those who might still be able to maintain hetero-sexual contacts and who are interested in doing so, there is little opportunity. There are no private facilities, and such interests generally get no encouragement from the staff. In those relatively few cases in which staff members are sensitive to the patients' needs for companionship, and even for sexual contact, the medical and administrative requirements of the homes generally prevent their offering support and encouragement.

In those few cases in which the husband and wife are both still alive and enter a nursing home together, they may be able to share a private room, but they may not. Even if they do get a room together, privacy does not extend to security from intrusion by staff. Their role as "patients" effectively strips them of the privacy of the marital relationship. Nursing homes are places where people without alternatives go to await death; they offer little opportunity for anything else.

Most people at this stage of life have had experience with death. They have buried a husband or a wife and, sometimes, children. They have seen their friends die off until few are left. They know, more urgently each day, that their own deaths are not far away.

The older people get, the more illness they suffer, and the fewer meaningful relationships they have left, the more resigned they become to dying (Gubrium, 1975). Death may be regarded merely as inevitable, and some people await it stoically, refusing to make plans for more than one day at a time. Others come almost to welcome it as a source of relief from pain and misery and meaninglessness.

At the same time, the depersonalization of death in modern society makes it more difficult for many people to die with dignity (Mannes, 1973). As the person becomes infirm or ill, for example, he or she

FACING DEATH

typically is placed in a nursing home or a hospital. In these settings, the full technology of modern medicine is employed to preserve life for as long as possible. The longer these life-extending procedures are used, the less effective do the patient's relationships with a surviving spouse and children become. They see one another only for brief periods, and then often through a maze of wires and tubes. Try as hard as they might to give love and support, both the patient and family members find themselves increasingly isolated from one another.

The patient, who needs all of the help that he or she can get in facing death, often encounters a wall of deceit and concealment. Physicians and other medical personnel, partly as a matter of professional conviction and partly because of their own personal anxieties about death, evade the patient's questions about what to expect. Family members, too, try to keep up a cheerful emotional front which, more often than not, fools nobody. The patient becomes depressed. Family members suffer torment as they vacillate between love for the dying person and longing for relief from the physical and emotional burden of the terminal illness. In the final days and hours, as gross physical deterioration occurs, it is increasingly difficult for those who would give comfort even to touch the dying person.

A growing number of people are protesting this dehumanization of the process of dying. Increasingly, people are asking whether the desperate prolonging of some signs of life should be encouraged when there is no possibility of the person's ever resuming an active life. Advocating medical restraint is not the same thing as advocating euthanasia, or mercy killing, which is an ethical and legal matter that goes far beyond the scope of this book. It is, rather, a reflection of a growing feeling that modern medical technology has unintentionally deprived the dying person of the right to say what measures should be taken to preserve life. Massive medical intervention has worked to isolate the patient from his or her family.

In the emerging view, hospitalization or institutionalization are not always the best thing, either for the dying person or for those who will be left behind. Death and dying must remain the most shattering of human experiences. But perhaps they can be tolerated best in the privacy of relationships with loved ones.

SUMMARY

As age advances, the prospect of widowhood becomes more and more likely. Beyond age 65, almost half of all women and one-fifth of all men have lost their spouses. At each succeeding age, the disparity in survival rates becomes greater; there are four times as many widowed women as widowed men.

Widows typically continue to live for a while in the homes they shared with their husbands. The devastation of their grief is eased somewhat by the resumption of the familiar routines of caring for the home. Many widows also have meaningful roles as grandmothers, and they find a growing corps of other widows with whom the sharing of grief gradually is replaced by friendship and the development of new interests.

The death of either spouse is traumatic, but widowers often are left without even the basic skills to care for themselves, such as cooking, cleaning, and doing the laundry. There is little room for them in their children's lives, and they are also victims of the lifelong expectation that men should be independent and able to care for themselves. The one advantage that widowers have is the large number of widows available with whom to form new relationships.

Widows are more likely than widowers eventually to live with their children and grandchildren. Most often, they live with their daughters, with whom they share strong bonds of affection and similarity of routines. A clear division of labor within the home avoids most conflict between the women, and in some cases the husband welcomes his mother-in-law almost as he would his own mother. The maintenance of some privacy for each family member often is tacitly agreed upon, and special joking relationships between the widow and her son-in-law often help to relieve tensions.

Many widows and widowers are healthy, vigorous people with continuing interest in people of the opposite sex. They may develop new relationships with brothers or sisters of their deceased spouses, with friends who also have been left alone, or even with childhood sweethearts who are rediscovered after many years.

Going together often leads to living together, with marriage or without. Existing social security regulations discourage remarriage, and grown children sometimes oppose it. Marriage contracts providing for the disposition of property to the children may ease some objections, and many children become more accepting of their parents' new romances when they see the happiness they bring.

Studies of remarriages following widowhood show them to be highly satisfactory, emphasizing companionship, sexual satisfaction, and the reaffirmation of masculinity and femininity. They also reflect the need to share incomes and to have someone to depend upon and to help around the home.

Some older persons and couples have begun to create communal living groups in which expenses, household chores, and companionship are shared. So far, older-person communes seem virtually confined to warmer sections of the country and use large, single houses as residences. Residents report them to be very satisfactory, but some objections have been raised by neighbors. Outsiders either object on moral grounds or who fear the loss of the single-family character of their neighborhoods.

Affluent oldsters, in either first or second marriages, can take advantage of suburban retirement communities created especially for them. These communities offer many amenities and special services. Unattached, but still affluent, old people can find comparable urban facilities organized around large apartment houses. These institutions may offer special care as the tenants move into extreme old age. The dehumanizing environment of the nursing home awaits those who can no longer care for themselves or be cared for at home or in a retirement community.

Ultimately, each person faces death. Modern medical technology has done much to delay death for many people and to make it less painful. It has also taken dying out of the home. Increasingly, it has isolated the dying person from intimate relationships, and prolonged some lives beyond meaning. Some families are seeking to reclaim the rights of their members to more humane deaths.

FOR ADDITIONAL READING

Blau, Zena Smith, *Old Age in a Changing Society* (New York: New Viewpoints, 1973). Examines the impact of exit from marital and work roles upon the self concepts, morale, and social participation of the elderly.

Cottrell, Fred, *Aging and the Aged* (Dubuque, Iowa: William C. Brown, 1974). Brief analysis of the many aspects of the situations of older people.

De Beauvoir, Simone, *The Coming of Age* (New York: Putnam, 1972). A distinguished writer's complaint about society's mistreatment of the aged.

Lopata, Helena Znaniecki, *Widowhood in an American City* (Cambridge, Mass.: Schenkman, 1973). Comprehensive report of research on widows over 50 years of age in Chicago.

Mannes, Marya, *Last Rights: A Case for the Good Death* (New York: Signet, 1975). An eloquent plea for the right to die with dignity.

STUDY QUESTIONS

1. Try to compare the adjustment problems faced by new widows and widowers. What oversimplifications does such a comparison encourage?

2. What special strains confront married women whose widowed mothers come to live with them? What can the widow do to help minimize those strains?

3. On the whole, older women who have lost their mates are sexually less active than comparable men are. Interpret this fact in terms of the development of masculine–feminine differences described in Chapter 2.

4. If an older couple wishes to remarry or to live together, and their grown children object, how should the older couple handle the situation? What disadvantages are there in your solution?

5. If you were trying to predict whether a proposed marriage between older widowed persons would be successful, what factors would you look for?

6. Should society encourage the formation of communal living groups by older people? Why or why not?

7. In what ways are retirement communities desirable places for old people to live? In what ways are they not desirable?

8. One day you will face death—your own death. What role do you want medicine to play in prolonging your life?

Glossary

abortion. Expulsion of the embryo or fetus before it is capable of living outside the mother's body. *Spontaneous* abortions occur without external causation. *Induced* abortions are medically caused.

affinity. Relationship by marriage.

alimony. Monetary payments ordered by a court to be made to a divorced spouse. Alimony may be in a lump sum or in monthly payments for a prescribed period. Payments generally cease with the remarriage of the spouse.

amniotic fluid. The fluid within which the fetus is suspended during pregnancy.

androgen. The general male sex hormone.

anomaly. A biological deviation from the norm.

antibodies. A general class of proteins, produced by the body to neutralize infections or other foreign substances.

anus. The rectal opening.

areola. The dark pigmented area directly surrounding the nipple.

artificial insemination. Introduction of semen into the vagina by means of a tube to induce pregnancy. The physician uses either the husband's sperm or that of the husband mixed with the sperm of an anonymous donor.

beneficiary. The person or persons designated to receive the proceeds of a life insurance policy upon the death of the insured.

breech presentation. A birth in which the baby's buttocks emerge first.

cash value (loan value). The equity that a person has accumulated in a permanent life insurance policy. The policy may be surrendered for the cash directly, or the policyholder may borrow that amount of money against the policy.

castration. The removal or loss of the sex glands. The testes in men and the ovaries in women.

cervix. The neck of the uterus.

cesarean section. A birth in which the physician delivers the baby surgically through the abdominal wall.

chauvinism. Originally, excessive patriotism. Now commonly taken to stand for ''male chauvinism,'' a belief in the superiority of men and things masculine.

child support. Payments that a court requires a divorced spouse to make for the care of his or her children.

clitoris. A small, erectile organ in girls and women, located at the junction of the labia minora.

coitus. Sexual intercourse.

collusion. Agreements made by a couple concerning the securing of a divorce. Such agreements are illegal in states that do not have no-fault divorce.

common law. The body of legal precedent brought to the American colonies from England and applying in the absence of statutory law. Includes common-law marriages that are established without benefit of legal sanction.

conception. The beginning of pregnancy; the moment when the ovum is fertilized by one of the sperm.

condom. A male contraceptive consisting of a sheath placed over the penis to prevent the semen from entering the vagina.

consanguinity. Relationship by blood.

cortisol. A hormone, produced by the adrenal cortex, which is essential to the maintenance of life.

cortisone. A form of cortisol, available in synthetic form, for therapeutic use.

counterculture. The youth-oriented movement of the late 1960s and early 1970s that encouraged the development of alternative life styles.

Cowper's glands. Small organs at the base of the penis which produce a pre-ejaculatory fluid.

cyst. A closed sac developing abnormally within the body.

defendant. The person accused of wrongdoing in a legal action, as in fault divorce.

demography. The statistical study of population.

diaphragm. A female contraceptive device, consisting of a bowl-shaped rubber membrane, placed within the vagina and covering the cervix, to prevent the sperm from entering the uterus.

disengagement. A process in which many of the relationships between an aging person and other people are severed or altered in preparation for death.

domicile. The legal residence of a person or married couple.

douche. A contraceptive technique consisting of flushing out the vagina with water and a spermicidal agent following sexual intercourse.

dower. The inalienable legal right which a woman has in her husband's property.

ejaculation. The sudden emission of semen from the penis during orgasm.

embryo. The term for the baby developing within the uterus during the first three months of pregnancy.

endowment insurance. An insurance policy in which the proceeds are paid to the insured upon the termination of premium payments after a specified time period.

epididymis. A group of oblong bodies attached to each testis in which sperm mature and are stored.

equity. The money value of one's interest in a property.

erection. The enlargement and stiffening of the penis during sexual excitement.

estrogen. The primary female sex hormone, produced in the ovaries and also in the adrenal cortex and the testes.

euthanasia. The painless putting to death of persons suffering from incurable diseases.

face amount (insurance). The dollar amount for which an insurance policy is written.

fallopian tubes. Tubes connecting the ovaries with the uterus, through which the ovum passes and in which fertilization usually occurs.

fecundity. The biological capacity to reproduce.

fertility. The actual rate of reproduction.

fetus. The medical term for the unborn baby after the third month.

field of eligibles. The groups of persons from among whom an individual is able to select a mate.

follicles. The small sacs, near the surface of the ovaries, within which the ova develop.

gender identity. The persistent definition of oneself as male or female.

glans. The head of the penis.

group insurance. The most inexpensive form of insurance, in which one policy is written to cover many people, usually company employees.

hermaphroditism. A condition in which the sexual structures are ambiguous, not clearly male or female.

heterogamy. The marriage of persons who are unlike one another in one or more respects.

homogamy. The marriage of persons who are like one another in one or more respects.

hymen. A thin membrane stretched across and partly covering the entrance to the vagina.

hypothesis. A suspected relationship between two or more things that forms a basis for the development of research.

hysterectomy. The surgical removal of the uterus.

infertility. The temporary inability to reproduce.

intrauterine device (IUD). A small metal or plastic device inserted into the cervix and left in place for long periods of time to prevent pregnancy.

labia majora. The outer lips of the vulva.

labia minora. The smaller, inner lips of the vulva.

laparoscopy. A technique for sterilizing women using high-intensity radio waves to destroy sections of the Fallopian Tubes.

lesbianism. Female homosexuality.

limited payment insurance. An insurance policy in which the proceeds are paid upon death, but premium payments are made over a specified time period.

masturbation. The manipulation of one's own genitals for sexual pleasure.

mating gradient. The pattern in which men select marriage partners with less education or from a lower social class position than themselves.

menopause. The time in the woman's life when ovulation gradually ceases and she can no longer become pregnant.

menstruation. The periodic discharge of blood and other materials from the uterine lining in sexually mature women.

miscarriage. The spontaneous, premature termination of pregnancy.

mons veneris. The fleshy mound located just above the vulva.

norms. Society's standards of behavior for its members.

normal presentation. The usual manner of birth, in which the baby's head emerges first.

orgasm. The sexual climax.

ovaries. The primary female sex glands, located in the abdomen adjacent to the uterus, which produce the ova.

ovulation. The periodic release of an ovum from one of the ovaries.

penis. The primary male sex organ, consisting of a tube of sponge-like erectile tissue.

perineum. The erotically sensitive area between the genitals and the anus.

pill. An oral contraceptive containing synthetic hormones that resemble those produced by the body during pregnancy.

placebo. An inert or innocuous medication.

placenta (afterbirth). The cake-like mass that connects the fetus to the uterus by means of the umbilical cord, and through which food and waste products are passed.

plaintiff. The person who brings charges in a legal action, as in fault divorce.

platonic relationship. A non-sexual relationship.

progesterone. The pregnancy hormone produced by the ovary and by the placenta.

progestin. A synthetic hormone that acts like progesterone.

prostate. A gland that surrounds the male urethra and the neck of the bladder. Produces part of the seminal fluid.

puberty. The stage in life when sexual maturity and the ability to reproduce is reached.

random sample. An ideal sample for the conduct of research, in which each potential respondent has an equal chance of being studied.

reference group. A group that is important to the individual and whose standards shape his or her behavior.

refractory period. The short period following orgasm during which the person cannot be sexually aroused.

residential propinquity. The tendency of people to select marriage partners from among those who live nearby.

Rh factor. A substance found in the blood. When there is a mismatch between that of the fetus and that of the mother, a type of anemia in the fetus may result.

rhythm method. A birth control method involving abstinence from sexual intercourse during the presumably fertile period.

role. A pattern of behavior that is socially appropriate in certain circumstances, as in masculine and feminine roles.

rubella. German measles; hazardous to the fetus if contracted by the woman during the first three months of pregnancy.

salpingectomy. The sterilization of a woman by destroying parts of the Fallopian Tubes.

scrotum. The pouch, hanging below the penis, which contains the testes.

secondary sexual characteristics. The physical characteristics not directly connected with reproduction but which distinguish males and females, such as body hair, body shape, and voice.

semen. The thick liquid, containing the sperm, which is expelled from the penis at ejaculation.

seminal vesicles. Glands on either side of the prostate which produce components of the semen.

sex ratio. The ratio of males to females, generally stated as the number of males per 100 females. The *primary* sex ratio is the ratio at the moment of conception. The *secondary* sex ratio is that at birth. The *tertiary* sex ratio is that at young adulthood.

sexism. Widespread cultural attitudes asserting the superiority of men, and of things masculine.

show. The vaginal discharge of mucus and blood which signals the onset of labor.

socialization. The formal and informal learning that results in personality development.

sperm. The male reproductive cells, produced by the testes.

spermicide. A chemical that immobilizes or destroys sperm. Used for contraception.

sphincter muscles. Ring-like muscles surrounding body openings, as around the cervix and the anus.

spontaneous abortion. A miscarriage; an abortion occurring naturally and without human interference.

sterilization. Rendering a person incapable of reproduction.

stereotype. A caricature, an over-simplified or erroneous set of beliefs about a class of persons, as in sexual stereotypes.

straight (whole) life insurance. A type of insurance policy in which the insured pays premiums for life and the face amount of the policy is paid upon death.

subculture. A culture within a culture, as in masculine, feminine, and youth subcultures.

term. The culmination of pregnancy at the end of nine months.

term insurance. The least costly type of life insurance, having no savings or cash value.

testes (testicles). The male sex glands, contained within the scrotum, which produce the sperm.

testosterone. The male sex hormone, produced by the testes and responsible for the secondary sexual characteristics.

thalidomide. A sedative drug; its use in pregnant woman was responsible for a large number of deformed babies.

transverse presentation. The condition in which neither the head nor the buttocks of the fetus will move in the birth canal. Often results in a cesarean section.

tumescence. The swelling and stiffening of the penis in sexual excitement.

unsecured loan. A loan made without collateral and generally at high interest rates.

urethra. The tube through which urine passes from the bladder; also carries semen in the male.

urological. Pertaining to the urinary tract.

uterus. The pear-shaped organ within which the fetus grows during pregnancy.

vagina. The elastic canal in the female which receives the penis in sexual intercourse.

vas deferens (pl. *vasa deferentia*). One of two tubes that carry the sperm from the testes to the urethra.

vasectomy. Sterilization of the male by destroying part of the *Vasa deferentia*.

vestibule. The area surrounding and including the entrance to the vagina.

withdrawal. An unreliable contraceptive technique involving the removal of the penis from the vagina before ejaculation.

References

Aldridge, Delores P., "The Changing Nature of Interracial Marriage in Georgia: A Research Note," *Journal of Marriage and the Family* 35 (Nov. 1973), p. 641.

Alexander, Tom, "There are Sex Differences in the Mind, Too," *Fortune* (February 1971), pp. 76–9, 132–35.

Almquist, Elizabeth M., and Shirley S. Angrist, "Career Salience and Atypicality of Occupational Choice Among College Women," *Journal of Marriage and the Family* 32 (May 1970), pp. 242–49.

Angrist, Shirley S., "Variations in Women's Adult Aspirations During College," *Journal of Marriage and the Family* 34 (Aug. 1972), pp. 465–68.

Arafat, Ibtihaj S., and Betty Yourburg, "On Living Together Without Marriage," *The Journal of Sex Research* 9 (May 1973), pp. 97–106.

Arafat, Ibtihaj S., and Wayne L. Cotton, "Masturbation Practices of Males and Females," *The Journal of Sex Research* 10 (Nov. 1974), pp. 293–307.

Ard, Ben N., Jr., "Premarital Sexual Experience: A Longitudinal Study," *The Journal of Sex Research* 10 (Feb. 1974), pp. 32–39.

Bacon, Loyd, "Early Motherhood, Accelerated Role Transition, and Social Pathologies," *Social Forces* 52 (March 1974), pp. 333–41.

Bahr, Stephen J., and Boyd C. Rollins, "Crisis and Conjugal Power," *Journal of Marriage and the Family* 33 (May 1971), pp. 360–67.

Bahr, Stephen J., Charles E. Bowerman, and Viktor Gecas, "Adolescent Perceptions of Conjugal Power," *Social Forces* 52 (March 1974), pp. 356–67.

Baker, Luther G., Jr., "The Personal and Social Adjustment of the Never-Married Woman," *Journal of Marriage and the Family* 30 (Aug. 1968), pp. 473–79.

Balswick, Jack O., and James A. Anderson, "Role Definition in the Unarranged Date," *Journal of Marriage and the Family* 31 (Nov. 1969), pp. 776–78.

Balswick, Jack O., and Charles W. Peek, "The Inexpressive Male: A Tragedy of American Society," *The Family Coordinator* 20 (Oct. 1971), pp. 363–68.

Bardwick, Judith, *Psychology of Women* (New York: Harper and Row, 1971).

Bardwick, Judith, "Infant Sex Differences," in Clarice Stasz Stoll, ed., *Sexism: Scientific Debates* (Reading, Mass.: Addison-Wesley, 1973), pp. 28–42.

Barrett, Curtis L., and Helen Noble, "Mothers' Anxieties Versus the Effects of Long Distance Move on Children," *Journal of Marriage and the Family* 35 (May 1973), pp. 181–88.

Bartell, Gilbert D., *Group Sex: A Scientist's Eyewitness Report on the American Way of Swinging* (New York: Wyden, 1971).

Bartz, Karen W., and F. Ivan Nye, "Early Marriage: A Propositional Formulation," *Journal of Marriage and the Family* 32 (May 1970), pp. 258–68.

Bauman, Karl E., and Robert R. Wilson, "Sexual Behavior of Unmarried University Students in 1968 and 1972," *The Journal of Sex Research* 10 (Nov. 1974), pp. 327–33.

Bayer, Alan E., "Early Dating and Early Marriage," *Journal of Marriage and the Family* 30 (Nov. 1968), pp. 628–32.

Bebbington, A. C., "The Function of Stress in the Establishment of the Dual-Career Family," *Journal of Marriage and the Family* 35 (Aug. 1973), pp. 531–37.

Bell, Robert R., *Social Deviance: A Substantive Analysis* (Homewood, Ill.: The Dorsey Press, 1971).

Bell, Robert R., and Phyllis L. Bell, "Sexual Satisfaction Among Married Women," *Medical Aspects of Human Sexuality* (Dec. 1972), pp. 136, 141–44.

Benjamin, Harry, ed., *The Transsexual Phenomenon* (New York: Julian Press, 1966).

Berardo, Felix M., "Survivorship and Social Isolation: The Case of the Aged Widower," *The Family Coordinator* 19 (Jan. 1970), pp. 11–25.

Berger, David G., and Morton G. Wenger, "The Ideology of Virginity," *Journal of Marriage and the Family* 35 (Nov. 1973), pp. 666–76.

Bernard, Jessie, *The Future of Marriage* (New York: World, 1972).

Bock, E. Wilbur, and Irving Webber, "Suicide Among the Elderly: Isolating Widowhood and Mitigating Alternatives," *Journal of Marriage and the Family* 34 (Feb. 1972), pp. 24–31.

Bohannon, Paul, ed., *Divorce and After: An Analysis of the Emotional and Social Problems of Divorce* (New York: Doubleday & Co., 1970).

Booth, Alan, and Elaine Hess, "Cross-Sex Friendship," *Journal of Marriage and the Family* 36 (Feb. 1974), pp. 38–47.

Bouvier, Leon F., "Catholics and Contraception," *Journal of Marriage and the Family* 34 (Aug. 1972), pp. 514–22.

Brandwein, Ruth A., Carol A. Brown, and Elizabeth Maury Fox, "Women and Children Last: The Social Situation of Divorced Mothers and their Families," *Journal of Marriage and the Family* 36 (Aug. 1974), pp. 498–514.

Breedlove, William, and Jerrye Breedlove, *Swap Clubs* (Los Angeles: Sherbourne Press, 1964).

Broderick, Carlfred B., "Sexual Behavior Among Pre-Adolescents," *The Journal of Social Issues* 22 (April 1966), pp. 6–21.

Broderick, Carlfred, "Sexuality and Aging: An Overview," in Irene Mortenson Burnside, ed., *Sexuality and Aging* (Los Angeles: The University of Southern California Press, 1975), pp. 1–6.

Broderick, Carlfred B., and George P. Rowe, "A Scale of Preadolescent Heterosexual Development," *Journal of Marriage and the Family* 30 (Feb. 1968), pp. 97–101.

Brody, Jane E., "Are Birth Control Methods Safe?" *The New York Times,* March 11, 1975.

Bruning, Fred, "Runaway Wives," *Newsday Service,* March 3, 1974.

Bumpass, Larry L., "Is Low Fertility Here to Stay?" *Family Planning Perspectives* 5 (Spring 1973), pp. 67–69.

Bumpass, Larry L., and James A. Sweet, "Differentials in Marital Instability," *American Sociological Review* 37 (Dec. 1972), pp. 751–66.

Burchinal, Lee, and Loren Chancellor, "Survival Rates Among Religiously Homogamous and Interreligious Marriages," *Social Forces* 41 (May 1963), pp. 353–62.

Burnside, Irene Mortenson, "Sexuality and Aging," in Irene Mortenson Burnside, ed., *Sexuality and Aging* (Los Angeles: The University of Southern California Press, 1975), pp. 42–53.

Busselen, Harry J., Jr., and Carroll Kincaid Busselen, "Adjustment Differences Between Married and Single Undergraduate University Students: An Historical Perspective," *The Family Coordinator* 24 (July 1975), pp. 281–87.

Butler, Edgar W., Ronald J. McAllister, and Edward J. Kaiser, "The Effects of Voluntary and Involuntary Residential Mobility on Females and Males," *Journal of Marriage and the Family* 35 (May 1973), pp. 219–27.

Cannon, Kenneth L., and Richard Long, "Sexual Behavior in the Sixties," *Journal of Marriage and the Family* 33 (Feb. 1971), pp. 36–49.

Carns, Donald E., "Talking About Sex: Notes on First Coitus and the Double Sexual Standard," *Journal of Marriage and the Family* 35 (Nov. 1973), pp. 677–88.

Carter, Hugh, and Paul C. Glick, *Marriage and Divorce: A Social and Economic Study* (Cambridge, Mass.: Harvard University Press, 1970).

Centers, Richard, Bertram H. Raven, and Aroldo Rodrigues, "Conjugal Power Structure: A Re-Examination," *American Sociological Review* 36 (April 1971), pp. 264–78.

Chevan, Albert, and J. Henry Korson, "The Widowed Who Live Alone: An Examination of Social and Demographic Factors," *Social Forces* 51 (Sept. 1972), pp. 45–53.

Cohen, Jerome B., and Arthur W. Hanson, *Personal Finance: Principles and Case Problems* (Homewood, Ill.: Irwin, 1972).

Cole, Charles L., and Graham B. Spanier, "Comarital Mate-Sharing and Family Stability," *The Journal of Sex Research* 10 (Feb. 1974), pp. 21–31.

Connell, Elizabeth B., "The Pill Revisited," *Family Planning Perspectives* 7 (March–April 1975), pp. 62–71.

Constantine, Larry L., and Joan M. Constantine, "Where Is Marriage Going?" *The Futurist* (April 1970), p. 44.

Constantine, Larry L., and Joan M. Constantine, "Sexual Aspects of Multilateral Relations," *The Journal of Sex Research* 7 (Aug. 1971), pp. 204–25.

Constantine, Larry L., and Joan M. Constantine, "Dissolution of Marriage in a Nonconventional Context," *The Family Coordinator* 21 (Oct. 1972), pp. 457–62.

Coombs, Lolagene C., and Ronald Freedman, "Pre-marital Pregnancy, Childspacing, and Later Economic Achievement," *Population Studies* 24 (1970), p. 389.

Cosneck, Bernard J., "Family Patterns of Older Widowed Jewish People," *The Family Coordinator* 19 (Oct. 1970), pp. 368–73.

Croake, James W., and Barbara James, "A Four Year Comparison of Premarital Sexual Attitudes," *The Journal of Sex Research* 9 (May 1973), pp. 91–96.

Culhane, John, "The Cases of the Runaway Wives," *The New York Times Magazine* (June 10, 1973), pp. 87–91.

Cvetkovich, George, Barbara Grote, Ann Bjorseth, and Julia Sarkiasian, "On the Psychology of Adolescents' Use of Contraceptives," *The Journal of Sex Research* 11 (Aug. 1975), pp. 256–70.

Darnley, Fred Jr., "Adjustment to Retirement: Integrity or Despair," *The Family Coordinator* 24 (April 1975), pp. 217–26.

Davis, Fred, "On Youth Subcultures: The Hippie Variant," (New York: General Learning Press, 1971).

de Lissovoy, Vladimir, "High School Marriages: A Longitudinal Study," *Journal of Marriage and the Family* 35 (May 1973), pp. 245–55.

Denfeld, Duane, "Dropouts from Swinging," *The Family Coordinator* 23 (Jan. 1974), pp. 45–49.

Denfeld, Duane, and Michael Gordon, "The Sociology of Mate Swapping: Or the Family that Swings Together Clings Together," *The Journal of Sex Research* 6 (May 1970), pp. 85–100.

Dodson, Fitzhugh, *How to Father* (New York: New American Library, 1974).

Driscoll, Richard H., and Keith E. Davis, "Sexual Restraints: A Comparison of Perceived and Self-Reported Reasons for College Students," *The Journal of Sex Research* 7 (Nov. 1971), pp. 253–62.

Duberman, Lucille, "Step-Kin Relationships," *Journal of Marriage and the Family* 35 (May 1973), pp. 283–92.

Duvall, Evelyn Millis, *Family Development* (Philadelphia: Lippincott, 1971).

Easterlin, Richard A., "Does Money Buy Happiness?" *The Public Interest* 30 (Winter 1973), pp. 3–10.

Eastman, William F., "First Intercourse," *Sexual Behavior* (March 1972), pp. 22–27.

Edmiston, Susan, "How to Write Your Own Marriage Contract," in *Readings in Marriage and Family 75/76* (Guilford, Conn.: Dushkin Publishing Group, 1974), pp. 136–42.

Edwards, John N., "Extramarital Involvement: Fact and Theory," *The Journal of Sex Research* 9 (Aug. 1973), pp. 210–24.

Ellis, Albert, "Group Marriage: A Possible Alternative?" in Gordon F.

Streib, ed., *The Changing Family: Adaptation and Diversity* (Reading, Mass.: Addison-Wesley, 1973), pp. 81–86.

England, J. Lynn, and Phillip R. Kunz, "The Application of Age-Specific Rates to Divorce," *Journal of Marriage and the Family* 37 (Feb. 1975), pp. 40–46.

Epstein, Gilda F., and Arline L. Bronzaft, "Female Freshmen View their Roles as Women," *Journal of Marriage and the Family* 34 (Nov. 1972), pp. 671–72.

Eslinger, Kenneth N., Alfred C. Clarke, and Russell R. Dynes, "The Principle of Least Interest. Dating Behavior, and Family Integration Settings," *Journal of Marriage and the Family* 34 (May 1972), pp. 269–72.

Fairfield, Richard, *Communes U.S.A.: A Personal Tour* (Baltimore: Penguin Books, 1972).

Fengler, Alfred P., "Romantic Love in Courtship: Divergent Paths of Male and Female Students," *Journal of Comparative Family Studies* 5 (Spring 1974), pp. 134–39.

Figley, Charles R., "Child Density and the Marital Relationship," *Journal of Marriage and the Family* 35 (May 1973), pp. 272–82.

Freund, M., and J. E. Davis, "A Follow-Up Study of the Effects of Vasectomy on Sexual Behavior," *The Journal of Sex Research* 9 (Aug. 1973), pp. 241–68.

Friedan, Betty, "Up from the Kitchen Floor," *The New York Times Magazine,* March 4, 1973, pp. 8–9, 28–37.

Furstenberg, Frank F., Jr., "Birth Control Experience Among Pregnant Adolescents: The Process of Unplanned Parenthood," *Social Problems* 19 (Fall 1971), pp. 192–203.

Gebhard, Paul H., "Postmarital Coitus Among Widows and Divorcees," in Paul Bohannon, ed., *Divorce and After* (New York: Doubleday, 1970), pp. 89–106.

Gelles, Richard J., *The Violent Home: A Study of Physical Aggression Between Husbands and Wives* (Beverly Hills, Cal.: Sage Publications, 1972).

Gelles, Richard J., "Violence and Pregnancy: A Note on the Extent of the Problem and Needed Services," *The Family Coordinator* 24 (Jan. 1975), pp. 81–86.

Glenn, Norval D., Andreain A. Ross, and Judy Corder Tully, "Patterns of Intergenerational Mobility of Females Through Marriage," *American Sociological Review* 39 (Oct. 1974), pp. 683–99.

Glick, Paul C., "A Demographer Looks at American Families," *Journal of Marriage and the Family* 37 (Feb. 1975), pp. 15–26.

Glick, Paul C., and Arthur J. Norton, "Frequency, Duration, and Probability of Marriage and Divorce," *Journal of Marriage and the Family* 33 (May 1971), pp. 307–17.

Glick, Paul C., and Arthur J. Norton, "Perspectives on the Recent Upturn in Divorce and Remarriage," *Demography* 10 (Aug. 1973), pp. 301–14.

Goode, William J., *Women in Divorce* (New York: The Free Press, 1965).

Grier, George, *The Baby Bust* (Washington, D.C.: The Washington Center for Metropolitan Studies, 1971).

Gubrium, Jaber F., *Living and Dying at Murray Manor* (New York: Saint Martin's Press, 1975).

Gubrium, Jaber F., "Marital Desolation and the Evaluation of Everyday Life in Old Age," *Journal of Marriage and the Family* 36 (Feb. 1974), pp. 107–13.

Hamburg, D. A., and D. T. Lunde, "Sex Hormones in the Development of Sex Differences," in Eleanor E. Maccoby, ed., *The Development of Sex Differences* (London: Tavistock, 1967).

Harvey, Carol D., and Howard M. Bahr, "Widowhood, Morale, and Affiliation," *Journal of Marriage and the Family* 36 (Feb. 1974), pp. 97–106.

Heath, Linda L., Brent S. Roper, and Charles D. King, "A Research Note on Children Viewed as Contributors to Marital Stability: The Relationship to Birth Control Use, Ideal and Expected Family Size," *Journal of Marriage and the Family* 36 (May 1974), pp. 304–6.

Heer, David M., "The Prevalence of Black–White Marriage in the United

States, 1960 and 1970,'' *Journal of Marriage and the Family* 36 (May 1974), pp. 246–58.

Henshel, Anne-Marie, ''Swinging: A Study of Decision Making in Marriage,'' in Joan Huber, ed., *Changing Women in a Changing Society* (Chicago: Univ. of Chicago Press, 1973), pp. 123–29.

Henze, Lura F., and John W. Hudson, ''Personal and Family Characteristics of Cohabiting and Noncohabiting College Students,'' *Journal of Marriage and the Family* 36 (Nov. 1974), pp. 722–27.

Hepker, Wilma, and Jerry S. Cloyd, ''Role Relationships and Role Performance: The Male Married Student,'' *Journal of Marriage and the Family* 36 (Nov. 1974), pp. 688–96.

Hicks, Mary W., and Donald Taylor, ''Sex on Campus: The Students' Dilemma,'' *Sexual Behavior* (March 1973), pp. 43–47.

Hobart, Charles W., ''The Social Context of Morality Standards Among Anglophone Canadian Students,'' *Journal of Comparative Family Studies* 5 (Spring 1974), pp. 26–40.

Hochschild, Arlie Russell, *The Unexpected Community* (Englewood Cliffs, New Jersey: Prentice-Hall, 1973).

Holden, Constance, ''Sperm Banks Multiply as Vasectomies Gain Popularity,'' *Science* 176 (April 7, 1972), p. 32.

Holmstrom, Lynda Lytle, *The Two-Career Family* (Cambridge, Mass.: Schenkman, 1972).

Horner, Matina, ''The Motive to Avoid Success and Changing Aspirations of College Women,'' in Judith Bardwick, ed., *Readings on the Psychology of Women* (New York: Harper and Row, 1972), pp. 62–67.

Hudson, John W., and Lura F. Henze, ''Campus Values in Mate Selection: A Replication,'' *Journal of Marriage and the Family* 31 (Nov. 1969), pp. 772–75.

Hunt, Morton M., *The World of the Formerly Married* (New York: McGraw-Hill, 1966).

Hurlock, Elizabeth, *Child Growth and Development* (New York: McGraw-Hill, 1970).

Hutchison, Ira W., III, "The Significance of Marital Status for Morale and Life Satisfaction Among Low-Income Elderly," *Journal of Marriage and the Family* 37 (May 1975), pp. 287–93.

Jackson, Erwin D., and Charles R. Potkay, "Precollege Influences on Sexual Experiences of Coeds," *The Journal of Sex Research* 9 (May 1973), pp. 143–49.

Jacoby, Susan, "49 Million Singles Can't All Be Right," *The New York Times Magazine* (Feb. 17, 1974), pp. 13, 41–49.

Johnson, Ralph E., "Some Correlates of Extramarital Coitus," *Journal of Marriage and the Family* 32 (Aug. 1970), pp. 449–56.

Johnson, Sheila K., "Three Generations, One Household," *The New York Times Magazine,* Aug. 19, 1973, pp. 24–31.

Johnson, Sheila K., "Growing Old Alone Together," *The New York Times Magazine* (Nov. 11, 1973), pp. 40–59.

Jones, Kenneth L., Louis W. Shainberg, and Curtis O. Byer, *Sex* (New York: Harper and Row, 1969).

Jones, Stella B., "Geographic Mobility as Seen by the Wife and Mother," *Journal of Marriage and the Family* 35 (May 1973), pp. 210–18.

Kaats, Gilbert R., and Keith E. Davis, "The Dynamics of Sexual Behavior of College Students," *Journal of Marriage and the Family* 32 (Aug. 1970), pp. 390–99.

Kafka, John S., and Robert G. Ryder, "Notes on Marriages in the Counter Culture," *Journal of Applied Behavioral Science* 9 (Nos. 2–3, 1973), pp. 321–30.

Kanin, Eugene J., "Selected Dyadic Aspects of Male Sex Aggression," *The Journal of Sex Research* 5 (Feb. 1969), pp. 12–28.

Kanin, Eugene J., Karen R. Davidson, and Sonia R. Scheck, "A Research Note on Male–Female Differentials in the Experience of Heterosexual Love," *The Journal of Sex Research* 6 (Feb. 1970), pp. 64–72.

Kanter, Rosabeth Moss, "Communes for All Reasons," *MS.* Magazine, as reprinted in *Readings in Marriage and Family 75/76* (Guilford, Conn.: Dushkin Publishing Group, 1974), pp. 132–35.

Kantner, John F., and Melvin Zelnik, "Sexual Experience of Young Unmarried Women in the United States," *Family Planning Perspectives* 4 (Oct. 1972), pp. 9–17.

Kantner, John F., and Melvin Zelnik, "Contraception and Pregnancy: Experiences of Young Unmarried Women in the United States," *Family Planning Perspectives* 5 (Winter 1973), pp. 21–35.

Karp, Ellen S., Julie H. Jackson, and David Lester, "Ideal-Self Fulfillment in Mate Selection: A Corollary to the Complementary Need Theory," *Journal of Marriage and the Family* 32 (May 1970), pp. 269–72.

Katelman, Doris K., and Larry D. Barnett, "Work Orientations of Urban Middle-Class Married Women," *Journal of Marriage and the Family* 30 (Feb. 1968), pp. 80–88.

Katz, Barbara J., "Cooling Motherhood," in J. Gipson Wells, ed., *Current Issues in Marriage and the Family* (New York: Macmillan, 1975), pp. 161–64.

Kephart, William M., "Some Correlates of Romantic Love," *Journal of Marriage and the Family* 29 (Nov. 1967), pp. 470–74.

Kephart, William M., "Why They Fail: A Socio-Historical Analysis of Religious and Secular Communes," *Journal of Comparative Family Studies* 5 (Autumn 1974), pp. 130–40.

King, Karl, Jennie McIntyre, and Leland J. Axelson, "Adolescents' Views of Maternal Employment as a Threat to the Marital Relationship," *Journal of Marriage and the Family* 30 (Nov. 1968), pp. 633–37.

Kinsey, Alfred C., Wardell B. Pomeroy, and Clyde E. Martin, *Sexual Behavior in the Human Male* (Philadelphia: W. B. Saunders, 1948).

Kinsey, Alfred C., Wardell B. Pomeroy, Clyde E. Martin, and Paul H. Gebhard, *Sexual Behavior in the Human Female* (Philadelphia: W. B. Saunders, 1953).

Knox, David H., Jr., and Michael L. Sporakowski, "Attitudes of College Students Toward Love," *Journal of Marriage and the Family* 30 (Nov. 1968), pp. 638–42.

Knox, David H., Jr., "Conceptions of Love at Three Developmental Levels," *The Family Coordinator* 19 (April 1970), pp. 151–57.

Knox, William E., and Harriet J. Kupferer, "A Discontinuity in the Socialization of Males in the United States," *Merrill-Palmer Quarterly* 17 (July 1971), pp. 251–61.

Kolb, Trudy M., and Murray A. Straus, "Marital Power and Marital Happiness In Relation to Problem-Solving Ability," *Journal of Marriage and the Family* 36 (Nov. 1974), pp. 756–66.

Komarovsky, Mirra, "Cultural Contradictions and Sex Roles," *American Journal of Sociology* 52 (Nov. 1946), pp. 184–89.

Komarovsky, Mirra, "Cultural Contradictions and Sex Roles: The Masculine Case," *American Journal of Sociology* 78 (Jan. 1973), pp. 873–84.

Komarovsky, Mirra, "Patterns of Self-Disclosure of Male Undergraduates," *Journal of Marriage and the Family* 36 (Nov. 1974), pp. 677–86.

Kovach, Bill, "Communal Living Becomes a Factor in the U.S.," *The New York Times,* Jan. 3, 1971.

Krantzler, Mel, *Creative Divorce: A New Opportunity for Personal Growth* (New York: New American Library, 1975).

Kuzel, Paul, and P. Krishnan, "Changing Patterns of Remarriage in Canada 1961–1966," *Journal of Comparative Family Studies* 4 (Autumn 1973), pp. 215–24.

Landis, Judson R., and Louis Stoetzer, "An Exploratory Study of Middle-Class Migrant Families," *Journal of Marriage and the Family* 28 (Feb. 1966), pp. 51–53.

Landis, Judson T., and Mary G. Landis, *Building a Successful Marriage* (Englewood Cliffs, N.J.: Prentice-Hall, 1973).

Larson, Richard F., and Gerald R. Leslie, "Prestige Influences in Serious Dating Relationships of University Students," *Social Forces* 47 (Dec. 1968), pp. 195–202.

LeMasters, Ersel E., *Parents in Modern America* (Homewood, Ill.: The Dorsey Press, 1974).

Leslie, Gerald R., *The Family in Social Context* (New York: Oxford University Press, 1976).

Levinger, George, "Sources of Marital Dissatisfaction Among Applicants for Divorce," *American Journal of Orthopsychiatry* 36 (1966), pp. 803–7.

Lewis, Robert A., "Parents and Peers: Socialization Agents in the Coital Behavior of Young Adults," *The Journal of Sex Research* 9 (May 1973), pp. 156–70.

Lief, Harold I., and Michael B. Guthrie, "What It's Like to Live in a Co-Ed Dorm," *Sexual Behavior* (Dec. 1972), pp. 20–27.

Lobsenz, Norman M., "Sex and the Senior Citizen," *The New York Times Magazine* (1974), as reprinted in *Readings in Marriage and Family 75/76* (Guilford, Conn.: The Dushkin Publishing Group, 1974), pp. 187–91.

Long, Larry H., "Women's Labor Force Participation and the Residential Mobility of Families," *Social Forces* 52 (March 1974), pp. 342–48.

Luckey, Eleanore Braun, and Joyce Koym Bain, "Children: A Factor in Marital Satisfaction," *Journal of Marriage and the Family* 32 (Feb. 1970), pp. 43–44.

McCall, Michael M., "Courtship as Social Exchange: Some Historical Comparisons," in Bernard Farber, ed., *Kinship and Family Organization* (New York: John Wiley & Sons, 1966), pp. 190–200.

McCary, James L., *Human Sexuality: Physiological and Psychological Factors of Sexual Behavior* (Princeton, N.J.: D. Van Nostrand, 1967).

McKain, Walter C., "A New Look at Older Marriages," *The Family Coordinator* 21 (Jan. 1972), pp. 61–69.

Macklin, Eleanor D., "Heterosexual Cohabitation Among Unmarried College Students," *The Family Coordinator* 21 (Oct. 1972), pp. 463–72.

Madigan, Francis C., "Are Sex Mortality Differentials Biologically Caused?" *Milbank Memorial Fund Quarterly* 35 (April 1957), pp. 202–23.

Mannes, Marya, *Last Rights: A Case for the Good Death* (New York: New American Library, 1973).

Masters, William H., and Virginia E. Johnson, *Human Sexual Response* (Boston: Little, Brown, 1966).

Mastroianni, Luigi, Jr., "Rhythm: Systematized Chance-Taking," *Family Planning Perspectives* 6 (Fall 1974), pp. 209–12.

Mazur, Allan, and Leon S. Robertson, *Biology and Social Behavior* (New York: The Free Press, 1972).

Mishell, Daniel R., Jr., "Assessing the Intrauterine Device," *Family Planning Perspectives* 7 (May/June 1975), pp. 103–11.

Monahan, Thomas P., "Are Interracial Marriages Really Less Stable?" *Social Forces* 48 (June 1970), pp. 461–73.

Monahan, Thomas P., "Interracial Marriage and Divorce in Kansas and the Question of Instability of Mixed Marriages," *Journal of Comparative Family Studies* 2 (Spring 1971), pp. 107–20.

Monahan, Thomas P., "Marriage Across Racial Lines in Indiana," *Journal of Marriage and the Family* 35 (Nov. 1973), pp. 632–40.

Monahan, Thomas P., "Some Dimensions of Interreligious Marriages in Indiana, 1962–67," *Social Forces* 52 (Dec. 1973), pp. 195–203.

Money, John, and Anke G. Ehrhardt, *Man and Woman, Boy and Girl* (New York: New American Library, 1972).

Money, John, "Developmental Differentiation of Femininity and Masculinity Compared," in Clarice Stasz Stoll, ed., *Sexism: Scientific Debates* (Reading, Mass.: Addison Wesley, 1973), pp. 13–27.

Money, John, "Human Behavior Cytogenetics: Review of Psychopathology in Three Syndromes—47,XXY; 47,XYY; and 45,X," *The Journal of Sex Research* 11 (Aug. 1975), pp. 181–200.

Moss, J. Joel, Frank Apolonio, and Margaret Jensen, "The Premarital Dyad During the Sixties," *Journal of Marriage and the Family* 33 (Feb. 1971), pp. 50–69.

Moynihan, Daniel P., "Peace—Some Thoughts on the 1960's and 1970's," *The Public Interest* 32 (Summer 1973), pp. 3–12.

Murstein, Bernard I., "A Theory of Marital Choice and Its Applicability to Marriage Adjustment," in Bernard I. Murstein, ed., *Theories of Attraction and Love* (New York: Springer, 1971), pp. 100–151.

Nye, F. Ivan, John Carlson, and Gerald Garrett, "Family Size, Interaction, Affect, and Stress," *Journal of Marriage and the Family* 32 (May 1970), pp. 216–26.

Oakley, Ann, *Sex, Gender and Society* (New York: Harper Colophon Books, 1972).

Olson, David H., "Marriage of the Future: Revolutionary or Evolutionary Change?" *The Family Coordinator* 21 (Oct. 1972), pp. 383–93.

Orden, Susan R., and Norman M. Bradburn, "Working Wives and Marriage Happiness," *American Journal of Sociology* 74 (Jan. 1968), pp. 392–407.

Orlinsky, David E., "Love Relationships in the Life Cycle: A Developmental Interpersonal Perspective," as reprinted in *Readings in Marriage and Family 75/76* (Guilford, Conn.: The Dushkin Publishing Group, 1974), pp. 11–15.

Otto, Herbert A., "Communes: The Alternative Life-Style," *Saturday Review,* April 24, 1971.

Packard, Vance, *A Nation of Strangers* (New York: David McKay, 1972).

Parelius, Ann P., "Emerging Sex-Role Attitudes, Expectations, and Strains Among College Women," *Journal of Marriage and the Family* 37 (Feb. 1975), pp. 146–53.

Peterman, Dan J., Carl A. Ridley, and Scott M. Anderson, "A Comparison of Cohabiting and Noncohabiting College Students," *Journal of Marriage and the Family* 36 (May 1974), pp. 344–54.

Petroni, Frank A., "Teen-age Interracial Dating," in *Readings in Marriage and the Family 75/76* (Guilford, Conn.: The Dushkin Publishing Group, 1974), pp. 32–36.

Pilpel, Harriet F., "Abortion: U.S.A. Style," *The Journal of Sex Research* 11 (May 1975), pp. 113–18.

Pitts, Jesse R., "On Communes," *Contemporary Sociology* 2 (July 1973), p. 352.

Pomeroy, Richard, and Lynn C. Landman, "Public Opinion Trends: Elective Abortion and Birth Control Services to Teenagers," *Family Planning Perspectives* 4 (Oct. 1972), pp. 44–55.

Pomeroy, Wardell B., "Playboy Panel: New Sexual Life Styles," *Playboy* (Sept. 1973), p. 86.

Porterfield, Ernest, "Mixed Marriage," in *Readings in Marriage and Family 75/76* (Guilford, Conn.: Dushkin Publishing Group, 1974), pp. 66–72.

Pratt, Lois, "Conjugal Organization and Health," *Journal of Marriage and the Family* 34 (Feb. 1972), pp. 85–95.

Presser, Harriet B., and Larry L. Bumpass, "The Acceptability of Contraceptive Sterilization Among U.S. Couples: 1970," *Family Planning Perspectives* 4 (Oct. 1972), pp. 18–26.

Price-Bonham, Sharon, "Student Husbands Versus Student Couples," *Journal of Marriage and the Family* 35 (Feb. 1973), pp. 33–38.

Rallings, Elisha M., "Family Situations of Married and Never-Married Males," *Journal of Marriage and the Family* 28 (Aug. 1966), pp. 485–90.

Ramey, James W., "Emerging Patterns of Innovative Behavior in Marriage," *The Family Coordinator* 21 (Oct. 1972), pp. 435–56.

Rapoport, Rhona, and Robert N. Rapoport, *Dual-Career Families* (Harmondsworth, Middlesex, England: Penguin, 1971).

Renne, Karen, "Correlates of Dissatisfaction in Marriage," *Journal of Marriage and the Family* 32 (Feb. 1970), pp. 54–67.

Rimmer, Robert, "Playboy Panel: New Sexual Life Styles," *Playboy* (Sept. 1973), p. 80.

Roache, Joel, "Confessions of a Househusband," *Ms. Magazine* 1 (Nov. 1972), pp. 25–27, as reprinted in John W. Petras, ed., *Sex: Male/Gender:Masculine* (Port Washington, N.Y.: Alfred, 1975), pp. 186–91.

Roberto, Eduardo L., "Vasectomy Responses," *Family Planning Perspectives* 5 (Winter 1973), pp. 5–6.

Robinson, Ira E., Karl King, and Jack O. Balswick, "The Premarital Sexual Revolution Among College Females," *The Family Coordinator* 21 (April 1972), pp. 189–94.

Rogers, Carl R., "Interpersonal Relationships: U.S.A. 2000," *Journal of Applied Behavioral Science* 4 (1968), as reprinted in *Readings in Marriage and Family 75/76* (Guilford, Conn.: The Dushkin Publishing Group, 1974), pp. 1–6.

Rosenthal, Erich, "Divorce and Religious Intermarriage: The Effect of Previous Marital Status Upon Subsequent Marital Behavior," *Journal of Marriage and the Family* 32 (Aug. 1970), pp. 435–40.

Rossi, Alice S., "The Roots of Ambivalence in American Women," paper presented at Continuing Education Conference, Oakland University, Michigan, 1967.

Rossi, Alice, "Deviance and Conformity in the Life Goals of Women," Unpublished Paper, Goucher College, Baltimore, Maryland.

Rossman, Isadore, "Sexuality and the Aging Process: An Internist's Perspective," in Irene Mortenson Burnside, ed., *Sexuality and Aging* (Los Angeles: The University of Southern California Press, 1975), pp. 18–25.

Russell, Candyce Smith, "Transition to Parenthood: Problems and Gratifications," *Journal of Marriage and the Family* 36 (May 1974), pp. 294–302.

Ryder, Norman B., "Contraceptive Failure in the United States," *Family Planning Perspectives* 5 (Summer 1973), pp. 133–42.

Ryder, Robert G., John S. Kafka, and David H. Olson, "Separating and Joining Influences in Courtship and Early Marriage," *American Journal of Orthopsychiatry* 41 (April 1971), pp. 450–64.

Ryder, Robert G., "Longitudinal Data Relating Marriage Satisfaction and Having a Child," *Journal of Marriage and the Family* 35 (Nov. 1973), pp. 605–6.

Safilios-Rothschild, Constantina, "The Relationship Between Work Commitment and Fertility," *International Journal of Sociology of the Family* 2 (March 1972), pp. 64–71.

Safilios-Rothschild, Constantina, *Women and Social Policy* (Englewood Cliffs, N.J.: Prentice Hall, 1974).

Saline, Carol, "Why Can't Married Women Have Men as Friends?" *McCall's* (January 1975), pp. 67, 132–33.

Salsberg, Sheldon, "Is Group Marriage Viable?" *The Journal of Sex Research* 9 (Nov. 1973), pp. 325–33.

Saxton, Lloyd, *The Individual, Marriage, and the Family* (Belmont, Cal.: Wadsworth, 1972).

Scanzoni, John, and Martha McMurry, "Continuities in the Explanation of Fertility Control," *Journal of Marriage and the Family* 34 (May 1972), pp. 315–22.

Schimel, John L., "Self-Esteem and Sex," *Sexual Behavior* (July 1971), pp. 3–6.

Schlesinger, Benjamin, "Remarriage as Family Reorganization for Divorced Persons—A Canadian Study," *Journal of Comparative Family Studies* 1 (Autumn 1970), pp. 101–18.

Schlesinger, Benjamin, "The Widowed as a One-Parent Family Unit," *Social Science* 46 (Jan. 1971), pp. 26–32.

Schmitt, Robert C., "Recent Trends in Hawaiian Interracial Marriage Rates," *Journal of Marriage and the Family* 33 (May 1971), pp. 373–74.

Schoenfeld, Eugen, "Intermarriage and the Small Town: The Jewish Case," *Journal of Marriage and the Family* 31 (Feb. 1969), pp. 61–64.

Schuman, Marion L., "Idealization in Engaged Couples," *Journal of Marriage and the Family* 36 (Feb. 1974), pp. 139–47.

Seidenberg, Robert, *Corporate Wives—Corporate Casualties?* (New York: Doubleday, 1975).

Sexton, Patricia Cayo, "The Feminized Male," in Clarice Stasz Stoll, ed., *Sexism: Scientific Debates* (Reading, Mass.: Addison-Wesley, 1973), pp. 61–73.

Sheldon, Alan, Peter J. M. McEwan, and Carol Pierson Ryser, *Retirement: Patterns and Predictions* (Washington, D.C.: National Institute of Mental Health, 1975).

Shuttleworth, Frank K., "A Biosocial and Developmental Theory of Male and Female Sexuality," *Marriage and Family Living* 21 (May 1959), pp. 163–70.

Simon, William, and John H. Gagnon, "Psychosexual Development," in John H. Gagnon and William Simon, eds., *The Sexual Scene* (Chicago: Aldine, 1970), pp. 23–41.

Social Security Administration, *Resources of People 65 or Over* (Washington, D.C.: U.S. Government Printing Office, 1971).

Spanier, Graham B., "Romanticism and Marital Adjustment," *Journal of Marriage and the Family* 34 (Aug. 1972), pp. 481–87.

Spanier, Graham B., "Sexualization and Premarital Sex Behavior," *The Family Coordinator* 24 (Jan. 1975), pp. 33–41.

Spears, Lawrence M., "How Children Survive Pain of Divorce?" *The National Observer* (Dec. 8, 1973).

Spicer, Jerry W., and Gary D. Hampe, "Kinship Interaction After Divorce," *Journal of Marriage and the Family* 37 (Feb. 1975), pp. 113–19.

Spreitzer, Elmer, and Lawrence E. Riley, "Factors Associated with Singlehood," *Journal of Marriage and the Family* 36 (Aug. 1974), pp. 533–42.

Statistical Abstract of the United States: 1975 (Washington, D.C.: United States Department of Commerce, 1975).

Stinnett, Nick, Linda Mittelstet Carter, and James E. Montgomery, "Older Persons' Perceptions of Their Marriages," *Journal of Marriage and the Family* 34 (Nov. 1972), pp. 665–70.

Straus, Murray A., "Leveling, Civility, and Violence in the Family," *Journal of Marriage and the Family* 36 (Feb. 1974), pp. 13–29.

Thomas, Darwin L., David D. Franks, and James M. Calonico, "Role-Taking and Power in Social Psychology," *American Sociological Review* 37 (Oct. 1972), pp. 605–14.

Thompson, Wayne E., and Gordon F. Streib, "Meaningful Activity in a Family Context," in J. Ross Eshleman, *Perspectives in Marriage and the Family* (Boston: Allyn and Bacon, 1969), pp. 592–600.

Toussieng, Povl W., "New Sexual Attitudes of Young People," *Sexual Behavior* (Sept. 1971), pp. 48–55.

Troelstrup, Arch W., *The Consumer in American Society: Personal and Family Finance* (New York: McGraw-Hill, 1970).

Udry, J. Richard, *The Social Context of Marriage* (Philadelphia: Lippincott, 1971).

Uhlman, Gerald, "Vasectomy Counseling by Private Physicians and Clinics," *Family Planning Perspectives* 7 (March–April 1975), pp. 92–93.

Veevers, J. E., "Voluntarily Childless Wives: An Exploratory Study," *Sociology and Social Research* (April 1973), pp. 356–65.

Vener, Arthur M., and Cyrus S. Stewart, "Adolescent Sexual Behavior in Middle America Revisited: 1970–1973," *Journal of Marriage and the Family* 36 (Nov. 1974), pp. 728–35.

Veroff, Joseph, and Sheila Feld, *Marriage and Work in America* (New York: Van Nostrand Reinhold, 1970).

Vital and Health Statistics, Series 21 No. 23, "Teenagers: Marriages, Divorces, Parenthood, and Mortality," (Washington, D.C.: DHEW) August 1973.

Vreeland, Rebecca S., "Sex at Harvard," *Sexual Behavior* (Feb. 1972), pp. 4–10.

Wake, Sandra Byford, and Michael J. Sporakowski, "An Intergenerational Comparison of Attitudes Towards Supporting Aged Parents," *Journal of Marriage and the Family* 34 (Feb. 1972), pp. 42–48.

Wakil, S. Parvez, "Campus Mate Selection Preferences: A Cross-National Comparison," *Social Forces* 51 (June 1973), pp. 471–76.

Waller, Willard, and Reuben Hill, *The Family: A Dynamic Interpretation* (New York: Dryden Press, 1951).

Weigand, Jonathan, "The Single Father," in *Readings in Marriage and the Family 75/76* (Guilford, Conn.: The Dushkin Publishing Group, 1974), pp. 172–75.

Weinstock, Edward, Christopher Tietze, Frederick S. Jaffe, and Joy G. Dryfoos, "Legal Abortions in the United States Since the 1973 Supreme Court Decisions," *Family Planning Perspectives* 7 (Jan.–Feb. 1975), pp. 23–31.

Weitzman, Lenore J., "A Proposal for Individual Contracts and Contracts in Lieu of Marriage," *California Law Review* 62 (July–Sept. 1974), pp. 1169–1288.

Weitzman, Lenore J., Deborah Eifler, Elizabeth Hokada, and Catherine Ross, "Sex-Role Socialization in Picture Books for Preschool Children," in Carolyn C. Perrucci and Dena B. Targ, eds., *Marriage and the Family:*

A Critical Analysis and Proposals for Change (New York: David McKay, 1974), pp. 155–78.

Weitzman, Lenore J., "Sex-Role Socialization," in Jo Freeman, ed., *Women: A Feminist Perspective* (Palo Alto, Cal.: Mayfield, 1975), pp. 105–144.

Westoff, Charles F., "The Modernization of U.S. Contraceptive Practice," *Family Planning Perspectives* 4 (July 1972), pp. 9–12.

Westoff, Charles F., "Coital Frequency and Contraception," *Family Planning Perspectives* 6 (Summer 1974), pp. 136–41.

Westoff, Leslie Aldridge, "Sterilization," *The New York Times Magazine,* Sept. 29, 1974, pp. 30–31, 80–89.

Whitchurch, Fay H., "Disengagement in Three Types of Communities," *Contributions: A Journal of Student Papers in Sociology* 1 (May 1975), pp. 13–23.

Whitehurst, Robert N., "Some Comparisons of Conventional and Counterculture Families," *The Family Coordinator* 21 (Oct. 1972), pp. 395–401.

Wilson, W. Cody, "The American Experience with Pornography," in George V. Coelho and Eli A. Rubinstein, eds. *Social Change and Human Behavior: Mental Health Challenges of the Seventies* (Rockville, Maryland: National Institute of Mental Health, 1972), pp. 111–35.

Winch, Robert F., *Mate Selection* (New York: Harper, 1958).

Wittman, James S., "Dating Patterns of Rural and Urban Kentucky Teenagers," *The Family Coordinator* 20 (Jan. 1971), pp. 63–66.

Wolf, Rosalind, "Self-Image of the White Member of an Interracial Couple," in Jacqueline P. Wiseman, ed., *People as Partners: Individual and Family Relationships in Today's World* (San Francisco: Canfield Press, 1971), pp. 58–63.

Yankelovich, Daniel, *The New Morality: A Profile of American Youth in the 70's* (New York: McGraw-Hill, 1974).

Zelnik, Melvin, and John F. Kantner, "The Resolution of Teenage First Pregnancies," *Family Planning Perspectives* 6 (Spring 1974), pp. 74–80.

Photo Credits

FIVE **Opener:** Joanne Leonard/Woodfin Camp & Associates. **Page 102:** Alice Kandell/Rapho-Photo Researchers. **Page 105:** Nancy Hays/Monkmeyer Press Photo Service. **Page 107:** Christa Armstrong/Rapho-Photo Researchers. **Page 111:** Chester Higgins, Jr./Rapho-Photo Researchers.

SIX **Opener:** Esaias Baitel/Rapho-Photo Researchers. **Page 121:** Bob Combs/Rapho-Photo Researchers. **Page 127:** Alice Kandell/Rapho-Photo Researchers. **Page 133:** Chester Higgins, Jr./Rapho-Photo Researchers.

SEVEN **Opener:** Alice Kandell/Rapho-Photo Researchers. **Page 142:** Esaias Baitel/Rapho-Photo Researchers. **Page 152:** Ray Ellis/Rapho-Photo Researchers. **Page 156:** Alice Kandell/Rapho-Photo Researchers.

EIGHT **Opener:** Christa Armstrong/Rapho-Photo Researchers. **Page 167:** Charles Gatewood/Magnum Photos. **Page 177:** Michal Heron.

NINE **Opener:** Joanne Leonard/Woodfin Camp & Associates. **Page 196:** Joel Gordon. **Page 200:** Springer/Bettmann Film Archive.

TEN **Opener:** Alice Kandell/Rapho-Photo Researchers. **Page 211:** Robert deGast/Rapho-Photo Researchers. **Page 215:** Hanna Schreiber/Rapho-Photo Researchers. **Page 227:** Ray Ellis/Rapho-Photo Researchers.

ELEVEN **Opener:** Ray Ellis/Rapho-Photo Researchers. **Page 240:** Ron Nelson. **Page 243:** Les Mahon/Monkmeyer Press Photo Service. **Page 252:** Sylvia Johnson/Woodfin Camp & Associates.

TWELVE **Opener:** Tom Myers/Photo Researchers. **Page 264:** Hanna Schreiber/Rapho-Photo Researchers. **Page 271:** Alice Kandell/Rapho-Photo Researchers. **Page 274:** Lucia Woods/Photo Researchers.

THIRTEEN **Opener:** Hanna Schreiber/Rapho-Photo Researchers. **Page 285:** Mimi Forsyth/Monkmeyer Press Photo Service. **Page 289:** Michael Philip Manheim/Photo Researchers.

FOURTEEN **Opener:** Bruce Roberts/Rapho-Photo Researchers. **Page 297:** Hanna Schreiber/Rapho-Photo Researchers. **Page 299:** Emily Harste.

FIFTEEN **Opener:** Michael Philip Manheim/Photo Researchers. **Page 320:** Christy Park/Monkmeyer Press Photo Service. **Page 325:** Alice Kandell/Rapho-Photo Researchers. **Page 332:** Ray Ellis/Rapho-Photo Researchers.

Opener: Dick Swift. **Page 343:** Susanne Anderson / Photo Researchers. **Page 349:** Christy Park / Monkmeyer Press Photo Service.

SIXTEEN

Opener: Thomas Hopker / Woodfin Camp & Associates. **Page 364:** Tim Eagan / Woodfin Camp & Associates. **Page 367:** Alice Kandell / Rapho-Photo Researchers. **Page 370:** Philip Teuscher.

SEVENTEEN

Opener: Eve Arnold / Magnum Photos. **Page 377:** Hanna Schreiber / Rapho-Photo Researchers. **Page 387:** Steve Eagle / Nancy Palmer Photo Agency. **Page 389:** Mark Jury / Rapho-Photo Researchers.

EIGHTEEN

NAME INDEX

C

D

R

SUBJECT INDEX

C